BF
637
.C45   Wells, Theodora.
W39   Keeping your cool
        under fire :
        communicating non-
        defensively

OCT 1 7 1985   DATE

Learning Resources Center
Santa Fe Community College
P.O. Box 4187
Santa Fe, New Mexico 87502

© THE BAKER & TAYLOR CO.

KEEPING YOUR COOL UNDER FIRE

Communicating Non-Defensively

Theodora Wells

Wells Associates
Beverly Hills, California

McGraw-Hill Book Company

**New York   St. Louis   San Francisco   Auckland   Bogotá   Düsseldorf
Johannesburg   London   Madrid   Mexico   Montreal   New Delhi
Panama   Paris   São Paulo   Singapore   Sydney   Tokyo   Toronto**

Learning Resources Center
Santa Fe Community College
P.O. Box 4187
Santa Fe, New Mexico 87502

KEEPING YOUR COOL UNDER FIRE
Communicating Non-Defensively

Copyright © 1980 by Theodora Wells. All rights reserved. Printed in the United States of America. No part of this publication may be reproduced, stored in a retrieval system, or transmitted, in any form or by any means, electronic, mechanical, photocopying, recording, or otherwise, without the prior written permission of the publisher and author.

34567890 DODO 83210

Library of Congress Cataloging in Publication Data

Wells, Theodora
    Keeping your cool under fire: communicating non-defensively.

    Includes index.
    1. Interpersonal communication.   2.   Success.
I.   Title.
BF637.C45W39   158'.1   79-12890
ISBN 0-07-069250-5

This book was set in Plantin by Holmes Composition Service. The editors were Robert G. Manley and Helen Kelly; the designer was Linda Marcetti; the production supervisor was Dominick Petrellese. The cover was designed by John Hite.
R. R. Donnelley & Sons Company was printer and binder.

ACKNOWLEDGMENTS

I wish to express appreciation for permission given to reprint the following illustrations:

Page 59 "Now go to sleep. There's nothing to be afraid of," by William O'Brian, 1965. Permission received from Random House, New York.

Page 60 "Why can't you behave like your Cousin Margery?," by William O'Brian, 1965. Permission received from Random House, New York.

Page 61 "And *stay* in your room, young man," by William O'Brian, 1965. Permission received from Random House, New York.

Page 63 "Of course he can go wherever he wants to college but naturally . . . ," by William O'Brian, 1965. Permission received from Random House, New York.

Page 66 "Peanuts," by Charles M. Schulz, 1977. Permission received from United Feature Syndicate, New York.

Page 78 "Power Plays," drawings by Tom Parker, 1976. Permission received from Tom Parker.

Page 82 "Now let me give you *MY* interpretation of your interpretation!," by Marvin Kuhn, 1977. Permission received from *VOICES*, New York.

Pages 101–102 "Organizational Profile," by Rensis Likert, 1967. Permission received from McGraw-Hill, New York.

Page 116 "The Rational Organization/The Real Organization," by *Systemation,* 1959 and Tom Parker, 1976. Permission received from Systemation North America, Denver, and Tom Parker.

Page 120 "The Fallacy of Facades," by Jim Cole, drawings by Tom Woodruff, 1970. Permission received by Dr. Jim Cole.

Page 124 "The Walking Wounded" from the cover of *Organizational Behavior: Research and Issues* by George Strauss, Raymond E. Miles, Charles C. Snow, and Arnold Tannenbaum, eds., 1976. Permission received from Wadsworth, Belmont, Calif.

Page 225 "Dooley's World, by Bradfield, 1975. Permission received from King Features Syndicate, New York.

Page 288 "Revenge is sweet," by William Steig, 1942. Duell, Sloan & Pearce, New York.

Page 292 "I do what is expected of me," by William Steig, 1942. Duell, Sloan & Pearce, New York.

Page 296 "I am blameless," by William Steig, 1942. Duell, Sloan & Pearce, New York.

TO MY PARENTS
Marjorie and Oscar Westmont

CONTENTS

PREFACE

Learning to communicate non-defensively is easier said than done. It involves looking at some of your own attitudes, inner rules and underlying beliefs that may contribute to feelings of defensiveness. In the process of becoming non-defensive, you are also in the process of becoming more of your own person. This improves the odds that other people will recognize you more as a person, less as a machine. As you exercise more choices, you will be redefining yourself, renegotiating your relationships, and revising the results you get. You'll have available a larger repertoire of behaviors to choose from for handling any situation, especially when you're in the subordinate position.

Use the strategies in this book to pick up ideas for coping when situations make you feel and act defensively. Use it for increasing your overall effectiveness as a person and in your work as well as in other areas of your life. The chapters are arranged to build on each other if you have growth as a goal. At the end of some chapters there are questions to ask yourself or suggested experiments.

In the first two chapters, you'll see the principles of non-defensive communication in action. In Chapters 3 and 4 you will see how defensiveness is learned and practiced among people and in organizations where it's vitually built into traditional systems. Chapters 5 and 6 describe in detail the processes of defensive communication, and ways to recognize your own patterns, and ideas about how to change them where you want to. Chapter 7 helps you visualize and create new options. At this point, the background and non-defensive skills you need will have been explored thoroughly.

You'll now be ready for action.

Chapter 8 offers some quick, non-defensive responses to "zaps" so you can soon cure yourself of the "I should've said . . ." disease. Chapters 9, 10 and 11 show the non-defensive process in action. The last chapter looks at the increase of power and energy that is possible when others join you in communicating non-defensively.

The thirty situations and the ninety people you will meet are all real, with one exception. Only the names and recognizable details have been changed. This material has come from women and men with whom I've consulted or who have been in workshops and classes I've conducted in industry, government and university extension courses across the country and my private practice.

Not only will you have the benefit of these people's experiences, you'll also have the benefit of authors from such diverse fields as non-verbal communication, human development, behavior in organizations, humanistic psychology, social change, creativity and philosophy. An annotated bibliography tells you more and is cross-referenced at the end of each chapter in addition to specific chapter readings.

I am indebted to the hundreds of women and men, probably thousands by now, who have learned from me while I learned from them, and whose experiences and encouragement have made this book grow to what it is today. Many additional people have been and continue to be a source of support and inspiration to me, although I would guess that some of them might be surprised to find their names here. They may have no idea how much they have influenced my thinking and self-perception through their writings, my personal contact with them (which in a few instances is brief) and the courage they inspire by the way they live their beliefs. Alphabetically, these include: Tony Athos, Ruth Bebermeyer, Warren Bennis, Dick Farson, Charles Ferguson, Wilma Scott Heide, Aileen Hernandez, Evelyn Knight, Gordon Lippitt, Rollo May, Charlene Orszag, Barbara Perrow, Elias Porter, Carl Rogers, Earldean Robbins, Ann Scott (deceased), Jane Walker, Marjorie Westmont (deceased), and Oscar Westmont.

Other people have been supportive in an ongoing mutual resource-exchange network. (Others with whom I have had less frequent, but just as significant, contact are not listed for lack of space.) These include: Nancy Albrecht, Ruth Austen, Margo Berger, Renee Branch, Ed Caprelian, Barbara DiPadova, Mary Fuller, Ev Chormley, Judy Glass, Natasha Josefowitz, Sylvia Jour, Winnie Kessler, Ray and Margie Leidig, Hannah Lerman, Sallie O'Neill, Joe Robinson, Bob Shearer, Wendy Tuller, Nora Weckler, Pat and Gene Wyskocil, and other friends and associates in professional associations and women's rights groups, particularly those who are also working for change that not only allows for, but actively encourages, human growth and excellence.

Another vital source of inspiration comes from family members who are always there when I need them, again, alphabetically: Dave and Steve Kuettel, Dolly and Gingee Molina, Art and Laurel Westmont, Oscar and Clare Westmont, Roger and Lois Westmont.

Now to the hard-working team who contributed to the actual writing process of this book. Early contributors who commented, criticized and helped me think through approaches include: Betsy Hogan, Chuck Leo,

Rosalind Loring, Jennifer McLeod and Betty Pellett. During the long and sometimes tortuous writing process, these people kept the faith, criticized, conceptualized, tore apart, typed, prepared graphics, edited, commented, demanded discipline, or were simply patient: Sandra Anderson, Ruth Austen, Marjorie Balazs, Vickie Basler, Jack Gibb, Catherine Hiekel, Helen Kelly, Suzanne Knott, Kyrene (who has one name by choice), Madaline Lee, Mary Lou Maneff, Bob Manley, John Morriss, Eileen Moskowitz, Joe Robinson, Bernie Scheier, Irwin Schorr, Jane Walker and Oscar Westmont.

As with most book projects, a few special people provide honest commentary, give their expertise and ideas, and offer encouragement when the going gets rough, even when their feed back is what made it rough! Without that honesty and sense of withness, this book would have been stillborn in the typewriter. Together we made non-defensive values come alive and thrive through the hard labor of creating this book.

Ruth Austen, a professional writer and editorial consultant, had been in several NDC workshops and was also experimenting with non-defensive writing. Patiently she taught me to appreciate the difference between expressing ideas while talking and expressing the same ideas on paper. You see, I was sometimes defensive about my writing when I overexplained the point. She suggested—non-defensively—that I practice what I preach.

Enter *Helen Kelly*, an independent professional editor retained by McGraw-Hill as a developmental editor. I didn't know what that was or what she would do, but I gave her my first draft, and we got to work developing a flow, this time for structuring the content of the book and creating my writing flow. Even when the first eight chapters landed on my desk for a complete rework, the turnaround of the content eventually became part of our non-defensive writing process. Thanks to Helen's necessarily incisive honesty, you have action examples instead of descriptions. Helen could visualize the finished product long before I could see it and kept saying, "Keep on going."

All during this process, assistant Kyrene kept typing and polishing. Communication consultant Joe Robinson kept saying, "Less is more." To Joe goes the credit for incubating the cool/fire idea in the title. He practices what he preaches. (Once I got into my flow, you couldn't turn me off.) Jane Walker also kept calling a halt: "You've already stated complex ideas simply. Stop! Enough!"

Now you, the reader, have the final word. If you also have grown through participating in the results of our non-defensive writing, we have all gained. That's the result we wanted.

Theodora Wells
Beverly Hills, Calif.
January 1979

AUTHOR'S NOTE

I tried to present an equal number of men and women in this book. However, the reality of the workplace—when up to now there are more men than women—prevented that. The ratio is about two men to one woman. I am also aware that the defensiveness created by racism, ageism, religious discrimination, and physical handicap is insufficiently reflected. As non-defensive communication touches more lives, I expect that future revisions will include more of these examples.

1

NON-DEFENSIVE COMMUNICATION

What It Is and Why It Is Important

Ten years ago I put my job on the line—and was fired. Here's their reason: "INVOLUNTARY TERMINATION: Employer unwilling to meet employee's salary demands." Here's what they meant: I had questioned a management decision—their right to control. They had given me peanuts for an annual raise; I had asked for more money and an officer title. There was no problem about the title, but money, well, that was something else again. For people like me, they had an automatic reaction: fire 'em. They thought they had won that round.

Actually I won, too. I had known all along I didn't want to stay more than another six months. Although there wasn't a name for it in those days, I was preparing for a midlife passage. All I needed was more information before deciding between continuing my education and starting my own business. My plans, priorities, children, and finances were in tolerable order.

With great relief, I left a company not fit for human growth, only for money growth. The top executive of that company was a rigid authoritarian, benign as long as you did what you were told and were properly grateful for any crumbs of recognition. Everything was fine if you didn't make waves. Question the apparently gentle giant, and the underlying tyrant emerged— hostile, cagey, crouched for action. I'd seen him pounce when questioned; it was predictable.

I had weighed the risks of being fired before I had raised my questions. I just didn't know what form the attack would take. But I had known for some time that I needed room to become more of a leader, less of a lackey. I knew chances were slight that I'd get enough room to sprout wings in that company, much less fly a little. Even the number of pencils in desk drawers were subject to after-hours count; having more than two was suspect. Those executives didn't trust *anyone* who might grow enough to act independently.

My next strategy matured when rumblings through my grapevine revealed that their sole remaining question was whether to fire me or let me quit. How to save themselves unemployment insurance points was their key concern. I decided to continue cheerfully delivering completed projects of top quality. If the quality of one's work is not in question, how do you fire someone whose only crime is asking for more money? All you have to do is say "No." (Let me add that the people at the unemployment benefits window found my exemployer's reason somewhat confusing, but eventually I collected. That's another story, but it's rather delicious to take home tax-free money by simply asking for more taxable income.)

Ten years ago I didn't call my part in those negotiations "non-defensive communication," but that's what it was. Here's what made it non-defensive for me. First, I did not feel threatened in the face of a direct threat. Instead, I was centered in my own values and priorities, which gave me a sense of security. I also took responsibility for myself by paying attention to my own needs for growth: arranging finances ahead of time, becoming willing to take more risks, developing some future directions.

If I had chosen to react to their actions, I would have given them control over me. They already had control over my job, and presumably they also had control over themselves. For me to keep control over my own choices seemed a basic minimum in an already uneven match.

Non-defensive communication is: absence of threat, centering, taking responsibility for oneself, planning, taking risks, and keeping control over self.

To be able to do this, I had decided many years before to become my own person, both personally and professionally. The two are so closely entwined they are inseparable. I had decided on the results I wanted—to be my own person in my professional work—and when faced with this conflict and the choices of action involved, I finally knew what this meant and how to do it.

Being my own person is not the selfish "me, me, only me" image of Tom Wolfe's *Me Generation*. Nor is it the competitive "me versus you" in the sense of looking out for Number One without considering others. Being my own person is "me *plus* you." It's taking responsibility for, and control of, my own choices and decisions while also considering yours. It's having control of myself balanced with consideration for you.

Being your own person is defined by: control of self, considering others, a sense of personal worth, self-confidence, self-esteem, and personal integrity

---

When you give control of yourself to others, you dance to their tune. When you keep control of yourself, you can at least choose the tune. If I had reacted emotionally to my grapevine information, I could have become angry that they were trying to get rid of me and might have vindictively sabotaged my assigned projects. However, that would have given them good reason to fire me, and I would have lost the tax-free benefits. That alternative didn't fit my strategy. So I chose to treat my grapevine rumblings as vital but impersonal information.

As it was, all I had to do to call my own tune was continue doing my job as I had all along. (I did allow myself an extra dash of cheer.) They couldn't fault me on my work, my attitude, or how I got along with others, including them. I was in control of "me," acting on my own choices instead of reacting to them.

Being your own person is having the sense of personal worth that comes from the power of self-confidence—confidence in your own competence, your own values, your own worth. It's also having the power of self-esteem—the power of being able to say, "I feel good about me." Feeling good about yourself comes from living what you believe and putting your actions where your mouth is. It's the power of personal integrity that doesn't include selling out or compromising yourself.

When someone wants to bend, fold, spindle and mutilate you, it's your decision when and where you plant your feet, put your hands on your hips and say, "No." This is not a declaration of war. It simply draws a line around the territory you choose to control: you.

NON-DEFENSIVE COMMUNICATION (NDC): WHAT IT IS

There were two processes going on in the situation leading up to my getting fired. One was the sequence of objective events—the meetings and conversations between myself, the executives, my friends in the informal grapevine—which culminated in the memo that delivered my demise. The other was the subjective, personal choices made by me and the top executives before and during the negotiations. I had an advantage because I had thought through the results I wanted, my options, some risks going for and against me, and I had made my choices. I was the actor; they were the reactors with no plan.

In fact, behind *every* sequence of objective events is a subjective process that people go through as they shape those events. The top executives concerned themselves with only objective events, having no apparent regard for subjective attitudes and feelings—their own or mine. When feelings, needs, emotions, beliefs, or personal priorities are not considered, people usually feel threatened. Then they become defensive and communicate in ways to protect themselves. I could communicate non-defensively because I had thought through my priorities, knew my feelings about possible events, and felt strong enough to hold out for what I wanted. No matter what they did, I felt in control of me.

Non-defensive communication meshes the people processes with the ongoing events. Figure 1-1 shows a picture of it. The process of communicating non-defensively boils down to consciously meshing the considerations of both objective and subjective processes—what you do and how you feel about what you do. Both processes happen simultaneously, but we often seem to think that the most important things are objective things. Somehow in less tangible, less visible processes, such as the people process, the feelings seem less important. Many people have a vague uneasiness that they can't control this potentially volatile process anyway, and they can't communicate what they feel, so they had best forget it. Yet most people are also aware that something's not quite right; perhaps they're not sure of what's really going on; but they suspect they're not really in control.

If you don't feel in control of yourself or if you have that vague sense of threat coming in from an unknown source, you're likely to feel some low-level anxiety.[1] This anxiety leads to many forms of defensiveness.

Feelings we have are neither good nor bad, just more or less useful.

Many people feel that they shouldn't have certain feelings, that they should have outgrown them. They evaluate what they should or should not feel. To me, there's nothing right or wrong about feeling anxious or defen-

---

[1]Rollo May discusses anxiety as being an emotion without a specific object and an inability to know "from whence the danger threatens," in *The Meaning of Anxiety* (rev. ed.), W. W. Norton, New York, 1977, pp. 60–61.

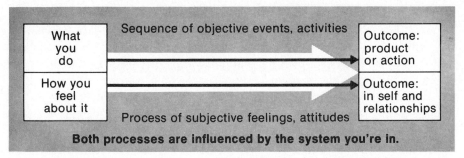

Figure 1-1. *Objective and subjective processes in a system occur simultaneously.*

sive. When I feel that way, that's how I feel. In fact, I doubt if it's possible *not* to feel defensive or anxious about a great many things in this changing, complex world. *It's what we do with such feelings* that makes the difference between saying to yourself "What's the use of fighting it?" and "I feel good about how I handled that." If I don't like what I'm feeling or what's happening or how I'm handling it, I can do something about myself, my relationships, or the situation I'm in. It may take a while, but it can be done.

Defensive communication results from having emotional fences between yourself and your problems. Non-defensive communication results from acknowledging the defensive feelings and turning that energy around so it can be used for constructive purposes. Here are some examples of what non-defensive communication looks like in action.

What Non-Defensive Communication Looks Like in Action

In this first case, engineer Jim Lansing was considering the risks of living by his principles. He hadn't yet learned to communicate non-defensively but wanted to be more of his own person.

I was asked by my boss to beef up the overrun costs on the government contract we were working on. I could go along with the one percent he wanted, even though I didn't like it. That was within sound engineering reasoning, which I could justify if asked. It turned out that I was asked. My boss called me in when the contractors came to audit our work. Later he asked me to up it another 2 percent. I think there was pressure from above. I knew that if I did what he asked, I'd be on the hotseat along with my professional judgment.

I don't like playing those games. I don't even want to know about what they're doing upstairs. You might say that I'm a craftsman, in Maccoby's language.[2] I just want to do the work well by sound engineering standards at reasonable costs. Sometimes I pay a price for being this way, but that's just the way I am. So I told my boss that he'd have to add the 2 percent himself and he'd have to justify it; I couldn't. He didn't like that, but I didn't get any more of those requests. [Jim's way of communicating with his boss was probably quite defensive, depending on the tone of his voice.]

Sometimes it's discouraging. I think you can do quality engineering at a fair price. I don't like gouging other people, even if that is the way the game is usually played. I just don't think you have to. [This is one of Jim's definitions of being his own person.]

Jim gives excellence a higher priority than gamesmanship even if it costs him some advancement. Knowing he can live with himself and his principles is very important to him. In his words, "That's success to me."

In this next case, Virginia Madison was working with her own inner processes before a scheduled confrontation.

I was in court getting a divorce, and I knew I would be attacked for not being a good mother. Even though my husband needed me in our accessories manufacturing business, he thought I should be at home available to the children. He knew I had some conflict about this even though I've worked it through fairly well. He also knows that sometimes I still rise to the bait when he attacks me on it. He was sure to try.

So while I waited for the judge to take our case, I wrote down the results I wanted and read them over and over to myself. I wanted a clean decision; I wanted decent child support and no alimony; I wanted to keep calm under any attack; I wanted to feel serene inside. So I sat there reading my list and letting myself feel calm and serene, and you know what? Every result I wanted happened. They never would have if I'd been sitting there thinking about what I was afraid of. He attacked me just as I expected, but I just didn't respond. I stayed calm and talked about the issues to be settled right there. I felt so proud of myself.

Virginia had good reason to feel threatened. By facing the threats and working with them, she turned her apprehensions into a new chunk of self-confidence. Even though she couldn't control the system, the judge, or the attorneys, she could have more control over herself.

---

[2]He's referring to one of the categories of corporate leaders described by Michael Maccoby in *The Gamesman: The New Corporate Leaders*, Simon and Schuster, New York, 1976.

Facing your own fears reduces their threat. Focus your attention on results you want, and you may get more of them.

In this third vignette, Teresa Adams, Finance Director of a substantial human services agency, needed some options for dealing with her manager.

Teresa had begun to notice a recurring pattern about 4 P.M. on Fridays. Her manager, Assistant Director Mark Saber [a name to fit his fantasies, according to Teresa], had taken to calling her into his office about that time and giving her a weekly verbal beating. He called it "constructive criticism." Other times during the week, Teresa would get an occasional nod of recognition or approval, but Friday afternoons were beginning to be painful. She took pride in the excellence of her work while adhering to her own code of personal ethics. She observed that Mark's stabs were always in one of those two areas, as if designed to hit where it would hurt most. Teresa was not clear what was really going on but had gradually come to dread the end of the week.

One Sunday she decided to write down some options. Here is her first unculled list of fifteen possibilities:

1. Go to his office as summoned and take the flogging.
2. Go to office and fight.
3. Go to his office and state, "This will stop." Expose his game.
4. Go to his office and change the subject. Save up a week's worth of important problems and bombard him.
5. Refuse to go to his office because, "I'm tied up."
6. Schedule every Friday afternoon off for vacation time and be alert to Thursday afternoon patterns.
7. Invite Mason [the director and Mark's boss] to join the Friday afternoon meetings. [Teresa had a good relationship with Mason as well as with his wife.]
8. Complain to Mason about my treatment from Mark.
9. Make an appointment for Mark to come to my office for staff meetings which I can schedule each Friday afternoon. My staff feels free to take Mark on here. They don't like him either.
10. Present Mark with another scapegoat in the agency, such as, "Are you aware of the mess in Personnel?"
11. Allow myself to be sexually seduced by him, which is working well for a few other executive women in the agency. (UGH!)
12. Resign my job and go somewhere else to work.
13. Take a leave of absence for several months while he finds another scapegoat.

14. Ask Mason to mediate the conflict.
15. Continue affirming for Right Action [her form of prayer].

We usually have many options, even though we may never choose to use some of them.

At the end of her list she penned "How to wreck Sunday." She resented having to deal with Mark's attacks, knowing that her reputation for excellence and commitment to the agency had long since been well established. She had good reason to suspect it might be related to her refusal of a proposition from Mark some three years before. If so, it was all the more galling. But there was no way to check that out.

Mark Saber was sending Teresa double meanings. Under the label of constructive criticism, he encouraged Teresa to reexamine herself and her work, even though there were no unusual problems needing attention. Underneath he was attacking two of her central values. She knew these attacks were not justified, having already reexamined herself several times before going on to analyze what else might be happening. The absence of similar comments during the week was another indicator that there was something different about Friday afternoons which, if effective, could sour her weekends. Whatever Mark's reason, neither of his double meanings was applicable as she saw them. So another meaning seemed likely, though unverifiable.

The result Teresa wanted was to work for someone who would value her work and value her as a person. While she worked for Mark, she used a combination of options 4, 5, and 15. This gave her distance from him. Her ethics didn't allow her to attack Mark or involve other people in his abusive tactics. Nor would she allow Mark to attack her any longer, once she paid attention to her feelings of dread. Then she began to analyze and plan strategies to get the longer term results she wanted.

Control, Power, and Authority

In each case described, notice that a central issue is *Control*. The questions raised are: Who is going to have control over whom? Who is controlling the situation? How much control can one keep over oneself? Can control be shared?

Also in each case, some form of *Power* or *Authority* is operating in the relationships and in the system where the events are acted out. For Jim, it's his boss, the government contractor, and his company; for Virginia, the husband, the attorneys, the judge, and the courtroom; for Teresa, her manager and the agency.

A person has power when he or she has the ability to cause or prevent change. Power can come from having access to physical resources such as money; it can also come from having influence, which comes from status or prestige. Power can be actual or potential.[3] Sometimes the *appearance* of power can be as effective as actual power.

A person has authority when she or he can gain consent from others to perform the desired action. "The decision as to whether an order has authority or not lies with the person to whom it is addressed and does not reside in persons of authority or those who issue orders."[4] Authority is generally more negotiable than power.

A person gains control through using power and authority for the purpose of controlling resources, a situation, or other people's behavior or activities. A person also controls oneself or one's own choices. The way that control is used has much to do with feeling defensive or non-defensive.

Control over others, over situations, and of self, are similar but different.

Most of us have had the experience of someone having control *over* us, which usually creates defensive feelings. We also control ourselves through self-discipline, which usually requires us to deny or push down some of our feelings. This can also create defensiveness.

Most of us have less experience with using control over ourselves as a way to deflect other people's attempts to gain control over us. Withholding consent can be one non-defensive way to disengage from top-down, competitive power plays. When Teresa sidestepped Mark's Friday meetings, she disengaged from his double meanings to retain control over herself. She acted, not reacted.

In the above cases we were focusing on the people processes behind the objective events. In each case a threat was presented. The actors dealt with their anxieties in constructive ways. They were staying centered in their own values, being their own persons. Even though they were in systems that could coerce them into compliance and even though others had the power to make decisions affecting important parts of their lives, these people, though *feeling* defensive, were true to themselves in the most non-defensive ways they knew. They had learned to keep their own identities and priorities separate from the

---

[3] Rollo May, *Power and Innocence*, W. W. Norton, New York, 1972, p. 99.
[4] Chester I. Barnard, *The Functions of the Executive*, Harvard University Press, Cambridge, Mass., 1938 and 1968, pp. 163–165.

expectations and pressures of other people, especially whose authority stemmed from a system's power and norms.

How Communication Is Influenced by the Systems in Which It Occurs

Let's take a moment here to consider a few key factors about the systems in which Virginia, Jim, and Teresa were communicating. The courtroom is clearly a hierarchy in which the judge has the power to exercise control over others. The court system culminates in the U.S. Supreme Court, the structure forming a pyramid with final decisions made at the top.

Work systems in which money is the grease on the wheels still use power, authority, and control in the pyramid structure of hierarchy.[5] The chain of command gave Jim's manager formal power to control him and the exercise of his engineering judgment, just as Mark Saber's position gave him control over Teresa's time and their relationship.

Position power is different from person power.

Positions within systems give people formal power and authority to control the activities of people. Formal power exists for people only as long as they hold those positions. Call it *position power*. Informal power and authority comes from the abilities people have developed within themselves to control their own choices and to influence others. Call it *person power*. Everyone has both, but when you're in the subordinate position, you have to rely more on your person power to make your way in the system because you may have little position power with which to work.

How people in authority positions use their power determines whether communication is mostly closed off and defensive or more non-defensively open. Perhaps the most common way authorities control subordinates is by calling forth basic values that motivate most people in their work. Three pervasive American values that have been strong motivators are:

---

[5] Although many other organizational forms are now being used—flatter pyramids, matrix structures, open systems—the pattern in most large systems is still the mechanical, bureaucratic hierarchy. Designed for industrial mass production, it is not as responsive to postindustrial technological rates of change and their social consequences.

- *The work ethic*—work hard, earn your way, strive to achieve your goals, one of which is financial success; respect the authorities who give you financial rewards.
- *Competitiveness*—maximize winning and minimize losing. Where neither side wins or loses, it's a draw, and both people save face.
- *Keep feelings out of the way*—suppress your feelings and be rational (don't feel or express anger, fear, frustration, or undue excitement); disclose little of yourself, get others to disclose more.

Although these values have contributed to giving us two cars in every garage, a TV in every room and an RV (recreational vehicle) in every other driveway, they also make it possible to manipulate millions of employees, Jim's and Teresa's experiences being a small sample. Jim and Teresa withstood the pressures by using their person power. Most employees become defensive if they rely only on position power.

Top-down communication can generate defensiveness.

One perceptive study showed how many executives used these three values to exercise control and take action.[6] They operated from the top down, designing and delivering goals, defining tasks and telling how the tasks would be done. They built a one-way street, giving little opportunity for subordinates to answer back or join in deciding how they'd do their own jobs. The executives' rule was "Do what you're told," just as Jim was supposed to add 2 percent more costs when told to, no questions asked. People with authority can win by manipulating the work ethic of subordinates to their own interests. It's persuasion through unquestioned shared values.

These executives also protected themselves by blaming others, stereotyping them, hiding their feelings, and intellectualizing. They acted out "the best defense is a good offense." Teresa got a dose of this under the label of "constructive criticism," which every good employee is supposed to be able to take, appreciate, and use.

They also played parent, protecting subordinates from being hurt by withholding information and creating rules to censor behavior such as not talking back "for their own good." Subordinates weren't sure whose "good" was being served, their own or the executives'.

[6] Chris Argyris and Donald A. Schön, *Theory in Practice: Increasing Professional Effectiveness*, Jossey-Bass, San Francisco, 1975, pp. 66–76.

These controlling actions communicated defensiveness to the subordinates, who felt little concern was being shown to them. Reacting defensively, they also become more dependent on the executives, participating less in meetings and helping each other less. As mistrust grew, they engaged in more rivalry and competitive power plays. Not having much freedom of choice or sense of involvement, they had little commitment to their work.

Few executives in the study had any way of breaking out of this vicious circle. If they opened up the subject, they might appear weak, as if losing instead of winning. Discussing the subordinates' defensiveness might have meant listening to some uncomfortable feelings, possibly rejection. Then things would really have been out of control.

If you, as a subordinate, accept the values of the work ethic, of competition, of suppressing your feelings, and of acting rational, you are likely to get caught up in protecting your position. That diverts your attention from your person power. If you're not using your informal person power, you are vulnerable to control by others. People with formal authority have power to control your position. That means your job is always on the line, whether you choose to put it there or not. Using your person power gives you some choice about what happens.

The power to define is the power to control—and the power to choose.

Teresa Adams' boss, Mark Saber, had caught her in this vicious circle of control for a while, and she would have stayed there if she had continued to suppress her feeling. As her dread of Friday afternoons increased, however, she listened to that feeling, using it as a warning signal. She didn't compete with Mark because he had more position power. She had worked hard, earned her way, and had achieved a fair amount of financial success, but she didn't respect this man.

Informal person power is used to renegotiate informal relationships.

Using her person power, she chose to make her share of the communications non-defensive, sharply reducing his control over her. She was changing the balance of informal power between them, while respecting the imbalance of formal power between their positions. She could be non-subordinate without being insubordinate.

People Are Changing and Non-Defensive Communication Can Make a Difference

More and more people are less and less ready to be obedient to traditional, top-down authority. More and more people in established, traditional authority positions—employers in particular—are becoming angry and frustrated with such changes. What their next moves will be—personally, in their work roles, and in reshaping the workplace—remains to be seen.

The Desire to Be One's Own Person Is Growing. As more people are wanting to act on their own authority, they are saying, in effect, "I want to be my own person, to make a dent in this world, to feel that I matter." A growing number of voices from all walks of life are saying the same thing. Here are some of them as they talked to Studs Terkel about their work.[7]

- Gary Bryner, young president of Local 1112, United Auto Workers, has different values than his father:

  Fathers used to show their manliness by being able to work hard and have big muscles. . . . Father felt patriotic about it. Whereas the young guy believes he has something to say about what he does. He doesn't believe that when the foreman says it's right that it's right. . . . He says, "I'll work the normal pace, so I don't go home tired and sore, a physical wreck. I want to keep my job and my senses."

  The almighty dollar is not the only thing in my estimation. There's more to it—how I'm treated. What I have to say about what I do, how I do it. . . . I can concentrate on the social aspects, my rights. And I feel good all around when I'm able to stand up and speak for another guy's rights.

- Sharon Atkins, receptionist, may yet get free of her machine:

  One minute to five is the moment of triumph. You physically turn off the machine that has dictated to you all day long... You're your own man [!] for a few hours. Then it calls to you every morning that you have to come back.

  My father's in watch repair. That's always interested me, working with my hands, being independent. I don't think I'd mind going back and learning something, taking a piece of furniture and refinishing it. The type of thing

[7] Studs Terkel, *Working: People Talk About What They Do All Day and How They Feel About What They Do*, Pantheon Books, a Division of Random House, Inc., New York, 1974. Quotes excerpted from Gary Bryner are on pp. 189–190; Sharon Atkins, pp. 31–32; Larry Ross, pp. 408–409 and p. 412; Kay Stepkin, pp. 465–470; and Tom Patrick, p. 589.

where you know what you're doing and you can create and you can fix something to make it function. At the switchboard you don't do much of anything. . .

■ Here's Larry Ross, ex-president of a conglomerate, now consulting with corporate officers. Here's why he left:

I left that world because suddenly the power and the status were empty. I'd been there, and when I got there it was nothing. Suddenly you have a feeling of little boys playing at business. Suddenly you have a feeling—so what?

■ About vice presidents, presidents, boards of directors, profits and people, Larry has these observations:

As he struggles in this jungle, every position he's in, he's terribly lonely. He can't confide and talk with the guy working under him. . . [or]. . . the man he's working for. To give vent to his feelings, his fears, and his insecurities, he'd expose himself. . .

[The president] can't talk to the board of directors, because to them he has to appear as a tower of strength, knowledge, and wisdom, and have the ability to walk on water. . . . So you're sitting at the desk, playing God.

You say, "Money isn't important. . . . What is important is the decisions you make about people working for you, their livelihood, their lives." It isn't true . . . To the board of directors, the dollars are as important as human lives.

■ Kay Stepkin, director of a bakery cooperative, is living out her ideas about work and her values about people:

We're a nonprofit corporation 'cause we give our leftover bread away, give it to anyone who would be hungry. . . . We never turn anybody away.

I get the same money as the others. I don't think that's the important issue. The decisions have been mainly mine, but . . . Now we have meetings, whenever anyone thinks we need one.

We try to have a compromise between doing things efficiently and doing things in a human way. Our bread has to taste the same every day, but you don't have to be machines. . . . I believe people will survive if we depend on ourselves and each other. Unless we do something like this, I don't see this world lasting. . . . There's such a joy in doing work well.

■ Tom Patrick's job as a fireman makes these concerns sharply clear:

Firemen, you actually see them produce. You see them put out a fire. You see them come out with babies in their hands. You see them give mouth-to-mouth when a guy's dying. . . . That's real.

I worked in a bank. You know, it's just paper. It's not real . . . You're lookin' at numbers. But I can look back and say, "I helped put out a fire. I helped save somebody." It shows something I did on this earth.

These people, some younger, some older, aren't dropping out. They're dropping away some of our earlier, traditional values of work. They want "daily meaning as well as daily bread."[8]

These are not lonely voices in the wilderness. They are joined by a new breed of Americans, born out of the social movements of the 1960s and grown into a majority in the 1970s. Out of his many years researching the workplace, Daniel Yankelovich concludes that "this New Breed holds a set of values and beliefs so markedly different from the traditional outlook that they promise to transform the character of work in America in the '80s."[9]

Values and beliefs are changing: being recognized as individual persons now matters; work matters less than leisure or family.

The most dramatic shift in what motivates the New Breed is the desire to become *recognized as individual persons*. They are on a quest for self-fulfillment, no longer getting a sense of identity from their work roles. They don't describe themselves as a car dealer, a salesman, a secretary. Instead they are saying, in effect, "I'm more than my role, I'm myself."

Almost as dramatic is the relative importance the New Breed puts on leisure, family, and work. They're in just that order: leisure first, work last. For people who lived through the Depression years, now over 40, such a reversal may be hard to absorb emotionally, even when they can agree with it intellectually. But for many under *and* over age 40, money and status are no longer the incentives they used to be. The old family pattern of husband as breadwinner and wife as homemaker in a family without divorce is now more memory than reality. The huge influx of women into the work force is not only due to economic factors; to many women, a paid job now represents "a badge of membership in the larger society and an indispensable symbol of self-worth. It is also a means of achieving autonomy and independence"[10] even when the job is menial or pays poorly.

Most of the thousands of over-30 working women with whom I've talked would probably put the desire for interesting, non-subordinate work close in importance to recognition as a person. They've done boring jobs long enough.

[8] Ibid., p. xi.

[9] Daniel Yankelovich, "The Psychological Contracts at Work," *Psychology Today*, May 1978, pp. 46–50.

[10] Ibid., p. 49.

Employers and Work Systems Are Slow to Respond. People in authority usually have a vested interest in maintaining their authority. At the very least they can be depended on to try to maintain the status quo. In the interest of stability, many executives consider social movements as possible passing fads, adopting an attitude of "It may go away, so let's not lose any sleep over it until we have to."

When there's a vested interest, many traditional men—and many women, too—will go to great lengths to protect that interest, whether from a minor threat or the usual threats of competition. My former employer did that, as did most of the executives in the study reported earlier. Protecting one's interests often means defending them. Therefore, defensiveness in management practices is usually a safe prediction.

The workplace has a reputation for being one of our most conservative institutions, highly resistant to change, particularly to social movements advocating stronger individual choice.[11] When people are primarily motivated by externals, such as paychecks and promotions, these rewards can be controlled by managers to serve their own interests and those of their systems. Now that many people are more motivated by internals, more rewards come from inside, out of the reach of employers. That doesn't leave as much to control.

Many people don't mind letting others take control and make the decisions as long as they have confidence or trust in the judgment of those to whom they give control. However, many people are questioning the old-style authority. According to one expert, Richard Cornuelle: "Authority is obsolete. It isn't working the way it once did; practically all Americans are losing confidence in practically all our institutions—highly structured, authoritarian, bureaucratic organizations—aren't working any more."[12]

Non-defensive communication is renegotiating control.

Much as managers may want to keep control, it still requires the consent of the controlled. With less of that around, the balance of control can now be negotiated more often. Considerable change is possible whenever enough people decide "they want to redefine their rights and force the front office to accept whatever definitions they devise."[13] We seem to be somewhere in that process now.

[11] Ibid., p. 50.

[12] Richard Cornuelle, *De-Managing America: The Final Revolution*, Random House, New York, 1975, pp. 7–17. He provides ample evidence to support these conclusions.

[13] Ibid., p. 144.

The Best Time to Make Changes Is When Change Is Happening.
The best time to negotiate changes in relationships is when many other
people are doing it, too. It becomes normal. If others are more demanding and
bumptious than you, the changes you want may seem tame and eminently
reasonable by comparison. Your odds improve.

Also the best time to negotiate a change is when a system is already
undergoing change. Virtually all our systems are in a state of flux. As a
consequence, people, products, and processes in most systems are also in
constant motion. Perhaps the most common symptom we have is "We're
going through a reorganization," at the end of which people say, "We've got
to get organized."

During change we unfreeze, add the change, and refreeze.

It doesn't matter whether the reorganize–organize cycle applies to marriage and divorce, going through a life passage, starting a second career,
being in an accident, or surviving in a work system—the process is the same.
You group your efforts around one cluster of activities and relationships, it
gets shaken up somehow, and you regroup around another cluster. All the
while, you have your own wants and needs to tend to, which by now may
include time for a breather, time to do nothing for a change!

Our common themes today are, "The only constant is change," and
"Nothings remains the same." Against that shifting background are also
these common themes: "I want to be my own person, to make a dent in this
world, to feel that I matter," and "I don't want to be alone while doing it."

For these crosscurrents to come together and make some sense, we
need more ways to stay afloat and roll with the tides, while also choosing and,
to some degree, steering our own directions. For these fluid situations, non-
defensive communication can be important.

WHY NON-DEFENSIVE COMMUNICATION (NDC) IS IMPORTANT

Many people spend quite a bit of time feeling defensive and would like
to be more of their own person. NDC not only describes and analyzes what
generates these defensive feelings; it also gives some approaches for changing them to some degree. Therefore, NDC is both an approach to communication as well as a problem-solving process. Its purpose is to make it possible
for you to be less defensive by being more of your own person, especially
when you're in a subordinate position.

When using NDC, you'll be listening to the inner dialogues you have with yourself—your intrapersonal communication—and considering some options for growing yourself. We'll also look at what occurs between yourself and other people—interpersonal communication—and consider some options for handling these relationships more non-defensively. Both intra- and interpersonal communication are influenced by the norms and relative power positions between yourself and others, so we consider options for how to minimize these factors while also respecting them.

NDC is both an approach to communication and a problem-solving process: within yourself, between yourself and others, and within the norms of systems.

As you can become more non-subordinate (without becoming insubordinate), you can feel more effective as your own person, in your relationships, and in doing your activities with a sense of pride and excellence. If you've done all you can where you are and you're not satisfied with what is happening, you can better identify another system in which your odds for gaining more results are better.

You can be non-subordinate without being insubordinate.

Not everyone is necessarily ready to change his or her situation. For some, maintaining a situation as it is may be more important right now. Sometimes that's difficult to do when so much change is occurring. Most of us, as Gail Sheehy suggests, have both seeker and merger selves, each of which has its time.[14] The seeker strikes out to reshape things; the merger self is more concerned with joining with others. When becoming non-defensive, both of these aspects of self are respected, since NDC is based on increasing your power to make your own choices according to your needs and desires.

[14] Gail Sheehy, *Passages: Predictable Crises of Adult Life*, E. P. Dutton, New York, 1974, pp. 35–37.

NDC is useful wherever you feel threat. How you deal with threat
is how you know yourself.

NDC can be useful, whether in handling surprise situations that put
you off balance or in making more extensive decisions about your life directions. It's useful in all aspects of living—at home and in your social life as
well as at work.

According to Rollo May, to realize one's self is to "avail oneself of new
possibilities in the meeting and overcoming of potential threats to his or her
existence."[15] Defensiveness is aroused by such threats. Non-defensive communication is one way of meeting and overcoming them.

READINGS

For additional background reading, see bibliography entries 1, 7, 9, 21, 25, 28, 31,
32, 33, 80, 82, 83, 88, 89.

---

[15] May, *The Meaning of Anxiety*, p. 391.

2

HOW NON-DEFENSIVE COMMUNICATION WORKS

Values and Principles in Action

NON-DEFENSIVE COMMUNICATION IN ACTION

Lori Landau, 26, handles the advertising for an employment agency owned by its founder, Mr. Charles Wilson, who wants his twenty-five employees to address him as Mr. Wilson, not Charles or Chuck. Three weeks after participating in a four-hour NDC workshop with the agency's four branch managers, Lori reports this experience:

> I was thinking of leaving. My opinions didn't seem to count for anything, even though that's the most important reason for my being here. Mr. Wilson gets these enormous ideas; I boil them down to ads. Then he gets five or six other people involved, everyone tears the ads apart, and round and round we go until he has nit-picked every detail with everyone. Since he was doing this all the time anyway, I figured he may as well write the ads himself and be done with it. He asks for my honest opinions and gets them. But if they're not what he wants to hear, we're off again, so why bother?
>
> After we had that workshop though, I got to thinking. Two of the branch managers kept telling me that he'd listen and try to do something if I'd just let him know how I felt. So I decided to try it.
>
> It took two weeks—he seemed to be avoiding me after I'd told him three or four times that I wanted to talk with him. I almost dropped the idea until we got into the same thing again, rewriting an ad at least ten times just to satisfy his ego. I was furious. This time, however, I sat down

and asked myself, "What results do I want?" I wanted to handle this to my advantage instead of just blowing up, but I wanted to get it off my chest. In a way, my feelings were running me, and I was starting to talk about him behind his back. So I also thought about, "What are my options?" Whatever I did, I had to be honest.

We finally got together. After going over the ads, I calmly told him how I was feeling. He was surprised, said it was all in my head, that he did value my opinions and I shouldn't feel that way. [Wilson's initial reaction to Lori's statements was a little defensive, as he tried putting her down by saying it was all in her head.]

But I gave him some examples, adding that perhaps I needed more tact and better timing with my honesty. He listened, but neither agreed with me nor admitted anything. That ended the discussion, but I guess he thought about it. The next ad that he wrote alone, he asked me twice if I liked it. I told him twice that I did, but he kept asking as if he doubted that I was telling him the truth. Finally, I asked him straight out if that's what was going on. It was and we got that cleared up.

Later we got to talking about the go-arounds again, and he agreed that perhaps too many people got involved and that he may have been spending too much time on details. He almost said he'd turn over the ad writing to me, but he kept the final say: "Show it to me and I'll try not to change anything unless I feel it's really important."

I felt so good I asked him if I could give him a hug—and did. He still didn't fully agree with me but that's okay. He's making the effort. I realize he won't change very much, but he doesn't have to. I needed to face it—for me. Now all that negative energy is gone. Being critical behind his back wasn't honest. I was hurting myself more than him.

You know, I have to give Mr. Wilson credit. He's made this agency a place where people can really talk with each other quite openly. I just didn't know that he was included, too.

No, I'm not going to leave. I can learn and do a lot more. When's the next NDC workshop?

NDC in Action: Growing Your Self and Increasing Your Options

Lori is growing into individuality and independence, taking responsibility for her own feelings, thinking about the results she wants and the options she has, and taking some risks after weighing the cost of leaving against the positive experiences others had had with Mr. Wilson. As she squarely faced her feelings and acted on them, she saw Mr. Wilson's behavior quite differently. Instead of expecting him to change, she's modifying her own behavior and is more willing to trust herself in the ongoing negotiation of their working relationship.

Ego needs can be met, control can be kept, others can be involved in decisions, and productivity and profits can also grow.

As for Mr. Wilson, who had contracted for the NDC workshop at the request of the director of branch operations, he does like getting everyone's opinions. He also recognizes that he likes to hear others admire his ideas, as most of us do. Now he can delegate responsibility more comfortably, get the ads done faster, get the support he wants from Lori, and keep necessary control over the final product. Strong commitment to the value of involving people in decisions allows him to balance other factors—a balancing act that varies from moment to moment. As he said, "When they're involved, they produce better and enjoy it more."

Growth and profits are high priorities of his, but so is the excellence of the services he provides through the collaborative efforts of the staff. His is one of the few agencies where employees are not on commission. Instead he pays higher salaries than most. He believes that employees who are competing for commissions won't produce the long-term results he wants.

The climate provided by Wilson's philosophy encourages people like Lori to be more of her own person and to increase her choices and control over herself. Figure 2-1 is a diagram of how this process might be shown graphically.

Think of yourself as having a door to yourself, a store of yourself, and a core of yourself.

You could call the *white giveaway area* a "door to self," where the door is open to others but you are not deeply involved. You keep little control over your choices here, playing out roles and meeting others' expectations without much questioning. People in subordinate positions may believe they have to give away control to others because of their formal position in the system. If so, they will use little of their potential person power.

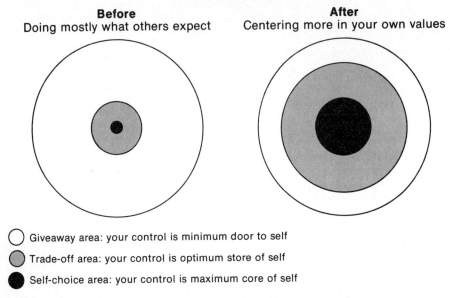

Before
Doing mostly what others expect

After
Centering more in your own values

○ Giveaway area: your control is minimum door to self

◐ Trade-off area: your control is optimum store of self

● Self-choice area: your control is maximum core of self

Figure 2-1.   *Increasing your areas of self-choice as you become more of your own person.*

The *shaded trade-off area* might be called a "store of self," where generally you share yourself with others and are willing to negotiate relationships, such as when Lori decided to try to work things out with Mr. Wilson. Here is where your person power becomes more active, and you can exercise optimum control over your choices. Optimum control means taking the risk of being yourself as much as possible while keeping within safe limits as you see them.

The *solid self-choice area* is like a "core of self," that center of yourself that you choose to discuss with others or keep to yourself. The core of self is where your vital values reside—values that give you a committed sense of purpose. Those values you will not compromise; to do so would be to compromise yourself. Refusal to compromise oneself was in Jim Lansing's refusal to pad the bill to the government. Over these values you exercise maximum control. They give your life meaning as you modify and reshape answers to universal questions such as, "Who am I?" and "What am I here to do in this life?"

At first, Lori was giving up on Mr. Wilson's behavior and giving away some of herself by saying nothing. She wasn't ready to risk talking with him (coming from her trade-off area), but she was committed to her honesty (her self-choice area). As in the Figure 2-1 "before" diagram, she had a relatively small self-choice area. But when she started talking to Mr. Wilson, she moved in the direction of "after." As she took more control over her own actions, she became more honest, using more of her person power as she accepted responsibility for making her own choices.

Mr. Wilson probably had a similar experience as he acknowledged what he was doing and made some different choices. Each became less defensive.

As you become non-defensive, you increase the size of your self-choice area as well as the trade-off area over which you maintain some control but in which you are willing to negotiate. As one or both of these areas is increased in size, there is a decrease in the size of the area in which you are willing to give yourself over to other people's control. Table 2-1 shows some consequences of changing the sizes of your self-choice, trade-off, and giveaway areas.

In thinking about making changes in yourself, there may be aspects in your life where you want total control. For example, you may allow no one to see the contents of your safe-deposit box, or you may feel that inquiry about your religious beliefs invades your privacy. For these, you can choose your own ways of saying "No," of not giving your permission to others to come into these self-choice areas.

In most aspects of life, however, total self-choice would mean self-isolation. You'd be all take and no give. In order to enjoy the normal give and take so essential for caring relationships, the door to self has to remain

Table 2-1. *Degree of Control Over Self and Consequences*

Degree of Control Over Oneself	*Some Consequences of Changing the Sizes of Self-Choice, Trade-Off, and Giveaway Areas*
Total Self-Choice	You isolate yourself. Self-choice based on your core values becomes confused with being selfish at others' expense. You become unwilling to consider others.
Much	You act as a person with strength, not compromising yourself on core values and negotiating most of your relationships in the trade-off area. Sometimes you risk temporary isolation, but you can live with that possibility.
Some	You are easier to get along with, negotiating many relationships, making more compromises, willing to give some of yourself away.
Little	You appear to be a pushover, using few trade-offs and more often giving yourself away.
None	You behave like a doormat, always giving yourself away. You do whatever anyone wants with no apparent convictions of your own.

partially open. However, you can choose when, how, and to whom you give permission to enter your psychological and physical space.

Once you have self-choice, you can choose to use less of it and still be non-defensive because you are guided by the strength of your core values and beliefs.

We're talking about moving *in the direction* of total self-choice without expecting to arrive there fully. When you're in your trade-off area, you may negotiate some relationships tightly, such as when contracting to purchase a home. In other relationships in which you feel more trust, you may negotiate more loosely, such as when agreeing on how work is distributed among your family or work group when you all feel a share of the responsibility.

When you have more choice and control over yourself, you can also choose to use less of it. The *act of choosing* to use less self-choice can also make you non-defensive.

When you feel you don't have any choice but to do what others expect of you or you're dependent on their fulfilling your expectations, you're more likely to feel defensive. You have fewer ways to protect yourself when necessary. However, when you know you can negotiate your relationships by extending yourself or holding your ground, you probably will feel less need to protect yourself. Trusting yourself to honor your core values and having conviction and skills to make them come alive acts as an inner non-defensive protection.

NDC in Action When Using Self-Choice Is a Risk

Growing your self is much easier when the climate is receptive. Not all systems are as collaborative as Wilson's agency. Let's see what happens when values conflict.

Leslie Stein, 44, has been personnel director of a privately supported, well-known medical center for sixteen years and more recently has also been functioning as its affirmative action officer. She believes in full compliance with the law, impeccable honesty, respect for the rights and worth of all people, and preservation of the integrity of the medical center in the community. In her position she often wears two hats at once: as a member of management and as an advocate of employees' rights. When her personal convictions conflict with what her bosses want, she is in a dilemma. For example:

Recently the chief of medical services fired Dr. Opal Miller, the only black woman doctor we had. True, there were some difficulties, but nothing that would cause her to be fired. The center was legally vulnerable, but Chief Administrator Bill Davis (my supervisor) didn't want to hear that. He didn't like opposing doctors' decisions.

Sure enough, Dr. Miller filed a claim and requested a hearing. Management decided to fight it with me as their representative, which I could not do. I advised Bill that the center was in the wrong and that it would lose the fight. He saw this as "fighting them and not being on the team." Nevertheless, I recommended they act legally by reinstating Dr. Miller without a hearing. That didn't sit well, as I knew it wouldn't.

I was considering bowing out and turning it over to our legal advisors when I was able to bring about another option—an internal hearing, which included attorneys from both sides. Management bought this idea, not because of Dr. Miller's rights, but out of fear of adverse publicity that might result in reduced funding. I didn't agree with their reasons, but a fair means to respect all interests was now possible.

The hearing resulted in Dr. Miller's reinstatement which, by this time, she didn't really want. During the delay, she had won a lucrative scholarship for postdoctoral study, for which she would have used the settlement money. However, she gained her point about improper termination.

The center avoided adverse publicity, but management expressed relief when Dr. Miller resigned to continue her studies. They lost a good doctor and some affirmative action points.

Personally and professionally, I felt good about the case having been handled fairly, according to the law, and within my ethics. Unexpectedly, I also gained credibility among black employees without loss of credibility among doctors or administrators. I like to think women and minorities will get more careful consideration in the future, but other managers have different values so I don't expect that will change very soon.

In this situation Leslie held the line, maintaining her ethics while doing her job in the manner she felt it deserved. The difference in values produced a climate that gave her little support or validation from her management, although she got some from employees.

Leslie's values more closely match those of the New Breed (even though she is older), the values of her bosses being more traditional. To get a picture of how these values come in conflict, several types of behavior are

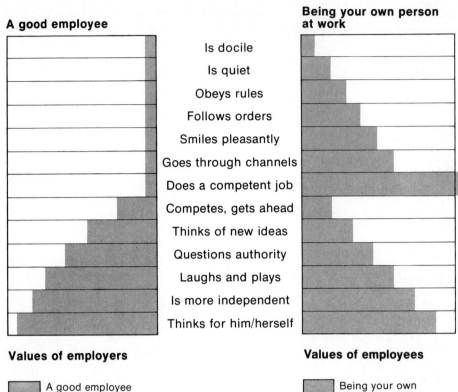

A good employee

Being your own person at work

Is docile	
Is quiet	
Obeys rules	
Follows orders	
Smiles pleasantly	
Goes through channels	
Does a competent job	
Competes, gets ahead	
Thinks of new ideas	
Questions authority	
Laughs and plays	
Is more independent	
Thinks for him/herself	

Values of employers

A good employee
Shaded area represents values that traditional employers do not want from employees.

Values of employees

Being your own person at work
Shaded area represents values that "New Breed" employees are likely to want when they are working. Notice they don't want just to do competent work; they want to do superior, sometimes inspired, work.

Figure 2-2. *Where values conflict: a hypothetical model of traditional employers and New Breed employees.*

shown in Figure 2-2, some of which are expected by traditional employers, some not so desired.

The first chart, "A good employee is," shows some typical expectations of traditional employers. The white area indicates desirable employee behavior, the shaded area undesirable behavior.[1] The first seven types are

---

[1] The types of behavior shown across the chart are somewhat hypothetical but are based on expectations of the more authoritarian styles of management described by Rensis Likert in his organization profiles of System 1 and 2 in *The Human Organization: Its Management and Value*, McGraw-Hill, New York, 1967.

highly valued in most employees, whereas competing to get ahead is valued in fewer employees. Continuing down, we see that being more independent and thinking for oneself are definitely not wanted. Leslie got that message when she gave an opinion and was then accused of "not being on the team."

The shaded area in the second chart, "Being your own person at work," shows an estimate of how much of these values New Breed-type employees are likely to go along with or want. Not only do they want to do a competent job, but many want to do a superior job. Even this can be an area of conflict, as we see in Figure 2-3, where the first two charts are superimposed.

The open, white areas in Figure 2-3 indicate values being practiced in a vacuum where employees don't do what is expected of them. For instance:

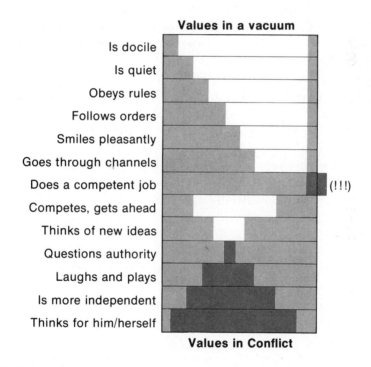

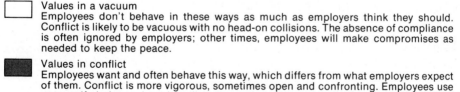

Values in a vacuum
Employees don't behave in these ways as much as employers think they should. Conflict is likely to be vacuous with no head-on collisions. The absence of compliance is often ignored by employers; other times, employees will make compromises as needed to keep the peace.

Values in conflict
Employees want and often behave this way, which differs from what employers expect of them. Conflict is more vigorous, sometimes open and confronting. Employees use more self-choice and are less likely to compromise themselves as they see it.

Figure 2-3. *The nature of conflict between traditional employers and New Breed employees.*

River City's volunteer office was run by Ella Randall, who was nearing retirement and had been a hard worker all her life. She would go to her retirement dinner unable to understand what motivated the three young women now on her staff.

Ella tries to set an example of "a good day's work for a good day's pay." A strong believer in proper discipline, she bemoans that "Those girls just don't work like they should. They socialize too much." (When pushed, Ella admits they get the work done.)

She feels she's dealing in a vacuum; she gets no response. The young women don't fight her, they do things their way and get the job done.

The conflict is indirect; it stems from their differences in some values. A result is that the younger women do not comply with the norm that they appear to be working hard and industriously. Their style is more relaxed while they get the work done—another important value they adhere to. It's hard to fault people who do what they're paid for, so some of these differences are ignored or tolerated by employers.

At the lower end of Figure 2-3 where values are in conflict, employees are doing things not wanted by traditional employers. Conflict is more direct, as with Leslie. She was very much her own person, operating from a strong core of self and a large store of self. Her door to self was not very open. As a result, she was more likely to come in conflict with her traditional managers. However, she had many more ways to develop and negotiate strategies for handling that conflict because she had so much control of self.

Leslie couldn't do what her management wanted, and she even considered bowing out but was able to find an option they could all live with. It was not particularly gratifying to her, since she expected the same kind of battle would be fought again. Bill, her boss, probably expected the same. It was an uneasy truce, since her ethics sometimes became threatening to others. These same ethics were also valued or she wouldn't have worked there so long, she reasoned.

To put your values into action, you need two or more options to choose from. If you know only one way you have no real choice.

Others in her place whose giveaway area is much larger (such as on the "before" diagram in Figure 2-1) would incur less conflict. They would be more likely to go along with requests from their supervisors, even when they didn't want to. Often such people avoid conflict because they don't know how to generate *options* for handling it well. They may feel their only choice is to go along. If they know only one option, they don't have a real choice.

We have to be able to visualize two or more available options, which we can imagine ourselves actually using, before we can make a choice between them. To be able to cook up more options can be critically important to people who want to be their own persons. NDC provides a way to do that.

NDC in Action: A Process of Choosing Among Options to Gain Specific Results

To stay off the defensive, the Choosing Process is a way to define the results you want and generate options for getting them. The more you become your own person, the more likely you are to come into conflict with traditional employers. You'll get most of your results through negotiating with your informal person power, combined with the power advantages (or disadvantages) of your official position.

The Choosing Process is a form of problem solving that helps get these results. It consists of seven steps:

1. Sensing Attitudes. Becoming aware of feelings, biases, assumptions, values, norms, priorities—your own, and others—within the system you're in.

2. Analyzing Content. Observing and gathering data about what is happening, what is not, and what might be occurring beneath the surface.

3. Formulating Results Wanted. Formulating a clear statement of what you want to be happening when action is completed and how you'd identify it.

4. Generating Options. Generating as many options as possible for how to get results you want. This includes those options you doubt you'd ever use. You'll get the most options when you don't evaluate any of them at this point.

5. Assessing Risks and Odds. Rating each option for what helps or hinders your using it; also assessing how well it will get the results you want and how much risk you can take with some safety to get those results.

6. Testing Choices. Making a tentative choice that you then test for mutual gain, worst possible consequences, and how well it fits your style and ethics.

7. Taking Action. Taking action with the choice you made, or making an action plan with others. When results are known, these are compared to results you want; then you learn how to sharpen your skills for next time.

This process can be used in great detail or almost instantly. Not all the steps are necessary in every situation. In the first case, Lori Landau simply focused on results she wanted and her options when she was getting ready to confront Charles Wilson. She also used all the other steps, in part, without thinking them through in detail. That was sufficient for her purposes.

On the other hand, Leslie Stein had more at stake, so she had to use all of the steps. She had to consider such factors as the medical center personnel director's status, the peculiar patterns of the medical center system—doctors' and administrators' struggle for control; the shifting relationships among nurses, union organizers, the board, and the fund raisers as each group exercises its power and authority; as well as her past and current relationships with people involved in Dr. Miller's dismissal.

Leslie wanted some specific results: to comply with the law, to respect employees' rights, not to participate in something that would violate her ethics, and to keep a decent working relationship with Bill, other managers, and the doctors. Not an easy order in this case. However, she had several options that she kept working on, with the least desirable always available— backing out. She was prepared to put her job on the line, if necessary.

As the situation developed, Leslie kept assessing the various risks, those risks which were working for her as well as against her, keeping several options available that were acceptable to her. Fortunately, she was able to take an action that resulted in some gain for herself, some for Dr. Opal Miller, and a somewhat negative gain for the administration—relief at Dr. Miller's resignation. The administrators and doctors got rid of Dr. Miller, which was both a win and a lose—that is, a draw solution. Even though Dr. Miller won her case, the others could save face by not facing that loss every day.

The strength of the Choosing Process is its flexibility. It can be used in any situation to increase control over your own decisions. However, this is also a function of your own priorities, some of which may be in conflict. You may want to stick to your convictions but not be willing to go all the way in that commitment if it means your job.

When you defend yourself, others name the game—and your worth. When you choose for yourself, your worth is measured by your own values.

For example, if Leslie had not been willing to put her job on the line, she might have become defensive when Bill told her she wasn't on the team.

With a not-so-hidden threat like that, many people protect themselves by going along with people in power. Once you put your attention on defending yourself *against* others, you are not likely to be thinking of ways to work through problems *with* others. When you defend yourself by going along, you put the location of your esteem and the evaluation of your behavior in the hands of the people with authority. You may become clay in their hands. Then they decide your worth by their values.

When you're non-defensive, you evaluate your behavior by your own standards. Since your energy is still centered in yourself, you can continue to put your attention on working through the problems with everyone's concerns in mind, even when you don't agree with their reasons. You are more likely to keep searching for options that fill the bill, knowing that if you have to, you will bow out from the immediate situation or from the job. At best, you may save the day; at worst, you may be a thorn in their side. But you decide your worth by your own values.

You may not feel you can take the risk of putting your job on the line. There are just too many mouths to feed and too many bills to pay. When that's the case, your options are fewer. However, when you consciously face that fact and make your choices accordingly, you are less likely to feel defensive.

If you can see your way out of that bind, it's even better. You may want to consider a plan to reshape your budget to get out of excessive debt and develop some options for increasing your income. Those plans take time, of course, and require patience, persistence, and perhaps more know-how. When you can move away from the fear of being fired and move toward some possible ways to cover your financial needs or increase your financial resources, you're building more security within yourself. When we can see more options for exercising our own choices, it becomes more tolerable to live with situations that aren't desirable. And sometimes when your personal security feels greater, the situation may not seem as undesirable.

It's not the action you take, it's the *choice* you make, that keeps you non-defensive.

After going through the Choosing Process, you may decide to take the same action you would when you felt defensive. But *if you choose to take an action because you expect it to get results you want, you are likely to be non-defensive by the act of choosing.*

The more you can control the choices toward results you want, the less defensive you become—as long as others also gain while you do.

NDC in Action: Changes in Management Norms Change the Climate

People's desire to be treated as persons and not as machines is long standing. A manager who treats a subordinate as a person can leave an indelible memory. Retired plant manager J. B. Montgomery, age 79, had this experience at a meeting of his former mining company's club for employees with over twenty-five years of service:

> The last time I was at our Quarter Century Club meeting, old Fred Hinkle—he used to be one of our welders—came up to me and said, "Monty, do you remember the time I was tugging on a heavy welding machine, trying to haul it up the ramp in the mill? You came along and got behind it and gave it a big shove. You kept at it 'til we got that rig up that ramp. Do you remember that?"
>
> After he reminded me of it, I can vaguely remember it. But what amazes me is that he would remember that after all this time. Why, that must have happened at least twenty years ago!

Apparently it was a rare event for the top manager to pitch in and lend a hand when needed.

Even today, it's news. A feature story on the changing management practices at National Can Corporation began with this incident:

> Escorting a top executive from headquarters on a walking tour of the plant . . . the manager noticed a puddle of oil on the floor. Instead of collaring the nearest worker, ordering him to mop the oil FAST before the executive spotted it, the manager, Fred Verschueren, grabbed a rag and mopped in up himself. Workers watching the scene didn't seem surprised. And if the executive had been looking, he would have been pleased with Verschueren. For the executive is Roland H. Meyer, National Can's senior vice president-operations, who is campaigning to break down the "king–serf" relationship between management and labor that he contends exists at too many manufacturing companies.[2]

According to the news story, chief executive Frank Considine attracted Meyer with this philosophy:

---

[2] Excerpted from Ron S. Heinzel, "I'm the Boss! But at National Can It Means Being a Good Guy, Too," *Los Angeles Times*, Outlook, Part IV, June 4, 1978, p. 1.

We want to grow through the use of people. I don't mean using people. I mean I want us to be a people-oriented company. I want to change the company.

By all the usual measures, the philosophy seems to be working. At the Vernon, California, plant, the accident frequency has reportedly been slashed by 48 percent, absenteeism dropped 1.8 percent to less than 2 percent overall, and union grievances are on the decline.

How does this happen? It seems that Fred Verschueren talks with the workers where they are. He doesn't believe in the open-door policy; he prefers to be out on the floor where he can find out how to help with problems employees are having.

When there are changes, "You tell them 'that's the way it's going to be BECAUSE . . .' The because is important. Years ago we were glad just to have a job, and we took things just because somebody told us to. But today you've got to take time to explain why."

Further, Verschueren reportedly asks workers for their ideas. When he couldn't get a handle on the scrap problem:

He stopped production one day and called a meeting of the hourly workers. "That accomplished two things," he says. "First I let them know we had a problem. Second, I got some positive feedback."

Not only does Verschueren get results this way, but so does Meyer, the visiting executive.

After complimenting a worker on a couple of days when production topped three million cans, the worker said: "Yeah, man, that was pretty good but it's going to get better."

Surprised, Meyer asked why.

"Because when you treat people like people that's what counts— that's everything. They treat us like people here and that's why things will get better," the worker said.

As he turned away, Meyer seemed a bit shaken by the response. He leaned toward Verschueren, smiled and said: "That's MY payoff."[3]

---

[3] Ibid. One thing which would have made this story more credible would have been the inclusion of the worker's name. The caption for a large photograph accompanying the story named Verschueren and Meyer, but gave no name to the pictured black worker.

According to this story, there is mutual gain all around—for the workers, for management and for the company—which is not an easy balance to establish and maintain. However it may be no more difficult than managing by traditional top-down, one-way communication and control, creating a more defensive climate; and National Can reportedly is getting better results.

NDC: VALUES AND PRINCIPLES IN ACTION

Next we will consider a few underlying values from the several cases, principles, and processes that have been introduced.

Respecting One's Rights As a Person

When becoming non-defensive, you have to respect your own rights as a person as well as those of others, not violating their sense of self, their feelings, or their choices. Each person must have the psychological space in which to maintain his or her personal dignity, even when you don't like what that person does. Let's see how this works in action.

> Tony Jamison, 15, had no regular home. His mother had custody but gave him little caring and had lost control. He landed in juvenile hall after a couple of years of deciding everything for himself. He was caught stealing.
>
> The parole officer contacted his father, Hal Jamison, who agreed to bring Tony into his family acquired by marriage, with the consent of his present wife, Carol, and her three daughters, ages 7, 10, and 14. The judge's terms to Hal were: "We'll try this arrangement for 30 days. If you can control his behavior, he won't have to be locked up."
>
> Tony had learned to hide his feelings. During that month, he used his usual non-responsive, controlling behavior, saying nothing to express "Thank you," or "I won't steal from you again," or "I like (or hate) being here"—no remorse, nothing. Participating little or not at all in family goings-on, he kept complete, total control over himself. Thirty days of that behavior generated endless strain among the rest of the family members. He had no give.
>
> Hal and Carol were wise enough to refrain from trying to control him, in spite of the judge's instructions. They gave Tony many opportunities to join in and knew that if anything worked out, Tony would have to voluntarily choose to give up some of his controlling behavior. After a month of stress, they put it to him straight:"We don't want you to stay if you continue to push us all to the limit as you've been doing." That's where it stood as they drove to court. The judge's terms were not met so it looked like lock-up for Tony.

On the way, he came to a tough decision. "I want to live in that house," he parried.

The answer came: "It's more than a house. It's a home with us living in it."

Slowly, tentatively, Tony ventured again. "I want to live with you." Carol and Hal handled his vulnerability gently, respecting his unease. Then they discussed what that might mean for Tony as well as the rest of them. They didn't feel they had won a victory as much as relief that Tony might try more ways to grow into the family.

In court, the judge agreed to Tony's staying with the family another thirty days.

This was a difficult negotiation for everyone. Hal and Carol had to insist on their rights and her daughters', yet they didn't want to take away Tony's right to make his own choice. Not controlling Tony didn't mean they couldn't say "No" to him. They were controlling their own limits. Control was the issue.

When options are few, defenses are many. The vicious circle is hard to break out of.

Tony's area of control was limited so his options were few. At 15, under a court order with only one family willing to accept him, he had to consider the constraints of two systems available to him: the legal system and the family system. To him, his options were: Give away no control to the family and lose his physical freedom or give up some control to the family and keep most of his physical freedom. Yet he wanted physical freedom with no control.

He had not yet learned how to negotiate his relationships, so he felt as if he were choosing between having total control or no control—a tug of war. Hal and Carol didn't want to play that game with him. They felt they had to draw the line and say "No." Yet they were willing to keep the door open if Tony would give a little respect. But that Tony had to decide for himself, since he had to live with the consequences of his actions.

Using Gain–Gain Values Works Better Than Win–Lose

First, let's see how the win–lose values work. Then we'll see how using gain–gain values increases your odds of gaining more results you'd like for yourself.

Because of the hierarchical, authority–subordinate structure of most work systems, you're one down when you're in a subordinate position. The further down you are in the organization, the more down you are. When win–lose, competitive values prevail, each down point becomes a losing point for you. To start counting your down points count how many levels down from the top you are. Then give yourself additional down points if you are:

- In a staff position[4]
- Too old or too young (Check the average age of recently promoted white males to find out what is not too much.)
- Working in any non-income-producing department
- A female
- Working in a slow-track department (Check the departments from which the better promotions are usually made. If you're not in one of those departments, you're one down.)
- Having a slow rate of promotion so far
- Not having skills that can be transferred to another system
- A minority (In some systems it's worse to be black than Asian. Check the evidence; occasionally you get a temporary up point if you're the "right" minority.)
- Working behind the scenes
- On a short career path
- Physically handicapped
- Without a college degree or with the wrong one
- A graduate of the wrong university (Check to see if many executives come from the same school. If so, that's the right one.)
- A supervisor who has lost momentum or clout
- In any other category that doesn't fit winning patterns peculiar to your organization

Now that you've counted your down points, you counterbalance these with your up points to calculate your win–lose position. Give yourself up points if you are:

- In a second-level or higher position (In a ten-level organization, give yourself one up point for every two levels above first-line supervision.)

---

[4] Staff people generally advise, assist, provide expertise, and support the line operations of a company. Staff functions are accounted for as an expense. These efforts do not directly produce income as do line functions, which produce the company's product or service. Consequently, staff roles are usually less valued when a primary value in the work system is making money. In government where profits don't govern, being in a staff position is only a half down point.

- The right age *and* white *and* male (It usually takes all three to make one up point.)
- Working in an income-producing department from which fast-track promotions are usually made (It usually takes both to make one up point.)
- Sponsored by a mentor who has already seen to it that you have established a beginning track record that is properly paced and who is introducing you to the higher level, informal "old-boy network" (It usually takes all three to make one up point.)
- A favored family member in a family-owned corporation (This is worth three up points all by itself, sometimes more.)
- A graduate of the right college (This is worth from one to three points, depending on the importance attached to certain schools in your company.)
- A member of some other favored category in your system

Another source of up points can come from outside these channels, such as participation in an action group of some kind or membership in certain professional and community organizations. However, the points to be made here are highly variable—sometimes volatile. Only you can estimate whether they will give you up or down points.

After totaling your down and up points, if you come out with more downs than ups, playing by win–lose rules isn't to your advantage. You're guaranteed to lose in most encounters. In competitive systems, you're usually a loser to start with. If you don't like those odds, playing by those rules isn't your game. You need more gain–gain rules.

Even from the down position, you can improve your odds. When you consider how you can gain some of the results you want while also considering what others want, you redefine your rules to gain–gain, which increases your odds of success. Since you're not trying to set up higher up point people to lose, they are less likely to become defensive and use their points to win over you. Better, you are trying to help them maintain their points while you increase yours. This improves your odds. Gain–gain values are based on non-defensive premises that reduce threat to others and increase the potential for more collaborative, mutually supportive relationships. Most people in subordinate roles could use more of that. Odds are increased when you offer it.

Power With Others Is Like Drawing the Circle Bigger

We're so accustomed to one person using power over another—win–lose use of power—that it may not be easy to visualize the idea of "When you and I decide on a course of action, we have power over ourselves together."[5] When our interests are bound together, even though they may not be the same, we are in one situation, not two. When we treat it as one situation, then the authority of the situation will appear, which can give power to participants who differ.[6] Let's see this in action:

> At a city council meeting, women representing both conservative and feminist views had been invited to discuss possible rape prevention programs for their community. The arguments were becoming heated when conservative Marcy Dilmont flatly announced her solution for the whole problem: "Get rid of dirty movies and dirty bookstores because pornography is the cause of rape."
>
> Rather than get sidetracked into arguing the relative merits of this simple solution for a complex problem, feminist Beth Teague quietly countered with, "We won't get rid of rape until we teach a whole generation not to be violent."
>
> Marcy Dilmont couldn't disagree with this statement. It included her views even though it didn't respond to them directly. By drawing the circle bigger to include all the issues, Beth Teague put rape in its context of violence. Then she redirected attention to the interrelated, feasible prevention programs, which was the reason for their being at the council meeting.

For a short time, the situation had authority. Marcy Dilmont's and Beth Teague's opposing interests were bound together in the context of the city council's interest in rape prevention programs.

By Building on Your Strengths, You Have More of Yourself

NDC builds not only on your own strengths but on the strengths of others, respecting their potential for more self-choice. Becoming non-defensive does not mean having no defenses. Nor does it mean being nicey-nice. It assumes the best, not the worst, from people, but it does not ignore conflicts and differences that exist. Instead of polluting relationships with blame, guilt, and buck-passing, differences are respected and brought out as much in the open as possible to be dealt with honestly. If productive energy is to be released, the parties need a background of caring and respect. We saw this happening at National Can.

[5]Mary Parker Follett, *Creative Experience*, reprinted by Peter Smith, New York, 1951, by permission of Longmans, Green, and Co., London, 1924, p. 186.
[6]Ibid., p. 187.

To really listen to others takes much more courage and strength than defending yourself by building façades of fear or shifting your responsibility to someone else. It takes real person power to hear what you may fear to hear, to face it, and grow with it. But when you do, you can have more of yourself through building a larger repertoire of behavior. Here's how that can happen.

A group of litigation attorneys were so well trained in adversary behavior that they had trouble getting necessary support from their staff. The staff felt like they were being prosecuted and had lost interest in "understanding attorneys." Here's what was happening:

Attorney Barry Swinbourne would ask for staff support from Jan Morris, the firm's editor, in this manner: "Edit this brief so it'll get past the judge." He didn't like the senior partner's rule that all briefs had to be edited and he expected Jan to know what to do with them.

Jan felt he was asking her to do his work because he didn't say what key points he wanted to make or what the judge's expectations were. No matter how she edited, if it wasn't what Barry needed, he could shift the responsibility back to her. When she asked him for more specifics, he'd tell her, "Editing is your job. You ought to know how to do it." He was playing adversary, putting her on the defensive, and not getting the editing done the way he had to have it.

Finally Jan told Barry he'd have to give her enough information to do the editing or she wouldn't be able to accept his work. [She knew she had the senior partner's backing to take this position.] Her powerful "No" required Barry to reconsider his position. But she did it with respect, not rejection, expecting both of them to gain.

When Barry started focusing on the results he really wanted, he realized he was taking out on Jan his frustration at the senior partner's rule. What he really wanted was a good brief. So he tried this with Jan: "Please edit this brief so it emphasizes these points with these as sub-points; gloss over here and lift out these two points with sharp clarity." Jan then had criteria for doing the job the way Barry needed it. She became more involved as she felt Barry working with her, not against her. Both got more of what each needed.

Adding a more explanatory, collaborative style to his repertoire of behavior didn't lessen Barry's adversary skills. There's a place for parrying and thrusting in the courtroom; at the same time there's a place for caring and trusting back at the office. Barry now had more ways of communicating when he wanted different kinds of results. He also began to see some benefits from having editorial services that saved him time at the office and in court.

The Power to Define Is the Power to Control—and to Choose

In most of the examples so far, we have seen that an underlying issue is control. We've seen how power and authority give legitimacy for exercising control over other people and for controlling situations. Now let's see how the power to define gives another person the power to control *you*—and also gives you the power to choose and gain more control over yourself.

Some people control by defining the rules of the relationship. You can choose to redefine the rules of how you will relate.

One way to control others is to define the rules of a situation or relationship. For example, if your supervisor says to you, "Now let's be fair," the hidden meaning is usually "by my rules." If you accept his or her definitions without being aware that you are doing so or if you're not negotiating the rules as you go along, your supervisor will define, and thus control, the rules of what's fair for you.

Listening for such power plays, recognizing them, and deciding for yourself whether or not they're acceptable to you is part of getting off the defensive. When Teresa Adams realized that Mark Saber's "constructive criticism" was actually destructive, she probably became aware of following one of her own inner assumptions; perhaps "I'm supposed to listen to constructive criticism and learn from others' experience to improve myself." As long as she believed Mark's comments were constructive she endured the pain, thinking there must be something there for her to learn.

Once she followed her feelings to identify her inner assumption, she found that she was not learning, only enduring, so something else must be happening. At that point, she used her power to redefine the rules so she could exercise more of her own options in that relationship. This is one way the power to define can also be the power to choose.

Some control by defining responsibility and authority. You can choose to state your desires or limits, drawing on higher authority when needed.

Another way that supervisors exercise control is by defining your work, which is an ongoing negotiation of your responsibility, authority, and accountability. Sometimes you may be given more responsibility than authority, yet be held accountable for your work as if you had enough authority to act. Jan Morris was given more responsibility than authority from the senior partner for editing Barry Swinbourne's briefs. From Barry she received little information with which to do it, yet he held her accountable for correct editing—correct by his definition. She renegotiated that imbalance by refusing to edit his work without sufficient information, knowing she was backed by the formal power and authority of the senior partner.

Some control by giving orders. You can choose to not follow orders.

Jim Lansing was asked to take responsibility for adding 2 percent overrun costs based on his engineering authority, though he didn't feel it was honest. He didn't want to be held accountable for something that violated his principles. He chose not to negotiate but simply to refuse. His supervisor could no longer lead him because Jim refused to follow.

Some control by unintentional confusion. You can choose to clarify by discussion.

Lori Landau was given more responsibility and authority for certain radio ads than Charles Wilson was willing to leave in her hands. As she interpreted his actions, he kept giving and taking back both her authority and responsibility. She renegotiated that confusion through direct discussion with him.

In all these cases, the people in subordinate positions were renegotiating their responsibility and authority by drawing on higher authority, by refusal to act, or by direct discussion. These are among the ways you can redefine the rules of your job so you have more room to choose how you perform it. Some rules are more negotiable than others, of course, depending on your supervisor's needs to control you or the situation.

Some control by defining your options. You can choose to generate more options.

Another way that some supervisors exercise control is to define your options. "It's either this . . . or that . . . Which is it going to be?" When you are given either–or options and neither one is acceptable to you, you can choose to redefine these limits by saying something like, "I think there are some other possibilities." For example, Jim Lansing had an either–or choice when his boss told him to either add the 2 percent cost overrun or (leaving an unstated threat). Jim might have found a less arbitrary way of refusing to add an across-the-board increase by offering to go over the cost breakdowns with his boss to identify places where costs were actually higher. By using a selective instead of an averaging technique, he might have found some ways he could honestly work with his boss's instructions. If there were none, he might have convinced his boss in the process that they had gone as far as was reasonable to go. He could take his boss's either–or into consideration while looking for a way to have more control over his own options.

Whenever you are exercising your power to define to get more power to choose, you are enlarging definitions. You can do this by extending the limits around yourself and giving yourself a wider field of operation, which may also benefit your supervisor. It's another way of drawing the circle bigger and operating from gain–gain values.

YOU KNOW YOU'RE ON YOUR WAY TO COMMUNICATING NON-DEFENSIVELY WHEN . . .

Your odds of becoming non-defensive are best when you focus on becoming more of your own person while getting more of the results you want, that others want, and that will move ahead the task at hand. Your odds are also better when you're prepared to offer to others what you'd like for yourself. Here are some of the directions in which you may grow.

You're Responsible to Yourself and WITH Others, as Well as TO and FOR Others

Consider these six kinds of responsibility, the first three being most useful for becoming non-defensive, the last three for getting along non-defensively in relationships and systems that invite defensiveness.

Responsibility to yourself and *with* others makes collaborative energy flow.

First, when you're responsible to yourself, you take ownership of your own feelings, attitudes, and behavior; you do not shift or project them onto other people by blaming or passing the buck. You also take responsibility for your own personal and professional growth, being true to yourself and not compromising yourself. Teresa Adams was responsible this way when she chose to distance herself from Mark Saber's tactics.

Second, when you're responsible *with* others, you share your knowledge and experience, listen, add, and build on ideas, and join efforts to co-create something more than you could do alone. Kay Stepkin did this as she balanced the desired economic and humanistic outcomes of the bakery she was managing collaboratively.

Third, developing your ability to respond is another way of being *with* others. You can listen and hear other people's concern and enthusiasm without feeling you have to do something about them. By giving and receiving feedback, you obtain clear information (without double meanings) and can trust the quality of your relationships. From a desire to be with others you become responsive while getting work done. You're on the same side of the fence. As Lori Landau and Charles Wilson renegotiated their relationship, they did more of this. It was probably also happening at National Can.

Responsibility *to* and *for* others can be exercised with more self-choice.

These first three kinds of responsibility are less likely to produce defensiveness because they are more on the same level, more mutual and reciprocal. More traditional definitions of responsibility lead to defensiveness because they use more top-down control. For example, when you're hired to do a job, someone else usually decides what you're supposed to do and evaluates you. You're responsible *to* the one who pays—a fourth kind of responsibility. You're down and may become defensive, as did Lori Landau when she felt like giving up on Mr. Wilson. As she saw it initially, he was defining everything.

Being on top doesn't necessarily relieve you of defensiveness either. As a supervisor (or parent) you're usually responsible to see that others are taken care of and do what they're supposed to do. Using this fifth form of responsibility, you decide *for* them on the assumption they need controlling and you're the one to do it. However, if they don't agree, they may not accept your control. Any attempt to control Tony Jamison would have invited his rebellion, leading to a vicious circle of more control and rebellion in which everyone would have become more defensive. This often happens between supervisors and subordinates on a more subtle basis.

Sixth, as an adult, you're expected to be responsible *for* yourself and your family, providing a living for all of you. Part of being responsible for yourself is your continued advancement on the job with increasing income. Do it and you're considered successful, worthy of social approval. Need help and you may be seen as a failure, leading to feelings of defensiveness. When you're non-defensive, you'll be less concerned by others judging you as a success or failure, knowing it's a strength to seek help when you need it.

Non-defensive people who are responsible in the first three ways also tend to be responsible in the last three, although their motive may not be as much for social approval as for their own personal integrity. When Leslie Stein handled the dismissal of Dr. Opal Miller, she was using these six kinds of responsibility, but in her own time and style.

Your Security Is Located More Within Yourself, Less in Others

As a non-defensive person, you have a healthy respect for yourself, a positive belief in your own worth, a commitment to your own growth, and more independence from others' approval. True, most of us need to get feedback from others to get some idea of how we're coming across. We can sort out these perceptions and use what seems to fit. Also, most of us need validation from other people—some acceptance and approval, but when you're non-defensive you can do without approval for a while when necessary. You have your core of self, that home-base that is your centering point. You can learn to rely more on yourself, just as you can rely more on others you trust. You can become more interdependent and increase your resources.

That core of self is your inner source of identity as a person, the source of your person power. It includes the values that guide your choices. Some of these values may not be clear enough to use; others may no longer apply. You can take responsibility for searching out new versions, studying, asking, and learning from others. You then adopt your own version of those values to which you can commit yourself.

A similar process applies to the expertise that is part of your person power. Through the years, Leslie Stein told me, she has continued to develop her expertise in human resources development. Today, she's an expert in labor–management law; yesterday it was preretirement planning and affirmative action. J. B. Montgomery saw his professional field of chemical engineering change its focus from applied chemical research in industry to large-scale chemical engineering applications for cleaning up pollution. He developed his expertise in cleaning the air around the mines for the health and safety of plant employees back in the 1940s and 1950s, long before the current concern for the environment.[7]

Today, whether you're staff, professional, technical, or management, continuing education is survival. Yesterday's information may be obsolete today; yesterday's children may make you obsolete today. Professional lifelong learning is now vital just to keep on top of the field or to keep up with a system's priorities, as well as to prepare yourself for promotion or a career change. Personal lifelong learning is also vital. Since the process of growing your self as a person and as a professional takes many years, sometimes a lifetime, you accept yourself as being in an ongoing process, subject to change as new interests arise.

In this process of becoming non-defensive, you increase your self-esteem and self-respect, continually becoming more confident in your decision-making ability even when others may see you as "wrong" or "square." Jim Lansing risked being seen as "square" when he wouldn't go for 2 percent add-ons. Leslie Stein was seen as "not on the team" when she recommended Dr. Miller's reinstatement. They gave themselves permission to do what they felt was right for themselves and their organizations, not for approval from others. Each was secure enough in his or her expertise, experience, and beliefs to risk disapproval while living his or her convictions. They allowed their beliefs to shape their experience.

You Accept Yourself and Your Feelings

When you're non-defensive, you can accept yourself and whatever feelings you're having as all right to have, even though you might not choose to express or act upon those feelings. If expressed, some feelings would be illegal (the urge to kill); some would violate another's sense of self (feeling someone is stupid); or some would be self-deprecating (thinking you're no good). Other feelings may seem too much of a risk to express (thinking your boss is incompetent) or may feel inconsiderate (expressing elation to someone who seems sad).

You may discover you're worth listening to.

---

[7] His company placed a high, long-range priority on clean air even then. Interestingly, though, he was never provided management training. People skills were apparently not yet considered worth the investment.

Whether or not you express a feeling externally, you can give yourself permission to feel whatever feelings you have internally. For example, an inner dialogue with yourself might go like this: "I'm feeling very confused right now. I don't want to let on that I am, but what is it that seems so confusing?" You acknowledge the feeling of confusion as legitimate, you decide to keep it to yourself, and you mentally ask yourself to gather more information.

In this way, feelings can be followed as clues for sensing more of what is going on. If you don't allow these feelings to register, you may miss some vital information. Teresa Adams followed her feeling of Friday afternoon dread and discovered destructive, not constructive, criticism. Virginia Madison accepted her feeling of fear of being attacked in court and could, as a result, choose to focus her attention on what she wanted to feel instead—calm and serenity.

You Accept Others as They Are, Even When You Don't Agree with Them

When you accept others as they are, you're not trying to change them. You're willing to accept their right to see the world through the light of their experiences and beliefs, not expecting these to match yours. You may not agree with others; you may not understand them; you may feel strong disagreement or personal offense; you may prefer to have little or no contact with them.

Accepting others as they are means you suspend making judgments about them. You can abdicate from playing God. Teresa Adams didn't judge Mark Saber by saying or feeling, "He's not worth respecting." She did form her own opinion that she couldn't personally respect him. Her conclusion was for herself. She did not define him as totally unworthy of respect, nor was she advocating that other people not respect him. She didn't try to change him; she simply chose to put distance between them as long as she worked for him.

Jan Morris didn't try to change Barry Swinbourne's way of using her editorial skills. She set her own limits and let him know what she needed. When he didn't respect that, she drew her limits by saying, "No." Knowing that with the position power of the senior partner added to her own, she could insist on respect for her work requirements and get it.

In each case, there was acceptance without agreement. No one tried to change the other nor judge them. But they did arrange to have their own feelings respected while setting limits within the relationship.

You Are Aware of Your System's Norms and Their Positive and Negative Risks

When you are non-defensive, you are attuned to the norms, customs, and values that operate in whatever system you're in, recognizing that there are often subtle differences within each grouping that can shift rapidly. There are the dominant cultural norms such as those used by the executives in the Argyris and Schön study—the work ethic, competition, rationality. Other such norms define appropriate behavior for men or women, older or younger people, line or staff positions, and others we saw in the down–up point analysis. These tend to operate in most systems, varying only in degree and intensity.

Other norms operate within each job level, such as the norms Larry Ross rejected at executive levels—being a tower of strength, playing God, and valuing dollars more than human beings. In Jim Lansing's system, the hierarchy of technical engineering groups had a norm to pad the bill to the government. In the authoritarian system from which I was fired, one norm was to never question a management decision.

Still other norms—such as who talks with whom about what subjects, degrees of permissible informality, and what must be kept confidential and what can be passed on—are unique to smaller groups or between two people. As you become more aware of these norms and how closely or loosely they are observed, you can get a feel for the payoffs for following them and penalties for breaking them, who is expected to know them, and which are reserved for certain groups. As you relate this information to your own values and your style of playing your role in the system, you can also become aware of how your inner rules lead you to adhere to these norms. Then you can better assess the positive and negative risks you personally take when you choose to follow, bend, or break a norm. These risks are factors within yourself, in other people, and in the system, which help or hinder you in getting the results you want.

As a subordinate, you may have to bend or break some norms just to get your job done, as Jan Morris did. She broke a typical norm by refusing Barry Swinbourne's work. However, she did it by observing a more powerful norm set by the senior partner that all briefs were to be edited.

Your Information Is More Available, More Complete, and Less Distorted

When you're off the defensive, you get better information because you're really listening and hearing other people: giving, asking for, and receiving feedback. You use your ability to respond rather than to put so much energy into defending yourself. If you feel threatened, you can treat the sense of threat more as data, recognizing that you are more likely to distort or misinterpret information at such times, perhaps attributing double meanings where there are none or misconstruing others' motives. You can take things less personally except when it *is* personal. Inner and outer information is clear and straight more of the time.

When you're non-defensive, you're likely to have more trusting relationships in which people give you confidential information you need. For example, I was given critical, timely information when friends in my grapevine told me that management wanted me to resign to save themselves unemployment insurance expense. We could trust each other for help when needed.

As trust builds, people are more likely to share ideas with you, knowing you're all in a situation together. Fred Verschueren reportedly got help on his scrap problem by asking for information, listening, giving reasons for decisions, and being out on the plant floor with an attitude of helping to produce cans. Working *with* people suggests having respect for them as persons, which creates a climate for more open and complete exchange. As people have less need to defend or protect themselves, they have less need to send double meanings or to control you by controlling information.

You Are Getting More of the Results You Want—and Have More Options

As you become more non-defensive and more centered, you'll be getting more results you want more often. When you don't make it, you're more willing to stop and assess what happened, learning from the experience instead of sweeping it under the rug, attempting to justify yourself, or castigating yourself. You stop looking for the one best way, the perfect solution to a problem. Instead you're looking for as many ways as you can find to get desired results. You integrate your creative thinking with your analytical abilities. You can acknowledge your desire to win; you can also recognize that losers are often strongly motivated to see that you lose next time. More often, therefore, you can keep to gain–gain values, building longer-term trust.

When you're functioning non-defensively, you can choose your actions, rather than simply reacting to what others say or do. Lori Landau got angry at Charles Wilson's go-arounds but chose to ask herself what results she wanted and what options she could think of. Beth Teague could have reacted to Marcy Dilmont's simplistic solution to the complex problem of rape, but

Beth chose to act by drawing the circle bigger. Both Lori and Beth chose to act out of their own centers instead of reacting to someone else's control.

ASK YOURSELF: DO YOU REACT—OR ACT?

When You React Defensively

- Others make your choices for you
- Others have power over you
- You defend your position against others
- You increase your odds of losing

When You Act Non-Defensively

- You make your own choices
- You have power over yourself
- You extend your resources with others
- You increase your odds of gaining

LET'S GET STARTED

Make some notes about a situation in which you became defensive. Jot down what happened, what you did, how you felt, whether you reacted or acted. Now state what results you would have liked to have gotten. Then list all the options you can think of. How might you have handled that situation non-defensively?

IN THE NEXT CHAPTER

Next we consider some of the ways people learn to become defensive within themselves and in relationships with other people. Then in Chapter 4 we will see some ways many systems operate which arouse defensiveness.

The purpose of these chapters is to make visible some defenses we've learned. In later chapters we see some ways to unlearn what is no longer useful. What you have learned you can unlearn. Then we see how to replace them with non-defensive attitudes and behavior that create communications that help you get more of the results you want with others.

READINGS

Cornuelle, Richard: *De-Managing America: The Final Revolution*, Random House, New York, 1975. "Authority is obsolete" is the central idea here, and he supports his position with ample evidence. Cornuelle proposes managing results, not behavior, which is compatible with non-defensive communication.

Fromm, Erich: *The Revolution of Hope: Toward a Humanized Technology,* Bantam Books, New York, 1968. The chapter on "What Does It Mean to Be Human?" is particularly relevant to the definitions and values for non-defensive communication.

Hampden-Turner, Charles: *Radical Man: The Process of Psycho-Social Development,* Doubleday, Garden City, N.Y., 1971. Hampden-Turner brilliantly synthesizes a massive body of research, primarily from psychological and management literature, to formulate his model of a healthy and creative psychosocial development, and what happens when people feel anomie—at loose ends, anxious, and defensive. He also reviews how formal systems encourage this anomie and how it can be changed. This book is especially useful to people who want to add depth to their conceptualization of non-defensive processes.

Maslow, Abraham H.: *Toward a Psychology of Being,* Van Nostrand Reinhold, New York, 1962. Maslow's direction of working from an assumption of health and moving toward desired personal growth goals is the same assumption underlying non-defensive communication.

Rogers, Carl: *On Personal Power: Inner Strength and Its Revolutionary Impact,* Delacorte Press, New York, 1977. Rogers clearly demonstrates the conflicts that can arise in organizations when people become more of their own persons, and how these can be worked through even from a relatively powerless position. He also discusses the revolutionary impact of developing human excellence, since this questions and threatens several basic American values. He incorporates ideas developed in his earlier writings, which are useful for background in non-defensiveness.

For additional background reading, see bibliography entries 1, 7, 21, 25, 31, 33, 80, 83, 88.

3

DEFENSIVE COMMUNICATION

How It's Learned, Recognized, and Practiced

Dick Christenson's new clerical assistant, Ellen Kimball, needed some answers. Here's how she asked:

"Are you busy right now? I only need a few minutes of your time and I hate to interrupt you because I know how busy you are and most of the things I have can wait but there are a few things I have to have your decision on before I can go ahead. I've been waiting a long time to see you when you weren't too busy [catching her breath]. Is this a good time— I'm not interrupting anything, am I?"

Dick Christenson, always one to get to the point, became exasperated with her long preamble and growled his abrupt reply. "Yes, you are but since you have, what is it?" All he wanted was to get this conversation over with and go back to work.

In her attempts to be considerate of Dick's time, Ellen took up more time apologizing, deferring, asking permission, and seeking approval by justifying herself. The normal requirements of the situation called for only a simple request, such as, "I need your decisions on three questions. Do you have time now?" Her excessive preamble was typical of one style of defensiveness often used by people under stress who feel subordinate.

One defense invites another, generating a vicious circle.

In turn, Dick reacted defensively, quelling his exasperation into a growl, cutting conversation to a minimum, answering her questions with the least information possible just to get rid of her. As a result, her on-the-job training was ignored or given sparingly and grudgingly. Ellen became even more defensive, wondering why she got so little help on her new job when she was being so conscientious. Their defensive reactions to one another became a vicious circle.

Another form of defensive communication occurred when Paul Masters, the director of the civic auditorium of a medium-sized city, seemed to abdicate his responsibility and authority without delegating these to others on his administrative staff. Not long before he had separated from his wife and filed for divorce, and the adjustment had been rocky and painful. Nonetheless, Paul had developed high community interest in the program he'd brought to the city, a program of outstanding artists, rock groups, dance companies, even poetry readings, which had been well attended. His fine sense of what people like, his ability to write exciting promotional announcements, and the profits from his programs earned the respect of the city council.

However, for the last eight months, his staff has been sympathetic to his erratic behavior, aware he'd had personal problems, but they were also frustrated. They'd been covering for him, but their patience had begun to wear thin under pressures of hourly deadlines, clients with erratic egos, and daily crises that are typical of this type of operation.

Doris Underwood, one of Paul's administrative assistants, tells us a few indicators of Paul's defensive communications:

1. At 10:30 Monday morning, Paul stalked in saying, "Just try to take care of things today, I can't handle it," and slammed the door to his office. He had already missed two client appointments and had thirteen calls to return.

2. The day before a major report was due to the city council, Paul had not begun to write it. Offers of assistance were turned down with, "That's my bailiwick." At 5:00, after a three-hour lunch and a two-hour fight with his ex-wife on the phone, he demanded that the staff stay to get the report done. He left for a dinner date.

3. On Labor Day weekend we had three separate events. On Wednesday after the holiday, the promoters were scheduled to pick up their checks. Paul is the only person authorized to sign checks. Without informing anyone, Paul took a vacation day without signing the checks. We had to deal with the promoters who were understandably upset, especially the one who drove 110 miles, when they couldn't get paid.

Not only was his presence unpredictable, but Doris and the other administrators never knew whether he would be dictatorial or ask for their participation. Feeling off-balance, unrespected and demoralized, they became less willing to cover for him and afraid to confront him about their need for delegation of authority to go with the responsibility he left behind.

Paul's style of defensiveness is more typical of people in authority positions who can shift responsibility to others when they themselves are under stress. His inability to talk about it set up a vicious circle. His staff's defensive reactions combined with his to create another vicious circle. These are just two kinds of defensiveness—one from a subordinate position, one from an authority position. Both Ellen Kimball and Paul Masters are expressing defensiveness from within themselves, defensiveness that closes like a noose, strangling the work at hand.

We don't know what inner rules, dialogues, fears, or threats rumble around in our own or anyone else's interior worlds that arouse defensiveness. We don't know specifically why Dick Christenson and Doris Underwood reacted with the particular defenses they chose. To ask "why" would take us down either of two paths, both of which lead nowhere. One path takes us into yesterday. We try to reconstruct a person's earlier experiences from which he or she learned to protect the self from what felt like attacks, or from self-doubts. Although this might be fascinating sleuthing, it's yesterday's paraphenalia. The other path is one of speculation. We play guessing games about what makes a person tick. As an amateur or arm chair psychiatrist, you could make some educated guesses, but there's no way to verify those guesses. Even if you asked the person if your speculations were accurate (and we usually don't), she or he may fortify the defenses—perhaps more so if your guess is accurate! "Why's" tend to invade a person's privacy.

For example, you might speculate that Ellen Kimball defends herself because she has a weak ego, that her father might have beat her as a child, and that she's anxious about a man in a superior position who unexpectedly might punish her. Even if you knew this history to be accurate, how does it help Ellen or Dick get their work done today? If it's mere speculation, you may add insult to injury, which simply raises more defenses. "Psyching out" a person's motives for the particular defenses he or she uses may be entertaining, but it's not useful for what to do next.

SOME WAYS THAT PEOPLE LEARN DEFENSIVENESS

Although it's not useful to "psych out" individual sources of a person's specific forms of defenses, a general idea of *patterns* that lead to defensiveness can help us be compassionate about people's need to defend themselves.

People usually defend themselves because they feel a threat. The threat may be real and present; it may be a carry-over from past experiences; it's often a mix of both.

Perhaps it's easiest to understand the threat of physical danger: being attacked by a large dog, being present at a bank robbery, discovering your car has no brakes as you approach a busy intersection. Other threats to your security are less obvious: fear of not having enough money to pay your living expenses as the cost of living goes up, fear of not being able to get the education you need, fear of extended illness, fear that someone else will get the promotion you're shooting for. These are threats to your need for security: physical safety and health, having the resources and means to take care of yourself and those close to you.

Threats that are carry-overs from past experiences are often labeled as imaginary or irrational. The threat is usually more psychological, less physical; however, it is no less real. Such threats can come from inside ourselves ("What's wrong with me?") or from others ("What ever gave you that idea?"). They involve feelings about how you feel about yourself and your adequacy as a person.

Each of us has a self and also a self-concept, an inner picture of one's self. Your self-concept is a network of perceptions you have about what you're like, what you can do, where you fit in, your values and beliefs, who you are—perceptions about your self that you know about. Any information about your *self* that you don't want to face won't be included in your picture of your self. These unacknowledged fears or aspects of your self that you dislike are likely to be hidden away where you don't have to look at them. They're also protected from the prying eyes of others. You're likely to defend your self against threats of exposure, whether or not you're aware of doing it. This is one source of defensiveness.

Paul Masters seemed to be protecting himself from prying eyes by his absences. A change in his marital status may be forcing him to face something he's hidden away or may be forcing him to question the accuracy of his self-concept. Such assumptions must be tentative, but many people derive a large part of their identity from their marriage relationships. Whether or not Paul does, we don't know. What you can learn to do is deal with such behavior as it affects you and your work.

Another source of defensiveness may come when other people don't see you the same way you see yourself. When these people are important to you, such as a spouse, parent, child, friend, or supervisor, you may want or need them to verify your self-concept in order to maintain your sense of identity. If instead they judge you negatively or try to change you, you're likely to defend strongly your picture of yourself. Your identity is under attack.

Ellen Kimball saw herself as conscientious and felt attacked (or at least not appreciated) when Dick was so abrupt with information she needed for her job. Her defensiveness, which took the form of excessive preambling, gave hints that she needed approval and permission from others—aspects of herself of which she probably was not aware. She defended herself (to herself but not to Dick) by focusing on her conscientiousness, which she seemed to want verified. Dick didn't have time to think all this through, however. He had to deal with her behavior quickly and move on.

What's Learned at Home Is Often Perpetuated at Work

A person's first experience with being in a subordinate role comes with being a child. No matter what style of parenting is used, children learn something about power, control, authority, obedience, and responsibility. *What* they learn results from how these energies were used in the family, the style of parenting.

Traditional, top-down, adjust-to-society patterns were prevalent when today's adults were growing up, until the mid 1950s. Many families still function this way, although most families have had to at least discuss other approaches, if not make major changes.

But old styles change slowly. When the pressures are on, it's tough to resist the urge to control others. Even young parents who deeply believe in developing the potential of their children surprise themselves. One such father, Gene Sandler, heard himself say to his son: "Never mind why—just do it." / "But why, Daddy?" / "Because I said so." Startled, he stopped himself, observing, "Just listen to me. I sound like my father." It may take a long time before we can consistently live our beliefs.

The same thing happens when supervisors and managers are under pressure. For example, when money gets tight, managers who have been delegating decisions and control down the line tend to take these back, making more top-down, arbitrary ones.[1]

Traditional patterns in the family are often perpetuated in work systems. To children, parents represent authority. To adults, supervisors, managers, and executives represent authority. Traditional parents and bosses define and enforce rules, give and withhold approval, make decisions "for your own good," control money (children's allowances, adult's paychecks and promotions), and control other resources (for children, home, clothing, food, caring; for adults, a workplace, tools, income, recognition).

If the employee handbook where you work talks about the company as "one big happy family," you can be sure that Big Daddy is at the top. Most large organizations still use paternalistic styles of management, in which managerial prerogatives strongly parallel parental rights and respon-

---

[1] Rensis Likert has graphically documented this process in *New Patterns of Management*, McGraw-Hill, New York, 1961.

sibilities.[2] As long as subordinates accept this pattern—because they think they have to or because they don't know what else to do—it works. It keeps most subordinates defensive and therefore easier to control.

Defenses Are Learned Early in Life

We start building self-concepts in the cradle, sending and responding to verbal, voice–tone, and touching messages from parents. Without going into a discourse on child development, however, I'd like to offer some samples of what you might have learned from some parental messages that were common in the days when parents felt it was their right and responsibility to control their children—back when today's adults were growing up. (Styles of parenting have swung from total control to virtually no control; only more recently are we finding ways of raising children between these extremes with more shared control between parents and children.)

Look at the following drawings and consider what you might have told yourself as a child if you had repeatedly heard these things when you were growing up. Then compare yours with the possible learning that occurred to me.

"Now Go to Sleep. There's Nothing to be Afraid of."   Picture yourself as the child in the cartoon and consider what you might learn about trusting your feelings. To you that bear is real. To your parent, it's just your imagination. You may assume that your parents know more and should be believed because they are bigger and older. Perhaps they use a reassuring tone. Even so, what might you say to yourself night after night?

- How can I "just imagine" this bear? It *does* exist, or does it?
- What's wrong with me? Can I believe what I'm seeing and feeling?
- They won't listen to me. (Maybe I'm not worth listening to.)
- They don't believe me. (Maybe I'm not believable.)
- I feel scared but I shouldn't.
- There's no out. I have to keep quiet.
- I have to be brave and swallow my fear.
- What I feel doesn't exist.
- I shouldn't bother them with it.

"Why Can't You Behave Like Your Cousin Margery?"   If you had heard this comparison with some frequency, what might you have learned about being judged or evaluated?

---

[2] Rensis Likert, "A Conversation with Rensis Likert," *Organization Dynamics*, AMACOM, a division of American Management Associations, New York, Summer 1973.

"Now go to sleep. There's nothing to be afraid of."

Source: From *No Dessert Until You've Finished Your Mashed Potatoes,* by William O'Brian. Copyright © 1965 by William O'Brian. Reprinted by permission of Random House, Inc.

- Who wants to be a stupid goodie-two-shoes anyway? My stuff is more fun.
- Why does she have to be so perfect? I hate her.
- Nobody will love me unless I behave in a way I hate.
- I'm supposed to be perfect and I'd rather be poisonous.
- I'm no good and there's nothing that can be done about it.
- I'll show them. I'll *act* perfect and *be* poisonous. Ha!

"Why can't you behave like your Cousin Margery?"

Source: From *No Dessert Until You've Finished Your Mashed Potatoes*, by William O'Brian. Copyright © 1965 by William O'Brian. Reprinted by permission of Random House, Inc.

Many parents may simply want the ease of more conformity, yet not really want conformity itself. But from this double message, some children could learn to manipulate their appearances if they find it gains them approval or if it means survival to them. To avoid being disappointed or disillusioned, some children learn never to reveal their feelings. They pull down the window shade, garnering what little choice and control over themselves that they can scrape together. They have little validation for being themselves.

"And Stay in Your Room, Young Man."   Have you noticed that parents say "young man" at times like this, but say you're "too little" when it's something *you* want to do? If this had happened often, what might you have

"And stay *in your room, young man."*

Source: From *No Dessert Until You've Finished Your Mashed Potatoes,* by William O'Brian. Copyright © 1965 by William O'Brian. Reprinted by permission of Random House, Inc.

learned about people with power over you? How would you feel about obeying authority?

- What's so bad about what I want to do?
- What I want, grownups don't want.
- When they don't want me, they lock me out.
- I feel helpless. I'm too small.
- When I get bigger, I'll be boss. Then I'll get back at them.
- You wait and see. Someday I'll win.

If he later adds anger to his sense of helplessness, the seeds of violence may be sown.

"Of Course He Can Go Wherever He Wants to College, but Naturally..." Overheard conversations among adults can be powerful indeed. On one hand, many parents talk about their youngsters taking responsibility for making their own decisions. On the other hand, they may want their children to make the same decision they themselves would, while making it *appear* as a free choice. The hidden meaning is that this child had better choose Yale if he's going to be accepted by these parents who give two signals: "Make your own choice" but "Choose my way." Given this pattern, what might you learn about making choices by the time you graduate from high school?

- What if my grades aren't good enough to get into Yale? Does that make me a failure?
- I don't want to have to live up to (or live down) Dad's college record.
- I want to make my own decisions and do it my way.
- They promised me I could decide, but they don't even give me a choice.
- My choices aren't respected.
- I'm not respected.
- If I don't decide their way, they might not send me to any college.
- They lied to me.
- So what? It'd be easier to just leave. I don't owe them anything.

What Parents Believe Helps Shape the Child's Self-Concept—and Self

Parents who believe their role is to socialize their children to cultural and social expectations will conscientiously do their best to raise them to be responsible—to authority. They are likely to subscribe to the idea that with-

"Of course, he can go wherever he wants to college, but naturally ..."

Source: From *No Dessert Until You've Finished Your Mashed Potatoes*, by William O'Brian. Copyright © 1965 by William O'Brian. Reprinted by permission of Random House, Inc.

out strong social control, the "beast in man" will destroy society. Consequently, they're more likely to use top-down control, deciding *for* their children what they should do and continually judging them on how well they're doing it. Using this kind of responsibility, parents make it difficult for children to believe them when they say, "It's not *you* that I don't like, it's what you *do*." If parents are being judgmental, their children will sense it.

The way these children see themselves—that is, the self-concept they form—is likely to be shaped by the evaluations of people who have power over them. They've learned that these people can punish and reject them, physically and psychologically, to elicit approved behavior. Their security and even their identity is defined and controlled mostly by other people, not by themselves.

When they want something different as adults—self-choice—they often experience inner conflict, self-doubt, and guilt. They may ask themselves, "Why *shouldn't* I do what *I* want?" But the built-in answer echoes back: "Because I say you shouldn't." The giveaway area is large, open to the entry of others. The store and core of self is small. Years later, they are likely to say, "I've done everything I was supposed to and I've made a decent life for us. But I'm not happy—I don't know why." They discover that meeting only others' expectations is not particularly soul satisfying.

On the other hand, parents who believe their role is to nurture into being the special qualities that make *this* child a unique individual are more likely to raise the child to be responsible to him or herself and others. They probably subscribe to the newer idea that the human organism is basically good and can be trusted to evolve in life-enhancing ways. They are more likely to develop their ability to respond to the child's curiosity, share their knowledge, listen, add to, and join *with* the child in her or his explorations. The child learns the parents' reasons for setting limits instead of learning blind obedience. Growing up becomes a process of self-discovery shared with parents who want to learn more about this new person—a partnership.

Such parents also teach their children what the larger society expects of them. However they're more likely to present these expectations as choices a person makes that have positive or negative consequences rather than "shoulds" that become built into a child's self-concept. As they live their values, they may talk about why they have chosen them, guiding instead of coercing their children to share those values.

Children raised this way may, and often do, have a stronger sense of self as adults. When the self-concept more closely matches the self, there is less need to defend hidden, hated or feared parts of oneself. These adults become more aware of who they are and can trust themselves. As a result, they also tend to assume that other people are basically good and trustworthy and to become less judgmental when others disappoint them. Years later they are likely to say, "It's been a rich life so far. People have been good to me, I've done most of the things I really wanted to do, and I'm still finding out what I'm going to be when I grow up." Their security and identity are in their own hands, shared with, but not controlled by, others.

The Larger Society Presumably Offers Security Outside Ourselves

People who have been raised to look outside themselves for security and identity tend to replace their parents' expectations with those of the larger society. They tend to believe in the conventional wisdom—What Everybody Knows—which says that marriage and family is the best way to fulfillment, that getting a college education is the way to earn more money, that adhering to the work ethic is the way to get ahead. Many people live their entire lives believing these so-called guarantees, sure that *if* they do what they're supposed to, *then* they can expect these results to automatically follow.

In the past these predictions happened more often than in today's rapidly changing society. Many people don't expect dreams to come true like they used to. The divorce rate suggests that marriage security is unpredictable. The surplus of people with college degrees in the labor market suggests that educational security is unpredictable. The unemployment rate suggests that job security is unpredictable. People who have invested themselves deeply in these or similar beliefs often feel that someone has pulled the rug out from under them when their guarantee evaporates.

Whenever we believe these if–then propositions, we may place ourselves in a dependent position—dependent on some undefined social force or some unnamed organization to keep a promise no one ever made. Whenever we look outside ourselves for security, we become dependent on others to deliver it. This creates a false sense of security because we've given away much control—and many choices—to others.

Let's look at some clues for recognizing defensiveness in ourselves and others. After that, we'll look at some ways people use to gain power over others. When we can recognize defensiveness, we can consider what to do with it.

HOW TO RECOGNIZE CLUES TO DEFENSIVE COMMUNICATION

As we've seen, we may have learned early and well to be defensive and to carry that behavior with us when it's no longer needed. Then it's easy to take an ordinary situation and give it a meaning that may not be there at all. This is the stuff of cartoonists. Consider this one:

PEANUTS   by Charles M. Schulz

© 1977 United Feature Syndicate, Inc.

It's not just kids who distort reality to fit their self-concepts. Grownups do it just as well. Consider this manager who sent copies of this memo to all his counterparts and to the executives above them:

> If you don't know the difference between getting upset and justifiable action, you're more stupid than I thought. My action was justified because you gave my staff an order you had no business giving them; you overstepped your authority and undermined mine; you messed things up so that my staff had to spend 27.33 hours trying to get it cleaned up. You should take care of your own shop as well as you interfere in mine. The next time you step out of line, I'm charging my staff time to your cost center.

Each of us brings our present collection of defenses—and the self that may need no defending—to our relationships.

Some Clues for Identifying Patterns of Defensiveness

If you've learned to feel subordinate to others, you may tend to defer to them beyond the normal expectations of courtesy. Decisions that you could make for yourself—decisions not requiring approval—are often referred upward as if they are questions needing higher approval. In your work role, you may be expected to do this.

On the other hand, if you think of yourself as having power over others, you may act paternally dominant, as if you were responsible for the behavior of others not fully capable of thinking for themselves—parent to child. Again, this style may be the prevailing one of supervising people in the system in which you work.

Among adults, both stances are usually defensive. Table 3-1 shows some patterns you may have observed, with some typical phrases for easy identification. If you want to score yourself on these twelve types of behavior, give each item *ten* points and divide them between the subordinate and dominant columns by how often you use each behavior. For example, in the first item, if you tend to explain, justify, and prove yourself much of the time when

Table 3-1. *Patterns of Defensiveness.*

Subordinate Defensiveness	*Dominant Defensiveness*
☐ Explain, prove, justify your actions, ideas, or feelings more than is required for results wanted.	☐ Prove that you're right. *I told you so.* *Now see, that proves my point.*
☐ Ask why things are done the way they are, when you really want to change them. *Why don't they . . . ?*	☐ Give patient explanations but few answers. *It's always been done this way.* *We tried that before, but . . .*
☐ Ask permission when not needed. *Is it okay with you if . . . ?*	☐ Give or deny permission. *Oh, I couldn't let you do that.*
☐ Give away decisions, ideas, or power when it would be appropriate to claim them as your own. *Don't you think that . . . ?*	☐ Make decisions or take power as your natural right. *The best way to do it is . . .* *Don't argue. Just do as I say.*
☐ Apologize, feel inadequate, say *I'm sorry* when you're not.	☐ Prod people to get the job done. *Don't just stand there . . .*
☐ Submit or withdraw when it's not in your best interest. *Whatever you say . . .*	☐ Take over a situation or decision even when it's delegated; get arbitrary. *My mind is made up.*
☐ Lose your cool, lash out, cry, where it's inappropriate (turning your anger toward your self).	☐ Lose your cool, yell, pound the desk, where it's inappropriate (turning your anger toward others).
☐ Go blank, click off, be at a loss for words just when you want to have a ready response. *I should've said . . .* (afterwards)	☐ Shift responsibility for something you should have taken care of yourself. *You've always done it before. What're you all of a sudden upset for now?*
☐ Use coping humor, hostile jocularity, or put yourself down when "buying time" or honest feedback would get better results. *Why don't you lay off?*	☐ Use coping humor, baiting, teasing, hostile jocularity, mimicry—to keep other people off balance so you don't have to deal with them. *What's the matter, can't you take it?*
☐ Use self-deprecating adjectives and reactive verbs. *I'm just a . . .* *I'm just doing what I was told.*	☐ Impress others with how many important people you know. *The other night at Bigname's party when I was talking to . . .*
☐ Use the general *you* and *they* when *I* and personal names would state the situation more clearly. *They really hassle you here.*	☐ Don't listen: interpret. Catch the idea of what they're saying, then list rebuttals or redefine their point. *Now what you really mean is . . .*
☐ Smile to cover up feelings or put yourself down since you don't know what else to do and it's *nice.*	☐ Use verbal dominance, if necessary, to make your point. Don't let anyone interrupt what you have to say.
☐ TOTAL Subordinate Points	☐ TOTAL Dominant Points

you're defensive, you might score it *seven*, with only *three* points for how often you try to prove you're right. Total each column separately.

Let your scores speak to you, telling you whatever they do about your styles of defensiveness. I have purposely not included a score-card to evaluate what the totals indicate. Evaluating oneself or being evaluated by others tends to raise defenses. *Experiment with simply observing the information about yourself; do not attempt to make an evaluation.* If this feels difficult or strange, you may have a habit of evaluating. Most of us do!

When Subordinate Thinking Gives Away Control Over Self

Perhaps you noticed in the self-test that many of the subordinate defenses included qualifiers such as "more than is required, when not needed, when it's not in your best interest." In these instances subordinate thinking goes beyond the limits of normal courtesy, taking you into your giveaway area. In this sense, you may give away power over self when you don't have to—deference to position. (There is a subtle difference when you defer to someone because of their expertise or excellence of leadership. This deference comes out of respect. You *are* subordinate, more like the student of a virtuoso. In this case, however, you'd come out of your trade-off area, giving of yourself in exchange for an opportunity to learn from a master. This is non-defensive subordinacy.)

"Why" Questions.   There are two kinds of "why" questions: (1) those that deal with series of events, such as "Why the slowdown in traffic?" (2) those that deal with people processes, such as "Why don't you try my way?" In the first, one can find a cause-and-effect relationship; remove the cause and traffic will move. This works with tangible events but makes little sense with people processes. "Why" questions between people usually stimulate defensiveness. Here's how it happens.

"Why don't you try/do. . .?" questions are likely to elicit a list of explanations why the other person doesn't. That's what the question asked. The question sounds like a reprimand, "You shouldn't do what you're doing," or a put-down, "My idea is better than yours." If others defend themselves by justifying their actions, you end up right back where you started. Nothing changes.

If you want things to move ahead, you might get farther with "what" questions, such as "What would happen if we did this?"

Some people turn "Why" questions inward: "Why can't I . . . ?" Faced with her first meeting of department heads as the only woman in the group,

Dodi Summers asked herself these questions: "Why am I so introverted at business meetings? Why the lack of participation on my part? Why am I so intimidated?" Outnumbered, she feared she would be coerced into thinking as the men did. Not only did she undermine her own self-confidence, she also arranged for the group to go on as if she weren't there. If Dodi wanted change, "How can we . . . ?" questions would improve her odds. She would have to complete the question with what she wanted to accomplish, not with what she wanted to avoid.

Most fruitless of all are "Why don't they . . . ?" questions, which are usually asked in the absence of "they." Dodi asked herself (and anyone else who would listen) questions such as, "Why don't the men give me equal time in the meetings?" More bemoaning than questioning, this behavior didn't change the fact that so far they hadn't. A better question to ask herself would be, "How can I get in what I want to say?" This question focuses on what she *does* want and leads to possible options, thus returning more control to herself.

"Don't You Think . . . ?"   If you ask me a question beginning this way, here's how I could take your power from you (if I were so inclined, which I'm not.) I could say "No" (which your question invited) without further explanation and squash your thought. Or I could say, "Yes, and what's more . . ." and take over your idea as if it were mine. In either case your idea evaporates as *yours*. I could probably get away with this take-over, especially if I do it in a good-humored style.

To keep the power of your ideas, you can take ownership of them by restating this way: "I think . . . Would you agree?" Then I'd have to give you reasons for a yes or no reply, which you could simply listen to, gathering information to think about. Either way, you would still have authorship of your own ideas. If I were not trying to take your power or control you, but instead wanted to connect with you, I would now have something to connect with.

"You Make Me Feel . . ."   This usually ends with some uncomfortable feeling—tired, inadequate, guilty, stupid, angry. It shifts the responsibility for your own feelings to the other person. In effect, it says, "You make me feel bad and it's your fault. You're responsible for how I feel. So you have to treat me better so I'll feel better." Whether you're on the sending or receiving end of this blame laying, you're likely to defend yourself. Discussion usually revolves around who's at fault, which leads nowhere.

You can turn it around by saying, "When you do that, I feel . . ." Better yet, say that to yourself and then ask yourself, "How do I want to feel?" Self-choice then returns.

Some Clues for Identifying Defensiveness in Voice Tones

Stanley Bennett, an engineer by training, and Nancy Oliver, a graduate student in women's history and athletics, were living together and were concerned about working out an egalitarian relationship—a partnership between themselves as people as well as in the mundane aspects of living. After listening to them, I suggested they tape-record some of the discussions they got into at home, replaying them later for the sole purpose of each listening to their own voice tones. Here's what happened.

> *Nancy:* "I couldn't believe it. The minute we got going good, I heard myself switch to a little-girl, pleading voice, almost whining. And he shifted to a patronizing, condescending tone that I reacted to by raising my pitch to a higher whine. It was just awful. I had no idea that's what we were doing."
>
> *Stanley:* "Yeah, it was pretty grim. I sounded just like my old man when he argued with my mother. And here all the time I was thinking I wasn't domineering. I really didn't like that in him and swore I'd never do it, but I am. I hate to admit it, but it's true."

It wasn't easy to face but they had live information about themselves to work with as they continued to work out their differences.

Simply changing one's voice intonations can substantially change a meaning. Having a music background, I tried graphing voice tones on a music staff. Here's how the down and up tones looked:

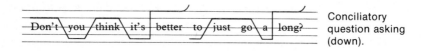

Conciliatory question asking (down).

Notice how the voice goes up when the person feels down.

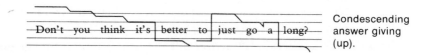

Condescending answer giving (up).

Here, the voice goes down when the person is in an up position.

This was the first time I noticed that a condescending voice had a descending tonal pattern. Seems obvious, once you see it. I just hadn't seen it presented graphically before.[3] Say these sentences out loud and listen to the intonations.

A "why" question with a possible response of someone who is annoyed by it might look like this:

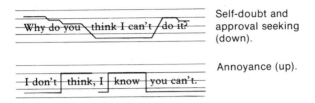

Self-doubt and approval seeking (down).

Annoyance (up).

When responsibility is shifted downward, it often sounds persuasive, looking like this:

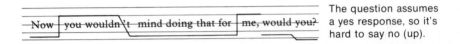

The question assumes a yes response, so it's hard to say no (up).

After responsibility has been shifted and the subordinate has gotten the blame (credit is rarely shifted downward), it might look like this:

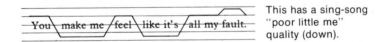

This has a sing-song "poor little me" quality (down).

These clues are only a few of the ways to recognize defensiveness. More will emerge as we consider some ways in which people use their defenses in practice.[4]

First we see a department head who is not getting assigned work from a professional staff person. As you read the situation, notice how the two processes—the series of activities for getting the work done and the people process—are working together. Notice which process seems most important and also notice how control is used.

---

[3]Later I found that linguists and phonologists have been using a similar technique without a music staff. In 1945 Rulon Wells and Kenneth L. Pike used it in their books about pitch and intonation of American English as reported in Ruth M. Brend's article, "Male–Female Intonation Patterns in American English," in Barrie Thorne and Nancy Henley (Eds.), *Language and Sex: Difference and Dominance*, Newbury House, Rawley, Mass. 1975, pp. 84–87.

[4]The language of body movements, facial expressions, tension and relaxation, size and use of space, standing and sitting, eye contact and touching now comprises a substantial body of literature that cannot be summarized here. However, such signals are used in the examples and will be discussed from time to time.

HOW TO RECOGNIZE DEFENSIVE COMMUNICATION AS IT'S PRACTICED

Let's listen in on a discussion in which Helen Henderson, 34, wants to get a special statistical report from her assistant, John Silberman, 38, for the third time. The report may locate where a critical variance from standards is occurring in production. In this high technology firm, some variances can be costly. This report was John's first assignment from Helen after she was chosen over him three weeks ago for promotion to chief of quality control. The final selection was made by Bill Bendorff, 52, to whom both of them formerly reported. John's only comment to her after the announcement was, "May the best man win."

John has recently earned a master's degree in mathematics and statistics, but Helen's ten years of departmental experience and her long list of specialized courses apparently counted for more. John has been there only two years but has eleven years of related experience. John's wife, Ruth, who went to work to pay for his graduate expenses, at some cost to the family, has been rubbing it in that a woman beat him out, especially one without a degree.

Bill Bendorff, to whom Helen still reports, says he needs this report "yesterday." Having been production manager, he knows the cost exposure. He's given her ten days to get John to deliver or to fire him and do the report herself. Helen suspects that Bill thinks women can't fire people; he's challenged her with: "It's up to you. You're a big girl now."

Helen badly needs John's expertise; it would take her much longer to do the correlations. She's anxious to prove herself in this job, which has never before been held by a woman, and she doesn't want the fact that she's a woman to get in her way, either in her own thinking or in her supervision of John. Here's how the discussion starts as John enters her office on Tuesday morning.

1*   "Have a seat, John. I want to find out what's holding up the variance report and how we can get it done by Friday noon." Giving him three days to produce, she's giving herself time for other options in case he doesn't come through again this time.

2   "You've been giving me so many projects that there just isn't time to finish up the leg-work on this one."

3   "Yes, you have a lot of work," she agrees, "but you also know the priorities," not letting him off the hook.

*Numbers are line references to be used in later discussion.

4   "You don't realize how much time it takes to analyze the backup data for that report," seeming to question her knowledge of the job. "There's no way it can be done without extra help to do the probability programming."

5   Not to be side-tracked, Helen sticks to the issue of timing: "It was due ten days ago. This is the third time we've talked about it and made schedules, but there's still no report. I *must* have it by Friday noon—or I'll have to take other steps."

6   Wary now, John asks, "Is that a threat of some kind?"

7   "No, it's a statement of fact," not wanting to talk yet about the pressures she's getting from Bill.

8   Not believing her, John confronts her: "If it's not done by Friday, what will you do?"

9   "That remains to be decided," she says, keeping her options open.

10   Taking another tack, he says sarcastically: "Well, it's impossible. If I don't get this report done, you'll 'take steps.' If I don't get the rest of your projects done, you'll hang me for that. You sure know how to squeeze a guy, don't you!"

11   Ignoring the implications of the last remark, Helen fires back, "Are you saying you can't even do the top priority report by Friday?"

12   Confident that he has her on the run, he calmly replies: "Not with the way you've arranged things. It's pretty clear you're trying to set me up to fail so you can get rid of your competition."

13   "I got this job fair and square, John. And I want to be fair with you."

14   Interrupting, he charges, "What's fair and square for a woman is dirty dealing for a man. And you don't even have a degree."

15   Angered, she puts it to him straight, "If you have some hangup about working for a woman, John, you'd better let me know now. I'm not going to put up with your insinuations. We're here to do a job, and I'm going to see that it's done." Fighting her anger, she shifts gears. "I need your expertise and I know you can work under pressure. You've done it before and you can do it again. Are you going to do it or aren't you?"

16   Pulling back, he notes, "What good is all that if *you* get the promotions?" Then, shaking his head, he mutters to himself, "It's not the right year for me."

17   "What do you mean by that?" she asks, rising to the bait.

18   Looking her square in the eye, through tight lips he states: "If I were female or black, I'd be sitting where you are now."

19   "That's enough of that, John," cutting him off. "Right now the only question is getting out that variance analysis by Friday noon. Are you going to do it or not?"

20   "If you put it that way, I guess I have no choice." Resigned, he stands, turns and says over his shoulder, "You'll have it," and casually strolls out.

21   Friday noon. No report. No word from John. Helen picks up the phone and dials his office. In clipped tones, she asks: "John, where's the report?"

22   "Oh, I forgot to tell you," he drawls, "I checked with Bill Bendorff and he said he could wait another few days. You'll have it on Tuesday like I promised him." Click.

What are you feeling right now? Put yourself in Helen's shoes and sense how you would feel. Then put yourself in John's shoes and sense how that would feel. Read the situation again from each point of view if you have difficulty identifying with one or the other actors.

Identifying the Transfer of Control

At the beginning of this scene, Helen had control; at the end, John has it. *Find the line number where you think control began to move out of Helen's hands. Then find the line number where you think control has been clearly transferred into John's hands.*

By line 12, John does, in fact, have Helen on the run. Given the norms of most work situations and the respect for authority due one's supervisor, John would not have accused Helen of setting him up to fail unless he thought he could get away with it. And he did.

At what point did you think Helen began to let control move out of her hands? At line 5, she decided to stick to the timing issue. She chose to not respond to his questioning of her knowledge or to his stated need for more staff. Closing off other avenues of discussion and focusing on deadlines only, she issued an ultimatum which she was not prepared to back up at line 7. Instead, she denied the threat that was actually there. From that point on, John gradually gained more control, Helen gradually lost it. By Friday, he had her holding the bag for the moment at least. How did he do it and how did Helen play into his hands?

Now read again the dialogue after control begins to shift. What information is missing? What is said that the other person doesn't respond to? What hidden meanings might be there? What power plays might be going on? What motives, if any, do you attribute to Helen or John? On what do you base your opinion? (Be aware of any assumptions you make and identify them as just that, assumptions that may be subject to change, given more information.)

Identifying Defenses in Action and Results They Produce

In this scene Helen's attention was focused on timing and production—the series of events necessary to produce the report. The people process part of the discussion—attitudes and feelings—she ignored, cut off, or denied, and John made several non-productive challenges. As a result of these defensive tactics, feelings became more intense and possible ways of getting out the work were passed over.

For example, Helen ignored, cut off, or denied several feelings and attitudes when she:

- Ignored John's reference to her job knowledge (4–5).
- Denied the element of threat of taking other steps (6–7).
- Refused to tell him other steps she might take, omitting to tell him that his job was on the line, per Bill's instructions to her (8–9).
- Ignored his "squeeze a guy" comment (10–11). She also questioned his ability to produce even one report (11).
- Ignored his charge of setting him up to fail (12–13).
- Acknowledged his insinuations but accused him of possibly having a hangup about working for women (14–15).
- Ignored his feeling of having no payoffs for good work (16–17).
- Cut him off on the reverse discrimination charge (18–19).

John employed a variety of other defensive tactics in the form of non-productive challenges, including:

- Shifting responsibility to Helen for not getting the report done (2, 4).
- Confronting and challenging her authority (6, 8, 20).
- Accusing her of motives to harm him (10, 12).
- Questioning the basis for her promotion (14, 16, 18).
- Not performing (report was not in after two talks and also in 21).
- Going over her head to Bill and appearing to get away with it (22).

Both Helen and John used the defense of *self-listening*—listening to the other only long enough to predict what's coming, tune out, and prepare rebuttals to protect their positions. Neither one was willing to risk listening to and really hearing the other.

Their combined defenses produced a vicious circle. At the end of the discussion, feelings were more intense than at the beginning. Possible ways of producing the report were not considered and wider implications were ignored. Among the questions not considered were:

- Is the workload actually too much, given the present staff?
- Are the right staff skills available at the right time?

- Have there been staff problems, such as absences, personnel problems, insufficient training, which affect productivity?
- What other staff resources can temporarily be made available?
- Are there possible shortcuts in collecting or analyzing the data?
- What is Bill Bendorff's role in this situation?
- How much extra production costs are being incurred because of this delayed report? What other production repercussions are there? How are other functions affected? How does all this affect the customer and profits?

Also unknown are the norms of this firm's system and the prevailing styles of management. In general, it may be safe to assume that traditional, competitive patterns prevail, but specifically, this assumption needs verifying.

When people get in the vicious circle of defending themselves, they engage in vying for control, power plays, charges and countercharges, insinuations, concealed information, distorted interpretations. The typical result is little production of actual work.

If you're thinking about what Helen or John should have done or if you're attributing motives or putting labels on them, be aware of what you're doing. If you're thinking that I am silently advocating one solution or another, be aware of that. If you're suspending judgment, waiting to see what comes next, take note of that. Whatever is going on within yourself is your own inner process—your own feelings, attitudes, and beliefs. Right now, just observe and notice them, without deciding whether they're right or wrong, justified or not.

In a later chapter we will replay parts of this scene to observe how the defensiveness occurs within each person. Later we will also see how Helen and John can each use non-defensive communication to get more results each one really wants, while allowing room for the other to get something of what he or she wants. Each will at least be able to save face and still get the report out.

At this point, however, our purpose is to recognize some of the ways defensive communication is used in practice. So next we build on the catalogue begun by Helen and John and possibly Bill.

HOW TO RECOGNIZE SPECIFIC DEFENSIVE TACTICS TO CONTROL OTHERS

Many defensive tactics are used to protect oneself from real or anticipated threat. Helen's defenses were mostly of this kind—fending off attacks. Other people use defensive tactics to control other people or a situation, believing that's the meaning of "being in control." Often they believe that the best defense is a good offense. They tend to use defensive power tactics that will put themselves in an up position or put the other person down. John did both.

Top-down defensive tactics are widely employed in many relationships and certainly in most work systems. Therefore, to know what you're facing, you have to be able to recognize them. The catalogue of these tactics is endless. What follows is only a start on some common forms.

Power Plays

Power plays, also called ploys,[5] are one kind of double meaning; there's a surface message with a hidden message. The cartoons on page 78 show some common examples of meanings that are unspoken but that are nevertheless there. This hidden meaning is sent through the tone of voice, certain body signals, perhaps a change of tension in the atmosphere, or by knowing the person's style.

The power to define is the power to control.

In these examples whenever there are two meanings, there is a power play. Some are virtually always power plays. "Now let's be fair" implies "I'll say what's fair," or "I assume that 'fair' means the same thing to both of us."

"What you *really* mean is" nearly always precedes an interpretation of your previous comment as if the other person knows what's going on inside you better than you do. An exception is when someone uses these words but intends to convey, in effect, "What I heard from you means. . . . Is that what you meant?" Then the statement is a request for clarification.

If you're on the defensive, you're more likely to hear double meanings. However, many apparent power plays may not actually be so. The surface meaning may be all there is. For example:

- *"Can you prove that?"* can be a clear request for information.
- *"Give an example"* can be a genuine desire for clarification.
- *"You just said . . . and now you say . . ."* can be a search for understanding two statements that seem to conflict.

[5]The term *ploy* was first introduced, as far as I know, by Stephen Potter, whose "gamesmanship" writings have been collected in *The Complete Upmanship*, Holt, Rinehart and Winston, New York, 1950.

Power Plays

Source: © Tom Parker 1976 (Drawings). © Theodora Wells 1975 (Balloons).

When you're non-defensive, you are less likely to hear double meanings when there aren't any. Or if you suspect there may be one, you can sense that possibility but test it further before deciding for sure.

Put Downs

Put downs are another form of power play in which there is almost always a hidden message. Whatever the reason, the hidden meaning is the same: *"You're worth less."* Because women are generally valued less than men in our society as well as being in subordinate roles, put downs they receive can be used to identify hidden meanings. From some 800 responses to *"I feel put down when . . . ,"* some common themes emerge. Although many refer to being female, others refer to being subordinate and would also be used with men. Here are some examples:

"I feel put down when . . ."	**Hidden Meaning**
■ I'm treated in a condescending manner. ■ Someone says, "Even Virginia can do it." I'm beginning to think my name is "Even Virginia." ■ Someone says, "Try to think like a man and you'll get it."	*You're not as intelligent, bright, smart.* *(261 replies)*
■ I'm ignored. ■ I'm asked, "Is it important?" ■ My suggestions and ideas are given little weight and acknowledgment and then, when the same goddam thing is said by some male, even a twerp, the group, usually men, says, "Oh yeah, that's a neat idea."	*You're not important.* *(240 replies)*
■ I ask what the potential is for a job and am "kiddingly" told: "For a man, GS-11, for you, GS-7." [Government pay grades.] ■ My boss calls us "lay personnel." ■ I'm told I shouldn't work because a man needs my job, with no consideration of my needs because I'm married.	*You're not a person.* *(114 replies)*
■ My boss discovers all the men will be out of the office for the afternoon and says, "Then *nobody* will be here in case a client calls!" ■ My boss blames me (indirectly) for things that went wrong. ■ I'm trying to communicate with my boss and he won't really listen to what I'm saying. He's saying what *he* thinks I want to say.	*You don't exist or are eligible to be the scapegoat.* *(97 replies)*

Speculating

You can recognize this potential power tactic by its lead-in, "It must be because . . ." What follows is a speculation about *why* someone does what she or he does. It can be idle wondering, not a power tactic. Said out loud, it has deadly potential for a power play since it usually casts suspicions.

Listen to George Digby, accounting supervisor, speculate about an error he just found, made by Sandy Jones, the new accounting clerk. Observe his line of reasoning.

George Digby's Dialogue	**Line of Reasoning**
■ "Now why did she do this? It doesn't make sense. Sandy should know you don't plug in a number to force the balance. Anybody who's worked in accounting for seven years knows that."	*George assumes a forced balance. He also assumes her training.*
■ "I wonder if that's why her references were vague. I'll bet she's had some trouble and nobody's talking. If this is any sample . . ."	*Without checking his assumptions, he speculates.*
■ "That's how Eddie got away with a few thou over a two-year period before they finally caught him embezzling. You sure don't know who you can trust and who you can't."	*Another incident leads to a generalization.*
■ "They say it's the innocent looking ones to watch out for. She sure looks innocent."	*Sandy gets the generalization.*
■ "Weeell, probably not—but you sure never know."	*Seeds of suspicion are now sown.*

George's thoughts may be speculations. However, they may tinge the way he sees future errors she makes. He's more likely to doubt her work, less likely to give her the benefit of the doubt.

Labeling With and Without Innuendoes

Labeling can be one of the more deadly power tactics, since it's often done by innuendo behind your back. Popular jargon for this game includes psychiatric labels, such as insecure, inferiority complex, paranoid; and pseudopsychiatric terms, such as losing his grip, gets cold feet, "on the sauce" (alcoholic). Once one of these labels sticks to you, it's hard to shake. Here are other ways:

- You can plant doubts about people by innuendo: "Have you noticed how touchy Joe's gotten lately?"
- A competitor for your next promotion might casually comment about you to your mutual boss, "Doesn't seem to have the same interest in the work. Wonder what's wrong?"
- You can box someone in by complimenting a strength until it becomes a liability. Prior to a very serious negotiation meeting on a big

sale of Sam Johnson's, he got this one behind his back: "Well, you know Sam—always full of jokes. Keeps 'em laughing." The back-slapping, joker image might cut him out of the meeting—and his commission.

- Innuendoes built on stereotypes can be used: "Yes, no question about it, Jane's good with details. About the bigger picture, well . . ."

Another form of labeling is often used face to face without innuendoes. "You're not ready [for the promotion]." "You're too hard-nosed. Relax a little." Judgments, evaluations, and interpretations can also raise defenses. They label behavior without describing it. Name calling can have the same effect.

Some labels may become part of one's identity, such as one's occupation, "I'm a carpenter." Comparing status or job levels also affects how we rate ourselves: "I'm a messenger" compared to "I'm vice president of operations." Sometimes we label ourselves: "I'm not good at statistics." Once we start believing these labels, whether we are consciously aware of them or not, they can become a self-fulfilling prophecy:

If I say you're a bad person
I can almost see you worsen
Funny how my words for you
Have a way of coming true.[6]

Raising Doubts

Doubts are more cruel than the worst of truths (Moliere). When someone can plant seeds of doubt in your mind about your knowledge, your abilities, your motivations, they can put you on the defensive, leaving them in control. You're down.

Whether it's used by supervisors or psychoanalysts, the process is the same. Here's one description of how analysts do it:

Doubt is, of course, the first step toward one downness. When in doubt the patient tends to lean on the analyst to resolve the doubt, and we lean on those who are superior to us. Analytic maneuvers [are] designed to arouse doubt. . . . For example, the analyst may say, "I wonder if that's *really* what you're feeling." The use of "really" implies the patient has motivations of which he is not aware. Anyone feels shaken, and therefore one down, when this suspicion is put

[6]Ruth Bebermeyer, "The Label Game," *I Wonder* (recording). Available from Ruth Bebermeyer, 218 Monclay St., St. Louis, MO. 63122.

"Now let me give you MY interpretation of your interpretation!"

Source: *Voices, the Art and Science of Psychotherapy*, vol. 13, no. 2. Summer 1977, p. 64.

in his mind [resulting in] suppressed fury and desperation—two emotions characterizing the one down position.[7]

Judging the Validity of Your Feelings

This one begins with, *"There's no reason . . ."* and ends with *". . . for you to feel that way."* You have just been judged as unreasonable, the judge being one up. If you defend yourself by giving reasons for your "unreasonable" feelings, you remain one down.

Again it's in your interest to look for what's missing. What the judge doesn't say are these possibilities in the middle:

"There's no reason ⟨ *that I can understand*
that I will accept ⟶ *for you to feel that way."*
because I won't recognize any

Mentally or verbally adding the missing middle can give you a starting point for stopping the up–down game, for getting off the defensive.

[7]Excepted from "The Art of Psychoanalysis," in Jay Haley, *The Power Tactics of Jesus Christ, and Other Essays*, The Viking Penguin, Inc., New York, 1969, pp. 15–17.

Breaking Confidentiality

Whenever the trust of confidence between two people is broken, the one who extended the trust tends to feel betrayed—defensive. Confidences between a supervisor and subordinate seem to be guided by a double standard: What Boss Bob tells Subordinate Sam is more confidential than what Sam tells Bob. If Bob thinks it's information Executive Ed might be interested in, he usually will tell Ed without thinking of asking Sam's permission. Sam would be expected to give it. "No" would not be considered an available option, according to the norms of most work systems.

If Sam discovers he cannot control his information through trusting Bob's confidentiality, he's likely to control it by not passing it on. Break trust and you break off receiving information that is likely to be important to you.

Offering Misleading Information

If you can persuade people to follow advice that will hurt them, you set them up to lose. You can abdicate and shift responsibility by saying, *"They didn't have to take the advice."* Although that may be true, shrugging it off has the effect of blaming the victim while you keep control.

If you happen to be on the receiving end of such advice, you have to base your actions on *your* weighing of the risks *you* take if you follow the advice. If you can't find out enough information about the risks involved for you, be aware of that. Absence of such information may be an alert to *beware*.

Scapegoating and Buckpassing

"Who can we blame?" is the name of this control game. Being in a subordinate position can make a person a natural target for scapegoating, finding a person to be blamed or sacrificed so a higher power person escapes the consequences for her or his actions. A low-power, low-status person who can easily be replaced is usually selected. For example, a messenger who runs errands for the president might be used as a scapegoat for information leaked by a vice president.

Passing the buck both downward and upward usually follows lines of responsibility and authority. Blame is usually passed downward; responsibility for making certain tough decisions upward.

You may be blamed or made the scapegoat before you know it—another good reason for having a reliable grapevine.

Joking and Play

Joking that is banter aimed at another person can also be a power tactic. The joker can say things he or she means without having to take responsibility for them. It's a defense against blame. If someone makes a joke at your expense, you may get the hidden meaning, but the humorous form makes it inappropriate or futile for you to confront the joker seriously. He or she can always claim it was only in jest.

Similarly, a person can deny a hidden meaning by saying, "Don't take it so seriously. I was only playing." By defining the communication as "play," people are not held accountable for their actions. Normal social rules are temporarily suspended, leaving you in a down position.[8]

Outright Lies and Other Deceptions

Other defensive ploys include lies, black, white, and all shades of gray. For example, in one survey chief executives admitted to consciously lying in these fourteen different ways:

- Outright lies
- Evasions
- Half-truths
- True statements that lead to false conclusions
- Silence
- Literal truth when it's known that the inference will be wrong
- The non-answer or non sequitur (answer doesn't follow the question)
- The knowing smile accompanied by silence
- An attack on the questioner to avoid answering
- Answering questions with other questions
- Ambiguity
- Postponement
- Obfuscation (confuse or dazzle) or gobbledygook
- Scatter grains of truth in a quantity of falsehoods[9]

[8]For the subtleties between joking and play, I am indebted to Joseph Alan Ullian, "Joking at Work," *Journal of Communication*, 26:3, 1976, pp. 129–33.

[9]From research reported in Otto Lerbinger and Nathaniel H. Sperber, *Key to the Executive Head*, Addison-Wesley, Reading, Mass., 1975, pp.51–52.

PULLING IT ALL TOGETHER

We've seen some ways that people learn to defend themselves, to protect their self-concepts. Sometimes the defense is against others; sometimes against the inner self. Many people defend themselves against threat and fears about being in control of themselves, of others, and of situations. These defenses can be short-term—using tactics to handle immediate situations— or long-term—developing strategies to control your own life.

There are non-defensive ways of keeping control over yourself and sharing control with other people. However, when you believe that you control your own life by controlling others or by controlling situations, you may become defensive and stimulate defensiveness in others. This may work for a while, but it can backfire. When it becomes a vicious circle, as it did for Helen and John, you, like Helen, may end up with less control than you thought you had. Others also want control.

The themes we've seen so far of ways that people use power to control other people are:

- Keep other people off balance by using double meanings that carry hidden threats.
- Appear to be open while disclosing little of yourself. Get others to react to you so they disclose or expose more of themselves.
- Don't really listen to the other person.
- Distort or omit information to suit your own purposes.
- Manage appearances, act "as if," using façades that give the impression you want when you know it's not the real thing.

When you're in a subordinate position *and you think subordinate,* you are likely to react to these control devices, giving away some control over yourself to others. As you become more of your own person, you can be in a subordinate position and *think as a person.* You can learn to see and hear these control devices, then make your own decision about when you choose to go along or when you choose to keep more control over yourself.

ASK YOURSELF

- Which patterns of defensiveness do you use most often?
- How do these relate to patterns you learned growing up?
- What results are you getting that you don't want?
- What results would you prefer to get instead?
- What defenses might be worth changing that would help you get different results that you *do* want?

Make some notes on these questions, keeping them in mind as we take a closer look at work systems, the context in which much of your time is spent. Other systems, such as the one in your home, is another context that may have similar or different norms. You have more choices about shaping the norms in your home than you do at work. In either place, however, the context affects your communications; it provides the background of norms, expectations, and rules of behavior that influence the way your meanings are sent and received.

IN THE NEXT CHAPTER

We've seen some ways that people learn to be defensive within themselves and how defenses arise between people. The context in which people relate also has much to do with how defensive they become. An atmosphere of high fear and low trust generates more defensiveness than a climate of lower fear and higher trust.

In the next chapter we will see how to recognize some values, norms, and rituals that contribute to the system's climate, and we will also consider some of the risks involved, both negative and positive, in adhering to or breaking from these customs and expectations. Such information is often critical in assessing various options for handling certain situations.

READINGS

Erikson, Erik H.: *Toys and Reasons: Stages in the Ritualization of Experience,* W. W. Norton, New York, 1977. This well-known psychoanalyst reviews how parents and society provide rituals at each stage of development in the life cycle. This ritualization gives an individual a group and personal identity, a sense of belonging while deflecting feelings of unworthiness onto outsiders, some definitions of what's right and legally good or guilt-producing, and sanctioned ways for doing daily activities.

Farson, Richard: *Birthrights,* Penguin Books, New York, 1974. A humanistic attitude toward raising children with deep regard for their rights as people and the kinds of needed supports for growth to develop as healthy, self-defining adults. It builds on belief in the essential goodness of the child.

Goffman, Erving: *The Presentation of Self in Everyday Life,* Doubleday Anchor, Garden City, N.Y., 1959. A classic on how people present themselves, as if on the stage of life; how we play out our roles and live our values; use of façades, games and self-protective enactment. Most insightful, interestingly presented, it is a "must" for seeing through the ways in which people present and preserve their personal dignity. Also see his *Interaction Rituals: Essays on Face-to-Face Behavior,* Doubleday Anchor, 1967.

Henley, Nancy M.: *Body Politics: Power, Sex, and Nonverbal Communication,* Prentice-Hall, Englewood Cliffs, N. J., 1977. Focuses on how nonverbal communication is used to maintain power in the social hierarchy, especially between men and women. Excellently researched and documented by the psychologist-author.

Jacobson, Wally D.: *Power and Interpersonal Relations,* Wadsworth, Belmont, Calif., 1972. An excellent review of the research on power, its bases, methods, attributes, group attributes, effect of the situation, leadership styles, and how it works in various types of systems. Summarizes power principles and provides exhaustive bibliography. Good reference text.

Scheflen, Albert E.: *Body Language and Social Order: Communication as Behavioral Control,* Prentice-Hall, Englewood Cliffs, N. J., 1972. Heavily illustrated with pictures showing facial and body expressions that connote social control of people and space, this book includes subtleties not found in the pop literature on body language. Useful for a good understanding of such behavior without getting heavily technical as in Birdwhistell.

For additional background reading, see bibliography entries 2, 3, 6, 8, 11, 17, 19, 21, 22, 26, 27, 28, 30, 34.

4

HOW ORGANIZATIONS CREATE A DEFENSIVE CLIMATE

Recognizing Some Norms, Values, and Power Factors That Affect Your Risks in Becoming Non-Defensive

Every organization or group creates a cultural climate for itself by the societal values it shares, the norms of appropriate behavior it generally agrees upon, and the rituals it performs to sustain its equilibrium through trials and tribulations as well as celebrations. Many people are not consciously aware of how strongly they may be influenced by these cultural norms and the resultant expectations, which usually come from the upper-level executives and managers—the norm setters—as they define appropriate behavior and attitudes for people in (and sometimes out of) their organizational roles. Expectations tend to trickle down through the organization as people play follow the leader.

Learning the values, norms, and rituals of a particular system is part of your indoctrination process whenever you enter or move within an organization. You are seldom a fully functioning, accepted member of the organization until you "fit in"—that is, until you can be trusted to generally adhere to the prevailing customs and expectations others have for you. Fitting in is often as important as the job you do, sometimes more so.

Many of the norms and practices in traditional systems have the effect of exercising power and control over you. You take risks when you choose to exercise more power over yourself as you are becoming more of your own person. In fact, this can be quite risky unless you know how to read some of the processes that are going on and can decide when and how you can effectively negotiate your way.

As a subordinate, you have more leverage if you are knowledgeable about the political realities in your system; if you have alternatives available to you;

if you have knowledge or influence that higher-power people depend upon; if there are others with whom you can link the power and influence you have; or if you've developed trusting relationships. You may also be able to negotiate a more open relationship with your manager than is usually the norm in your system. (Other factors were reviewed in Chapter 2 when we counted up and down points.)

Let's start with the values, norms, and rituals that are typical of traditional systems.

RECOGNIZING SOME VALUES, NORMS, AND RITUALS

Let's see what the climate of an organization, Country Stores, Inc., looks like in action. As you read its history and growth, think about what values and norms may have grown up in this system, both from the external culture as well as the internal one. These will be only indicators, but see what you can pick up about what life is like at the corporate offices and at the stores. Also observe what values or norms seem to differ between the officers and the new data processing manager.

Development of Values and Norms at Country Stores, Inc.

Country Stores was started thirty-two years ago by its current president and senior vice president, Tom Hudson, now 60, and Jack Willitt, now 55. Both started as lettuce growers who had difficulty making profits because of a federal clampdown on the illegal entry of Mexicans for jobs as farm laborers. So they formed a partnership as grocers and built a highly successful chain of small-town grocery–specialty stores in several Western states. The layout of their stores is designed to encourage socializing and visiting while people shop.

How the company was started, the kinds of people who helped build it, use and selection of experts tell something about what is valued in the company.

Both Tom and Jack are self-made men who learn fast from experience. Tom's the outgoing one, Jack is more interested in internal operations. The other corporate officers and store managers are much like them: hard working, conscientious, and cost conscious. Store managers are respected and involved in their local communities. Little they do escapes the scrutiny of Tom, Jack, or the other watchdog of Country Stores, controller, Peter Gross, 57, a long-time friend of both Tom and Jack. Sometimes, half humorously, the three of them are referred to among store managers as "the Trinity" or "Father, Son, and Holy Ghost."

Lack of formal education hasn't been a hurdle. Jack Willitt is particularly strong on hiring experts in areas of technology that will make them money. They've recently hired a replacement for their data processing (DP) manager to install scanners for the Universal Product Codes (UPC).[1] Dave Eliot, 26, is bright, has just graduated summa cum laude with his M.B.A. and is also quite personable.

A New Man Comes In

Dave has now headed up the computer operation under Pete Gross for five months. He's been given fairly free rein and has been working assiduously installing new UPC scanners, converting store inputs, and working closely with internal auditing to control discrepancies. Pete, Jack, and Tom have all told him how pleased they are with the way he's coming along.

Dave's additional activities and the speed at which he works have stretched both his day and night crews to the limit. But they don't complain. They respect Dave's quick grasp and innovative approaches, and they also like the way he says what must be done without ordering them around. He gives them ideas for shortcuts but lets them work out their own routines and schedules.

Dave's day and night supervisors, Mary Galloway, 27, and Juan Martinez, 30, see him more as a technical resource than a manager, and they supervise the same way. Both crews regularly come through; in fact, they take a certain pride in being able to pour out the work on time and still maintain documentation. They feel appreciated when Dave occasionally takes them out for drinks after an especially heavy run. This practice has drawn comment from Pete, Dave's direct supervisor.

An Unexpected Conflict Develops

Here's how Dave sees what's been happening:

I think we deserve something special. We all enjoy drinking together, and I pay for it out of my own pocket even though I think it should be a

---

[1]UPCs are the computer codes composed of lines, bars, and numbers that are on the labels of many grocery products.

business expense. But Pete and even Tom keep telling me that fraternizing with my employees will lead to discipline problems. So far I haven't paid much attention to these comments because we don't have discipline problems. We keep it friendly and my people produce.

But lately my night supervisor, Juan Martinez, has been punching in late. I talked with him about it and his reasons seemed okay. He sees to it that one of the crew knows what to do so the work keeps moving. As I say, they're a great bunch—they haven't missed an important deadline yet.

So I got pretty annoyed last week when Ed Jones, 52, came by. He's that old-timer in payroll who checks time cards. He stuck his head in my door and abruptly announced, "I've reported you to Pete Gross for your failure to put disciplinary memos in Juan's personnel file." He jerked the door shut and briskly walked out of DP before I had a chance to say anything and he hasn't returned my calls.

I spoke to Pete about it and all he would say was, "I've been telling you what would happen if you fraternize too much." With a cool stare he added, "You know the rules about disciplinary memos." End. He wouldn't listen to my side of it.

I know they insist on complete personnel records in case we have to fire someone, but I'd never fire Juan or anyone else for such minor infractions. You have to bend the rules a little to keep good men like Juan around, and you can't split hairs if you're going to keep up the *esprit de corps* for long.

All of a sudden they seem to be pulling in the reins on me and I don't like it one bit. Now I'm wondering if they'll hold back on those two people I need for researching discrepancies because of this. You don't think they'd make *that* much fuss over a few memos-to-file, do you?

What do *you* think, reader? Would they?

Identifying the Confronting Issue and the Underlying Conflict of Values

Let's identify the confronting issue and then trace back to the underlying values that may be operating at Country Stores. The confronting issue was this: Dave broke a rule; he didn't put the required memos in Juan's personnel file. Dave doesn't seem to think this is very serious; just look at how his people are producing. Dave may be assuming that getting the work done is more important than following rules. Surely, as DP manager, he has the right to make that decision, doesn't he?

It appears he may not; Ed's abruptness plus his boss' lack of support suggests that he has overstepped some boundary. Could there be a norm that says "Everyone must follow all the rules all the time?" This would be hard to enforce even for lower-level, inexperienced people, much less for supervisors on up. As a loosely enforced general rule, it can be strictly invoked when bosses want to draw someone up short, which seems to be happening to Dave.

Let's look beneath the confronting issue for an underlying conflict. Dave disregarded Pete's and Tom's warnings not to fraternize with his employees and continued having after-work drinks with them. Maybe it's also fraternizing when, as a manager, Dave doesn't give orders. Also Pete would probably expect Dave to warn Juan about tardiness in the future and not just accept his reasons without a reprimand. It appears that at Country Stores one unwritten system value is: Don't get too close to your employees if you expect to stay in control of them. Dave's managerial style includes a different value: Work with your employees if you expect them to produce.

At this point, you may be thinking that Dave could solve this problem by simply talking with Juan: Tell him what's happening, ask him to punch in on time to take off the pressure, and assure him that the memo Dave has to put in his file will be innocuous. That might seem to take care of the confronting issue, and it perhaps would. However, if the conflict of underlying values is not considered now, there's likely to be another confronting issue before long. So let's continue looking at the larger context to see Dave's position in it, assuming that you have only this information to work with.

We now have some indicators that the executives believe a good manager keeps distance from his employees to better control them, while Dave has demonstrated that friendly teamwork, information sharing and some socializing keeps people feeling good and producing well. When Dave doesn't manage in a similar style as the executives, when he doesn't share their same values, they may eventually decide to bring him into line, as they seem to be doing now. If Dave doesn't shape up, they will probably tighten up more until he comes around to their way of thinking.

This process is quite typical of traditional managers who, like traditional parents, feel that respect for authority comes from firm but fair control of the subordinate's behavior. And respect often means that the example should be followed: "Manage like I do—it's the best way." Father knows best.

Probable Prevailing Norms at Country Stores, Inc.

Most organizations have basic norms about age, seniority, experience, education, and learning the ropes in that system. Additional norms tend to evolve into large networks as a system matures and as traditional management extends its control. Reviewing Tom's, Jack's, and Pete's backgrounds and the development of Country Stores, what would you consider some of their basic norms? Consider these:

- Young people have to prove themselves (like we did).
- New people have to prove themselves (like we did).
- College kids, even smart ones, are wet behind the ears. They think they know everything when they only know some things. (We built Country Stores without college educations.)
- They don't know what goes on in the Real World. They've never had to meet a payroll. (We've made it through the rough times.)
- They should defer to, listen to, and do what the top men tell them. (We came up the hard way, so why should you have it any easier? We know how to run a business.)

Such norms as these are probable because they reflect traditional small-town patterns that Tom and Jack who began as farmers and have been successfully building the country business for thirty-two years might hold. We know that Pete is an old friend of similar thinking; store managers are probably conservative and over-40 or they're not likely to be respected in small-town communities. They also seem to accept the tight controls of corporate officers who may like to see themselves as having a tight hold of the reins. Keeping control is of central importance. The friendliness among the top three men probably rests on a commonly held value—belief in centralized control over policies and profits and of policing people.

If you know the local customs, you can usually predict many norms in businesses that grew up in that locality.

Other norms might coincide with regional or national cultural values, including some conservative stereotypes about people. For example, if the summa cum laude M.B.A. had been female, she might not have been hired as DP manager here. Mary Galloway, as day crew supervisor, is the highest level woman. Odds are good that store managers are male Caucasians and Protestant. Juan Martinez is the highest level minority. They can joke about "the Trinity" but might not include Juan in that humor, even if he were in a higher-level position. He is probably Catholic. In addition, Juan is an Hispanic who would probably be accepted only formally. In regions in which the labor of Mexican illegal aliens is used, Hispanics are often segregated both physically and socially. Some of the concern about Dave's fraternizing could be related to ethnic prejudice of this kind. Traditional norms usually hint that one doesn't mix with "them," a value Dave doesn't seem to share.

Without being inside this system, we have no way of knowing if these norms actually exist except by looking for what's missing, knowing local and regional mores, and drawing some tentative opinions, always recognizing these rely on assumptions that are subject to change with more information. However, it's well to be aware of their potential existence, since breaking a norm, whether it's explicit or implicit, involves a risk. The more power the norm breaker has in the system, the less risk; with little power the risk might be high.

Assessing Dave's Power Position in Country Stores' Power Structure

Let's start with some power signals that may be indicators of Dave's power position. Ed, the old-timer in payroll who checks time cards, doesn't seem to have high position power. However, he has seniority; he's in the same age range as Pete, Tom, and Jack; he serves as a watchdog, a valued function, and could have a private assignment to monitor Dave. He clearly assumes he is a high power person as shown by his body language. When he delivered his personal announcement to Dave, he stuck his head into Dave's office, indicating his presumed right to intrude or interrupt. He did not wait for a response, and his brisk exit indicated his power to close the discussion. His not returning Dave's calls indicated his power to ignore a less powerful person. Dave's discussion with Pete Gross carried similar power signals, although these would be expected since Pete is Dave's supervisor. However, his "I told you so" manner, his cool reminder about the rules, and his refusal to hear Dave's side of the incident, all indicate the role of the stern father teaching his naughty son how to behave.

Power seems to be distributed rather narrowly at Country Stores; it's tightly held at the top. Probably whatever power is acquired is by means of long tenure, shared values about control, adherence to norms, receiving the fathers' blessings, long-term loyalty, and other similar means. Competence and continued productivity are probably considered to be so basic as not to merit recognition beyond the paycheck—that's what people are paid for. Recognition probably comes only when productivity drops off, which may be accompanied by a fall from grace.

So Dave isn't likely to gain power by doing the job well or because his crews continue to produce well under pressure. That's expected. He's going to have to prove himself, which in this system means he has to show he can follow the rules and accept the authority of his superiors. As long as he assumes authority, as long as he thinks for himself, he's likely to be considered naive or a renegade. The rules will be enforced, and he will be punished until he learns to conform.

It takes time to prove you can be trusted not to rock the boat. Until then, your power is low and your risks are high.

Conformity to rules and not appearing to think for himself may well be the way for Dave to get early access to the power system here. After a suitable period of conformity, which proves he has become properly indoctrinated, he will have earned the right to bend the rules—an indicator of some power in this system.

Dave does not now have that power. Given what we know, what is Dave's power position? His substantial staff position may not be as powerful as a comparable line position. He produces well so he has no minuses there. His technical knowledge is highly valued but is offset by nonconformity to the basic norms in the system. He's young, has only five months' tenure, is college educated, has no previous business experience, and is not obeying authority. Odds are Dave's power position is very low, at zero, or even at a minus level. It's likely to remain so until he proves himself while going through the initiation rituals—the rites of passage from novice to initiate to member status in the system.

Initiation Rituals in Traditional Systems

These rituals are not unlike fraternity rites of passage for pledges, which include hazing, testing of loyalties, testing willingness to perform certain feats, some distasteful, and foremost, demonstrating willingness to obey all orders given by full members. In due time, having passed all the tests, pledges are received into membership as new initiates. Their loyalty and endurance is celebrated by solemn candlelight rites; swearing of undying fealty is exchanged; and a few inner secrets of the fraternity are opened to initiates, with promise of greater things to come as they continue to prove themselves. Similar rites are performed in the military, in athletic teams, churches, lodges, and other tribal groups.[2]

Rites in work organizations are far less visible, but the company code is no less real or secret. Different orders of membership are defined by the job

---

[2]See Bill Owens, *Our Kind of People: American Groups and Rituals*, Straight Arrow Books, San Francisco, 1974, for a remarkable pictorial array of some national rituals in action.

level at which the novice enters. At Dave's level, the length of testing time is likely to be from one to five years. One to two years take him through the annual cycle of his functions. One to three years more allow him to learn how things actually work in this system and to build a personal investment in maintaining that status quo.

Dave has started off on the wrong foot, and it may take him six months or more to recoup his loss of power—whenever he can show that he has learned his lesson to the executives' satisfaction. Then he will be ready to start again as a full-fledged novice approaching the status of initiate. He will not be informed of the date of his initiation, nor will it be formally announced. The candlelight service may be replaced with an unprecedented invitation to a high-level meeting, to break bread with selected executives, or perhaps to perform a junior ritual such as giving a briefing. At this event he "enters the men's hut" as an initiate.[3]

In a later chapter we will pick up the threads of Dave's situation. Right now, he is on the defensive in his down position. If he compromises himself, if he violates his self-choice area, he's likely to remain on the defensive for a long time. One compromise of self tends to lead to another—like lying—and the oftener you do it, the more difficult they are to untangle.

Later we'll also see how Dave might design a plan of action in which he doesn't compromise himself but can make some compromises that weigh the risks that go with breaking norms in this traditional system. First, he will have to be clear about what results he wants to achieve.

RECOGNIZING HOW PEOPLE PROCESSES CREATE THE PREVAILING CLIMATE

Let's get a larger perspective now on how a system can be described. When you can recognize some of these subjective patterns that operate in organizations, you can make better predictions of what helps or hinders you in achieving your career goals and in becoming more of your own person. Instead of focusing on production processes, we are considering the people processes that are necessary for production to occur and that affect people's productivity. Some of the functions that occur in all organizations are leadership, motivation, communication, decision making, goal setting, and exercising controls.

One way of describing an organization's climate is in terms of how these people processes are used, ranging from exerting strong control to

---

[3]The briefing ritual is played out in R. Richard Ritti and G. Ray Funkhouser, "Part 1—Enter the Men's Hut," *The Ropes to Skip and the Ropes to Know: Studies in Organizational Behavior*, Grid Publishing, Inc., Columbus, Ohio, 1977, pp. 24–47. To read more revealing narratives of these ritualistic processes, I recommend *Ropes* very highly.

providing a supportive climate for human growth, as shown in Rensis Likert's Organizational Profile in Figure 4-1 on pages 100–101.

The four systems described by Likert are:

System 1: Authoritative–Exploitative (Chew 'em up and spit 'em out) Control is tightly held at the top, and little concern is shown for people's growth or needs. This produces a climate of high fear and low trust, which results in much defensive behavior.

System 2: Authoritative–Benevolent (Salute the flag and Big Daddy, too) The paternalistic father knows what is best for people, so the system and its members are controlled for their own good. People compete for favorable attention at the top, which produces defensive behavior in the climate where fear is almost as high as in System 1 and trust almost as low.

System 3: Consultative (Ask 'em and listen) People are encouraged to be more involved with organizational goals and are taken more seriously as responsible adults. Goal setting and decision making are still done near the top, but people further down are consulted, their expertise being valued and used where feasible. Lower fear and higher trust produces a less defensive climate.

System 4: Participative (Let 'em do it) More people can influence decisions by using their competence and initiative. More decisions are made further down in the system, which are more coordinated than controlled at the top. Of the four systems, this one is least defensive because of the trust shown in people and the low-fear learning environment.

The Authoritative–Exploitative Climate[4]

The exploitative climate of System 1 requires obedience from employees, much like the obeisance due the Japanese liege lord. Power and control belong to management by virtue of their position more than their problem-solving abilities. Subordinates are expected to do what they're told, not to ask questions, and to be quietly respectful, well-behaved and obedient,

---

[4]The following descriptions of organizational climates are drawn heavily from Rosalind K. Loring and Theodora Wells, "Managerial Climate," Chapter 4 in *Breakthrough: Women into Management*, Van Nostrand Reinhold, New York, 1972, pp. 74–84. Although much of this material may seem basic to some readers, I find that many people are not familiar with how to read an organization's climate and have not made the connection between the climate and the degree of defensiveness they feel or the risks to be considered and weighed.

honest and trustworthy, and, of course, efficient. Conformity and dependency are valued because they confirm management's right to control.

Management believes that security is what motivates people, so the assumptions of McGregor's Theory X tend to prevail: the average person inherently dislikes work and will seek to avoid it; therefore, people must be coerced, controlled, directed, and threatened with punishment to get them to give adequate effort. People prefer to be directed, do not want responsibility, and have little ambition. They want immediate satisfactions and rewards.[5]

In these systems, you're likely to find shelves full of policy and procedure manuals. People who survive in this authoritarian climate tend to become more childlike than adult because "organizations are willing to pay high wages and provide adequate seniority if mature adults will, for eight hours a day, behave in a less than mature manner."[6] When people become more dependent on others with less power over themselves, they tend to protect and defend themselves by engaging in rivalries, competing for favor, hiding or manipulating information, and generally contributing to a climate of distrust.

The Authoritative–Benevolent Climate

The benevolent or paternalistic climate requires deference from its employees. In these systems, you're likely to find employee handbooks that talk about one big happy family, and you'll also find Big Daddy at the top. System 2 managements assume that they know what's best for their organizations and the people in it and that they are responsible to see that people conform to their "one right way." These managers may be more gracious in their relationships, but they expect subordinates to be grateful if and when they are included in decision making or sharing of information. The underlying assumptions about people are generally Theory X, although modified.

This climate usually breeds yes-men and -women who tend to pass the buck, protect their positions, and be competitive in their relationships. An active grapevine supplements information not officially dispensed from above, which is often shared among subordinates for self-preservation. An admixture of competition and collaboration may evolve among subordinates as a protection against the common enemy of upper management; yet this becomes unstable when someone is currying favor upstairs. Vicious infighting can occur as people maneuver for position in the pecking order, seeking visibility to make points for promotion.

[5]Douglas McGregor, *The Human Side of Enterprise,* McGraw-Hill, New York, 1960, pp. 33–34.
[6]Chris Argyris, *Personality and Organization,* Harper & Row, New York, 1957, pp. 66.

People processes	System 1	System 2	System 3	System 4	Item number
Leadership					
How much confidence and trust is shown in subordinates?	Virtually none	Some	Substantial amount	A great deal	1
How free do they feel to talk to superiors about job?	Not very free	Somewhat free	Quite free	Very free	2
How often are subordinate's ideas sought and used constructively?	Seldom	Sometimes	Often	Very frequently	3
Motivation					
Is predominant use made of 1 fear, 2 threats, 3 punishment, 4 rewards, 5 involvement?	1,2,3, occasionally 4	4, some 3	4, some 3 and 5	5,4, based on group	4
Where is responsibility felt for achieving organization's goals?	Mostly at top	Top and middle	Fairly general	At all levels	5
How much cooperative teamwork exists?	Very little	Relatively little	Moderate amount	Great deal	6
Communication					
What is the usual direction of information flow?	Downward	Mostly downward	Down and up	Down, up and sideways	7
How is downward communication accepted?	With suspicion	Possibly with suspicion	With caution	With a receptive mind	8
How accurate is upward communication?	Usually inaccurate	Often inaccurate	Often accurate	Almost always accurate	9

Category	People Processes	System 1	System 2	System 3	System 4	Item number
Communication	How well do superiors know problems faced by subordinates?	Not very well	Rather well	Quite well	Very well	10
Decisions	At what level are decisions made?	Mostly at top	Policy at top, some delegation	Broad policy at top, more delegation	Throughout but well integrated	11
Decisions	Are subordinates involved in decisions related to their work?	Almost never	Occasionally consulted	Generally consulted	Fully involved	12
Decisions	What does decision-making process contribute to motivation?	Not very much	Relatively little	Some contribution	Substantial contribution	13
Control	How are organizational goals established?	Orders issued	Orders, some comments invited	After discussion, by orders	By group action (except in crisis)	14
Control	How much covert resistance to goals is present?	Strong resistance	Moderate resistance	Some resistance at times	Little or none	15
Goals	How concentrated are review and control functions?	Very highly at top	Quite highly at top	Moderate delegation to lower levels	Widely shared	16
Goals	Is there an informal organization resisting the formal one?	Yes	Usually	Sometimes	No—same goals as formal	17
Goals	What are cost, productivity, and other control data used for?	Policing, punishment	Reward and punishment	Reward some self-guidance	Self-guidance problem-solving	18

Figure 4-1. *Organizational profile. (Source: Rensis Likert, The Human Organization: Its Management and Value. Copyright 1967. New York: McGraw-Hill Book Company, Inc. Used with permission of McGraw-Hill.)*

This creates a climate of comparatively high fear and low trust, which invites those defensive vicious circles so costly in paid time. Such costs are offset by those people who disdain competition—people whose goal is to perform their tasks according to management's expectations—the dependable plodders who keep operations going while others play win–lose games.

The Consultative Climate

The consultative climate of System 3 expects involvement from employees. Management assumes that people are motivated more like McGregor's Theory Y: It's natural for people to want to put forth work effort. People will exercise self-direction and self-control when they feel personal commitment to goals. Through that commitment people gain satisfaction from achieving these goals. People will accept and go after responsibility, given the right climate. Many people, not just a few, have capacities for imagination and creativity in solving organizational problems.[7]

In a System 3 climate, people's ideas are more valued. There is less punishment for mistakes or non-conformity. Communications are exchanged more freely and with more accuracy. More delegated work stays delegated, and there is more authentic teamwork. There is less reading of rules, more active productivity. With more room for self-direction, there is more reason to commit oneself to organizational goals. With more trust and less fear, self-confidence and self-esteem increase; defensiveness decreases.

The Participative Climate

The participative climate of System 4 encourages people to collaborate in problem solving and decision making. Theory Y assumptions are extended further down in the organization. Not only do managers believe that what's good for the company is good for its people, but they also believe that what's good for its people is good for the company. Self-interest and organizational goals intertwine; there is more collaborative use of power that comes from the interdependency created by the shared goals. Loyalty is more freely given because it is authentically present not because "that's what a good employee does." Personal security comes more from within. Paradoxically, as a person's need for security in the organization lessens, the desire to participate in it often increases.[8]

[7]McGregor, *The Human Side of Enterprise*, pp. 47–48.
[8]Loring and Wells, *Breakthrough: Women into Management*, p. 82.

Managers of these systems have learned that they cannot command people to give of themselves in these ways; such giving comes from authentic, personal experiences of feeling genuinely valued and respected as persons. Defenses can be lowered where there's low fear and self-reliant people can trust and listen to each other. Although difficult to achieve and maintain, a few organizations are developing their climates in these directions. Some tend to be more socially responsible, balancing social and political concerns with productivity and profitability. Self, system, and society all gain—a non-defensive outcome.

The Traditional Paternalistic Climate Is the Most Common One

Look at Figure 4-1 again; notice the vertical line in the middle of System 2. According to an interview with Rensis Likert, the climate of most large work organizations is in the median range of system 2—a benevolently paternalistic climate.[9] Since most people have to work in this environment, it's important to know its norms, values, rituals, and risks. Country Stores is probably somewhere between 1.5 and 2.5, a little more conservative than most systems.

Such systems are resistant to change; they are deeply invested in maintaining the status quo. Many professional managers are motivated more by a need for power than a need for achievement and even less from a need for affiliation.[10] This tends to generate feelings of defensiveness in others, often unrecognized since others may have higher needs for achievement or affiliation.

Power to Influence Is Partly Based on Who Depends on Whom

Sometimes a subgroup within a system will be able to operate on different norms. Dave Eliot's DP group is an example. But it will survive only when the leader of that group has the power to influence the more powerful leaders, when his group members do not have a large amount of interconnected work with other groups, and when they go through the forms of

[9]Rensis Likert, "A Conversation with Rensis Likert," *Organization Dynamics*, AMACOM, a division of American Management Associations, New York, Summer 1973, pp. 42, 44.
[10]David C. McClelland and David H. Burnham, "Power Is the Great Motivator," *Harvard Business Review*, March–April 1976, pp. 100–110.

generally conforming to prevailing norms. Their more liberal norms usually must be exercised in private. Public deviation would be seen as undermining the morale and discipline of the system, an unforgivable breach of behavior in System 1 and sometimes in System 2. It would challenge the control of the top leaders.

On the other hand, managers are dependent on subordinates to do the organization's work, whether they care to admit it or not. At Country Stores, the executives depend on Dave Eliot's expert knowledge for the UPC scanner installation. Their estimate of how available that knowledge is in other people determines how dependent they feel on Dave right now. Likewise, Dave, with his credentials, may have available alternatives elsewhere, especially if he is keeping close contacts with his university and computer professional groups. These factors—dependency and availability of alternatives—help determine how much influence Dave has, even as a new man, when conflict develops.[11]

In some management positions, the manager is dependent on only a few others to do the job well. In other positions, there are many people or groups the manager must depend on to be able to function; it's in the nature of the job. How well a manager can influence those on whom she or he depends for cooperation determines how well that position is managed. So, in positions in which you depend on many others, you need skills in working with others so they'll work with you—power-oriented behavior. In positions in which there are less dependencies, you can spend less time consolidating your resources and allies. "Successful managers use their power, along with persuasion . . . with a sensitivity to what the various kinds of power can accomplish, to what risks they are taking, and to others' beliefs about what constitutes the legitimate or illegitimate use of power."[12] When we develop Dave's plans of action for handling his position, we will see how he does this when he has different ideas about the use of power than his bosses and how this affects his risks.

Even though traditional managers tend to be autocratic, they sometimes respond more flexibly when you show initiative and self-reliance.

---

[11]Daniel F. Toomey, "The Effects of Power Properties on Conflict Resolution," *Academy of Management Review*, January 1978, pp. 144–150.

[12]John P. Kotter, "Power, Success and Organizational Effectiveness," *Organizational Dynamics*, AMACOM, a division of American Management Associations, New York, Winter 1978, p. 35. Kotter develops these concepts in considerable detail.

Dependency on subordinates can provide yet another avenue for influencing the climate around you. There is some evidence that traditional, autocratic leaders may become more democratic when their subordinates don't behave in the usual passive–dependent way that authoritarian climates stimulate. Instead, when a subordinate shows initiative and self-reliance, behavior more common in consultative and participative climates, some autocratic leaders accommodate their style to the subordinate's, behaving more democratically. This is likely to occur when the subordinate's productivity, which is often greater in the more open climates, is important to how the manager is rewarded for productivity.[13] For example, if Dave's boss, Pete Gross, can gain something from Tom Hanson or Jack Willitt because of Dave's productivity, Pete may be persuaded to give Dave more latitude in the way he manages the DP department. Jack Willitt is also a possible candidate for this change, since he recruited Dave and may want his choice to be a winner. Later we'll see more about what Dave might do with this power factor to reduce his risks.

If you feel you are invisible and have little or no power in your system, remember that there is a "power of no power." Because you have less to lose (in your system, if not personally), you may be able to take more risks. Also you may be able to build some influential alliances under your cloak of invisibility. Some of the most influential people don't appear in boxes in organizational charts. They may be gatekeepers to power, such as a president's secretary, or may have approval or veto power, such as administrative assistants who decide who gets technical assistance on special projects.

Whether you have such influence or depend on it from others, these are among the additional resources and allies for adding to your power potential, and they are often appropriate to the norms in many systems.

Now let's look further into how norms are formed, what they generally concern, how they become taboos, and how rewards and punishments may be administered in paternalistic systems.

HOW NORMS BECOME FORCES FOR CONTROLLING BEHAVIOR

A norm is a cluster of expectations that is shared throughout a system or within a group that determines what behavior is appropriate, right, good, allowable, or rewardable. It also defines what is inappropriate, wrong, bad, not allowable, or punishable. A taboo is like a norm, but is much stronger with more serious consequences. Punishment is sure to follow, ranging from

[13]Bruce J. Crowe, Stephen Bochner, and Alfred W. Clark, "The Effects of Subordinates' Behaviour on Managerial Style," *Human Relations*, vol. 25, no. 3, July 1972, pp. 215–237.

temporary social ostracization to permanent termination of membership in the group or system.

Rewards—the positive risks from adhering to a norm that increases your odds of getting what you want from the system—can range from a subtle nod of approval to entry into the inner power group. Initiation rituals can provide a series of increasingly valuable rewards to conformers to the system.

Punishments—the negative risks of breaking a norm or taboo—can range from a raised eyebrow of warning to dismissal. Intimidation rituals can provide a series of increasingly painful punishments to reformers of a system, with the sole responsibility for final expulsion being placed upon the reformer.

Norms Always Exist for Relating to People with Power and Control

There are always norms about how subordinates are expected to relate to power and control. Top executives who must always be given deference are identified to new employees during the initial orientation period. New supervisors, staff people, and managers are expected to assume deference until they learn the specific norms for each upper-level manager or executive and for each work group. These norms form a complex network, subtly shifting and changing with the political climate. You need to be constantly in tune with these if you want to wend your way upward or even just to maintain credibility in a typical paternalistic system.

Norms define how power is distributed, who is in control, and how authority is handled.

Norms are sometimes established quickly, perhaps by a single exchange in a meeting. For example, let's say someone challenges the leader by strongly complaining how the meeting is being run. Everyone falls silent, waiting to see what the leader will do. What he or she does in the next few moments will strongly influence subsequent norms about how this group will handle its power and authority issues in the future. If the leader fights back and the group supports him or her, either by siding with the leader or by remaining silent, a norm has been formed that "We don't challenge the authority of the leader." If, on the other hand, the leader permits the challenge and encourages others to voice their opinions, a norm has been formed that "We can talk openly about how authority is exercised in the group."[14]

Notice that only the challenger was using power over self (although complaining is not a useful intervention). All the others played follow the leader, letting her or him decide how power was distributed.

Norms About Group Behavior Reflect the System's Climate

Other norms are more generally known and not regularly tested. Almost any work group can readily list its own norms if they take time to list them. In a paternalistic system group norms create deference and caution, which create a defensive climate. Some of these norms might be:

- We wear suit coats to the meeting.
- We are on time or a few minutes early.
- We are on hand to greet the leader who arrives three minutes late.
- We let him speak first since he controls the agenda.
- We do not question his statements or challenge him.
- We participate and make a contribution but pay attention to what the leader wants.
- We appear informal but are generally cautious.
- We do not swear or use foul language.
- We keep things pleasant or humorous and keep our cool at all times.

In a consultative or participative system, group norms allow more exchange of differing viewpoints and seeking of consensus, which creates a more non-defensive climate. Some of these norms might be:

- We can dress informally at meetings among ourselves.
- We are on time although five minutes late is acceptable.
- We help ourselves and each other to coffee.
- We put our own items on the agenda.
- We assume leadership when the subject concerns us.
- We openly disagree as long as we listen to others' views.
- We do not attack each other when we vigorously disagree.
- We work toward consensus and do not fall back on voting.
- We make an important decision only after we know everyone is committed to carrying it out.

[14]Adapted from Edgar H. Schein, *Process Consultation: Its Role in Organization Development,* Addison-Wesley, Reading, Mass., 1969, p. 60.

These are explicit norms; they can be written down and discussed. Other norms may be implicit; they are ones no one talks much about, but they can be seen by the way people react when the norms are violated. Implicit norms are more common in Systems 1 and 2, since obedience and deference take priority over involvement and participation. In a climate of high fear and low trust, implicit norms tend to be part of the semisecret information, which is gradually shared with initiates to the inner power groups.

Norms That Create Distrust Are Easily Recognized

Most people can easily recognize a climate of low trust and high fear. When asked what they would do if they were going to create an organization in which there was maximum distrust, one group of managers quickly came up with these practices:[15]

- Require frequent reports.
- Maintain a tight security system.
- Make lots of inspection trips.
- Keep a tight rein on expense vouchers.
- Hire relatives.
- Make inconsistent policies.
- Issue frequent orders without explanations.
- Have checkers watch the time clocks.
- Have strict rules about coffee breaks and personal phone calls.
- Withhold information from subordinates.
- Insist that people follow channels when making appointments.
- Go out of channels when visiting others.
- Classify information as secret.
- Make people sign requisitions for things like pencils.

Notice that these practices all deal with exercising control over people, while giving privilege to make exceptions for higher-level people. They may be loosely or strictly enforced, but they remain available to use when convenient. Many others are common; perhaps you can think of additional ones you've noticed.

---

[15]Adapted from J. R. Gibb, "Fear and Façade: Defensive Management," in R. E. Farson (ed.), *Science and Human Affairs*, Palo Alto, Calif: Science and Behavior Books, 1965, pp. 197–198. Dr. Gibb's work is among the first to deal with the defensive aspects of communication and its effect on organizational climates.

Norms That Become Taboos Are Few But Powerful

Virtually all work systems have norms against disclosures about money, promotions, and feelings. The strength of these norms vary, but often they come into the taboo area—those areas that are ruled out in advance as a subject for discussion.[16]

Most systems don't allow discussion of salaries or whether or not you have stock options and other selective fringe benefits. Usually this is policy as well as part of the informal norms. You know it's a taboo when discussing salaries "just isn't done." If you ask anyway, some aspersion may be cast on your motives, such as that you have an obsession with money. If you pursue the topic, you may be reported to a higher-level person for reprimand or worse.

The money taboo may reflect a wider attitude in American society about keeping personal finances private, discussing them only with impersonal financial or legal advisors. However, it has some organizational effects, such as keeping people in the dark about the pay for certain jobs even when a person wants to know the payoff for aspiring for a different job. Discussion could also expose any pay differentials between men and women or between whites and minorities. Some organizations won't even release information about your own pay range or approved pay ranges for other job classifications.

Another taboo surrounds the selection of people for promotions. You may not even know how promotable you are in the eyes of executives. In most traditional systems, executives hold this information secret until publicly announced, although as an aspiring candidate, you may informally talk about it. Who the candidates are, the strengths and weaknesses of each, and reasons for the final choice usually are not discussed with candidates before the official announcement. If you're not selected, the reasons given afterward may or may not be the real ones. You may not be considered mature enough to cope with the actual information. It may be possible that the decision makers don't feel that their logic would stand up under open scrutiny.

Having control over people's economic lives may appeal strongly to executives who have a high need for power. They can use the system as a chessboard on which to play a human chess game. As a result of their secrecy, the pawns usually spend time speculating, looking for subtle signals, milking every source of information vital to their futures. Dependency doesn't enhance their self-esteem or sense of confidence, so their efforts will be spent in politically defending themselves, seeking ways to regain some control over themselves.

[16]In this section I am indebted to Fritz Steele, *The Open Organization: The Impact of Secrecy and Disclosure on People and Organizations*, Addison-Wesley, Reading, Mass., 1975, pp. 98–111, for his perceptive handling of this complex subject.

The third taboo—discussion of feelings—is virtually universal in the more closed systems. How you feel presumably has no relation to the work you do, so it is considered a waste of time. "Let's keep personalities out of this" is a way of enforcing this taboo, often followed by "Let's get on with the job to be done."

Keeping focused on the task—the series of objective events and activities—eliminates dealing with the people processes—the subjective feelings, attitudes, communication patterns, processes of making decisions. Task focus is considered to be rational, emotions and feelings irrational. What is rational is narrowly defined, even though it would be more rational to include all the energies that are operating—both task and people processes.

Once again, we see that *the power to define is the power to control.* Define a taboo against feelings and most people will publicly play it cool. Underneath, the feelings go on, often surfacing in double meanings and as power plays. By respecting this taboo, people learn to maintain the *appearance* of controlling their feelings, while shifting or denying responsibility for the way they use their hidden feelings. Emotional energy is then channeled into maintaining appearances, acting "as if," and staging impressions they want to make on others.

The effort to control tasks by suppressing the subjective side of people has just the opposite result. Many people become so embroiled in managing impressions and images that relatively little energy is left for attention to the tasks. Again, we see the price paid for creating defensiveness.

The risks you take in breaking or bending norms and taboos will be considered further when we discuss the risk considerations you have to weigh when choosing non-defensive options to get results you want. The sanctions for not respecting these invisible rules need to be tested and checked so you can accurately predict the risks you take. Then you need to find out how you can offset these negatives with positive risks, so you can act when the odds are in your favor. Being sure other people gain while you gain is often how you improve your own odds.

Violating a Norm Is Sometimes a Positive Risk—Though Rarely

Occasionally there can be a positive risk in violating some norms: when creative non-conformity signals your courage or daring and when it produces results that are highly valued by upper executives. Consider the risks Don Mitchell took when breaking some norms.

At Adler, Benson & Cutler Advertising, a strategy session was in progress with their most lucrative though tempermental client, Bart Holman, president of Apex Foods. Annual billings ranged from $400,000 to nearly $1 million, depending on the whim of Holman, who frequently threatened to move the account, just to keep the agency on its toes.

Every account executive assigned to Apex was present on orders from Ben Adler, the senior partner. Only Don Mitchell was missing, a fact duly noted by Ben for swift action later. In the midst of the agency's film presentation of their three-year campaign plan, Don slipped in, carrying a few paste-ups under his arm, drawing Ben's frown.

At the end of the film, Bart seemed pleased but not fully satisfied. Soon Don got his opening when Ben growled his annoyance, "What have you been up to? Where have you been?"

Moving in quickly, Don rose with a deferential bow to Ben; then turning to Bart, he placed the first paste-up directly in front of him, confidently stating:

"The concept you just saw, summarized here, is excellent—on that we agree." With a flair, he placed the second paste-up on top of the first and conspiratorially continued, "By adding this one new twist—just off the drawing board—I suggest your campaign will go *way* over the top!"

Silent suspense. How dare he do this without Ben knowing! How dare he take Ben's lead. This could cost us millions of dollars! All hold their breaths awaiting Bart's verdict. Leaning back in his swivel chair, he pronounced his decision:

"Perfect. Just what we need." Then to Ben, "You've done it again. We've got a winner here."

Relief flooded the group as they got ready to leave for lunch. Ben was elated at buttoning down Apex for another three years but was also angrily calculating what to do about Don. This mustn't happen again!

Don gambled and won. He'll likely get a token punishment for his outrageous behavior. However, landing the account for another three years was Ben Adler's objective and that was accomplished with Ben getting the credit. Bart had looked at Ben when he said, "You've done it again." But they all know who did it, so Don will have to stay assigned to Apex to satisfy Bart, tying Ben's hands if he wanted to do anything else.

Had Bart rejected his concept, Don could have been on the street. Making big money was a stronger goal than violating the norms of not being at the meeting, taking over Ben's role, and risking the Apex account. Don had assessed his risks well; he now has some new ones to juggle.

If You Don't Act Within the Norms, Others May Activate Intimidation Rituals

Fitting in, in personal style as well as in work priorities, can be critical to your survival in a system. Whether you're just entering a system or moving within it, you will be evaluated by others on how well you fit in with the existing people and norms.

Check how well the system fits your goals if you want to survive and do something you value. In particular, watch out for special forms of upward mobility. They could be dead-ends.

You can also evaluate the system. Can you accomplish what you want to do in the climate created by the people you will work with and for? Is it a climate that gives you the resources and supports you need to perform somewhere near your capacities? Or have you built your political gamesmanship skills so much that you need an authoritarian climate in which to operate—enjoying those challenges as much as the work challenges? Or do you just want to do a job without thinking much about it, so you can do more interesting things away from work? Whatever your personal goals, reading the climate can tell you how well these goals fit with the norms of the system or group you are considering.

You also can avoid other common traps: being shelved in a dead-end job, kicked upstairs with little to do, or promoted beyond your capabilities. These things happen in systems where it's difficult to fire people, where management wants to retire not fire someone—but can't (or won't) do either, or to punish someone in such a way that she or he eventually leaves. All of these tactics are used by people who use the system to reward or punish others, thus escaping personal responsibility. You can be rendered ineffective and then be blamed for it: You had your chance but you didn't fit in.

The human resources director at Precision Manufacturing (PM) tells us how this worked with Elmer Mullins, 59, after he was promoted from machine shop foreman to chief of safety and security.

Elmer was our machine shop foreman for ten years before he got the safety and security job two years ago. As a young man, he lost a finger on an unshielded lathe, so he had strong feelings about such hazards. He'd seen plenty of them at PM, so he thought he would finally have the chance to do something about them. He said he didn't want others to have to go through life with mutilations like his, and he acted like he'd found his mission in life.

Elmer reported to Carl Deutsch, 58, vice president of Manufacturing, and was responsible for Occupational Safety and Health Act (OSHA), fire regulations, and other preventative measures to keep down worker compensation claims. Carl doesn't like being bothered with this stuff.

Elmer didn't have much success, but he was dedicated to PM for their recognition of him, and he was even more committed to doing a conscientious job, perhaps because of Carl's disinterest.

Carl Deutsch is a traditional Theory X manager, expecting the worst from people, believing his subordinates are lazy and stupid and need to be managed through fear, and Carl often says so to anyone who will listen. He makes some exceptions with department heads he likes. One of these is the chief engineer, Bruce Barker, 38, Elmer's former boss. Bruce is highly regarded for his technical competence. A while back he left PM but was back in two months with a good pay hike. They begged him repeatedly to come back, as if they couldn't get along without him. I suspect it was because Bruce is so much like Carl. They both are Theory X managers and have volatile tempers, which they use frequently. Anytime Bruce acts like Carl, Carl seems pleased, as if Bruce is his fair-haired boy.

Bruce can do no wrong, it seems. Even before he came back, his credibility was high. For example, we had a severe acid explosion that damaged two floors of the building. Bruce was responsible for preventative maintenance, but Carl never criticized him for this incident. Instead, both Carl and the president praised him for his calmness in neutralizing the acid, stopping the immediate danger. So Bruce knew at the time that he didn't have to pay attention to Elmer's safety efforts.

Both Carl and Bruce could intimidate Elmer any time. Not only was Elmer unsure of himself, but he was getting more frustrated and touchy from the way they ridiculed and put him down. Elmer sent Bruce work orders demanding correction of breaches of safety standards, quoting the laws, and Bruce did nothing. Bruce was backed by Carl, who sent Elmer memos telling him not to give silly, inconsequential work orders to Bruce. (I've seen them.)

When Elmer presented his recommendations at department head meetings, Carl would say, "You just don't have any sense of prioritites. You have to be realistic and fit these details in with the main job of getting the product out the door." Other times Carl's remarks were more personal, "You mean well, Elmer, but you irritate people. You just don't come across right around here." After several of these incidents, Elmer got more defensive, and he became heavy-handed and did irritate people more.

Bruce and Carl would tell the others behind Elmer's back "Don't pay any attention to him. He doesn't know what he's doing! He's dumb. The only thing he's good at is running the fire fighting classes, and any damn fool can do those." (I wouldn't have believed this if I hadn't heard it myself.) When asked why he kept him, Carl would say, "We have to look like we're complying with the law. He'll do as well as anybody. He's not much good anywhere else."

During fire fighting classes, Elmer would light actual fires and have people practice putting them out. Carl and Bruce would jokingly accuse him of lighting them too close to the buildings. One time someone called the fire department during his training class, making him look like an utter fool in the only area he had any credibility left. Elmer hung on but it wasn't hard to see his discouragement and defeat.

They finally nailed him by using his work orders as evidence for his ineffectiveness in improving safety. Elmer wrote these in a brusque, military style, much like Carl's and Bruce's memos. They accused Elmer of not having rapport with people, so it was his fault that other people didn't complete his work orders. The day the worker's compensation insurance agent came out to explain the huge increase in premiums— employee injuries had risen at an appalling rate—Elmer was fired. The perfect scapegoat.

Only then—after Elmer was gone—did we get an effective safety committee. Bottom line is what did it.

What you've just witnessed is a standard intimidation ritual commonly used by middle management people on reformers, whistle blowers, well-intentioned non-conformists, or people who question the status quo. It's a four-step process, characterized by the following attitudes:

- *Nullification:* You don't know what you're talking about, but thank you for telling us. We'll certainly look into it for you.
- *Isolation:* If you insist on talking about things you don't understand, we'll have to stop you from bothering other people with your nonsense.
- *Defamation:* Don't listen to him. You can't trust a person like that. He's no good, crazy, or grossly incompetent—a loser.
- *Expulsion:* Unfitness is the reason, backed by legal evidence for dismissal, which has been collected to assure the permanent removal of this threat to power, control, and authority.[17]

---

[17]The adaptation is reproduced by special permission from *JABS*, "Intimidation Rituals: Reactions to Reform," Rory O'Day, vol. 10, no. 3, 1974, pp. 373–386, NTL Institute for Applied Behavioral Science.

All this was done at PM under the label of rationality—you just can't keep someone around who doesn't fit in. What "fitting in" *really* means in any given system or department is what you need to find out *before* you get into it. Often it will look like the cartoon on page 116.

If Elmer had been able to interpret past events and sense current double meanings, he might not have stayed long enough to be so cruelly crucified. The irony, as so often happens, is that a person like Elmer, who really cared about safeguarding the workers, will often stay longer and try harder *because* they sense that the Carls and Bruces don't care. Elmer would have had to be consciously aware of these feelings to be able to assess the risks he encountered. When feelings are taboo, this is hard to do.

Caring needs an environment where it can be effective. At PM, an underlying value was expediency—profit at the expense of people, until people cost too much. Only then would caring be possible—unless the taboo on feelings was so strong that safety would slowly sink back to its past neglected status. Much will depend on whether or not a new norm is formed by the president to which Carl and Bruce conform and by which they expect others to perform.

RECOGNIZING SOME UNDERLYING VALUES THAT INFLUENCE NORMS

Norms change slowly because they usually reflect more widespread societal values that we simply take for granted. These are even slower to change. Two of these values that have profound effects on the way most systems operate are competition and masculine identity, both being closely intertwined. Here's one description of this pattern:

> God knows how many times you have been told that competition is the American way and the only way; how you have heard it from lecterns and pulpits, and how you have almost come to believe it . . .
>
> When you come down to it, all competition is, is a behavior. A piece of behavior that builds on the need of individuals to be faster, cleverer, richer than the next guy. And, undeniably, this need to be unequal is of great value to society. Because one way of getting things done is to get everybody to outdo each other.
>
> So society encourages that kind of behavior by reward structures where the guy who ends up fastest or smartest gets everything, the others nothing.[18]

Concern for winning creates a fear of losing, which may well underlie the concern for power and control that is so evident in most systems. One has

[18]From *The Gospel According to the Harvard Business School* by Peter Cohen. Copyright © 1973 by Peter Cohen. Reprinted by permission of Doubleday & Company, Inc., pp. 249–250.

THE RATIONAL ORGANIZATION

The One that People SAY is There

THE REAL ORGANIZATION

Source: *Systemation*, January 15, 1959, published by Systemation, North America, Denver, Colo. (Artist Tom Parker modified the top cartoon from the original at the bottom.)

to be in control to win, according to this thinking. How can you trust some-one when you're afraid you'll lose to that person? The result is often "Don't trust anybody."

Competitiveness and winning are central to our American stereotype of masculine identity—the idea of what makes a man a real man. Some of these expectations are that men become:

- *Successful in business,* having a high position with responsibility and status
- *Financially productive,* having a house, two cars, good clothes, in-vestments
- *Sexually attractive,* being in good physical condition, attractive to more women than his wife
- *Physically productive,* able to build things, repair cars, father attrac-tive children
- *Knowledgeable* about business, politics, his own goals[19]

In order to accomplish these ideals, our society places emphasis on expecting its young men to absorb and develop these aspirations and learn to believe in these ideas:

1. *A high need for achievement* brings status and acceptability. Achievement means successful performance in the work world, which is preceded by academic achievement.
2. *Competitive score keeping,* based on "beating someone else," is the way to achieve success. Most men are rated (and may rate them-selves) on "How am I doing compared with others?" Few major aspects of men's lives are not affected by scorecards: school (grades), sports (athletic prowess), sex (how many, how often), work (promotions, pay, title), possessions (home, cars, family), even re-tirement (travel).
3. *Power and success* means having influence, sometimes arbitrary power, over others and over decision making. This means most men are striving toward some goal in the future, thus becoming rela-tively unaware of, or denying, the relationships and tasks of today.
4. *Conflict* arising out of this competitiveness calls for men to use combative, rather than collaborative, techniques to solve problems. The role does not expect them to distinguish between functional

---

[19]These points and the rest of the discussion in this section are abstracted from Patrick Canavan and John Haskell, "The Great American Male Stereotype (GAMS)." Reprinted from Clarke G. Carney and Sarah Lynne McMahon (eds.), *Exploring Contemporary Male/Female Roles: A Facilitator's Guide,* La Jolla, Calif.: University Associates, 1977, pp. 150–166. Used with permission.

and dysfunctional competitiveness, encouraging them to advance themselves over others by crippling the competition.

5. *Task orientation* is emphasized over process orientation. To achieve successful performance at work, men are expected to "come to grips" with day-to-day problems, "take the bull by the horns" and come to "tough-minded" decisions in an orderly, rational manner. So much focus is placed on concrete things and activities that many men do not develop the ability to deal with intangibles and processes, such as planning or building trust.

These masculine ideals are learned in school and reinforced on television through presentations of building the railroads, winning the West, opening up new frontiers, shoot-'em-ups, and facing death with steeled nerves (with only one slight twitch allowed).

Some Consequences of Male-Role Competitiveness on Personal Behavior

The term, "male role competitiveness," refers to the complex set of expectations that many, if not most, men learn so they can win in the game of life, which becomes defined as a competitive game. In work systems and other hierarchies the consequences are often defensive.

- Consequences of competitive score keeping:

  A sharp sense of analysis is developed. Others' strength, vulnerability, and potential is quickly assessed. The defensive nature of this process makes it extremely difficult to develop collaborative and intimate relationships.[20]

- Consequences of defensively assessing the competition:

  The person who behaves defensively, even though he also gives some attention to the common task, devotes an appreciable portion of his energy to defending himself. Besides talking about the topic, he thinks about how he appears to others, how he may be seen more favorably, how he may win, dominate, impress, or escape punishment, and/or how he may avoid or mitigate a perceived or an anticipated attack.[21]

- Consequences of intensive task orientation:

  Because decisions must be (or appear to be) fast, perfect, and irrevocable, the need to be defensive of one's positions and abilities is paramount. Therefore, the brittleness of these processes and of the individual is well hidden and rarely,

---

[20]Ibid., p. 151.
[21]Jack R. Gibb, "Defensive Communication," *Journal of Communication*, vol. 11, no. 3, September 1961, p. 141.

if ever, is perceived by others. The capable male never shows how afraid or fragile he is while operating in this mode.[22]

- Consequences of denial of feelings:

Because feelings are not permitted free expression, the male lives in a constant reaction against himself. What he is on the outside is a façade, a defense *against* what he *really* is on the inside. *He controls himself by denying himself*.[23]

- Overall personal consequences of adhering to these and related values:

Following traditional patterns and external guides, basing one's life on competitive striving and the rewards of the marketplace, modeling oneself after people in authority or with high status, the individual no longer knows who he is. He does not mean what he says and does not do what he believes or feels. He learns to respond with surface or approved thoughts. He learns to use devious and indirect ways, and to base his behavior on the standards and expectations of others. He moves toward falsehood, fakery, pretense, and being on guard, often without being aware that this is not a truthful existence. His values and convictions do not emerge from real experience but from a feeling of danger and anxiety, from a fear of not keeping pace, a fear of being minimized, and a desire to be protected from rejection and attack. Cut off from his own self, he is unable to have honest experiences with others . . . His life is predicated on appearance, deceptions, and controlling behavior . . . He does not know his place in the world, his position, where he is or who he is.[24]

All of these may be defensively denied, producing the fallacy of façades shown on page 120.

That possible denial also comes out of adhering to another sex-role expectation: People are expected to police others of the same sex to adhere to their assigned sex role. This pressure is strong in systems in which males are in control. They use the system's power in addition to their own person power to reward or punish men for how well they demonstrate the accepted male attitude.

Since a man is expected to tie his masculine identity to occupational achievement (among other things), his human strivings for becoming his own person can be delayed or lost in the role playing demanded of him in most systems. This may partially account for the late development of personal independence—between the late 30s and early 40s—that Daniel Levinson found among the men he studied. Becoming one's own man, with

[22]Canavan and Haskell, "The Great American Male Stereotype," p. 152.

[23]Herb Goldberg, *The Hazards of Being Male: Surviving the Myth of Masculine Privilege*, Nash, New York, 1976, p. 69.

[24]Clark Moustakas, *Creativity, Conformity, and the Self*, Harper & Row, New York, 1956, pp. 92–93. Reprinted in the *Journal of Applied Behavioral Science*, vol. 2, no. 2, April–June, 1966, p. 242.

The Fallacy of Façades

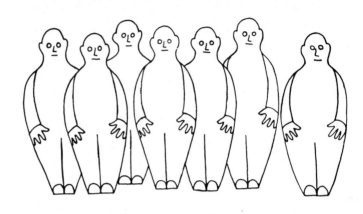

The more I build the façade, the less others really know me and the less I really know myself.

Many times I fool myself and believe the façade is real.

Source: Jim Cole, *The Facade: A View of Our Behavior*, illustrated by Tom Woodruff, distributed by Ed & Janet Reynolds, Mill Valley, Calif. 94940, 1970, unnumbered pages.

affirmation from others, was difficult. Men higher up in organizations who were their mentors were also maintaining and protecting their own territories (a competitive practice that has been attributed to male biology). These mentors gave their juniors this double message: "Be a good boy and you'll go far," together with, "Make trouble and you're dead."[25]

This dilemma—be a good child or out you go—seems to be a continuation of a parent–child relationship, which may be prolonged through the mentor relationship many men enjoy. If so, it may be no surprise that many men approaching age 40 are still dealing with unresolved "little boy" conflicts. They haven't had a chance to integrate their playful, imaginative, idealistic selves into their self-concept during earlier stages of development.[26] Their role didn't permit it.

Some Consequences of Male-Role Competitiveness on Organizational Behavior

One of the more remarkable aspects of executive and organizational research is the *absence* of making a connection between male-role expectations and what occurs in the system. For example, Chris Argyris and Donald A. Schön sought to find out what underlying assumptions (espoused theories) guided the actions (theories in use) of executives and the effects of these actions on organizations. As you read this, notice the similarity between the underlying assumptions and male-role competitiveness discussed above.[27]

Underlying Assumptions	Action Strategies	Consequences in the Organization
1. Define goals and try to achieve them.	*Design and manage the environment* unilaterally, be persuasive, appeal to larger goals.	Executive is seen as defensive, inconsistent, incongruent, controlling, fearful of being vulnerable, manipulative, withholding feelings, overly concerned about self and others or underconcerned about others.

---

[25]Daniel J. Levinson, *The Seasons of a Man's Life*, Knopf, New York, 1978, p. 145.

[26]Ibid., pp. 144–149. In this excellent study American male-role expectations were not specifically discussed as a factor in shaping men's developmental periods over their life courses.

[27]Adapted from Chris Argyris and Donald A. Schön, *Theory in Practice: Increasing Professional Effectiveness*, Jossey-Bass, San Francisco, 1975, pp. 68–69.

2. Maximize winning and minimize losing	*Own and control the task*, claim ownership of the task, be guardian of definition and execution of task.	Defensive interpersonal and group relationship dependence on executive, add little of own ideas, little helping of others.
3. Minimize generating or expressing negative feelings.	*Unilaterally protect yourself*, make judgments without describing behavior that led to judgment, be blind to impact on others and differences between own words and actions, use defensive actions such as blaming, stereotyping, suppressing feelings, intellectualizing.	Defensive norms, such as mistrust, lack of risk-taking, conformity, external commitment, emphasis on diplomacy, power-centered competition, and rivalry.
4. Be rational.	*Unilaterally protect others from being hurt*, withhold information, create rules to censor information and behavior, hold private meetings.	Low freedom of choice, low internal commitment, low risk taking.

With this kind of leadership, many vicious circles result in little feedback, little testing of the validity of one's assumptions, and the system's effectiveness is decreased—a defensive climate.

In his study of executive gamesmen, Michael Maccoby also made no connection between male-role expectations and what he called the separation of head and heart. But he did note one organizational effect of the intense competitive strivings that characterized these leaders:

> The process of bending one's will to corporate goals and moving up the hierarchy leads to meanness, emotional stinginess, but not full-blown sadism. Although more than a third of the managers expressed sadistic tendencies, they are controlled and channeled, employed . . . in the form of jokes and put-downs or in the service of the team against opponents. There is just enough fear and humiliation to keep the hierarchy glued together. If the corporation is destructive, it is because its products are harmful and its human effects damaging, not because those who conscientiously fill their roles and further their careers wish anyone ill.[28]

[28]Michael Maccoby, *The Gamesman: The New Corporate Leaders*, Simon & Schuster, New York, 1976, p. 189.

Because organizations tend to emphasize intellectual skills, other skills involving human caring often remain underdeveloped. Gamesmen tended to be low on social consciousness and apparently took little cognizance of the larger social effects of their behavior. "Most important, the managers made no effort to learn the social/human effects of their actions in the United States and the rest of the world. So long as they remain unaware and unrelated they avoid having to accept responsibility."[29]

Avoiding responsibility apparently has the blessing of one of the best known management consultants, Peter Drucker. In his compendium on management, his primary statement about an ethic of responsibility for members of the professional leadership groups is: "Above all, not knowingly to do harm."[30] Fear, detachment, and separation of head and heart can keep many managers unaware of possible harm they may be doing, and yet they apparently can be excused and still be seen as ethically responsible leaders; they didn't *knowingly* do harm. Some of these consequences were apparent at Country Stores and at Precision Manufacturing.

Some Larger-Scale Consequences of Male-Role Competitiveness

As stimulating and appealing as the thrill of winning the game may be for many people, the larger effects may be clouded or lost under the hoopla of winning. Consider this:

> Everybody forgets that despite its undeniable advantages, competition is a wasteful process, that every winner comes at the cost of a hundred, a thousand, a hundred thousand losers.
>
> And this is where the American society is at; it talks of competition as if it had never heard the word "co-operation." It refuses to see that too much pressure doesn't move people; it kills them.[31]

Studs Terkel summarized these effects this way:

> Work is, by its very nature, about violence—violence to the spirit as well as the body. It is about ulcers as well as accidents, about shouting matches as well as fistfights . . . It is, above all . . . about daily humiliations. To survive the day is triumph enough for the walking wounded among the great many of us.[32]

[29]Ibid., p. 197.
[30]Peter Drucker, *Management Tasks, Responsibilities, Practices*, Harper & Row, New York, 1973, p. 368.
[31]*The Gospel According to the Harvard Business School*, Cohen, p. 250.
[32]Studs Terkel, *Working: People Talk About What They Do All Day and How They Feel About What They Do*, Pantheon Books, a Division of Random House, Inc., New York, 1974, p. xi.

The Walking Wounded

Source: Book cover from *Organizational Behavior: Research And Issues* by George Strauss, Raymond E. Miles, Charles C. Snow, and Arnold Tannenbaum, eds. © 1976 by Industrial Relations Research Association. Reprinted by permission of the publisher Wadsworth Publishing Company, Inc., Belmont, Calif. 94002. Colors used are *red* ties, *white* collars, and *blue* suits!

When masculine identity is equated with competitive power and control, when responsibility can be shifted to others who are required to defer to those higher up in the hierarchy, and when these patterns can be defended as the natural order of things, the status quo in traditional systems is not likely to change very soon.

If you consider the character of male actions in the vast past and the immediate past, then you will see that the overwhelming preponderance of men in important posts across the board of the American scene is more than an accident. It is a large part of the male system of control.[33]

No one has caught on to the depth and length and grip of the male on our total culture. It is to be understood only in the light of history and will take a long, long time . . . . The notion that the male attitude will change when exposed or that the present situation can be solved like a mathematical equation or problem is naive.[34]

[33]Charles W. Ferguson, *The Male Attitude: What Makes American Men Think and Act as They Do?*, Little, Brown, Boston, 1966, p. 25, by permission of Charles W. Ferguson.
[34]Charles W. Ferguson, personal communication, September 23, 1977.

PULLING IT ALL TOGETHER

We have been focusing on traditional systems and their values, norms, and rituals, since most work organizations are still run this way. A rigid hierarchy with extremely tight control at the top is probably an appropriate structure when a fire department is fighting a fire, in a direct military engagement, in a football game, in a life-and-death case in the hospital emergency ward, or in a symphony performance. The control structure is appropriate to the function. To violate norms in these situations is extremely high risk, probably not worth doing for most people.

However, when the fire department is back at the station, when war has shifted to peacetime, when the team is in the locker room, when sickness has abated, or when musicians are off duty, the need for strict obedience to the leader is no longer appropriate to the function. In many such systems, rules often are relaxed at such times but may be reactivated whenever it suits the leader. These norms become established as appropriate to the system, whether or not its most critical function is being performed. Violating norms here is only slightly less risky than when the system is geared to critical performance.

Other systems that have less critical functions to perform are often run as if their everyday functions are, in fact, life-and-death issues. This would justify the need for control and the other consequences we have just reviewed. Although system norms may not change, you may be able to bend some rules as you negotiate with those who depend on you.

A few organizations have been experimenting with more consultative or participatory styles of managing systems, but they tend to revert to more authoritarian styles when money gets tight. This signals emergency and thus the legitimacy of tighter controls. Economic survival, it is said, is at stake. And well it may be, but the prevailing values admit to only one best way to survive. As long as these values prevail, as long as we haven't learned other ways to cope with crises, we will respond with competition and conflict, dominance, and control. Other ways to use power will remain unexplored.

> Before anyone can be expected to move from a competitive value system to a collaborative one, one first has to be conscious of the inadequacy of the old value system; second, be aware that there is an alternative; and finally, be convinced that one can choose between these value systems.[35]

[35]Reproduced by special permission from *JABS*, "An Evolving Definition of Collaboration and Some Implications for the World of Work," Dee G. Appley and Alvin E. Winder, *Journal of Applied Behavioral Science*, vol. 13, No. 3; p. 281, 1977, NTL Institute for Applied Behavioral Science. This was a special issue on the theme, "Collaboration in Work Settings."

Different people function better in different climates. Those who have been raised traditionally and are comfortable with obedience and deference are likely to prefer the more authoritarian climates or at least know how to function well in them. It may take them a while to learn some of the skills needed to participate in more consultative systems. On the other hand, people who prefer to be their own persons are likely to want open climates and the supportive trust that more often occurs in consultative and participative systems. Even though they may be able to survive in more closed climates, they're not likely to enjoy such climates nor feel they are growing as persons.

Given this bleak picture of life in traditional systems, you may feel that you need to learn more defensive strategies to survive well. Indeed, these are important to know. However, if you want to grow as a person and influence some of the people in the systems you are in, the non-defensive communication skills and values can work in that direction. As you add to your repertoire of behaviors that you can choose to use, you are likely to find that, even though you can't change a system single handedly, you can strongly influence your relationship to it and others with and for whom you work. More about how to do this comes after we develop quick responses and then see how to use the Choosing Process for longer-term non-defensive plans of action.

ASK YOURSELF

1. What are some of the norms and taboos in:

   - The organization where I work?
   - My home?
   - The group or association where I enjoy being a member?

2. What would the negative risks be for me to break some of the norms or taboos at work? At home?

   - Name the norms or taboos and describe the risks, assigning them weights from −1 to −10.
   - Are there any positive risks in breaking any of these norms?

3. What effects of male-role competitiveness have I observed in the organizations to which I belong, in other people's behaviors, or among my own values?

IN THE NEXT CHAPTER

In these last two chapters, we have completed a review of some ways that defensiveness is created within ourselves, between ourselves and others, and in the competitiveness of work systems. Now what do we do with it? In the next few chapters we develop information and attitudes that are needed for getting off the defensive. In Chapter 5 we sort through the complexities of communication to basic exchanges between the speaker and the listener and how meaning is transferred, first without and then with double meanings. Later, we revisit Helen Henderson and John Silberman to see how their underlying competitive values worked so John would win by *not* producing the variance report.

READINGS

Argyris, Chris, and Donald A. Schön: *Theory in Practice: Increasing Professional Effectiveness*, Jossey-Bass, San Francisco, 1975. Reveals how executives' espoused theories are often different from their theories in use, resulting in double messages that get results they didn't expect or want. Also shows a specific program for identifying the differences and how to move to more effective communications and results. Provides models for moving from defensive to nondefensive values.

Ferguson, Charles W.: *The Male Attitude: What Makes American Men Think and Act as They Do?*, Little, Brown, Boston, 1966. Probably the most important book written on the subject; he gives an historical review of the American development of male attitude. The section on "The Sea" shows the total control of sea captains over our early founders and their impact on values in early communities. "The Gun" deals with the effects of war on Western development and the present-day views toward guns. "The Slave" shows the effects of slavery on male attitudes of power, dominance, and control. "The Scribe" shows male control over the writing of history, the educational process, language, and the written word. "The Machine" holds out a faint hope that the interconnectedness of our technology might lead to more interconnectedness in the attitudes of men, as an alternative to the power/dominance/control. Ferguson is an historical novelist, and this book reads like one. (Now out of print, but available from University Microfilms.)

Harragan, Betty Lehan: *Games Mother Never Taught You: Corporate Gamesmanship for Women*, Rawson Associates, New York, 1977. Addressed to women, it will also be useful to many men since it covers "the unwritten rules that men use to play the power game and everything else you'd like to know that your male colleagues will never tell you." Most men won't talk to women competitors at all, and often don't talk with each other either. Written in game language, it outlines "the Game, the Board, the Rules," "the Players, the Penalties, the Objectives," and "Symbols, Signals, Style, and Sex," all of which is an excellent interpretation of what goes on and the ways to cope with it.

Maccoby, Michael: *The Gamesman: The New Corporate Leaders*, Simon & Schuster, New York, 1976. The "gamesman" is the competitive American male at his best or worst, depending on your views and values. The core chapter is about the separation of head and heart, which is what we are bringing together in non-defensive communication. Readable, revealing, and cause for reflection.

Ritti, R. Richard, and G. Ray Funkhouser: *The Ropes to Skip and The Ropes to Know: Studies in Organizational Behavior*, GRID, Columbus, Ohio, 1977. A delightful unorthodox textbook, *Ropes* reads more like a novel. You'll recognize key organizational types engaging in typical types of behavior. For example, Ben Franklyn, production manager, is always "Getting the product out the door." Stanley, the universal subordinate, (which is why he has no last name) is guided by Dr. Faust, consultant and Stanley's former university professor. Bonnie is the universal woman—secretary. Ted Shelby is the staff man always promoting a new program .... and others. A realistic guide about what really goes on through the organizational maze in 55 brief chapters, summarized in 7 sections showing some principles.

For additional background reading, see bibliography entries 10, 17, 27, 46, 56, 57, 58, 59, 61, 62, 63, 64, 65, 67, 71, 73, 75, 76, 77, 78, 80, 81, 84, 86, 87, 89, 90.

5

THE COMMUNICATION PROCESSES OF DEFENSIVENESS

How to Sort Out Complexities of Defensive Communication

Everyone uses defenses to protect themselves from threat. That threat can come from many sources: from an internal difference between your real self and your picture of your self, from a difference between your present picture of yourself and how you want to appear to others, from an external threat from someone else, from expectations in systems that create norms to control you and your behavior. You may have other ways in which you personally experience threat, as well as self-protections you use just in case a threat might arise unexpectedly.

When façades are common, when maintaining credibility or appearances becomes important, when keeping control and suppressing feelings is a priority, when winning becomes more important than performance, defenses will play a major part in communication.

All of these motives involve fear—fear that façades may fall, fear that someone may find out what's *really* going on under the façade, fear of losing control, fear of forces you know you can't control. Fear and anxiety are the energies that build defenses. It takes a great deal of energy to maintain these defenses, energy that is used in ways that can tie you into knots like this:

> There is something I don't know
>   that I am supposed to know.
> I don't know what it is I don't know,
>   and yet am supposed to know,
> and I feel I look stupid
>   if I seem both not to know it
>   and not know *what* it is I don't know.

Therefore I pretend I know it.
   This is nerve-wracking
   since I don't know what I must pretend to know.
Therefore I pretend to know everything.[1]

In this chapter we develop some ways to untangle these knots by becoming more aware of, and being able to see, the people processes going on underneath the surface that contribute to defensiveness in communication. By understanding the complexity of it, some of the results it produces, and *where* you can begin to make some changes in yourself, you can then see how to increase your options for becoming less defensive.

COMMUNICATION IS COMPLEX WITH OR WITHOUT DEFENSES

Let's stop a moment and consider some of the ingredients of a typical communication in which neither you nor I feel defensive. Let's also assume we are in a private space where norms of a system are not operating; we make our own. To make our scenario even simpler, let's assume we don't know each other, so we start fresh. Here are a few of the perceptions that will occur:

- I bring my self and my view of myself.
- You bring your self and your view of yourself.
- I have my view of you as a person.
- You have your view of me as a person.
- I have my view of you in this situation.
- You have your view of me in this situation.
- I have my view of my action.
- You have your view of my action.
- I have my view of your view of my action.

Each of these views of self and the other, the situation, our actions in it may or may not be accurate. We may attribute things to each other; we may compare ourselves to each other or evaluate the other by standards of some kinds.

As you can see, our communication will become increasingly complex, and we've not even mentioned the norms we may develop as we go along and whether or not we find out what differences and similarities we have in how we see what's occurring—giving and receiving feedback. Nor have we mentioned body language and voice intonations and our respective interpretations of these that contribute to the nonverbal communication. Even the size

[1]R. D. Laing, *Knots*, Pantheon Books, a Division of Random House, Inc., New York, 1970, p. 56.

of the space we're in, its colors and furnishings will subtly influence us. So even without defenses, our communication is complex indeed.

If either one of us feels threatened—which could happen simply because we are two strangers in a private space—another set of complexities would be added by our respective defenses and façades. One or the other of us might be reacting as shown in Figure 5-1.

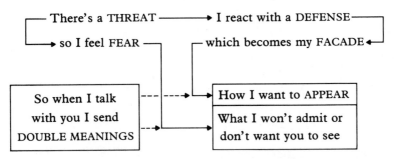

Figure 5-1. *How threats create facades.*

If we both do this, our communication will become even more complex. Now the façades become important to maintain. Efforts to get feedback will produce less accurate information. We may not believe each other; soon we won't trust each other very much. We may start attributing motives to the other without finding out if these motives are actually operating, and if they are, who will admit to them by now? Eventually, the investment in appearances may become greater than the investment in accuracy. The urge to hide, to avoid disclosure, to protect oneself, to win over the other can easily become primary.

We've already seen how this produces vicious circles out of which little work—or mutual concern—occurs. Recall the examples of defensiveness in Chapter 3: Ellen Kimball's preambles cut off by Dick Christenson's impatience, Paul Masters abdicating responsibilities, leaving Doris Underwood and other administrators without power to act, Helen Henderson and John Silberman reaching an impasse on the variance report.

As complex as ordinary communications are, it is possible to use some simple pictures of them to help see where you can make your communication more open, more honest, clearer—less defensive—without undue risk to yourself.

SORTING OUT SOME COMMUNICATION COMPLEXITIES

In interpersonal communication we are talking about the process of transferring meaning from one person to another. Now "meaning" can mean many different things. We'll classify it into two key elements: (1) the content of the message—facts, data, information, and (2) the feelings connected with that message—attitudes, opinions, biases, preferences, priorities. Content is expressed through words and sounds, feelings are expressed through voice tones, facial and body expressions, use of space, timing, pacing, and so on.

Content Plus Feelings Equals Meaning

Figure 5-2 shows the simultaneous flow of both content and feelings; it is similar to Figure 1-1, which showed the simultaneous flow of objective activities and subjective people processes. Both content and feelings have to be included if the full meaning is to be transferred. Let's see how this works in detail.

When I am communicating with you, I am transferring my meaning to you. I'm likely to choose words that say *to me what I mean*, and I'll express my feelings in ways that come out of my experiences, inhibitions, and personal style. The meaning I am transferring is *my* meaning—the speaker's meaning S1 in Figure 5-2. What you as listener perceive as my meaning (meaning L1) will be different in some ways from what I meant; you are a different person. You will perceive me—my words, voice tones, body and facial language, timing and other subleties—through *your* experiences, inhibitions, and personal style. Whatever expectations you have for me—as you know me personally, my role, appropriateness of my behavior and expressions—will also affect the way you perceive my meaning. You won't hear *me;* you'll hear me filtered through your expectations.

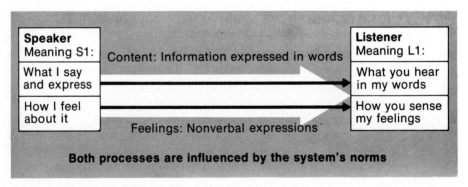

Speaker's meaning S1 will not have the same exact meaning as Listener's meaning L1 because they are two different people.
Meaning is in the person, not in the words or nonverbal cues.

Figure 5-2.   *Objective and subjective communication occur simultaneously. Content + Feelings = Meaning.*

Suppose one of your expectations is that, "People should say what they mean," by which you mean "Use the dictionary meanings of words." If you believe that *words* have meanings, (not that *people* have meanings when they use those words), you will select your dictionary meaning for the words I chose to express the content part of my meaning. You won't hear *me* or my feelings; you'll hear your dictionary meanings of my words. Here's the problem with believing that words have meanings: If I select my dictionary meaning for the word I want to use and if you select your dictionary meaning for my word, we may not select the same meaning.

Consider this: "The number of non-technical words that an educated adult uses in daily conversation is about 2,000. Of these, the 500 most frequently used have 14,000 dictionary definitions."[2] The odds of our selecting the same dictionary definition can sometimes become slim. To some degree, especially in person-to-person communication, we do some of what Humpty-Dumpty did: "When I use a word, it means just what I choose it to mean—neither more nor less."[3] My selection of words is influenced by my feelings and other content I may not express. To get my meaning—my content and feeling—you may have to ask me for feedback to see if what you heard is what I meant. Let's see how this works.

Suppose your supervisor hands you a piece of work and says, "I need this right away." What does "right away" mean? Does it mean to give it priority over your other assignments? Does it mean to drop everything and do it now? Does it mean to have it done in an hour, by lunchtime, before the afternoon meeting? Obviously, "it" doesn't mean anything—only your supervisor means.

Be careful about making assumptions. Whenever you ASSUME, you may make an ASS out of U and ME.

If your supervisor's body language is harried, rushed, and tense, you might assume that the meaning is, "Drop everything and do it now." Even though you are working on another project your supervisor calls urgent, you might stop and do this latest work, just to be safe or helpful. When you assume a meaning and don't check it out by asking for feedback, you may find out too late that your supervisor meant: "No, don't stop working on that

[2]Don Fabun, *Communications: The Transfer of Meaning*, Glencoe Publishing Co., Inc., Encino, Calif., 1968, p. 27.
[3]Lewis Carroll, *Through the Looking Glass and What Alice Found There*, Chapter 6.

urgent job. It's much more important than this. I just wanted you to give this a high priority. I don't need it until tomorrow."

Feedback Clarifies Meanings

So you have to find out your supervisor's meaning of "right away" when he or she uses these words (at that time, in that situation). When your supervisor's meaning is clear to you, when you both know that the work is needed and that you can complete it by 3:00 P.M. the next day, your feedback loop is complete. The supervisor's meaning has been clearly and accurately transferred to you and back again. Meaning S1 and meaning L1 in Figure 5-2 are now the same.

In a later chapter we'll discuss how to give and receive feedback in more detail as part of developing listening skills. However if you want to practice now, try this experiment.

> The next time you become involved in a lively or controversial discussion with another person, stop for a moment and suggest you both adopt this ground rule for continued discussion: Before either party can make a point or express an opinion, she or he must first restate aloud the other person's previous point or position. This restatement must be in his or her own words (merely parroting the words does not show that both content and feelings have been heard, but only the words). The restatement must be accurate enough to satisfy the first speaker before the listener can respond to the speaker's initial statement.[4]

When you have listened this way, both you and your listener will have completed the feedback loop, which can be diagrammed as in Figure 5-3.

Before feedback, the loop is incomplete as shown by the broken line. However, when you ask for and get feedback, the speaker's meaning is clarified when it goes through the completed loop. Both of you speak and both of you listen until you both *hear* each other.

It has been estimated that we speak at an average rate of 100 to 150 words per minute and listen at about 500 to 650 words per minute. The difference of 400 or 500 words per minute gives the listener plenty of time to perceive, speculate, evaluate, and prepare rebuttals—if he or she is so inclined.

How you use that gap of 400 or 500 words per minute strongly determines the degree of defensiveness or openness you create. You can *react* to the speaker, or you can choose the action you want to take. The faster you

---

[4]Carl R. Rogers and Richard E. Farson, *Active Listening*, University of Chicago Press, 1957, pp. 12–13.

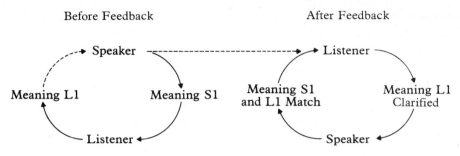

Figure 5-3. *The feedback process.*

think, the more options you have. Your thinking rate is your hidden asset. It is probably many times faster than the speaking or listening rates. It may not even be measurable in words per minute if you think in pictures and images. We will discuss this in more detail in coming chapters.

Norms Can Distort Meaning

As we saw in Figure 5-2, both the content and feelings must be transferred if the full meaning is conveyed. In traditional systems we noted that the usual norm is "Thou shalt always keep thy cool." Priority emphasis is placed on intellectual objectivity by not letting personalities get in the way. Emotions are often considered irrational, therefore not appropriate to discuss or express.

This tendency, along with a strong motivation to control information as well as other people, often leads to considerable deception and distortion of information—defensive communication. Most of us are aware that complete honesty is often not the best policy even though we consider ourselves honest people. In one study about how people control information, researchers asked 130 people to write about conversations they had with friends and relatives, then to tell whether they had been fully honest in those conversations. They admitted that they consciously tried to control information in almost two-thirds of their conversations.

How did they do it? Diversionary tactics and lies and half-truths were used 92 percent of the time, exaggeration and silence the other 8 percent. Why did they do it? Over half—55 percent—did it to save face. Maintaining a positive sense of their own worth and protecting others' self-images was the most important, followed by 22 percent who wanted to avoid conflict or tension. (Others wanted to control the relationship or the situation [10 percent each], with only 3 percent wanting to attack or exploit others.) They reported that their intent was benevolent: "Our respondents stressed over and over again that relationships are more important than truth."[5]

In social relationships where expression of feelings is more appropriate than at work, this research showed much face-saving and conflict-avoiding communication. Relationships were maintained by distortions and deceptions covered by façades. Relationships at work may be maintained even more by the intentional use of façades because people are expected to get along well with others whether they like them or not, and many people use others or the system to achieve their personal goals. When norms make competitive behavior legitimate and expression of feelings non-legitimate, the effect is to legitimize façades as the norm. Communication then becomes less face to face, more façade to façade.

We've already seen some instances of how much energy can be used in defensive façade maintenance and how organizational norms encourage, even reward, such efforts. Dave Eliot was dealing with façades during his initiation ritual at Country Stores. Elmer Mullins was intimidated by façades at Precision Manufacturing until he was fired. Façades can sometimes be dangerous if the people behind them refuse to come out and make authentic contact with you once in a while. Façades may cover the untrustworthiness of the one who says "Trust me." On the other hand, when you can see these processes more clearly, you have more information with which to assess what results are possible.

Filters Influence Meanings

Because each of us are such complex beings, in Figure 5-2 we've only touched the tip of the iceberg. Now let's look beneath the surface to some of the inner processes that influence our outer expressions.

As you'll notice in Figure 5-4, we filter meanings through a set of inner expectations, rules, and underlying values. Today's filters emerge out of things we've learned in the past and act like rules for deciding—guides, rules of thumb, even conscious censorship—that we use more or less consciously in our day-to-day communication. They form a way of seeing what is going on as well as a way of responding to it. Each person's total set is unique and is subtly changing as today's experiences are added to yesterday's. Some of the sources of filters from yesterday are:

- Family customs and practices, styles of parenting
- Sex and expected social roles

[5]Ronny E. Turner, "Information Control in Conversations: Honesty Is Not Always the Best Policy," reported as "The Social Art of Lying," *Human Behavior*, March 1975, pp. 31–32.

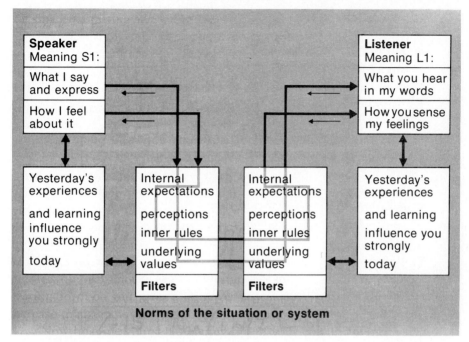

Figure 5-4. *Filters influence meanings when transferred and when fed back.*

- Race and ethnic background and expected social roles
- When you were born and the social meaning of your age today
- Socioeconomic class in geographic area where you grew up
- Education: amount, subjects, degrees, status and quality of schools
- Military experience, exposures to hierarchy, authority, violence
- Being single and dating; marital and parental experiences of your own
- Religious, spiritual, moral and ethical learnings
- Work experience, habits, values, kind of jobs held
- Cultural exposures to music, art, dance, reading, television
- Unknown repressed material

Out of these and other past life experiences—and what you learned from them—come today's inner expectations, perceptions, inner rules and underlying values that generally guide your decisions, consciously or not, such as:

- *Honesty:* when it's best to lie a little, to use tact, to be brutally honest, to say nothing, handling moral dilemmas
- *Valuing yourself:* how you see your value in relation to others, how

you compare yourself now with where you were earlier, how much you listen to yourself, your body, your hunches
- *Perception of others and their value:* whether you look for their strengths or their vulnerabilities, and whether you tend to evaluate others or accept them as they are
- *Assumptions and stereotypes:* assumptions about the right ways to do things or that there is one best solution, stereotypes about people with different educational backgrounds than your own
- *Attitudes about work:* work habits, what motivates you to work, how you feel about unions, your values of physical labor compared to head work, whether work can be pleasurable or if it should hurt
- *Relating to authority:* if and when authority can be questioned, how your behavior may change from when you're with peers or subordinates
- *Manners, courtesy, what's appropriate, right, in good taste:* whether you use these for personal graciousness or as standards against which you measure other people
- *How the world works:* truisms, adages, pearls of wisdom garnered as conventional wisdom that you don't question

These are only a few of the many kinds of subjective feelings, beliefs, attitudes, and convictions we each hold. Some might be very pervasive in your thinking. For example, if you were raised on the religious dictum, "An eye for an eye; a tooth for a tooth," you may now believe in retributive justice, in capital punishment for murderers, and you may see yourself as a dispenser of justified punishments when others need it. If you were the child who was told, "And stay in your room, young man," you might feel justified in getting back at others with the same measure of punishment you received. You might even occasionally play God.

Other learnings may not be so pervasive, but we can make insistent demands through expectations we call reasonable. Consider the potency and frequency of this expectation, "If you loved me, you would . . ." This common manipulation says, "Prove you love me by doing what I want." It comes in many versions: "If you think I'm doing good work, you'll give me a promotion"; "If you like the food I fixed, you'll have seconds"; "Since I won the sales contest, I should be able to pick my territory." These conditional expectations are designed to define, control, and limit other people's choices so they give you what you want, often at their expense.

Consider this one: "I helped you out, so you should help me when I need it." This seems so eminently reasonable that it's hard to refute, but it imposes a unilateral bargain to which you didn't consent. They helped you at their convenience but don't consider your time demands nor your willingness to help them.

How we're trained affects how we see and speak. 20/20 vision for engineers isn't the same as 20/20 vision for artists. Scientists go from the specific to the general, managers go from the general to the specific.

Consider also some of the differences in perceptions when engineers and artists try to communicate. Many engineers (as well as other professionals) have been trained to think in logical sequences, sorting, culling, narrowing, until they find causal links and corrective solutions. They use analytical, diagnostic and prescriptive modes of thinking to arrive at regularity and predictability.

Some artists might do the same, depending on the style of art they produce. However, artists are more likely to learn to break through patterns, to see new shapes, textures, abstracts, unusual linkages, to create simplicity out of the complex, or to allow distortions and misalignments to speak. They value the ability to see things in new ways, to arrive at non-predictability and singularity. With such different ways of approaching their work, these people aren't likely to see things the same way—personality conflicts, some might say.

Through our experiences, we absorb a number of inner rules—have-to's can be quite powerful in influencing our choices. Fifty of these rules are listed here. You may have others to add.

What Are Your Inner Rules?

Score the intensity of these rules as they apply to you. 0 = Don't have this rule. 1 = Often feel this urge. 2 = Yep, that's me!

I Have To:

____Be in control of the situation
____Be a good team player
____Be right
____Be loyal
____Justify myself
____Not make waves
____Have the answers
____Be persistent
____Break rules to see what happens
____Decide for myself
____Keep peace at any price
____Make the boss look good
____Be the expert
____Be logical and rational
____Stick to my principles, ethics

I Have To:

____Be convincing
____Do it by myself
____Appear confident and cool
____Be objective, unemotional
____Be a success
____Be responsible for others
____Do the best I'm capable of
____Take the initiative
____Follow orders
____See that things are done right
____Be dependable
____Be a nice girl/guy
____Finish it
____Go through channels
____Make a track record

I Have To:	*I Have To:*
____Stay ahead of the pack	____Keep this job, not get fired
____Be above average	____Prove myself
____Produce, perform	____Be consistent
____Be respected	____Make myself visible
____Be perfect	____Be liked, accepted
____Improve, develop myself	____Be in control of myself
____Conform to what's expected	____Not question authority
____Be "In the know"	____Be first
____Be on time	____Be prepared for anything
____Come out on top, win	____Be able to take it

Total your score which will be between 0 and 100. Again I don't know how to tell you what your score means. You'll have to let your rules speak to you personally. Do you observe any patterns in the rules you scored? Do you have many rules scored 1 but not many 2s? Or are most of your scores 2s? See if there are any patterns in those you didn't score. As you review these rules, think about the ones that help or hinder you in important situations or relationships. Also be aware if you are evaluating yourself about having these rules.

Notice if any of your rules are in conflict with each other, such as having to be in control of the situation but also having to follow orders. For example, if you have the urge to break rules to see what happens but also feel the need to keep peace at any price or to be liked, your inner conflicts may confuse others by double meanings you are likely to send.

Also consider what would happen if you have the same rules as other people. For example, if you and a coworker both have to "do it by myself," you'll probably have trouble coordinating your work. On the other hand, if you both have to be "in the know," you may tell each other a lot about what is going on, unless you both have a rule about coming out on top. Then you are more likely to tell the other only what doesn't help him or her get ahead of you.

Some rules are helpful in one situation but not another. "I have to be perfect" may be useful to the lab technician conducting sensitive tests but not at home taking care of an active three-year-old.

These fifty rules came from what many people have learned from male and female role expectations and the work ethic. Undoubtedly, the list could be expanded almost infinitely if we added the rules from other sources of our learnings. Every system has its rules—their shoulds and oughts and no-no's. When system rules match your own inner rules, you are likely to do what others expect even when it's not in your best interest. For example, if you and the system you're in agree on the rule, "You have to not make waves," you will probably voluntarily go along with what others say most of the time. Sometimes this won't serve your self-interest if, let's say, you're asked to be patient about receiving a raise that everyone agrees you've already earned.

Generally speaking, the more rules you have, especially those you rated as 2, the more likely you can be controlled by others and the more likely you'll respond to matching norms and expectations in your organization. A few exceptions to this statement are those inner rules that give you more power over yourself such as, "I have to decide for myself, stick to my principles and ethics, and be in control of myself." These are more likely to put you in conflict with traditional system norms.

Other inner rules will have varying results, depending on how you act them out with specific people. For example, if you "have to produce and perform" to the point of compulsion, you may put in unnecessary extra time and effort. You may feel you're being conscientious and loyal; your boss may see you as having to work that hard to do what should be done in a normal eight-hour day.

To gain recognition, you and your boss can negotiate what reasonable performance means. Then when you go beyond the loyalty of doing the little extras and coming through in crises, you will both know you've earned recognition. However, as long as your inner rule is compulsive, you're not likely to initiate that negotiation, and you can be fairly sure your boss won't. A common attitude is: If you're so dumb that you have to work that hard to do your job, you're already being paid enough; if you're dumb enough to work that much extra without pay, go ahead—it's a good deal for the company.

This is not in your self-interest. If you don't take care of your own interests, no one else is likely to. One way to gain more control over yourself is to occasionally review your inner rules to check their usefulness to you today.

Go through the list of inner rules again. *Underline all the rules that you know you want to keep, even though they get in your way sometimes. These will be the rules that are part of your core values and your identity as the person you want to be. These you won't want to change and you consciously choose to live with the consequences of these rules for now. Then go through and circle the rules you would like to change, modify or make less strong, like changing from a 2 score to a 1. Cross out the ones you have that you'd like to get rid of if you could.*

Even if you don't know *how* you're going to make these changes, you're at least identifying *what* rules you want to change, with some idea of *what* better results you'd like to get. This is like cleaning out a clothes closet, sorting out the items to take to the tailor, which to discard, which to start wearing again and making room for new clothes that fit your current interests and activities. We'll see some ways of how to revise old rules as we go along. Right now we're bringing them to conscious awareness and review.

When we're dealing with the complexities of communication, this kind of self-assessment is one way to see how some of your beliefs, rules, attitudes, and experiences can filter your communications as well as your need for façades. The more rules you have and the more compulsive they are, the more you need façades.

Filters of expectations and rules are fairly easy to identify. Once you become attuned to their themes, you may observe many subtle variations operating in yourself. More difficult to identify are the filters of underlying values that are often unconscious, so much a part of ourselves that we don't think about them or observe them in action. Some values are rich in human concerns; other values have the effect of using or exploiting other people. Since we're focusing on defensive communication, we'll narrow our attention to values that tend to generate defensiveness in ourselves and others.

Identifying Underlying Values

Identifying underlying values in defensive communication is important because these guide your habitual reactions. They are part of your core of self. Some values tend to generate more defensiveness than others. In the Argyris-Schön findings (page 122), we saw four underlying values that produced much defensiveness in other's behavior: (1) define goals and try to achieve them, (2) maximize winning and minimize losing, (3) minimize generating or expressing negative feelings, and (4) be rational.

As a way of observing values in action, let's review a segment of the conversation between Helen Henderson and John Silberman in which she was trying to get him to produce the variance report by Friday noon (Chapter 3). We know their verbal dialogue was defensive and resulted in no report as agreed. So let's see to what extent the above four values seemed to be operating in the inner dialogues of Helen and John when control was beginning to move out of Helen's hands into John's. We'll listen in on their respective inner dialogues as they engaged in their verbal dialogue and identify which of these values were being used.

Much of the inner dialogue here may have occurred in quick flashes, which are not fully thought through during the situation, as you can do while reading it. When the pressure is on, when you feel threatened, when you feel you're losing control, or when you have an old score to settle these reactions are likely to be almost automatic or habitual. When we react, we usually draw on inner rules or the guidance of values that have become part of the core of self, almost predetermining our reactions. If these reactions are defensive and we want to become non-defensive, we first have to be able to identify those values.

Verbal Dialogue	John's Inner Dialogue as Helen Verbalizes (Underlying Values)	Helen's Inner Dialogue as John Verbalizes (Underlying Values)
Helen (at Line 3)★: "Yes, you have a lot of work, but you also know the priorities."	"That bitch—giving me all this work, trying to make it look like I can't do it all. She's gloating over getting the promotion." **(J1)** *(Minimize losing. Minimize feelings.)* "It can't be done without more help but I'll be dammed if I'll ask her for anything and give her the chance to refuse." **(J2)** *(Minimize feelings. Minimize losing.)*	
John (at line 4): "You don't realize how much time it takes to analyze the backup data for that report. There's no way it can be done without extra help to do the probability programming."		"I know perfectly well what it takes. You just haven't done it. Sure I know you need extra help; you haven't asked for it. Now it's your problem. I have to have the report or it's your neck. If you only knew." **(H1)** *(Maximize winning. Be rational.)* "I'll buy some time and see if he can come through. He's too good to fire, and it's my neck too." **(H2)** *(Define goals. Be rational.)*
Helen (5): "It was due ten days ago. This is the third time we've talked about it and made schedules, but there's still no report. I *must* have it by Friday noon—or I'll have to take other steps.	"Hey, maybe she's sweating it now. She really needs that report. I bet my friend Bill has put the heat on her, like he does so well. Now what's she going to do?" **(J3)** *(Minimize feelings. Maximize winning.)*	

★Line numbers are those used in Chapter 3 (see pages 72–73).

Verbal Dialogue	John's Inner Dialogue as Helen Verbalizes (Underlying Values)	Helen's Inner Dialogue as John Verbalizes (Underlying Values)
John (6): "Is that a threat of some kind?"		"Let him sweat a little, like I am from Bill's pressure. I've got to make good on this job. It's not just for me, it's for women." **(H3)** *(Minimize feelings. Define goals. Maximize winning.)*
Helen (7): "No, it's a statement of fact."	"Ha! She's not talking. She's running scared. Well, let's just push that a bit farther." **(J4)** *(Minimize feelings. Maximize winning.)*	
John (8): "If it's not done by Friday, what will you do?"		"I don't want to fire him, but if he doesn't come through, Bill will think I can't fire someone." **(H4)** *(Be rational. Minimize feelings.)* "I shouldn't have let it go this far. I won't be pushed into an ultimatum. Best to keep my options open until Friday." **(H5)** *(Be rational. Minimize losing.)*
Helen (9): "That remains to be decided."	"Ahhh, she doesn't know what to do with me. Now I'll get her just like she thinks she's got me." **(J5)** *(Minimize feelings. Maximize winning.)*	
John (10): "Well, it's impossible. If I don't get this report done, you'll take steps. If I don't get the rest of your projects done, you'll hang me for that. You sure know how to squeeze a guy, don't you!"	"Watch her wiggle out of that." **(J6)** *(Maximize winning.)*	"This is getting out of hand. I have to regain control." **(H6)** *(Minimize feelings. Minimize losing.)*

Verbal Dialogue	John's Inner Dialogue as Helen Verbalizes (Underlying Values)	Helen's Inner Dialogue as John Verbalizes (Underlying Values)
Helen *(11):* "Are you saying you can't even do the priority report by Friday?	(John continued his pattern of confrontation where he was maximizing his efforts to win and minimizing his expression of negative feelings.)	(As we know, Helen had lost control by line 12 and did not get the report by Friday noon.)
Effects of playing this competitive win-lose game:	To win, John is now invested in *not* having the report done by Friday noon. This will make Helen lose.	To win, Helen is now invested in forcing John to meet the Friday noon deadline. This will make John lose.

Let's take a closer look at the underlying values and how they earned the label given them.[6] In J1 and J2 John seems to have some intense feelings some of which might be resentment about his workload, jealousy or anger about Helen's promotion, loss of face or a sense of injustice at having to work for a woman or for a former colleague, perhaps feeling demoted, fear of rejection. These are all so-called negative feelings, none of which John expressed in any direct way. Thus, the label: minimize feelings (which summarizes the value of minimizing the generating or expressing of negative feelings).

John also attributed some feelings to Helen—gloating over getting the promotion—suggesting that he sees her promotion as his loss. He may want to minimize the pain of losing by minimizing the promotion itself—or Helen. He chose to minimize Helen by saying she didn't know how much time was involved in preparing data. Thus, the label: minimize losing.

Maximizing winning and minimizing losing go together, resulting in dependence on the other person, offering few ideas and little help to others. This seems to be what John did when he told Helen that the report couldn't be done without extra help. He shifted responsibility for that to her, offering no ideas of his own.

In turn Helen, at H1 and H2, also offers no help to John. She's intent on winning. She's going to win by being rational, protecting John by *not* telling

[6]In this case the inner dialogues are composites from people working through this situation in workshops where disclosing inner dialogue and underlying values is part of the work. You can sense much of this through interpreting another's actions—actions speak louder than words. But your interpretations must remain tentative until you can have them verified by the other person through feedback. If you are working with another person on identifying her or his values, that person must have the final say about what applies to them.

him he could be fired nor that she considers him too good to be fired. She decides to buy time, her goal being to get out the report with or without John's help. If he doesn't produce it, she'll have time to do it another way. (She may also be minimizing—not expressing—her own feelings of frustration from not being able to get the report done and her apparent ineffectiveness in relating to John.)

You may want to continue rereading through the outer and inner dialogues, checking to see if you agree with how the underlying values have been labeled. You may identify them differently. Neither of us can be sure we're right; we can't talk with Helen or John. But we can clearly state our own perceptions. That step comes first—being aware of our own values and *tentatively* aware of values we think others hold until we can check them out.

Identifying the Interplay of Underlying Values and Their Results

If we put together the values underlying Helen's and John's inner dialogues, we can see how the battle for control shifted from Helen to John. For the moment, let's focus on the win–lose values that were operating and when those shifted.

John's Underlying Values	Helen's Underlying Values	
J1. Minimize losing Minimize feelings **J2.** Minimize feelings **Minimize losing**	**H1. Maximize winning** Be rational **H2.** Define goals Be rational	
J3. Minimize feelings **Maximize winning**	**H3.** Minimize feelings Define goals **Maximize winning**	**At Line 5, both try to maximize winning, starting the vicious circle that led to the job not being done.**
J4. Minimize feelings **Maximize winning** **J5.** Minimize feelings **Maximize winning** **J6. Maximize winning**	**H4.** Be rational Minimize feelings **H5.** Be rational **Minimize losing** **H6.** Minimize feelings **Minimize losing**	

At the beginning, John played loser while Helen played winner. At Line 5 their winner motives came into collision, after which John played winner and Helen played loser, although she later tried to regain her winning position.

Both hid their feelings behind their façades, built bigger ones, and listened mostly to themselves, not to each other. As they became more closed off from each other, each became set on winning and on not revealing his or her real thoughts or feelings to the other. Each competed for different goals; each became less rational and created more distortions about the others' motives. The net effect was that John *won by not producing* the report by Friday noon.

If John could get support for not producing from another power source, he would cement his win. So John called on "his friend Bill" to back him up. (We don't know Bill's real role and where his influence makes a difference. He may be John's friend only in John's eyes. He may be a personal friend who doesn't let that influence business decisions. He may be rooting for Helen but not wanting John to know that. This risk could be either positive or negative for John or Helen. So far, it *appears* he's on John's side, but our assumption must remain *tentative* until we know from Bill what was behind his action.)

With Bill as an unknown factor, Helen and John create a self-sealing vicious circle that, at each turn, becomes increasingly difficult to break out of. John ends up winning, Helen loses and so does the job—at least in its timing. It was the game that won:

> We are playing a game. We are playing at not
> playing a game. If I show you I see we are, I
> shall break the rules and you will punish me.
> I must play the game, of not seeing I see the game.[7]

FILTERS THAT PRODUCE FAÇADES PRODUCE DOUBLE MEANINGS

Of the samples of filters we've seen—expectations, perceptions, inner rules, underlying values—many are valuable and do not contribute to defensiveness. Filters can often lead to misunderstandings because of different interpretations or incomplete information. If these differences can be cleared up with feedback, the threat/fear-defense/façade reactions are not stimulated. Simple clarification is all that is necessary.

However most of us have tender spots we conceal from public view or motives that we think others might not find fully honorable, or we don't want to give others the advantage of knowing. When people work in competitive systems, when many people "look out for Number One" with less concern

---

[7]Adapted from R. D. Laing, *Knots*, Pantheon Books, a Division of Random House, Inc., New York, 1970, p. 1.

for others, when people have aspects of themselves they don't want others to see, when norms encourage maintaining defensive façades, a multitude of double meanings will be communicated—surface meanings that conceal hidden meanings. This is a powerful way to control others or situations although not the only one. However, it is so common that it's worth analyzing.

Figure 5-5 is a simplified version of Figure 5-4 so the double meaning can be more easily seen; however, both meanings still go through the filter systems of the speaker and the listener, producing "normal" distortions. Picture the two meanings going through those filters of expectations, perceptions, rules and values. When the speaker feels threat and fear, which create a need to defend him/herself with a façade, a double meaning occurs, as we saw at the beginning of the chapter. The surface content and feelings come from the façade; the hidden meaning comes from fear or from withholding information that the speaker wants to keep hidden.

For example, let's look at the double meaning John sent Helen when he said (at Line 4):

Surface content:	"You don't realize how much time it takes .... There's no way it can be done without extra help."
Surface feelings (unspoken):	"I'm justified in the report not being done. It's your fault."
Hidden content:	"You don't know what you're doing."
Hidden feeling:	"I'll show you up. I should be sitting where you are."

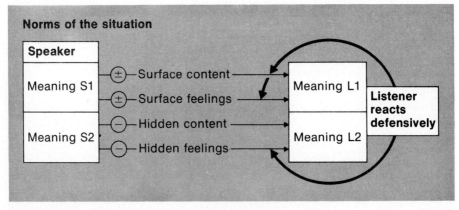

= A positive or negative meaning is said or implied.

= A negative meaning is intended so it is hidden.

Figure 5-5. *How the listener reacts defensively to double meanings.*

In this case, the surface content is negative and the surface feeling is self-serving, perhaps neither positive nor negative, but not very useful in getting the job done. Fixing the blame doesn't fix the problem. The hidden content and feelings are negative, which is usually the case. It would be too risky to openly state them. Remember John's remark when Helen's promotion was announced: "May the best man win." That might have been a declaration of war that John was going to come out winner over the woman in the long run but that could be denied under the guise of a figure of speech if he were questioned.

Now let's see how John's double meaning affected Helen, who we know was becoming defensive. As shown in Figure 5-5, the listener, Helen, becomes defensive when she reacts to the surface meaning and the hidden feeling and when she doesn't deal with the hidden content.

Helen's reactions to John's double meaning were similar to these:

To the surface content:	"I know perfectly well that it takes extra help."
To the surface feeling:	"You haven't asked for extra help so it's your fault." (Notice how each blames the other.)
To the hidden content:	—
To the hidden feelings:	"It's your neck—but it's also mine. I'm scared."

Helen reacted to all but the hidden content: "You don't know what you're doing." At some level, she probably sensed John's message; she got the emotional load of it even if she didn't identify the content. When it's not dealt with, the listener often reacts defensively to the threat in a way that makes that threat actually occur—a kind of self-fulfilling prophecy.

Helen felt quite sure about what she was doing. She wanted to keep John, buy time for herself in case he didn't come through and could fire him if he didn't, but she didn't know how to get him to produce except by threatening him, which she did in her next line. This fed the threat/fear–defense/façade cycle, generating more double meanings, less contact, more win–lose action, and less attention on getting the report done.

As long as the underlying values of maximizing winning and minimizing losing were present along with minimizing the expression of negative feelings, this pattern is likely to continue in most situations. Façades are necessary when other options are not yet available. Accurate feedback is often difficult to get until threat is reduced. The hidden meanings may be denied by the speaker or attributed to the listener. Sometimes immediate non-defensive options are limited to a draw where saving face (or saving the façade) is the least threatening result possible at the moment.

Awareness of Hidden Content Is Important For Getting Off the Defensive

The detail in which this example is presented is usually not necessary to do in practice. However, it is important to be aware of the necessity of identifying the hidden content. It can hold important information for getting off the defensive. For example:

- A person acting as a threatened adversary, such as John, often can nose out the vulnerable spots of the opponent. (In the last chapter, we noted this as among the skills many men learn from male-role competitiveness. Many women also learn it from female-role expectations. Men may share vulnerabilities that they can't share with men with women close to them. When they get in conflict, she knows how to hit him where it hurts.)

  What if they declared a war and nobody came? If you can sense where your potential adversary may strike, you can consciously plan ahead how you want to handle it or how you might prevent it, not as much by building façades as by considering the many other options you can make available to yourself and the other person if you are willing to see the threat in a non-defensive way. When you move away from defending yourself toward getting more of the results you want for yourself, your relationships, and the job to be done, many more options become available.

- Attacks are often built on grains of truth. If you have a vulnerable spot where you can be threatened, you may want to face that threat (where it's safe), so you can become less vulnerable. John's hidden content, "You don't know what you're doing," had some truth in it; Helen didn't know how to handle John's non-performance except to threaten him. If she had faced that and thought through additional options before she met with John, she might have had different results, provided she didn't get caught in the win–lose game.

- You can't be responsible for someone else's agenda. If you feel the threatened person wants to dump on you by shifting his or her pain or responsibilities to you, you can develop options that will leave responsibilities where they belong and still let you keep an empathic ear. If you can keep communications open and the threats impersonal, your odds of finding non-defensive possibilities are much better than those we've seen so far.

- You can manage results non-defensively, but not behavior. If the norms of your system require you to play parent when you supervise and you find that adults begin to act like children under this treatment, you may want to consider breaking those norms so you can have more adult-to-adult supervision. Although many systems insist on it, you cannot be responsible for the behavior of your subordinates. They are the only ones who can be responsible for their actions. You can be responsible for defining goals and limits, but you can only be held responsible for others' results. If they don't produce, there are consequences they have to face. If you don't tell them those consequences, you assume responsibility for them and are back in the parent–child stance, as Helen did with John.

As we saw earlier, many people do not respond to authority the way they used to. Gaining cooperation or collaboration is far more important today than it was in the past. Moving away from threat and fear, moving toward trust and openness are the directions for more effective, non-defensive relationships. We'll see more about how to do some of these things in the next chapter.

ASK YOURSELF

1. Think of some communication you had in the last few days in which you can identify double meanings that aroused defensiveness in you.
    - What was the hidden content? The hidden feelings?
    - How did you react? What inner rules did you use?
    - What results did you get? Were they what you wanted?

2. Think about the risks of your becoming more open or more honest. Consider doing it gradually where it might be appropriate, where it nudges at the norms without seriously violating them, with someone with whom your relationship is important.
    - What are the worst things that might happen?
    - What might this person's reaction be to you?
    - What do you hope this person doesn't find out about you?
    - How might you protect yourself from the worst that might happen and still open up the communication a little bit?

IN THE NEXT CHAPTER

Next we get into action, starting with yourself. You can't change the system you're in very soon; you can't change other people very much; but you can change the way you relate to other people, which usually influences the way they relate to you. As you become more of your own person, you'll keep finding more and more options for continuing growth, both professionally and personally.

In the next chapter the first action step is gathering information about yourself: what you're doing now, what you'd like to be doing instead, and what you're doing when you tell yourself, "I made it!" We continue to build on self-affirming attitudes that lead to becoming non-defensive.

READINGS

Fabun, Don: *Communications: The Transfer of Meaning,* Glencoe Publishing Co., Inc., Encino, Calif., 1968. Originally developed for Kaiser Aluminum and Chemical Corp. (who hold the copyright), this colorful pamphlet makes visible many common communication problems with options for clearer transfer of meanings. Now a classic, it is an excellent summary of a complex process.

Gordon, Thomas: *Leadership Effectiveness Training, L.E.T.: The No-Lose Way to Release the Productive Potential of People,* Wyden Books, New York, 1977. Dr. Gordon draws on many of the same principles that are used in non-defensive communication. However, L.E.T. addresses people in leader roles; NDC addresses people in subordinate roles. L.E.T.'s underlying values are directed toward no-lose results; NDC moves toward gain-gain results. Most readers will find rich additional material in this book.

Rogers, Carl R., and Richard Farson: *Active Listening,* University of Chicago Press, Chicago, 1957. Among the first materials on how to actively listen to others with the idea of hearing their feelings as well as their words. Risks of really hearing the other person's meanings are discussed.

Rogers, Carl R., and F. J. Roethlisberger: "Barriers and Gateways to Communication," *Harvard Business Review,* July–August 1952, pp. 28–34. Now a classic, this early article focused on the tendency to evaluate as a key barrier to mutual understanding. Active listening is illustrated.

For additional background reading, see bibliography entries 5, 12, 14, 19, 22, 33, 55, 67, 72, 73, 74, 78.

6

STARTING TO GET OFF THE DEFENSIVE

Recognizing Your Own Patterns, Developing New Attitudes, and Other Starting Points

We have defenses and façades because we need them. Looking at the self behind the façade is always a risk. If you lower or drop your defenses or façades before you have something of equal or greater value with which to replace them, you might violate yourself. That you don't need!

Respecting, accepting, and valuing yourself, no matter how you now see yourself, is a precondition of becoming non-defensive and of becoming your own person. So we build on strengths and develop new ways to see strengths, resources, and allies that may be blocked from view by the façades. We work with strengthening the real self behind the façade so it's a safe risk when you decide to come out from behind it. Taking risks safely is part of becoming non-defensive.

To gain a clearer picture of where you are now and where you want to go, you'll be collecting information about what you feel and do when you are both defensive and non-defensive. The Incident Card is your tool for recording these moments. This record helps you analyze your patterns so you can take steps toward becoming non-defensive. A companion tool, Notes to Myself, helps capture your thoughts about the incidents and other concerns.

Your Incident Card information will also help you identify and see how you've been using your strengths, inner rules, and beliefs. You might be using them against yourself instead of for yourself. For instance, let's look at your strengths. Compare a cluster of your strengths to a hammer. With this hammer you can build a house, but in the process you could also hit your thumb. If you're afraid of hitting your thumb, you may focus so much attention on the fear of hitting your thumb that you never get your house built.

This behavior is defensive. But if you focus on the house, you will probably build that house, even though you will probably hit your thumb a few times.

This is one way you can become non-defensive; you draw the circle bigger. You do this by defining and focusing on the results you want—the house. Your attention is then on using your strengths to gain that end so you're more likely to hammer the nails than your thumb. You can use the same approach for inner rules and beliefs. Part of becoming non-defensive is through reviewing your rules and reexamining your underlying values and beliefs that may be limiting the end results you could be gaining. You might also add some rules or values that you can draw on as you need them.

Let's start with a situation in which people became defensive and angry and then see how they might have used the Incident Card and Notes to Myself.

USING THE INCIDENT CARD AND NOTES TO MYSELF

Consider this situation in which everyone arrives defensive and becomes more so. Then we'll see how one person, staying non-defensive, might take the lead that could change the outcome, and we'll see how they get off the defensive afterwards.

> The meeting is just starting. Reluctantly, the eight men and one woman from XNG's corporate industrial relations sit down to the job they dislike most—recommending people for layoff. Jack Angelo, 36, the affirmative action officer, is particularly tense. The lost contract means that many support people—clerical workers, administrators researchers—will have to go. Many are women and minorities, which he is sure Marie Taylor, 44, will point out. As wage and salary director, she's critical of XNG's treatment of women. Jack feels she overemphasizes women and ignores what white and minority men face.
>
> Bob Olsen, 47, the director, is aware of this and many other related conflicts. He knows it's tough to find the right balance between qualifications and government requirements without stepping on somebody's toes. He suspects he will probably have to cut his staff and has no idea yet who to peg. If it's Marie, the newest to his staff, he'll probably get a sex discrimination complaint. If it's any of the men, he may get charges of reverse discrimination. It's a no-win situation.
>
> Marie walks into the meeting as if going to an execution, Jack clowns around a little, and Bob seems quietly cautious, perhaps wary. The others bring a wait-and-see attitude. Before they've gotten very far down the payroll list, Marie begins to suspect a pattern—they're targeting older women more than any other group. Her indignation at Jack rises; he's

often told her that minority men have it much worse than women of all colors at XNG. About halfway through the list, she angrily accuses all of them:

"I know what you're doing. You've got it in for the older women. You're not touching the men or the 'cute chicks,' as you call them." There had been too much talk through the grapevine about how Denise got her last promotion for Marie not to be sure there was something to it.

Working hard to keep his cool, Jack jumps in. "Now listen here, Marie," he warns her, "you're taking this too personally. Just be patient until we're done and you'll see you're wrong." Forcing himself to keep it light, he adds, "You know there're no male chauvinists here!"

Thud. Marie just stares at him. Nervous chuckles from a couple of the others. Marie resents Jack talking down to her by suggesting she's defending her own age group and by glibly denying any possible bias, but she holds her fire. "I'll wait," she tells herself, "they'll hang themselves yet," turning her attention back to the list.

Very little discussion ensues as they continue down the list, most of it being about seniority or performance reviews. Marie sees the pattern emerge even more clearly—over-40 women clearly predominate. Few males, white or minority, are targeted and among the younger women, the "foxy ladies" escape. Loaded with now-justified anger, she hits hard:

"There now, see? Just like I said. You and your industrial relations," her lip curling, "You're prejudiced against older women."

Boiling mad, Jack explodes, "Oh, f--- all those g--d--- broads." In the shocked silence of the group, Marie furiously grabs up her papers and stomps out in a flurry. Two of the quieter men quickly follow her back to her office, but she won't talk to them. She leaves for the rest of the day.

At the disrupted meeting, the men wind up agreeing that Marie got too emotional, but Jack shouldn't have used that kind of language in front of a woman.

The issue of possible bias was lost in the jungle of stereotypes. Both Marie and Jack were feeling threatened when they came to the meeting. So they attacked each other and defended their own positions. When this happens everyone loses: Marie, her credibility; Jack, his objectivity; Bob, his selection of whom to target from his own staff. All were worse off than when they began, and the list of recommended layoffs was still not done.

If just one person had spoken non-defensively, the tension might have been eased. For example, in Bob's role as director, he could have led off with, "We have a job that I expect none of us like doing—cutting off people's paychecks. I don't know how we're going to do it with a good balance between qualifications, skills no longer needed, recent promotions, seniority, affirmative action requirements, and whom we like. I'm asking you to be as objective as you can, not only about the recommendations you make but also about your conflicts about them. How are the rest of you feeling about this assignment?" Or he might have ended with, "We have to recommend $700,000 in cuts. Before we get into it, let's talk about what criteria we'll use, as well as our own ground rules." Using his position power, Bob could have given permission to talk about the conflicts, which would have legitimized discussion of feelings that would usually be excluded by prevailing norms. Whether or not the others would do so would depend on how much they trusted each other before the meeting took place.

One person can change the entire situation. The leader can legitimize expression of conflicting feelings. Someone's humor can release tensions. When someone lowers her or his façade, others may lower theirs.

If Bob had been preoccupied and started the meeting abruptly, Jack might have voiced his concerns early in the discussion: "I'm worried about the effects on our affirmative action program, especially the last promotions. Support people are going to get hit the hardest and that's where we've promoted so many women and minorities." To ease the tension, he might have added, "I could be run out of here, once they find out I'm at this meeting!"

Even further into the meeting, if no one had yet cut through the gloom, Marie might propose, "The last layoff seemed to hit the lower-pay categories rather hard. By now we might be top heavy some places. Let's start with higher-paid people and work down. Fewer people will get the axe that way." She might risk disclosing a little of her fear by adding: "Besides, I'd rather start on other people before getting to support staff like me."

When one person begins to disclose his or her feelings, lowering a façade, others sometimes take a similar risk. If one person had lowered his or her façade at the meeting, the job of identifying people for layoff would probably have proceeded on a less defensive basis. When Marie was sure of her data about the predominance of targeting over-40 women, she might have called attention to it in a fact-finding way. "It seems to me over-40 women are hit hard. Let's see if our selections are unduly heavy on any one group, such as men/women, older/younger, minority/non-minority, high/low job levels." By pointing toward criteria and involving others in data analysis, she can leave the way open for the men to see patterns and discuss inequities without attacking them with accusations. In that way, even if they were prejudiced, they could deal with the effects of that prejudice more objectively. They could save face. Not only would there have been no explosions, but the list probably would be completed sooner.

Recognizing the Feelings of Being On and Off the Defensive

To report their concerns or apprehensions, Bob, Jack, or Marie would have to recognize them first, which is often difficult. Here's one way it can be done in a small group. The group brainstorms this statement: "When I'm on the defensive, I feel . . . and I do . . ." People build on each others' experiences, making a group list of all the ways they have been defensive. No one judges or evaluates; this exercise is a recognition one. The longer the list, the better.

People discover they are not alone with their defensiveness. This makes it easier to recognize your own defenses and claim them as your own, even if you're not too proud of some of them. This step is the first one toward taking responsibility for them.

Table 6-1 shows what some people feel and do when they are defensive. Remember that these feelings and reactions are not always defenses. Many can be non-defensive choices when used for purposes of mutual gain. The first column lists feelings some people have when they are defensive. Not everyone feels defensive about the same things. For example, you may feel excited when challenged, but others may feel threatened. When you feel inadequate, you may withdraw; someone else might needle or bait other people. The last two columns show some patterns of what people do when

Table 6-1. *When I'm On the Defensive*
Match your feeling (1) to what you do inwardly (2) or outwardly (3).

1. I feel	2. I do (Inward)	3. I do (Outward)
Challenged	Rationalize	Get deliberative
Nervous	Sweat	Scheme
Resentful	Back down	Evaluate and choose
Uncomfortable	Withdraw	Find fault—shoot down
Put down	Go blank	Get hostile
Angry	Lose my cool	Get logical
Frustrated	Eat, drink water	Prove my point
Dumb	Smoke	Buy time
Guilty	Say silly things	Go to the bathroom
Inadequate	Come up with excuses	Retreat and regroup
Hassled	Talk too much	Get condescending
Confused	Get apologetic	Scream, yell
Threatened	Talk without thinking	Compute
Unprepared	Postpone the situation	Fire back a wisecrack
Like leaving	Get anxious	Become sarcastic
Insignificant	Say nothing	Needle somebody
Trapped	Blush	Give 'em the finger
Self-protective	Cry	Try to get off the spot
Blabbery	Put foot in mouth	Blame others
A need to justify	Chew on pencil	Ask questions
Evaluated, judged	Cut my head off	Take offensive—do battle
Violated	Become tense in the stomach	Get evasive
Slow simmer	Become illogical	Kill 'em with data

they feel defensive. Some turn it inward, as if they were punishing themselves. Others turn it outward, reacting to other people, sometimes aggressively. Others switch back and forth between both lists.

You may want to experiment with tracking your own behavior. Brian Benson, a director of a governmental social service agency, tracked what he did when he felt challenged and found this pattern: First he smokes, then computes, says nothing, asks questions, retreats and regroups, then kills 'em with data. For him, the best defense is a good offense. What do you tend to do?

Think of the defensive things you often do, then say them out loud to yourself. Recognize and own your feelings and reactions without trying to justify them. Just name them out loud. For many people, recognizing and owning these feelings is a relief, like opening the closet door and discovering the skeleton is just a bag of bones. You, like others, may eventually chuckle at the games you play in the name of defending yourself, even when they were—or still are—useful in the short run.

Recognizing and owning these feelings and reactions is just one step toward getting off the defensive. The next step is to replace them with something more non-defensive. Visualizing yourself when you're feeling centered, invigorated, or turned on is one way to start. For example, imagine what would have happened if Bob, Jack, and Marie had approached that meeting feeling refreshed, as if they'd just had a vigorous swim.

One way to get into a non-defensive mood is to brainstorm another list, one that describes When I'm Off the Defensive, I Become (Table 6-2). To get started with this list, people often find it easier to define what off the defensive means to them. Some say it's feeling turned on, centering in myself, or having my act together.

As you look at this list, you'll notice that there is no separation between "I feel" and "I do" as there was in the When I'm On the Defensive list. Non-defensive feelings and actions seem to be so blended that most people don't separate them. They almost always end up with a single list of experiences and sensations. See if any of these ring a bell with you. Perhaps you can add some of your own.

Visualizing and describing feelings and habitual reactions are among the ways to recognize your own defensive and non-defensive patterns. Now it's time to get specific, objective data about yourself—how often and in what way you act and communicate, both defensively and non-defensively, and in what kinds of situations.

Unfortunately these incidents are often like elusive gnats that buzz, bite, and zoom away. But you can capture them before they disappear. Your net is the Incident Card. Just write down what bugs you and what you do about it—whether you do nothing or use a steam roller to squash your gnats.

Table 6-2.   *When I'm Off the Defensive, I Become*

Centered in self (not necessarily meaning connected with others)	More outgoing; my energy flows out and wraps around others
Turned on	In control of the situation, not the situation in control of me
Alive, awake, gung-ho	Sure I can do most anything I make up my mind to do
Sharing of a lot of thinking, of seeing as I see it	Excited with a sense of inner peacefulness
Stimulating to myself and others	More able to work with others, not for/or against them
Freer from distress	Filled with a deep sense of joy
Able to see reality clearer	More open; unafraid of new ideas
Able to see other realities from different angles	More able to make positive statements about myself, not what I think others want to hear
Able to make odd, unusual, different connections between events and feelings	Freer with my sense of humor
Visual and able to use my imagination more	Able to listen without critiquing
More courageous	More sensitive and responsive to underlying fears and concerns in others, not needing to criticize their behaviors that irritate me, able to work with real issues
Less fearful, more confident	Able to tune out irritations and annoyances
Able to feel fun in the challenge	Intense with more concentrated attention
Creative—willing to experiment	Able to work faster, things click
Anxious that my experimenting mood might go away, that I can keep it going, that I can stay in control of myself, focused.	

The Incident Card and Notes to Myself

The Incident Card is a way to keep book on yourself. All you do is make notes on situations in which you feel defensive, as well as on those situations in which you feel ten feet tall because you made it. Notes to Myself are used to capture fleeting thoughts as they occur. Figure 6-1 shows the basic tools Jack and Marie would have been using if they had been keeping book on themselves.

INCIDENT CARD	Date _____ Number ____

Situation

What I did was

My feelings were (or, what I said to myself was . . .)

What I want to be ready to do next time is

So I can feel (or, so I can tell myself . . .)

☐ **I made it**   My next step is: Scheduled for
Do nothing _____
☐ **I avoided it**   Work on it_____   _____
Think about it later ____   _____
☐ **I blew it**   Other_____   _____

Additional comments

Copyright © 1974 by Theodora Wells

Figure 6-1(a). *Incident Card.*

Date	NOTES TO MYSELF

Figure 6-1(b). *Notes to Myself.*

After the meeting, recognizing the defensiveness, their Incident Cards might have looked like the one shown in Figure 6-2.

When feelings are running high, you may need some cooling off time before you can decide what to do next time. Just starting to capture these situations is enough. Lots of things may happen in the course of a day or a week that you wish were different. Some are loaded, as above; others may seem relatively insignificant. Size doesn't matter; recording them does. In Figure 6-3 we see some other things that also concern Marie and Jack.

In addition to collecting Incident Cards, you can catch fleeting thoughts that occur to you as you go about your day. Using Notes to Myself, you might write down hunches, questions that come to mind, or possible options for an incident you're thinking about. Some thoughts won't seem to be related to anything in particular. Other thoughts about an incident can refer to the number of that Incident Card. Figure 6-4 shows us what might be on Marie's and Jack's notes.

When people start using these notes and incidents, they often write down only those things that go wrong. Although it's important to take responsibility for your own actions, it's equally important to include what goes right. Recording off-the-defensive experiences keeps you in touch with those turned-on feelings, so you can savor and remember how you made it. Marie and Jack might have had such experiences on which to build more successes. Figure 6-5 shows how they recorded them.

When you capture one of these, celebrate! Pat yourself on the back, savor it, read it over and over, let it grow. Each time you claim a success, it spreads to other things. Arrange some incidents that are predictable winners. Cheat all you want on the "I made its." Set yourself up for all the real successes you can, no matter how small.

Make copies of the blank Incident Card and start making your own collection. While you accumulate these on your own, let's focus on attitudes and ways you can use them to create more options. This way you'll know more about yourself before you work on the Incident Cards you collect. Then, whether you do nothing or use a streamroller, you'll make your choices from your own center of strength—your core of self—and you'll be on your way to becoming non-defensive.

DEVELOPING ATTITUDES THAT LEAD TO NON-DEFENSIVENESS

To communicate non-defensively, you have to *be* non-defensive. When you are centered in a core of strength and confidence, it will show. If you act *as if* you are centered there but aren't, that thin veil can easily be pierced when the battles begin. We're after the real thing.

First, we will consider some attitudes that lead to getting off the defensive. Then we'll explore some ways to work with your inner resources and filters so that when threats come along, you're ready, not with thicker armor and sharper weapons but with more options to increase the odds of gaining results you want. When threatened, many people react with either fight or flight. But there are many more options. Here we will see how non-defensive attitudes can open these up.

Naming and Claiming Your Strengths

Developing an attitude of honoring your strengths as a source of inner person power is one way of becoming centered. What's a strength? It's not only physical strength; it's also having strong convictions, persistence, courage, astuteness, knowledge. Using strengths is using yourself in ways that give you inner pride so you can say to yourself, "I like me." It's living the best of you, feeling worthwhile, being true to your own self. Whatever gives you this sense is a strength for you.

When Marie checked "I made it" on her Incident Card, she used strengths of accepting others, choosing her own responses (to Jack's language), and giving herself approval instead of depending so much on others to give it to her. By choosing to take more control over herself and taking responsibility for this control, she used some of her strengths.

Jack used different ones. He took a risk that his children would come through even when he didn't think they would. His ability to trust—a strength—was becoming less conditional on whether or not they *always* came through. As he begins to feel better about his way of being a father—another strength—he will probably feel prouder of Dan and Deena. As they feel his pride, little by little they also will probably use more of their strengths. It's contagious!

Here's a brief lopsided inventory for naming your own strengths as well as your need to improves (which we'll talk about later). Remember, *whatever you call a strength is a strength for you.* Never mind if no one else you know calls it a strength. If it's a strength to you, that's enough.

Remember: The power to define is the power to choose.
Strengths spread just as fears do.

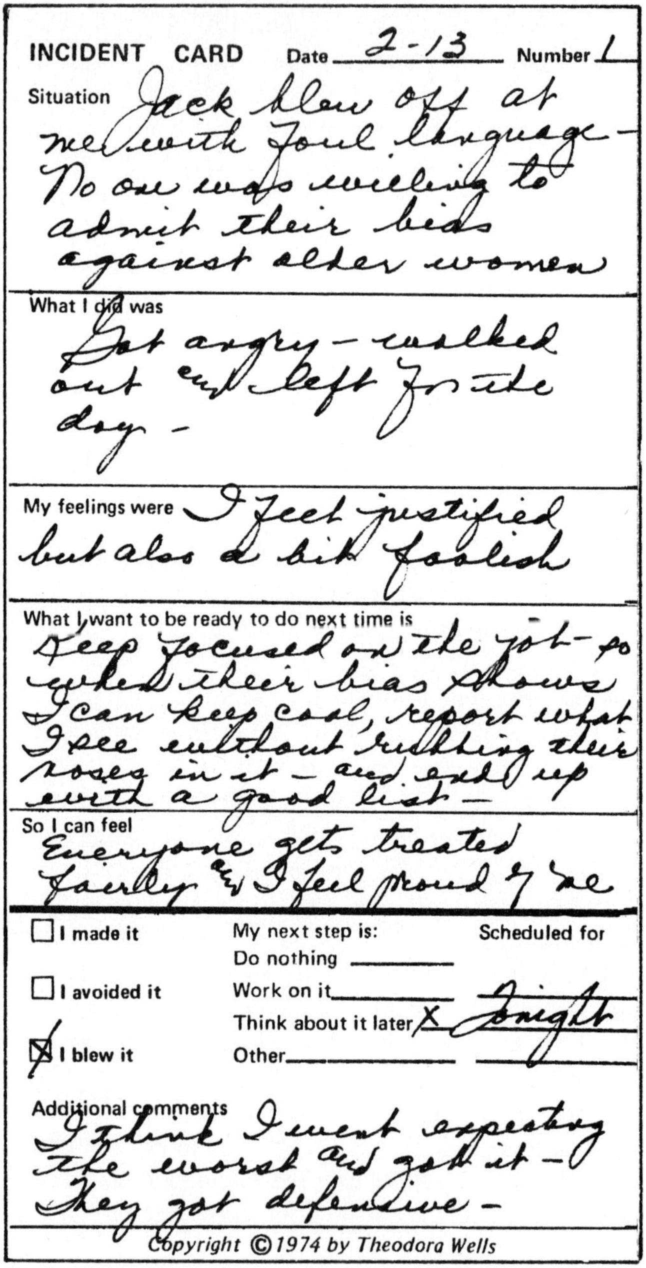

INCIDENT CARD   Date __2-13__   Number _1_

Situation _Jack blew off at me with foul language — No one was willing to admit their bias against older women_

What I did was _Got angry — walked out and left for the day —_

My feelings were _I feel justified but also a bit foolish_

What I want to be ready to do next time is _Keep focused on the job — so when their bias shows I can keep cool, report what I see without rubbing their noses in it — and end up with a good list —_

So I can feel _Everyone gets treated fairly and I feel proud of me_

☐ I made it   My next step is: Scheduled for
              Do nothing _____
☐ I avoided it   Work on it_____
              Think about it later _X_ _Tonight_
☒ I blew it   Other_____

Additional comments _I think I went expecting the worst and got it — They got defensive —_

Copyright © 1974 by Theodora Wells

Figure 6-2(a).   *Marie's Incident Card number 1.*

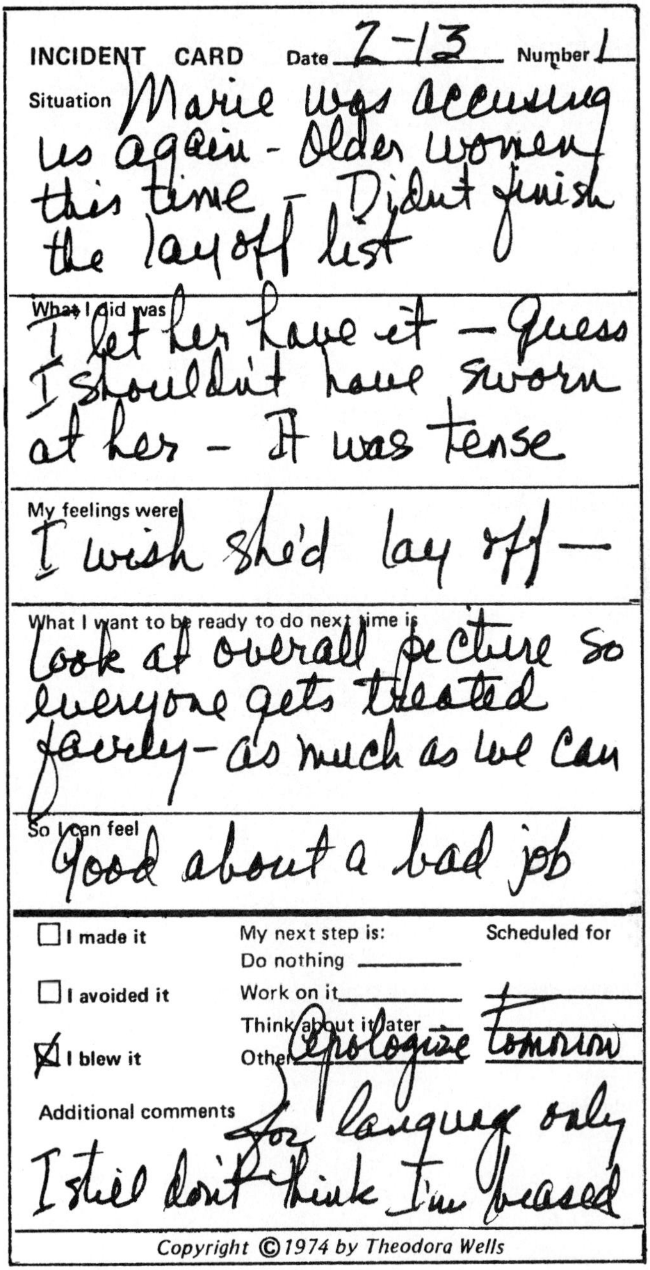

INCIDENT CARD   Date 2-13   Number 1

Situation *Marie was accusing us again - Older women this time - Didnt finish the layoff list*

What I did was *I let her have it - Guess I shouldn't have sworn at her - It was tense*

My feelings were *I wish she'd lay off -*

What I want to be ready to do next time is *look at overall picture so everyone gets treated fairly - as much as we can*

So I can feel *Good about a bad job*

☐ I made it   My next step is: Scheduled for
                  Do nothing _____
☐ I avoided it   Work on it_____
                  Think about it later
☒ I blew it   Other *apologize tomorrow*

Additional comments *for language only*
I still don't think I'm biased

Copyright ©1974 by Theodora Wells

Figure 6-2(b). *Jack's Incident Card number 1.*

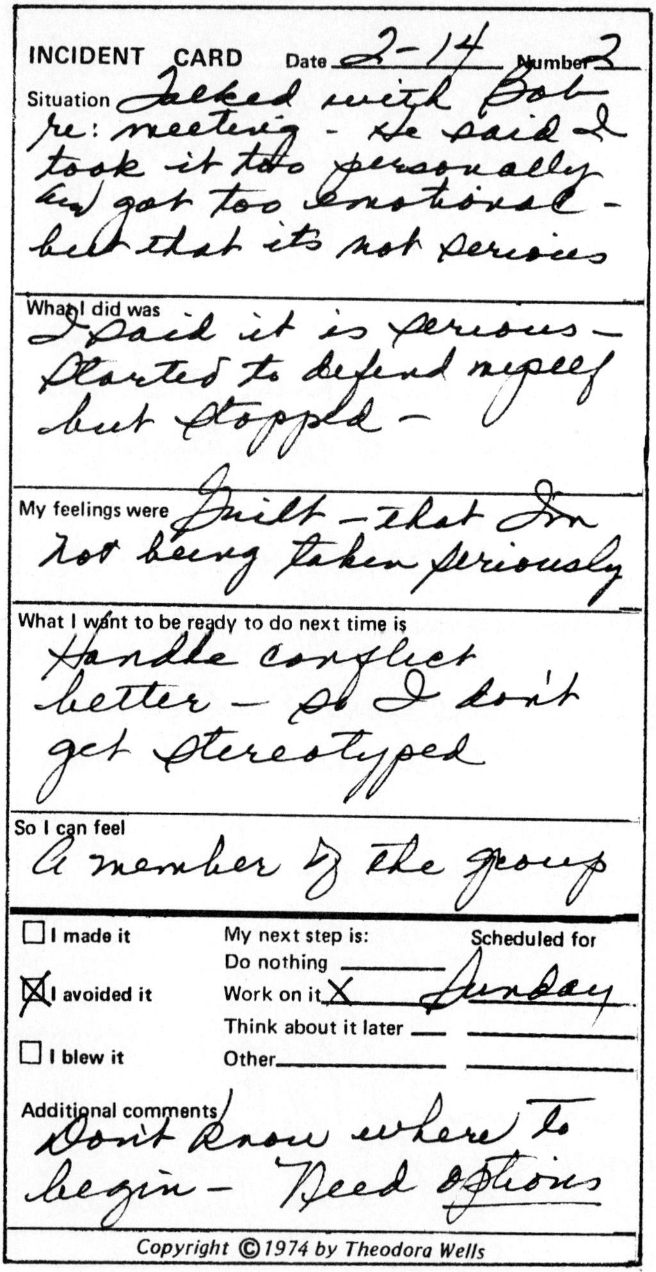

INCIDENT CARD Date *2-14* Number *2*

Situation *Talked with Bob re: meeting - He said I took it too personally and got too emotional - but that it's not serious*

What I did was *I said it is serious - Started to defend myself but stopped -*

My feelings were *Guilt - that I'm not being taken seriously*

What I want to be ready to do next time is *Handle conflict better - so I don't get stereotyped*

So I can feel *A member of the group*

☐ I made it

☒ I avoided it

☐ I blew it

My next step is:
Do nothing ___
Work on it *X*
Think about it later ___
Other ___

Scheduled for *Sunday*

Additional comments *Don't know where to begin - Need options*

Copyright © 1974 by Theodora Wells

Figure 6-3(a). *Marie's Incident Card number 2.*

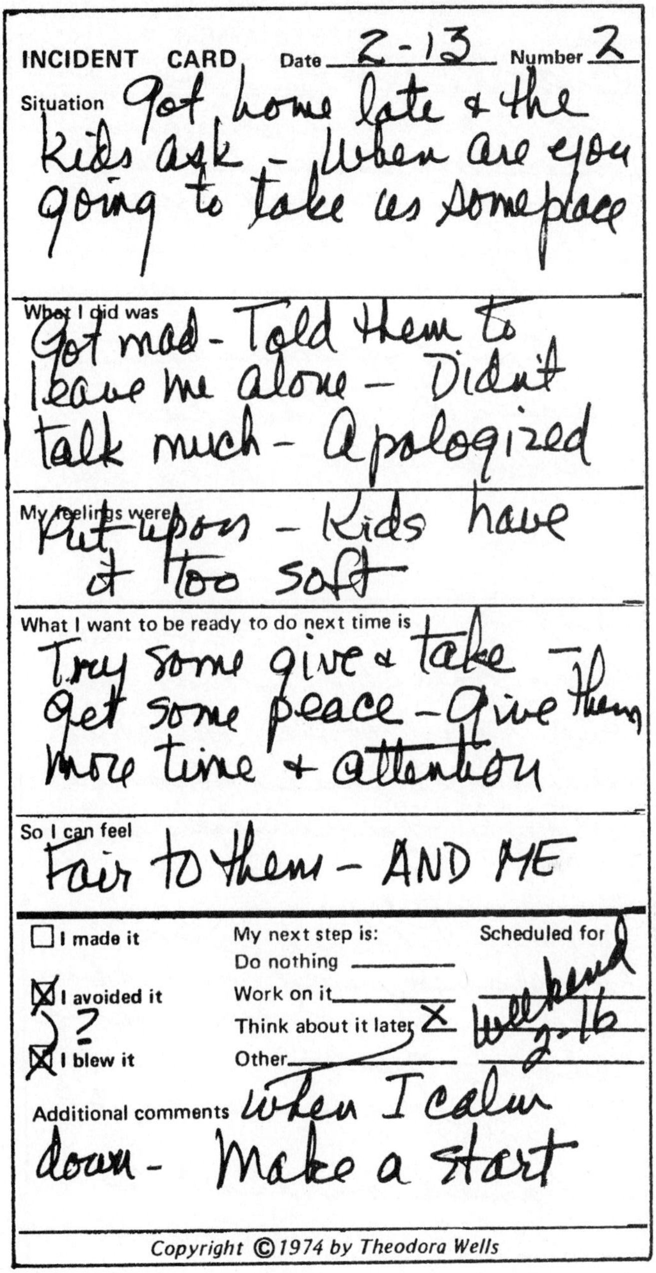

INCIDENT CARD Date 2-13 Number 2

Situation: Got home late & the kids ask - When are you going to take us someplace

What I did was: Got mad - Told them to leave me alone - Didn't talk much - Apologized

My feelings were: Put upon - Kids have it too soft

What I want to be ready to do next time is: Try some give & take - get some peace - Give them more time + attention

So I can feel: Fair to them - AND ME

	My next step is:	Scheduled for
☐ I made it	Do nothing	
☒ I avoided it ?	Work on it	weekend
	Think about it later X	2-16
☒ I blew it	Other	

Additional comments: When I calm down - Make a start

Copyright © 1974 by Theodora Wells

Figure 6-3(b). *Jack's Incident Card number 2.*

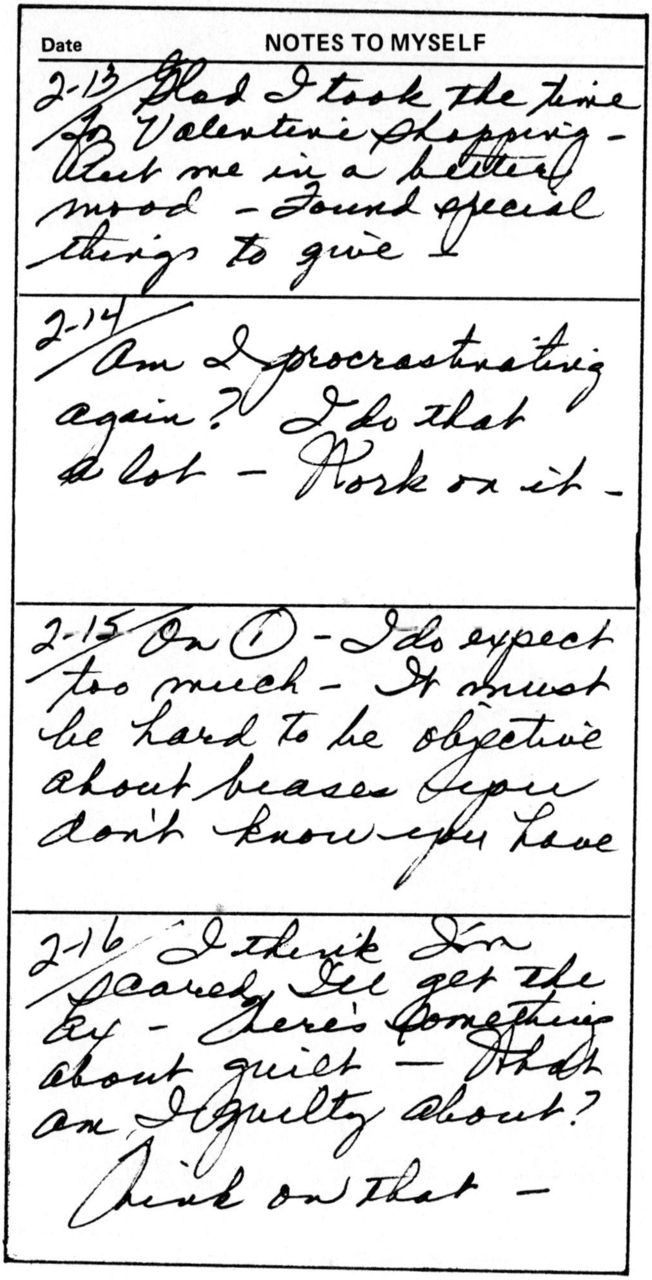

Date	NOTES TO MYSELF
2-13	Glad I took the time for Valentine Shopping - Put me in a better mood - Found special things to give -
2-14	Am I procrastinating again? I do that a lot - Work on it -
2-15	On (1) - I do expect too much - It must be hard to be objective about bosses if you don't know you have
2-16	I think I'm scared I'll get the ax - There's something about guilt - What am I guilty about? Think on that -

Figure 6-4(a). *Marie's Notes to Myself.*

Date	NOTES TO MYSELF
2-14	Time keeps getting away from me + Start Controlling it more — GET STARTED
2-14	Pick up Valentine candy on way home — Also champagne for in front of the fire —
2-15	On ① & ② — I got angry a lot that day — Marge says I've been touchy lately — What's going on?
2-16	On ② — Get the kids to clean up tools they left out — then play ball with them awhile — Give + take Negotiate more

Figure 6-4(b). *Jack's Notes to Myself.*

INCIDENT CARD   Date *2-15*   Number *3*

Situation *Jack apologized for his language — and said he still didn't think he's biased —*

What I did was *Told him I believe him — and that he can use what language he wants to — I can respond to it or not!*

My feelings were *I'm beginning to control me — not others*

What I want to be ready to do next time is *Maybe if I let him be the way he is — I'll get some in return — Even if I don't, I feel better*

So I can feel *Less in need of their approval*

☒ I made it !!   My next step is: Scheduled for
                  Do nothing *X*
☐ I avoided it   Work on it_____   _____
                  Think about it later _____
☐ I blew it   Other *Enjoy success!*

Additional comments *It wasn't his language — It was his control — Now, I'm more in control*

Copyright ©1974 by Theodora Wells

Figure 6-5(a).   Marie's "I made it" Incident Card.

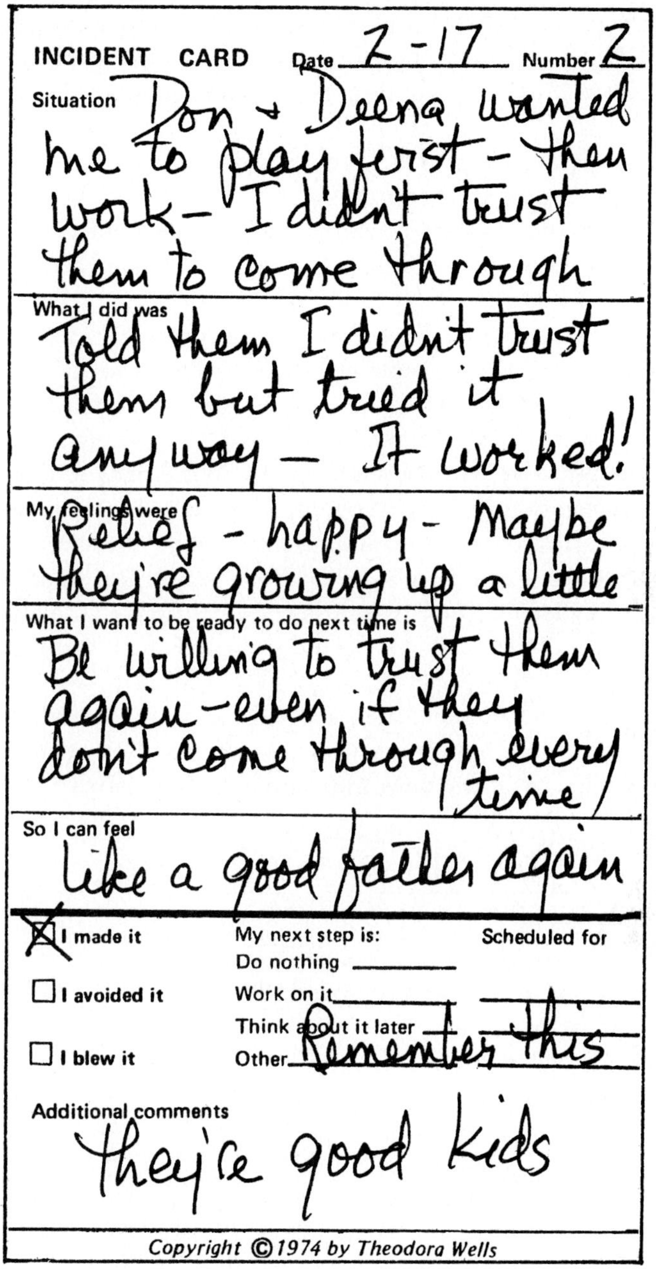

INCIDENT CARD   Date 7-17   Number 2

Situation *Don + Deena wanted me to play first — then work — I didn't trust them to come through*

What I did was *Told them I didn't trust them but tried it any way — It worked!*

My feelings were *Relief - happy - Maybe they're growing up a little*

What I want to be ready to do next time is *Be willing to trust them again - even if they don't come through every time*

So I can feel *like a good father again*

☒ I made it

☐ I avoided it

☐ I blew it

My next step is: Scheduled for

Do nothing _____

Work on it _____

Think about it later _____

Other *Remember this*

Additional comments *they're good kids*

Copyright © 1974 by Theodora Wells

Figure 6-5(b). *Jack's "I made it" Incident Card.*

Get a piece of paper, check the time and give yourself three minutes to do this exercise. List ten strengths. Then list five things that you think you need to improve. Stop in three minutes (ask someone to time you).

- How many strengths did you get down?
- How many need to improves?
- Did you start on your strengths, then switch to the need to improves?
- If so, what were you telling yourself that made you switch?

Whatever barriers lie between you and your strengths are filters that you don't need anymore. Many people learn to name their need to improves over and over again. Many of us learn that we should be willing to work on improving ourselves. Nothing wrong with that. But we also need to learn to claim the strengths we will use for working on the need to improves!

Here are some strengths that people have named themselves. Underline the ones you can call your own, adding others that you have.

What are you feeling right now? Most people feel good about themselves when they look at their lists. Some seem surprised they have so many strengths. Others didn't know they could feel good about themselves without feeling guilty.

Among the thousands of men and women who have taken this inventory, many have some filters that say no to looking at their own strengths. See if you've learned any of the ones they found in themselves:

Table 6-3. *Strengths I Can Claim Are*

Positive approach to people	Honest, ethical
Good body, keep in condition	Ahead of my time
Generally in a good mood	Keep my word
Sense of humor	Ability to pace myself and my work
Good listener	Can keep cool under stress
I'm a good risk taker	Good cook
Have and use a good vocabulary	Not afraid of change
Think clearly	Meet deadlines, like pressure
I care about people	Proud of my children
Dependable	Flexible
Good in bed	Can conceptualize well
Honest about my faults	People like to work for me; I'm fair
Take the initiative	Can communicate what I really mean
Keep confidentiality	Can separate what's important
Have good timing	from what is not
Considerate of others' feelings	Never been fired
Attend to details	Fired for my strengths
Keep on learning	Keep on growing
Take criticism well	Accept myself
Good taste and manners	Admit my mistakes without much delay
Good problem solver	Do my research well
Willing to say what I think	Make decisions easily
Know how to enjoy myself	Handle money well

- Would others consider it a strength, too? (If not, I can't either.)
- One word covers lots of things (so I can't put down ten).
- Some strengths become weaknesses when I use them too strongly. (Are those strengths or need to improves?)
- You don't talk about those things.
- It would be bragging.
- It would be immodest.
- It's easier to look at what needs improving.
- You're supposed to work on improving yourself.
- I don't use it every time I should, so it's not really a strength.
- It would be a sin of pride. Pride cometh before a fall.

The majority of people taking this inventory were able to write down a few strengths, then one of these filters got in the way and they went to their need to improves. Few were able to write down ten strengths without making this switch. In fact, not many were able to write down ten strengths!

When filters sap your strengths, question the filters, not the strengths.

I fear the faith to let my knowing grow
But why is it commendable to name
My failures? Can I be to blame
For failure to acknowledge strengths also?
I fear the faith to let my knowing grow.[1]

If you want to see some of their need to improves, here are a few. No need for you to add to this list unless you're a glutton for punishment. You may find enough of your own when you start reviewing your Incident Cards and Notes to Myself.

- Procrastination
- Tendency to justify myself
- Be more accepting of my shyness
- Dealing with anger, frustration
- Balance between work and social life
- Attitudes toward my children
- Correspondence, especially thank you's
- Remembering birthdays
- Setting priorities

[1]From Ruth Bebermeyer, "I Fear the Gift," *Good Mornin', Pain* (recording), 218 Monclay St., St. Louis, Mo, 63122 1970.

- Follow-through on business contacts
- Selling myself
- Being firm with people who drain energy
- Letting people take my time when I need to say no

Sometimes these vulnerabilities become deep, dark secrets, something people hope no one ever finds out about. Here are some secrets that people at a management workshop on authority–subordinate relationships hid from prying eyes.[2] See if any sound familiar to you.

- My habit of resorting to my expert mask and not being open, real, and risking.
- How overbearing and domineering I become, how frightened I really am.
- How difficult it is for me to really count on other people for support.
- How much I need others to believe in me, even when I sometimes don't.
- I've battled with requiring 100% performance from myself, which has carried over to employees and home relations.
- My strongest defense against facing a problem is hostility.
- How sometimes I feel despair and think nobody will ever understand how alone I feel.
- I only have a high school education. I'm smart but not brilliant. I haven't got a Ph.D. For all my ambitions and successes, a part of me is childish.
- I'm terribly impatient with people who don't cooperate, participate, follow the rules, and GET IT ON!
- I care only about myself.
- I'm self-destructive when all else fails. I'm brutal to others when I get tired of being brutal to myself.
- I am a first-class fraud. I cultivate an appearance of strength and assuredness, but am almost totally devoid of both.
- How desperately I need to be loved, and how I'm not willing to take the first step: loving myself.
- My very cold, calculated decisions to get exactly what I want at others' expense.

Notice that most of these people kept their secrets, fears, or inadequacies hidden from others and often from themselves. However, other people often sense your fears, even when you think your secrets are carefully hidden. Others may be careful not to let you know they know, recognizing

---

[2]These secrets were written anonymously as completions to the sentence, "Something I hope no one finds out about me is . . ."

your need for a façade. They, in turn, may build a façade to protect you from their knowledge. Façades, like billboards, clutter up the landscape of your relationships and get in the way of your growth.

You certainly don't have to reveal your secrets publicly, but to continue your growth, you do have to accept that you have them, know what they are, and that you can do something about them. As you know and nurture yourself more, as you take care of yourself so you can say, "I like me," you'll have less need for façades. You'll be cleaning out the filters of your expectations, rules, and underlying values.

Accepting Yourself, Your Feelings, Filters, and Façades

Accepting yourself means giving yourself permission to be the way you are right now, to have your fears, guilts, doubts, defenses, and secrets as well as your strengths, courage, ethics, and excellence. Give yourself permission and consent by telling yourself:

> Whatever I am feeling right now is all right for me to feel even if I don't like it, even if no one else would feel the same way, even if others think I shouldn't feel this way. This is my feeling right now. Because it exists in me, it is mine. I do not have to evaluate whether my feeling is good or bad, right or wrong, reasonable or not. It simply is, and I accept its existence.

When you give yourself permission to have your own feelings, you fear them less and hide them less from yourself and others. Every secret, every façade, every defense is evidence of a fear or guilt or doubt—your fear of your own fears or your fear of how others will see and evaluate you.

Sometimes you can't identify these fears; perhaps they are anxieties that come unbidden from some vague, shadowy distance. Many people become more anxious when they try to avoid their anxieties. You can give yourself permission to feel anxiety and avoidance. Once you accept these anxieties, you can release them. Compare acceptance to going outside in winter weather holding your body tight with teeth clenched, shivering and chattering and barely breathing, avoiding contact with the cold. When you decide to relax and *go into* the chill, your shoulders, jaws, elbows, and knees loosen and you walk more freely, discovering that the chill stimulates your body and blood to warmth and deeper breathing. Your breath's visible trail is the result of the chill circulating through your lungs. No longer an enemy, the cold now fuels your energy.

For example, suppose you had written as your secret, "How overbearing and domineering I become, how frightened I really am." To keep your secret, you would keep the façade to hide your fright from yourself, not liking either the façade or the fear.

When you decide to experiment with accepting your façades and feelings in a non-defensive way, you might start by telling yourself:

> I am aware that I am frightened. I don't know why but I accept that I am. The fear exists. I give myself permission to feel fear. I also give myself consent to have my façades of overbearance and dominance to hide my fear from others. I don't like feeling frightened, and I don't like scaring off other people. But right now these feelings exist in me. I have been avoiding them and that's also a feeling I don't like but can now see and accept.

Once you accept these feelings and give yourself permission to have them, you don't have to have a façade in front of yourself, even if you want one for others. You may begin making some connections, such as this:

> When I'm frightened, my overbearing dominance scares off other people and then I get scared they won't like me—I don't like me when I do that.

Listening to and Describing Feelings

By going into your fears and anxieties and listening to them, you can gradually release their hold on you, turning them around so they can be energy sources, not energy drainers. Your feared feelings—conflicts, defenses, confusions, anxieties, angers, and frustrations—are all part of being you, of being alive. They can also be used as barometers to tell you when you're becoming aroused, to warn you of dangers from others, to give you hunches and cues when you will listen. To listen, however, a language that gives names to feelings is needed.

Many people have little language for identifying or listening to feelings. They've placed so much attention on the rational, objective, intellectual language that they know less of emotional, subjective, sensing language. Without names, feelings are hard to hear. Table 6-4 lists some words to describe feelings: one part for when your wants are being satisfied, the other for when your wants are not satisfied. *As you read through the two lists, underline the feelings that would be inappropriate to express at work.*

Count the feelings you checked as being inappropriate at work. Out of the 56 satisfied feelings on the first list, how many would be inappropriate? How many of the 76 non-satisfied feelings would be appropriate? What does this tell you about the norms where you work?

Check the feelings you can visualize yourself feeling and expressing. Pick one and consider how you would express this feeling. Is your style of expression similar to or different from the way your supervisor might express it? Your spouse? Your child? You lover? What do your answers tell you about the communication between you and those people close to you?

Table 6-4. *Words to Describe Feelings*[3]

1. When Wants Are Being Satisfied

absorbed	eager	grateful	peaceful
affection	elated	helpful	proud
alive	encouraged	inquisitive	radiant
amused	engrossed	inspired	refreshed
appreciation	enthusiastic	intense	relieved
astonished	excited	interested	secure
breathless	exhilarated	invigorated	spellbound
calm	expansive	jubilant	stimulated
cheerful	fascinated	keyed-up	surprised
complacent	friendly	mellow	thrilled
concerned	fulfilled	merry	tranquil
confident	gleeful	moved	trust
curious	glowing	optimistic	wide-awake
delighted	good-humored	overwhelmed	zestful

2. When Wants Are Not Satisfied

afraid	discouraged	hesitant	nettled
agitation	disgusted	horrible	passive
aloof	disheartened	hostile	perplexed
angry	dismayed	humdrum	provoked
animosity	disquieted	impatient	rancorous
annoyance	disturbed	inert	reluctant
anxious	downcast	infuriated	resentful
apprehensive	dread	insecure	restless
aversion	edgy	intense	scared
beat	embarrassed	irked	shaky
blah	exasperated	jealous	skeptical
bored	fatigued	jittery	sleepy
chagrined	fidgety	lassitude	sour
cold	frightened	let-down	spiritless
confused	furious	listless	startled
cross	gloomy	lonely	suspicion
dejected	guilty	mean	thwarted
despondent	hate	miserable	troubled
detached	helpless	nervous	uneasy

[3]Excerpted from Marshall B. Rosenberg, *From Now On: Without Blame and Punishment,* Community Psychological Consultants, Inc., St. Louis, Mo., 1977, pp. 35–38.

Suspending Judgments and Evaluations

To become non-defensive means to become non-judgmental by developing a non-evaluative attitude of listening and speaking to yourself and to others. As we've already seen, defenses and façades go up in the face of threats. Perhaps the most common threat between people is the fear of being evaluated—which people do to each other most of the time. You can be just as hard on yourself when you carry around unexamined rules and expectations that act as an inner committee of Parent/Priest/God/Judge/Jury. (That PPGJJ committee is the one to suspend from a rope—before it hangs you.)

Let's see how you can get around this fearsome committee and gain access to your own feelings. The purpose is to identify your feelings as facts that exist, as data to acknowledge. The method is to ask questions that gather data without evaluating the data by the way the question is asked. Fact-finding questions are those that ask *what, who, when,* and *where.* Evaluative, judgmental questions ask *why* and *how.* Consider these questions:

"What" Questions

- What am I feeling or experiencing right now?
- What feels threatening in this situation?
- What is the worst that might happen and what do I feel about that?
- What events were occurring before my feelings changed? What events changed about the same time that my feelings changed?
- What did my body tell me before and after the change?
- What is missing? What belongs in this situation but isn't here?
- What hunches or intuitions do I have right now?

Notice that these questions do not ask for right/wrong, good/bad, rational/emotional evaluations. Nor do they judge for validity, accuracy, or testing for some measure of reality. They simply identify.

"Who" Questions

- Who are my allies, my competitors?
- Who would gain what if the worst happened to me?
- Whose interests might be advanced by keeping me in the dark?
- Whom can I trust with what?
- Who else might be involved? What could they gain?

Notice again the absence of evaluation. These questions identify your feelings about the people in your situation. They resemble the "what" questions and supplement them by asking:

- What signals am I getting that support my perceptions of what is occurring and from whom? What signals don't fit?

"When" Questions

- When did I first feel a threat? Some other change?
- When have I had this feeling before? What is the similarity?

Again, there's no evaluating. These questions simply link your present feelings with past events. They do not dig up past feelings to justify present ones; they only pick up possible connectors from the past that could prove useful.

"Where" Questions

- Where was I when I felt this way before? Is there a relationship?
- Where are my feelings picking up a threat (if any)?

These question location of places or feelings without evaluating relevance or accuracy. Evaluation comes later.

"Why" and "How" Questions.

"Why" questions are analytical, evaluative, and judgmental and are most useful when you are looking for cause-and-effect relationships. *After* data are gathered, you can work back from effects to causes. *During* data gathering, "Why" questions tend to stop the flow of information because of the search for causes, which leads you to analysis paralysis.

A similar thing happens with "How" questions. If you find threatening information, you're likely to start figuring out how to protect yourself, thus stopping the flow of data again.

Recall the XNG incident. Let's see how Marie Taylor probably used inner "why" and "how" questions that resulted in passing judgments and stopping the flow of information.

Inner Questions	Answers That Shut Off Data
■ Why are they targeting so many over-40 women?	They're prejudiced against them. (After this judgment, no more data was gathered except under pressure.)
■ Why should I trust any of these men?	No reason; they're biased. (Her mind was made up, closed to further information.)
■ How can I stop them?	She confronted them with accusations, followed by Jack's explosion and her own. (No more data were gathered, the whole group judged Jack's and Marie's behavior, and the layoff list lay there listlessly.)

"How" questions can be quite useful when used collaboratively: "How can we (get a fair layoff list)?" points toward getting wanted results. Marie's inner question, "How can I stop them?" emphasizes winning or minimizes losing. She can't control the behavior of eight men. All they have to do is nothing—just go on the same old way—and they win. She loses a round whenever she gives away her power to influence the group.

Jack's explosion had the same results for him. His unrealistic option for controlling women—maximizing winning for men—temporarily lost him his power to influence the group.

Managing Anger and Emotional Energy

When feelings are running high, as in the XNG incident, the scene predictably ends as this one did—with a stereotypic, conventional curtain. Marie got too emotional; Jack shouldn't have used that language in front of a woman. The other men didn't conclude that Jack got too emotional, even though he, too, was boiling mad. Notice that the language issue won out over the issue of possible prejudice, a stereotypic façade that people use to avoid facing a threatening issue.

When people are supposed to keep their cool and they feel hot, when people are not experienced in accepting or handling their feelings, these soap opera finales will continue to occur, and little work will be accomplished. Denial and misdirection of emotional energy probably create the most costly hidden losses in payroll and human expenditures. These costs will remain hidden as long as the norms of male-role competitiveness prevail, denial of feelings being so imbedded in these values.

Since these norms aren't scheduled to change next week, what can you do about becoming non-defensive when your anger is aroused? Well, you can sit on your anger and repress it, as many people do. However that's more defensive than not. Your organization may like it, but it's bad for your health.

> Feelings suppressed
> Become compressed
> When not expressed
> You get depressed.

It is more healthy for you to manage your anger when it is first aroused so it doesn't continue to rise, and to be able to direct its energy into the task to be done. With some practice you can do this, once you accept your anger as energy instead of as a destructive force. Anger is destructive only when people use it that way. In and of itself, it is energy we can choose to use as a source of person power.

Raymond W. Novaco at the University of California, Irvine, is one of the few researchers to develop a method for self-management of anger.[4] It

---

[4]Reprinted by permission of the publisher, from *Anger Control: The Development and Evaluation of an Experimental Treatment* by Raymond W. Novaco (Lexington, Mass.: Lexington Books, D. C. Heath, Copyright 1975, D. C. Heath and Company).

Table 6-5. *Six Functions of Anger*

Anger Against	Anger For
Disrupting. Shoot first and ask questions later. Associated with danger or competition. Disrupts task performance, attention is scrambled, reactions impulsive.	**Energizing.** Stay in the arena. Increases options for responses and increases vigor in challenging or competitive situations. Gives effective assertiveness.
Defending. Attack when threatened, physically or in ego. Anger feels better than anxiety and moves the conflict outside of oneself where it's easier to *appear* in control of the situation with personal power.	**Expressing.** Composed expression of negative feelings ("I'm disappointed that . . ."). Tends to resolve conflict in non-attacking manner, exercising personal power with calm competence. Centered.
Instigating. Act aggressively. Combine agitation, thwarted expectations, hostile internal dialogue. Releases tension, but may provoke anger in others.	**Discriminating.** A cue to choose. Using anger as a barometer, early pressure is cue to choose among pre-learned options to get desired results. Aware of arousal states.

consists of three basic steps: (1) getting educated about one's anger; (2) learning alternative ways to construe provocations; and (3) telling oneself to focus on the task while positively redirecting the energy from the anger.

The first step toward managing your anger is understanding more about the functions anger serves. Novaco found six functions.[5] Table 6-5 shows them arranged by their energy flow: anger used *against* and anger used *for* a person or a task. Notice the functions for which you usually use your anger.

If you often use anger for one of the *against* purposes, you can start your move toward non-defensiveness by pausing and asking yourself, "What results do I want?" or "What options do I have right now?" You may recall Lori Landau doing this when she began to get angry with Charles Wilson's runarounds with radio ads (Chapter 2).

Such a small step may seem like an inauspicious way to harness a mounting surge of explosive anger; indeed, there is more to it. However, if you can make this turnaround while your anger is just starting to rise, you can probably move over to the *for* side. You can probably channel your energy into the energizing discriminating function. If you express your mounting anger without recognizing its arousal and making a conscious choice to channel it, you may lose your cool.

Many people have learned to repress their feelings; some do so without being conscious of it. As a result, they may be carrying around a substantial backlog of compressed feelings that can often be aroused. If you have pushed down your feelings this way, you can probably put your emotional energy

[5]Ibid, pp. 3–6.

into a task, more as a survival technique than a rechanneling of that energy. To get the results you want and to be able to generate many options, you may have to cut back the size of your backlog. Until then, it may be easy for a stray spark to start a bonfire!

Claiming strengths and building your core of self adds to your self-esteem and reduces how angry you become. According to Professor Novaco's findings, when people are confronted with personal provocation, those who have high self-esteem respond with lower levels of anger; those with low self-esteem respond with higher levels. He defines self-esteem as being able to make enhancing, positive statements about oneself and to behave accordingly in many situations.[6] Because you will continue to add to your self-esteem and sense of confidence and competence in handling your feelings and relationships as you become more non-defensive, you can expect to use more of your feelings' energy to get the results you want.

Listening—and Hearing—Other People's Meanings

Self-listening is a common listening habit of competitive people. They predict what you're going to say from your first words, nod as if listening to you, then plan their own story as you're talking. When your mouth stops moving, they move in with their own points, taking the focus away from you to themselves. They haven't heard you; they have designed their power plays in the 400 to 500 w.p.m. gap between your speaking rate and their listening rate.[7]

Self-listening is just one of several listening habits that come out of competitiveness and that contribute to defensiveness. In the two lists in Table 6-6, you'll see more of them, as well as with a non-defensive alternative for each one. We've already discussed some of these, and we'll see more of them in action in subsequent examples.

In the first column underline the defensive habits you've learned. In the second column underline the non-defensive habits you frequently use; circle the ones you want to develop.

Notice how the defensive dominance habits shut out other people. When you focus on winning, your attention is usually on your own interests, excluding the interests of others, or on manipulating theirs to serve yours. This harnesses adversary win–lose energy. In some situations you may want to consciously choose this method if you think it will gain the results you

[6]Ibid, pp. 8–12.
[7]I first read the term, *self-listening*, in Warren Farrell, *The Liberated Man, Beyond Masculinity: Freeing Men and Their Relationships with Women*, Random House, New York, 1974, pp. 11–12.

Table 6-6. *Ways of Listening*

Listening and Not *Hearing Others* (*Defensive Dominance*)	*Listening and Hearing Others* (*Non-Defensive Negotiation*)
1. List your rebuttals	1. List others' points
2. Defend your position	2. Hear others' feelings
3. Use logic on others' feelings	3. Name the feelings you hear
4. Challenge others' views	4. Accept others' views
5. Evaluate others by your opinions	5. Disclose your opinions
6. Assume you know what they mean	6. Give and receive feedback
7. Overcome objections	7. Respect differences
8. Push for agreement	8. Respect similarities
9. Strive to win	9. Focus on mutual gain
10. Make your points now to build your track record	10. Build relationships to create mutual benefits over time

want. You might assume that some situations require it. Some people enjoy the challenge, but others resent not being heard and may not play with you.

Shut people out and they shut up. Bring people in and they open up.

Notice how the non-defensive negotiation habits include others; their views and feelings are respected and made part of the process of building longer-term relationships in which you both benefit. This harnesses collaborative, mutually supportive energy, which, when there's trust, increases the odds of gaining results you both want with every exchange.

When people's feelings are aroused, they listen more to themselves than they do to others, which is what happened at the XNG meeting. When these situations occur, ideally the group will be able to discuss both their subjective and objective processes so they can develop options for getting better results the next time they work together. However, this is not likely to happen in the XNG group right now. They have come to a stereotypic conclusion that doesn't lead to studying their people processes as a group; their conclusion is a temporary barrier to performing their task process.

However, as a group member you can consider how to get better results for yourself next time. Part of the Incident Card's potency is the section,

"What I want to be ready to do next time." What you write there is a first try at a statement of results you want, and it reflects feelings you express in the next section, "So I can feel . . ." To get off the defensive, both your actions and feelings require your attention and coordination. When your results-wanted statement includes your relationships with others and your task goals, you are more likely to move ahead in that direction instead of rehashing and evaluating the past.

After the heat of the XNG meeting had cooled, both Marie and Jack took more responsibility for results they could influence, as shown on their Incident Cards (Figure 6-6).

As the days passed, they privately considered their actions and feelings more fully. Jack made his apology; Marie dealt with being taken seriously, defending herself less, exploring guilt feelings, needing options for handling conflict better, fear of being fired, and becoming more of a group member. As she works through these concerns and takes more responsibility for her own actions and feelings, she'll develop more confidence in herself so she's less dependent on others for approval. More of her identity and self-esteem will be in her own hands.

Figure 6-6(a). *Marie's Incident Card number 1.*

Jack's priorities are mostly on family issues; however, as he develops more trust with his children and feels more competent as a father, these experiences may carry over into job issues, as we'll see later.

Learning to Take Risks Safely

We've seen that defensiveness is common in traditional systems because they create higher fear and lower trust climates. People tend to become wary of each other; they are never sure when others will use them or take advantage of them. In some systems, such as in courts, adversary rules define the legal process. Sales and marketing functions are often designed this way to meet market competition; promotions and other rewards are often based on how well people manipulate others. As a result, many people simply assume others cannot be trusted, and they are suspicious when trust is offered.

In such systems you can go along with the prevailing practice—*minimize* your risks by trusting no one and *maximize* your payoffs by using others for your own gain. As we've already seen, this is a good way to become

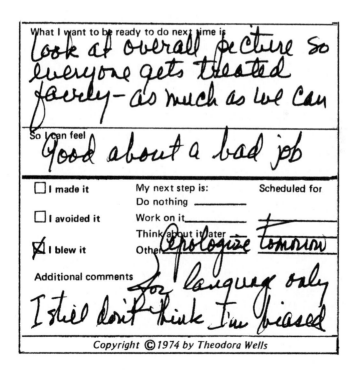

Figure 6-6(b). *Jack's Incident Card number 1.*

one of the walking wounded. It leads to compromising your core values, going beyond making compromises, accommodations, and trade-offs. If the system chews you up and spits you out, your identity is involved. Your core-of-self values, now small, may have to be put back together and reinforced before you can go on.

When you minimize risks and maximize payoffs, you may compromise yourself. When you optimize risks and optimize payoffs, you optimize yourself.

But in such systems you can also be centered in a willingness to trust others and offer trust, always testing the willingness of others to respond in kind. You have to be aware of the tendency for others to use you; that's part of their game. So you have to keep you bases covered, your back and your flanks protected. Once you've taken care of yourself and your position this way, then it's reasonably safe to extend your trust. When you do this, you *optimize* your risks—that is, you take the most risk you can while giving yourself these protections. In this way, you *optimize* your payoffs—for yourself, with others, and for the immediate task at hand as well as for the long-term personal and system goals. Your perspective is toward long-term gain, using daily gains in that direction, building on trust. If the system chews you up and spits you out, you still have your core of self and can go on.

In the XNG scenario, the payoffs for making a layoff list are negative. The only available way to maximize payoffs is to minimize negative reactions to the list. The industrial relations group can do this by being impeccably fair and clear about how they select and apply their criteria. When decisions are implemented non-defensively, all their needs for fair criteria will be satisfied. Then they can deal more openly with concerns of all employees as well as their own because their defensiveness is reduced.

We saw some options that Bob, Jack, or Marie might have used to make some tentative offerings of trust, thereby inviting others also to open up a little. Had Bob legitimized the expression of feelings, Jack might have expressed his concerns about affirmative action consequences more easily. He also seemed concerned that women and minorities would think he'd be the bad guy if support staff were hit hard. Fair criteria would have lent legitimacy to Marie's observation about over-40 women and created a climate of acceptance in which anger arousal would have been less likely.

Feelings would have been treated as facts to consider, even though many feelings might remain undisclosed. When people begin to listen and to *hear* each other, the trust level among them often rises. Even a small increase in trust often produces a large increase in achieving their work goals. A few drops of oil on the wheels of productivity allows them to turn much more freely. This *optimum* result is more likely to occur when people take *optimum* risks instead of the minimum risks we saw played out in the XNG scenario.[8]

Separating Subordinate Identity from Self-Identity

Many people strongly identify with their positions in a hierarchy or with performing roles, which give them recognition and a sense of importance. Sometimes this identification becomes so strong that they begin to think of themselves as *being* the position or role: "I'm Head Honcho," or "I am a manager/supervisor/operator/negotiator/businessman/etc."

The male-role which society expects of men is to acquire such occupational identities. Many men do, particularly when they move into higher-level positions, to signify their competitive ability to achieve financial success and thus to prove their masculine identity. Women may adopt these forms of identification as their work patterns change (it pays well); however, traditional roles have required women to acquire identities in relation to men—wife, mother, secretary to, assistant to—always as subordinates.

Organizational hierarchies structure relationships into dominant and subordinate and value the dominant more. Some people are dominant, everyone is subordinate. Every system has its norms for appropriate behavior and different ones for subordinate behavior. When your position calls for both dominant and subordinate behavior, you may find yourself treading a delicate line between the two in order to maintain your occupational identity.

When you have a strong occupational or relational identity, you usually have exchanged some of your self-identity for it, which leaves you vulnerable to control by people in more dominant positions. When they exert control, you are cast into the subordinate aspect of your position from which you are expected to behave in less valued ways.

Being defined by others gives them control. Defining yourself gives you choices.

As you become more non-defensive, you will be choosing to express more of your unique identity as your own person. You will identify less with

---

[8]The Latin roots for minimum and maximum (*minimus* and *maximus*, least and greatest) refer to *quantity*. The root for optimum (*optimus*, best) refers to *quality*. Competitive people often use maximum to mean optimum: If some's good, more's better. Again this shows that words don't mean; people mean.

either dominant or subordinate positions and roles. Making that transition, however, is easier said than done, especially if you have thought of yourself primarily as subordinate. Habits of deference, of obedience, of giving your power away to authority representatives may be hard to break.

When you are in a subordinate occupational position and dominant people expect you to act subordinate, you may need some ways to keep yourself from slipping into "thinking subordinate." As you move away from that mental stance while still in the physical position, your direction is toward becoming non-subordinate without becoming insubordinate. This is another delicate line but worth treading because it moves your identity away from others' control back into your own control and choice. The long-term payoff is optimal for you. However, if you go too far and become insubordinate, you may get fired.

A separate self is freer to choose.

One way to keep separate from others' control is to have a stock of separator phrases—words you mentally add to the end of judgments and evaluations others make about you. For example, suppose someone tells you, "You expect too much too soon." Mentally add "in your opinion." Consider your own opinion later after you've dealt with any subordinate tendency you have to accept the dominant person's verdict as automatically right.

Separator phrases that help you depersonalize an attack might be, "He's hurting and is striking out. I'm convenient." You may decide later to respond, but momentarily you can distance yourself, listen to his distress, take the distress into consideration as you decide whether or not to respond and how. This kind of separator keeps you from automatically reacting without first thinking how you choose to act. Instead of saying something like, "What are you attacking me for?" which could escalate a bad situation, you might choose to say, "Sounds to me like it's a bad day." As you depersonalize the attack, you also feed back an impersonal response.

Separating the speaker's process from the words can give you invisible protection. It's like observing a verbal tennis game while playing. When you're served a smash, you observe the non-verbal preparation, the manner of serving, the speed and direction of the ball. You don't return the ball; you return a report of the serve. It's naming the game instead of playing it.

The low expectations a dominant person may have for you are more subtle. These are highly communicable but difficult to observe. When you pay conscious attention to the expectations others seem to have for you, you can keep these expectations separate and not allow them to enter your consciousness until you choose whether or not you want to let them in.

We noted some of the assumptions authoritarian managers make about subordinates—all low expectations. If you don't consciously deal with these, you may find yourself reacting to them, turning them into a self-fulfilling prophecy. Here's how low-producing salesmen reacted when their manager treated them as losers:

> Unsuccessful men have great difficulty maintaining their self-image and self-esteem. In response to low managerial expectations, they typically attempt to prevent additional damage to their egos by avoiding situations that might lead to greater failure. They either reduce the number of contacts they make or avoid decisions which might result in further painful rejection, or both. Low expectations and damaged egos lead them to behave in a manner that increases the probability of failure, thereby fulfilling their managers' expectations.[9]

How did these managers communicate low expectations? Livingston found two potent ways:

- Managers are more effective in communicating low expectations than high ones, even though most managers believe exactly the opposite. Low expectations are most often communicated through indifferent or noncommittal (cool) behavior. The way the manager behaves communicates more than the words. (Actions speak louder than words!)
- What managers believe about themselves subtly influences what they believe about their subordinates, what they expect of them, and how they treat them. This is particularly potent in connection with the confidence they feel in their ability to develop the talents of their subordinates.[10]

What if your boss thinks people are no damn good? To protect yourself from reacting to your manager's possible low expectations—to choose to act from your own high expectations—you need to be aware of what your manager really expects. Cool behavior on his or her part may not mean low expectations, even though many subordinates apparently interpret such behavior that way. Develop a sense for what your manager believes about himor herself, especially about his or her abilities as people developers. Keeping

---

[9]Excerpted from J. Sterling Livingston, "Pygmalion in Management," *Harvard Business Review*, July–August 1969, p. 83.

[10]Ibid., pp. 84–85.

these beliefs separate from your own except when they enhance yours can keep you from unconsciously becoming part of a negative self-fulfilling prophecy. A positive one will do a lot of your work for you!

In these examples of ways to separate yourself from dominance, your ear must remain empathic—attuned to the other person's processes and beliefs. Instead of "thinking subordinate," you are giving yourself mental space and time to gather information and to choose your actions instead of reacting. Many more options are discussed in Chapter 8; however, keeping yourself separate as your own person is essential for being non-defensive, whether you're thinking of ways to cope with a short-term incident or developing a long-term direction.

STARTING TO APPLY NON-DEFENSIVE ATTITUDES TO YOURSELF

One way to become non-defensive is to have a wide variety of options. Some of your filters, such as inner rules, may limit today's options and need some updating. The more flexibility you can give your rules, the more options you can have.

When you work with the questions for flexing your rules (Table 6-7), be aware of any rule you have that suggests that being able to flex rules means you must flex them. You may find another rule that says, "If I *can* do it, I *must* do it," or "I have to be consistent." If you come across rules like these, write them down and question them in a similar manner as is shown with these ten rules selected from the list of fifty inner rules in Chapter 5.

These are samples of questions you can use. As you get started, you may find other questions more personal to you, ones that lead to areas you may have been hiding behind a façade. If a question is uncomfortable to answer, that's a hint there may be more. If no answer comes, set the question aside and come back to it later.

You may want to select one of your own rules that you would like to make more flexible from the list in Chapter 5. After asking yourself questions to help flex this rule, experiment with describing how you now use this rule and what happens. Then describe what would be happening when it becomes more flexible. Think of how you can practice making changes where you take little risks.

If you come across an uncomfortable feeling in this process, try giving yourself permission to go into that feeling to discover what it is saying to you. Simply listen to it and let it speak to you. If nothing happens at first, leave your listening attention open and wait for some hunch to come to you. By accepting your inner rules, messages, and energies, you'll gradually find a wealth of inner information and intuition available to you.

Table 6-7. *Ways to Flex Your Rules*

I have to	*Questions to ask yourself (and others you think of)*
Be in control of the situation	What for? Can I allow someone else to control part of it? Who? Can I share control? If I lose control, what is the worst that might happen? Does this situation matter this much to me?
Be loyal	To whom? At what cost or gain to myself, if any? What for? Is it reasonably well returned? Would it be disloyal to act in my own interest if I choose to? Would I be punished for that? Is there a way to be loyal to others and myself at the same time?
Keep peace at any price	Does this kind of peace come at a cost to me but a gain for others? Am I really willing to pay *any* price for it? Does this mean I have to go along with whatever anyone says? What if I question that? What might happen if I stir up a little trouble? Can I try rocking the boat somewhere safe?
Stick to my principles, ethics	Is this a rigid stand that I take at all times? Do I ever call opinions principles when I'm afraid of revealing something? Do I use these as weapons sometimes? Do they help me get centered under pressure? Can any be bent a little if the issue is relatively minor? Can I not state them, still hold them, and feel I've not compromised myself?
Come out on top, win	Every time? What for? Is it always worth the effort? When would it be okay to come out on the bottom? How would that feel? What if the situation calls for joint effort? Can I set aside winning?
Do it by myself	Do I think the only way to get it done right is to do it myself? Who could help me or do it instead? What would happen if I were less independent or more interdependent? Whom can I trust? Is it hard for me to ask for help? If so, what does that say to me? Am I trying to prove something?
Follow orders	All orders? Even those I don't agree with? What about those I don't understand? When can I make an exception? What if this rule conflicts with another one? How do I choose which to follow?
Finish it	When is this important and when not? What if usefulness or timeliness is past? When I don't finish, what holds me back? Have I lost interest or am I procrastinating? What might happen if I do finish? Can I dispose of it and go on to other things?
Keep this job, not get fired	How important is this job to me right now? Can I arrange things so I could quit if I chose to? What would that take so I could put my job on the line? How can I increase income or reduce expenses?
Be liked, accepted	Do I like and accept everyone else? Would respect do just as well? How would I feel if I were rejected by someone I don't like, by someone I do like? Am I avoiding pain? Do I like myself most of the time? Could I like myself more? How?

Ways to Identify Resources and Allies

Many people have inner rules, such as *Do it myself* or *Finish it,* that tend to isolate them from the resources and energies of other people. If you have some loner tendencies, consider these questions:

- Who else might be interested in what I'm doing?
- What resources—information and people—do they have that would help?
- What resources could we offer each other whereby we could both gain—and that would help me in what I'm doing?
- Who is blocking my effort? Is there a way to make that person an ally?
- Who outside of my work group or organization might also be resources? Family, family connections, people in same line of work or professional groups? Friends and their connections? People I know in community organizations? Casual acquaintances whom I could get to know better?

Ways to Use the Incident Cards and Notes to Myself

When you've collected several cards and notes and feel like looking for patterns, here are some suggested approaches.

As you arrange the Incident Cards by situations, you may find some patterns. Perhaps you're using only a few ways of reacting to your incidents. Certain feelings may repeat, such as usually "feel hurt," or "got irritated but didn't say anything." These can suggest to you possible rules that may be getting in you way. Perhaps you react very strongly to one particular kind of situation. You may be carrying around a backlog of old feelings that are getting in your way. Perhaps you react very strongly to one particular kind of

Check for notes on what you think other people should do. Do you have rules for *them*? If so, you may be giving your power away to them instead of focusing on what *you* can do.

Start on a pattern that occurs frequently, leaving the other incidents for another time (or not at all). If you are an analyzer, you may like to start by asking yourself:

- What is the situation and what is it *not*? When does it occur? How serious does it get? (This narrows down your pattern. Check to see if you have a single pattern going, or if two are present.)
- What feelings are barriers? How would I like to feel? How can I get there? (Analytical people are sometimes more comfortable identify-

ing feelings instead of experiencing them. Whatever your approach, consider your own feelings as well as what others may be feeling.)

- What results do I want? What is essential and what is optional to me?
- What options do I have? What would I really like to do or say if I thought I could get away with it? (List options, don't evaluate.)
- What is working for me? What is hindering me? How important are these in getting results I want?

This approach is based on part of the Choosing Process, as you may have noticed. You can add to your information by doing some free floating, which is letting one idea lead to another, even when there is no apparent reason or connection. If you're trying to find out, "Why do I do what I do?" start with "What is it that I do?" (Be sure to focus on what you *do* do, not what you *don't* do.) Then let the connections come. See where it leads. For example, you might discover that one thing you do is to give loyalty until it hurts. That may connect with a rule one of your parents had. Although you want the commitment that loyalty provides, you might look for ways you can commit yourself without hurting yourself.

Another kind of free floating can start with just sitting quietly, asking yourself, "What am I feeling right now?" Or, "Where in my body am I feeling some tension?" Try asking these kinds of questions to yourself, as if there is another self inside you who will answer back. Wait expectantly for the answers to start coming. Whatever comes into your head, write it down, even if it doesn't seem particularly relevant. Trust that it will take its own shape and evolve its own meaning.

This process may lead you to find out some things about yourself before you have a chance to decide whether or not you want to know them! If you discover that you are screening or editing what comes, try to let go of that and allow the flow to continue. You may gain some insights, find new ways of connecting information, see different angles from which to look at repetitious situations.

If you try this and nothing seems to happen, stop trying so hard. Go do something else, try another approach, or just forget it for a while. Come back to it only when you feel anticipation, excitement, or turned on to trying it again. It's more likely to happen when you expect and want it to.

IN THE NEXT CHAPTER

Next we explore some ways to use both sides of the brain. Most of us have learned to emphasize intellectual development at the expense of our expressive, creative capacities. Analytical thinking tends to be favored over imagery, which uses all the senses, and sometimes adds the sixth, intuitive sense. The more we can call forth images, the faster we can make associations and connections, thinking in flashes instead of words per minute. You can also redirect your energy to focus on results you want, setting a positive self-fulfilling prophecy in motion.

You might be able to become somewhat non-defensive if you used only analytical, non-evaluative logic. However, it comes more quickly, with many more options, and with more delight when you gain access to the pictures of your mind or pictures you plant in its fertile soil. So let's play a little.

READINGS

Bebermeyer, Ruth: *. . . And Master of None*, Ruth Bebermeyer, 218 Monclay St., St. Louis, Mo., 63122, 1976. (Order directly. Not sold in stores.) Short poems, mostly four-liners, that succinctly go to the core of humanistic, non-defensive ways of being yourself. A short, short course in non-defensive communication.

Cole, Jim: *The Façade: A View of Our Behavior*, cartoons illustrated by Tom Woodruff, distributed by Ed and Janet Reynolds, Mill Valley, Calif. 94940, 1970. A collection of drawings and captions that show the processes of acquiring façades, fears of dropping them, and how taking the risk of dropping your own leads to others doing the same. A clear simple portrayal of the complex process toward growth away from hiding.

Cole, Jim: *The Controllers: A View of Our Responsibility*, cartoons illustrated by Tom Woodruff, Shields Publishing, Ft. Collins, Colo., 1971. More drawings and captions show how we learn to be controlled, not taking responsibiltiy for our own behavior, how we try to get others to control (and take responsibility) for what we do, and how to let go of controllers so we can grow and choose.

Cole, Jim: *The Helpers: A View of Our Helpfulness*, cartoons illustrated by Tom Woodruff, Shields Publishing, Fort Collins, Colo., 1973. Helpfulness can be another way of controlling others or arranging to be dependent on others, shifting some responsibililty for yourself. These drawings and captions spell out how this works and show how the idea that "sometimes no help is the most help" can lead to growth. It also includes the value of helping that is not manipulating.

Rosenberg, Marshall B.: *From Now on: Without Blame and Punishment*, Community Psychological Consultants, 1740 Gulf Dr., St. Louis, Mo., 63130, 1977. (Order directly. Not sold in stores.) A deeply perceptive book, gently written, to help be in touch with your feelings as a means of becoming more capable of intimacy and personal effectiveness.

For additional background reading, see bibliography entries 5, 6, 7, 9, 12, 16, 17, 18, 20, 29, 67, 72, 73, 74, 78.

7

VISUALIZING INVISIBLE PROCESSES

Using More of Your Capacities for Gaining More Results

Do you ever think to yourself:

- I can see it in my mind's eye.
- The deal smells bad to me.
- Can't you just hear the reaction when this news breaks!
- How can such a smooth person be so abrasive at times?
- I don't like the flavor of that report.
- I can't tell you why, but I'm buying this stock. It's going up.

Sound familiar? We're using all our senses, all six of them—seeing, hearing, smelling, tasting, touching, and *hunching*—much of the time. When we do, we are also using both sides of the brain, the functions of which researchers generally describe as the verbal, logical, defining, analytical left side, and the picturing, creative, sensing, global right side. Much is yet to be learned about how the brain works, but if we use these descriptions, we can say that most of us have been schooled to emphasize the logical left brain functions. Most of us have also learned to discount or ignore the value of the imagination, sensing, perceptiveness attributed to the right brain, which seems to use illogical or archaic languages that are more symbolic than the literal, yet are also both, like dream symbolism.

We're also taught to believe that intellectual development, not emotional development, is central to proper growth. Until the recent popularity of jogging and running, postadolescent physical development was also placed lower in priority. Consequently, many people have learned a basic mind-body-energy split, which sorely limits their creativity and convinces them to shut down their imagination. This is one of the prices of conformity that helps maintain the status quo.

Becoming non-defensive requires breaking dysfunctional habits such as these, and choosing more ways of becoming your own person. We need more access to visualizing and experiencing what we want before it appears in actuality. Thought precedes action. In this chapter we're talking about working with our thoughts—states of mind or energy—that come before the actions that can get more of the results you want. We'll be doing *more valuing* and *less evaluating, judging,* and *comparing* against standards or against other people. Most of the examples that follow are ways you can expand your ability to visualize, but they do not show ways to expand your other senses because we're limited to the printed page here. However you can add ways of sensing, smelling, touching, tasting, and hunching to make the visualized processes more real.

First, we'll see some of the characteristics of our more familiar intellectual, logical, linear, left-brain thinking and compare it with the less familiar creative, multiple-image, multiple-sensory, symbolic right-brain thinking. Then we'll experiment with visual fantasizing as a way of developing more ways to handle yourself in relation to other people and for changing some inner pictures of yourself. These may stimulate other visual processes of your own with which to experiment.

After seeing these action examples, we'll consider how a different blend of capabilities can help solve problems and increase options.

LINEAR LEFT-BRAIN THINKING COMPARED WITH GLOBAL RIGHT-BRAIN THINKING

As we've seen, both sides of the brain operate as a unit without conscious effort. As we go about our normal lives, the two sides are inseparable. For convenience of discussion, however, let's compare each side's contributions to different kinds of thinking. Edward de Bono's comparison is quite useful for describing the processes of linear and global thinking, which he calls vertical and lateral thinking. Some of their characteristics are shown in Table 7-1.[1]

Vertical thinking is a narrowing process, sorting and evaluating to come down to the best solution. It intentionally limits options and is most useful for *solving* problems that deal with mechanical situations, such as locating the cause of backlogged work. On the other hand, lateral thinking is

---

[1]Data from pp. 39–45 in *Lateral Thinking: Creativity Step by Step* by Edward de Bono. Copyright © 1970 by Edward de Bono. By permission of Harper & Row, Publishers, Inc.

Table 7-1. *Characteristics of Thinking.*

Vertical, Linear Thinking	Lateral, Global Thinking
Selective	Generative
Moves only if there is a direction in which to move	Moves in order to generate a direction in which to move
Analytical	Provocative
Sequential	Can make jumps
One must be correct at every step	One doesn't have to be correct at every step
Uses the negative in order to block off certain pathways	There is no negative. The positive is used to open new pathways
One concentrates and excludes what is irrelevant	One welcomes chance intrusions—the apparent irrelevancies
Categories, classifications, and labels are fixed	Categories, classifications, and labels are not fixed
Follow the most likely paths	Follow the least likely paths
Is a finite process	Is a probabalistic process
One uses information for its own sake in order to move forward to a solution	One uses information *not* for its own sake, but provocatively in order to bring about repatterning

more exploratory and global, circling 360° at once, looking for probabilities and options. It's more useful for problems about *resolving* tensions between people with conflicting interests and sometimes for *dissolving* dilemmas. Results are more likely to be flexible checks and balances rather than one final answer.

You'll need both vertical and lateral thinking for the Choosing Process

Both types of thinking are necessary and valuable, and both sides of the brain are used in the Choosing Process. The lateral thinking is more valuable for sensing feelings and attitudes, for imagining results you want and what these results might accomplish, and for generating ways of attaining those results. On the other hand, vertical thinking is more useful for gathering and analyzing data about the objective content of a problem, for evaluating the risks associated with each option, for making choices, and for deciding on what actions to take.

When some problems are to be solved, others resolved, and some dissolved, we need both the looping, overlapping, imagining, and exploring of lateral thinking as well as the logical, rational, selective, definitive, and solution-mindedness of vertical thinking. Later, we'll discuss how to match thinking modes to kinds of problems.

SOME DIFFERENT WAYS OF IMAGINING YOURSELF

Let's play a little. Imagine action pictures of ideas, concepts, and ways of thinking. Play with feelings and different perspectives; play with different angles of looking at the same thing. Experiment with allowing yourself to play, to suspend your evaluations until after you've had the experience. Play can produce puns, paradoxes, and moving montages that convey symbolic information.

Imagine that when you feel defensive, you feel exposed to threats and would like to have some protection you can control. My picture is of you standing in open space, vulnerable to whatever comes your way from other people—barbs and jabs, shifted responsibilities and buck-passing; some compliments and rewards; some unknowns that keep you guessing; and some uncomfortable feedback that you know you need but don't want to look at. I see it all coming toward you, unsorted and swirling around you.

In one scene, I see you crouching, trying to protect yourself by wrapping your arms around yourself and ducking your head. Somehow the storm seems heavier and soon you're going to be buried in it. Shifting to a second scene, I see you standing tall, facing the storm with an energy that seems to thin it out, as if you're surrounded by an invisible wall of power that disperses the storm, but that picture flickers on and off, as if you can't maintain that energy output for very long at one time. So we decide to build you a personal space bubble that gives you control over what comes your way.

Your Personal Space Bubble Comes with Control Screens

Our culture gives you rights to personal space of about an arm's length all around you, so we'll use that for the general size of your bubble. When you are in a subordinate role, you have less right to this space than people higher up do, but we're going to build the bubble as if everyone has total control over the same amount of personal space.

Picture your bubble as a bell made of a clear, impermeable substance with a midsection of screens you can control from inside, as shown in Figure 7-1. (What's it made of? Choose what suits you—plastic, electricity, glass, invisible energy.)

The screens are in layers that instantly respond to the control selector levers (a), so you can create screens of varying sizes of mesh to allow different amounts of input from outside to enter the space. The screens have numbered settings that let you choose what enters your space. You can design your own, which might be like this:

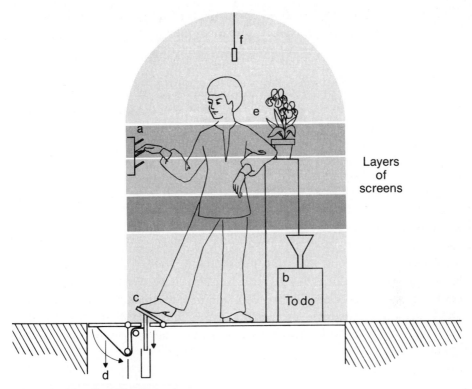

Layers
of
screens

To do

Legend: (a). Control selector levers
(b). Storage box: things to do on good days
(c). Pedal to drop outer pile
(d). To bottomless pit
(e). Flowers and people grow in safe places
(f). Pull cord to burst bubble (one pull) or create bubble (two pulls)

Figure 7-1. Your personal space bubble with control screens.

1. Let it all in (for sunny days when all is well at work, or when you are in the midst of a storm and a ray of sunshine flickers through, you can let it in).

2. Let in most of what's out there (for decent weather days when you also want to be able to shut out occasional clouds from gloomy people).

3. Let in only those energies that feel good, as when people express caring or give compliments.

4. Let in that constructive criticism you don't want to hear right now but you know you need to pay attention to. You take it in but will decide to look at it in your own time. This setting has a connection to a special chute that funnels these hard nuts into the to-do box (b), giving you responsible delay.

5. Let in very little, barely keeping contact and withdrawing into the safety of your bubble (for when it's dangerously stormy out there).

6. Let in nothing, closing off all contact and isolating yourself (not recommended, but an option to reserve for rare emergencies when the lightning of the electrical storm outside may split you in two unless you hide inside).[2]

On good days when you feel chipper and on top of the world, you may leave the screens quite wide open, sorting out the usual stuff of blame games, accusations, shifted responsibilities, energy drainers, put-downs, and other foul plays. As you see these coming toward you, you automatically adjust the controls to let these drop to the ground outside. When the droppings pile up, you just press pedal (c) to drop them into the bottomless pit (d).

Your bubble is a safe place of your own creation that you control. You have to value yourself enough to give yourself such a place in which to function and grow (e). At times you may feel it closes you in too much and limits your range of speed and action, such as when your energy is so powerful that no electrical storms can get near you. Even though the bubble is highly mobile, at these times you may want to move without it. Simply pull cord (f) to burst the bubble. When you want it back again, just give two pulls and it instantly reappears. Or you can invent your own model that protects your backside and flanks, leaving the front part open for more face-to-face contact.

As you fix the problem, you won't need to fix the blame.

One feature of this picture deserves consideration: you're at the controls and you choose what to let in. No longer can you legitimately blame other people when they do what you don't want them to. For example, if your manager has low expectations for you, if you don't let those low expectations into your personal space, they can't get to you. As you gain control over yourself, you lose the option of blaming others.

Perhaps this device seems elaborate. It takes longer to describe than to visualize (a picture is worth a thousand words). Once you can see it, you can recall and redesign it in an instant so you can see what's coming and choose what to let in. It's no more elaborate than hiding behind a façade or feeling caged up in an organizational zoo.

One person's image was driving a carnival electric car, covering it with an energy bubble and lining it with transparent bumper cushions to absorb

[2]The weather analogy for describing a system's climate has been well developed by Fritz Steele and Stephen Jenks, *The Feel of the Work Place: Understanding and Improving Organization Climate,* Addison-Wesley, Reading, Mass., 1977.

the shocks of hitting and being hit by other cars. Design your own picture to fit your needs. Whatever gives you control, protection, and mobility makes a good visual as long as you also have a way of stepping out of it when you want. The more playful you can make it, the more fun you'll have, which is likely to keep you more relaxed with your sense of humor available.

Distancing Changes Your Perspective on Authority

Physical distance can move you out of a danger zone. Emotional distance can also give you safety. Visualize the organization chart of your system.[3] Imagine yourself sitting in the box assigned to you on the organization chart. As you sit there, look at all the boxes above you; each one becomes bigger at each successive level, just as do the offices and the images of their occupants. Sitting underneath all those boxes, you begin to feel smaller and smaller, almost smothered by the sheer size and weight of the hierarchy bearing down on you. There are fewer boxes above you, but the higher ones increase in size, and they acquire more position power over you.[4]

Now imagine yourself stepping out of your box and facing a man who occupies a higher, bigger box: Put both of you on ground level. To look at the man of the bigger box, you have to look up rather steeply, like the 45° shown in Figure 7-2 (a). Now give yourself some emotional distance. When you move away you decrease the angle of elevation to 15° so you don't have to crane your neck to make eye contact with him (b). Sense how that feels to you—in your body, in your mental and emotional stance in relation to him, and in how you feel about yourself. Hear, smell, savor, intuit the difference.

You might go one step further and take the authority person out of the box. Perhaps you imagine that you are bigger than your own box, that you are a person with potential who will eventually be recognized in the organization. Imagine, too, that the person in the bigger box may not be as big as his box, that he's a person who has greater access to position power than you have. Then your perspective may be an eye-to-eye one, with a person-to-person perspective on your organizational positions (c). Experiment with these images and sense their effect on you.

Notice that these images are made inside yourself as ways to release yourself from limiting images and thoughts you may have learned. They are

---

[3]In many organizations this chart is not widely circulated because it shows only formal relationships that are usually out of date. Although the chart does not show how the system really works, it does show who has authority over whom, which is the perspective we're looking at.

[4]If your position isn't shown on the chart or if it's connected by broken lines to indicate your lack of formal power in the system, draw in a box for yourself using solid connectors so you have a base of operations.

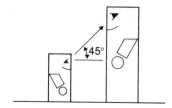

a. Up close you have to look up at a steeper angle...

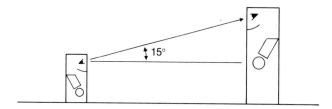

b. than the angle of elevation when you are further apart. Emotional distance changes your perspective. The position box is not the person.

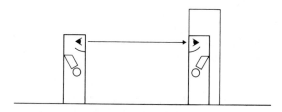

c. Stepping out of the boxes and seeing the person out of the box gives yet another perspective.

Figure 7-2. Changing your perspective of authority.

not yet a basis for external action for relating to authority. To take such action requires a decision that must include *consideration* of the norms and expectations existing around you. You may or may not follow them. However, when you are freer within yourself to make choices, instead of being *controlled* by others' expectations, you'll feel less defensive. You can give yourself a larger personal space bubble within which to operate, which reduces the pressure from above and increases your internal space for visualizing and making choices.

Seeing the World from Another Perspective

Now let's experiment with another analogy. This time you will do more imagining with less explanation from me. While playing with this picture, see if you can sense the general, global feel and pick up only the details that accent this larger picture.

Imagine that you have just been promoted to supervisor of a group in which you were formerly a member. You now supervise people who were your peers and with whom you shared social and work confidences. All of a sudden, your perspective has changed; you're in strange territory. Experiment by drawing a picture of the old and the new departmental relationships. See yourself climbing up the ladder to the bigger box above the others. Sense how it feels to be in the upper box compared with being in the lower one. Visualize and sense this experience in full detail. Embellish it and embody it, making it an indelible image on your mind.

Capture one picture in your mind, superimpose another experience, and notice how links seem to appear.

Now read and feel the following experience without predicting or evaluating what might happen. Simply fantasize and superimpose these images over your promotion experience, allowing links to form in your own imagination.

Changing position on the earth's surface carries a whole range of implications and consequences, particularly if the change is from one continent and language to another; it is not the disturbance of different constellations in the night sky or the curious new flora and fauna so much as a reapportioning of the whole world. The center from which one sees is here, and everything becomes relative to that here. At first, one searches, out of anxiety, for similarities—for houses, places to eat, human contacts—but that does not conceal for long the differences and strangenesses, the relative alteration of everything. From the house I occupy in Costa Rica, I look out on a giant rubber tree, recognizable as the ancestor of valiant offspring I have seen surviving dustily in New York apartments. It sheds leaves so huge and firm that they might be used as serving dishes. The insects seem big enough to be taken in as domestic pets, and I have to begin again to give names, as Adam did, to the natural world. That change is manageable; the more difficult one is that of having to see the world from a change so different that the world itself is a different one. Some people resist this change and unpack a world they have brought with them, as the occasional English-language newspapers throughout Latin America attest; but that misses the point of change, which is to see from a deflected angle, with a different focus, what has been familiar and habitual.[5]

[5]From "Notes from Latin America," by Alastiar Reid in the February 6, 1978 *New Yorker*. Reprinted by permission; © 1978 The New Yorker Magazine, Inc.

Experiment with imagination: superimpose this experience on your promotion experience. What links, analogies, parallels, paradoxes do you see? Now relax your reasoning mind. Close your eyes and let the images roam around just under your eyelids. You may see some moving shapes, some detailed pictures, some symbolic images. They may be in color or in black and white. Perhaps a word or two comes to mind that may not seem immediately relevant. Pay attention to whiffs of fragrances or odors that your nose uses for making analogies; notice any tingling or tensions in your face or body; notice any changes in your breathing or body temperature.

Put all your attention on what is happening; observe only, don't speculate or evaluate. (If nothing is happening, notice that, too. You may be working too hard to make something happen. You may be analyzing or wondering what it means. If so, that's similar to evaluating, which usually stops the flow of image formation.)

When no more image flow is coming, stop the experiment and consider what links you made between the two experiences and other personal experiences, sensations, or emotions that may have surfaced within you. Listen to these, recall any whiffs of smells that stimulated memories of past scenes, bring into focus body sensations that were aroused, and let these sensation messages feed information into your awareness. These are legitimate data to help you deal with your new supervisory situation.

Not only is image sensing a rich source of information, it can be a way to greatly increase the speed of your thinking. According to Jean Houston, psychologist and director of the Foundation for Mind Research:

> Much research indicates that thinking need not be limited by the slow pace of our physiological being or by the linear inhibitions of our verbal thought. When we examine high-level creativity, we note that the mind races over many alternatives, picking, choosing, discarding, synthesizing, sometimes doing the work of several months in a few minutes. . . . [T]here is much evidence to suggest that by thinking in images, solutions can be found and ideas expressed that are not possible when thinking is purely verbal. . . . Margaret Mead, an exacting scientist . . . by the use of vivid daydreams . . . explores alternative scenarios of problems and programs. She might begin by thinking, "If this should happen, what would follow?" She then sits back and watches the images and story unfold in her head. . . . Visualizing is apparently a creative process that tends to gather meanings and seek out solutions. When images are observed long enough, they cease to be random or disconnected and organize themselves into symbolic dramas, narratives, or problem-solving stories.[6]

> Her memory files are kept as current and available as her office files. . . . There is a constant reinforcement between the objective files and her

[6]Jean Houston, "The Mind of Margaret Mead: How She Democratizes Greatness," *Quest/77*, July–August 1977, pp. 26–27.

interior memories. In her mind's eye (and ear and nose and mouth and skin) she can walk around in a memory of 1907 just as vividly as she can in a memory of 1937 or 1977 . . . probably because much in her memory is tied to sensory images and bodily feelings.[7]

As images joined images, themes and words emerged and apparently made links from her experiences that selected themselves into a focus that served her purposes for the day. The speed with which she could make these connections was so rapid that some people have questioned how thorough she was. Her experience of thinking in and linking images was apparently much faster and richer in detail than our usual linear, verbal memory recall.

Belief opens the door to imaging your sensing resources.

Visualizing multiple images and developing the ability to see, sense, fantasize, and link these images is probably within the general potential of most people. However, to be able to give yourself permission to experiment with using it, it is necessary to believe in the possibility and to value it. The energy of *belief* seems to be vital to developing and valuing these sensing experiences and languages, for making these unusual connections and relationships from past experiences, for projecting probable scenarios to see effects of several possible courses of action, or for quickly generating many instantly available options when you need them.

Material from your subconscious may come through as you need it simply by your requesting it. Some people have learned to draw similar material from their dreams, receiving unexpected answers to questions they have asked into their deeper layers of consciousness.[8]

If your have barriers, ask to see them, own them, and then dismantle those you no longer need.

Some of you will already have more experience than others with this multiple or symbolic imagery. If you have doubts about it but are willing to experiment, close your eyes and ask into your consciousness for some visual sensings of your barriers and what they're made of. Don't require literal

---

[7]Ibid., p. 76.
[8]For additional information see bibliography entries 38, 46, and 49.

pictures; sensing may appear more as thoughts that remind you of something or a sense of following a memory. For example, when you ask for information about barriers, you may sense or see a two-foot thick adobe wall around a California mission, maybe a louvred redwood fence around a house you once lived in, perhaps strings of beads hanging in a doorway that you saw while traveling abroad. Or perhaps it's a parent.

Each of these can symbolize various thicknesses, densities, or textures of barriers, which may suggest how powerful or porous your personal inhibitors may be or may suggest where, when, or with whom your barrier arose. Symbols and associations tend to be highly personal so, for you, they may have other meanings. Even universal symbols seem to be influenced by your personal experience. See how your barriers have been useful to you and how new ways of thinking about yourself can make the barriers unnecessary. Notice, too, that each person who thinks about barriers has a unique experience. My reality is different from your reality because it's personal. Both are valid. We each live in our separate realities.

Now that you have experimented with some trips into your inner space and experimented with simply *valuing* your images rather than *evaluating* them, you may now be asking, "So what?" or "What's it good for?" To answer that question, let's consider the nature of problems. Then it will come clearer how using both reason *and* sensing can help deal with many, if not most, of life's problems.

USING BOTH REASON AND SENSING TO WORK WITH PROBLEMS

Most people assume that problems are basically alike and can be solved in basically similar ways. When a problem doesn't stay solved, we tend to use the same methods more energetically. We tend to see the problem as the problem, without considering that the *method* we are using may not match the problem. To consider this, we would have to consider that problems may not all be similar.

The predominant method we have for solving problems is mechanistic and is ideally suited for mechanical problems. However, many problems involve people, and we are not as mechanistic as some would wish. For example, we can analyze the volume of work flowing through a department and locate where too few resources are available to process it, thus locating the cause of a bottleneck. If the work is automated, the solution may be to add machine capacity.

If the work is processed by people, more people may not be the solution. Conflicting interests and motives may have to be resolved. Human conflict does not respond well to a mechanistic approach but usually requires a more organic, sensing, intuitive approach that allows for competing motives and provides a more dynamic balance among competing tensions and interests.

The mechanistic method relies more on the advantages of logical, reasoning processes; the organic method relies more on the sensing, intuitive processes that can influence and mediate reason and logic.

First, let's look at these two types of problems and how to recognize them. We'll look at the two different methods for working with each kind of problem, matching method to problem. Then, we'll see what happens when there's a mismatch between the nature of the problem and the method used to work with it.

Two Types of Problems

Let's think of a problem as consisting of two thrusts of energy. One thrust is the status quo or the present conditions—what *is;* the other thrust is the new desired condition—what *should be* or what *could be*. These energy thrusts can represent a condition that exists in things, within yourself, or between two people. Of course, there can be more than two such thrusts, but for clarity we'll limit them to two.

A convergent problem is one in which these two energy thrusts come together, converging on the same point. For example, if the department mentioned above were automated, you would analyze what is causing the bottleneck and compare this with how work should be flowing through the system. The more you work with it, the more the cause and the answer move toward a single solution—add machine capacity. Figure 7-3(a) shows this process. The more you work with it, the more it can be reduced to a single goal and a set of instructions until it is solved—a static condition.

A divergent problem is one in which the more you work with it, the more the two energy thrusts move apart. For example, if the bottleneck occurs where people process the work, the more you work with the problem, the more you may find passive resistance, absenteeism, or even sabotage. As you trace the data back to when the bottleneck started to appear, you may find a change in company pay policy or a change of supervisor. Conflicts or tensions between employees and authorities may diverge more widely as opposing or competing interests intensify. Figure 7-3(b) shows this dynamic. The tendency toward divergence occurs whenever there are opposing forces, such as a thrust for individual freedom of choice opposed by a thrust for obedience to authority—a dynamic condition.[9]

[9]These concepts of convergent and divergent problems are based on the philosophical analysis of E. F. Schumacher, *A Guide for the Perplexed,* Harper & Row, New York, 1977, pp. 120–136. (Dilemmas, Catch-22s and double-binds are my own additions to his definition of divergent problems.)

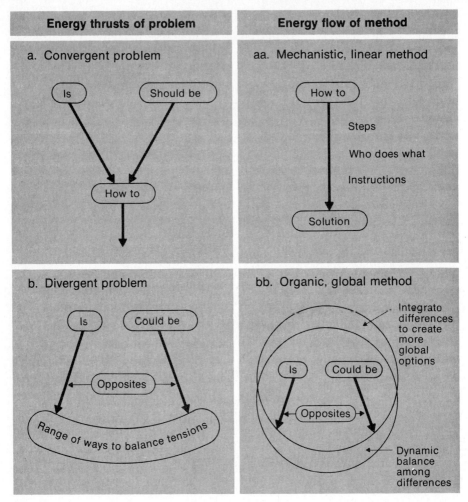

Figure 7-3. *Matching problems and methods.*

To diverge is to discover dichotomies. The more you work with this type of problem, the stronger the opposing forces become until you seem to be dealing with opposites. The energy thrusts move away from each other when forces push them apart. They can also collide head-on when the opposing forces rush toward each other, as on a collision course when an irresistible force meets an immovable object. Opposing forces may also cross each other, as in situations where you're hung if you do and hung if you don't, where you lose no matter what you do. Unless you have ways of handling divergent problems, you're likely to feel inadequate and thus defensive.

Let's consider a few examples of convergent and divergent problems. Dave Eliot, whom we left at Country Stores (in Chapter 4), has to deal with both types of problems. The convergent problems he deals with involve installing scanners to translate the universal product codes on the merchandise. These are mechanical, technical problems that can be reduced to steps, alternatives, clearly measurable results, ways of analyzing how and where errors occur, and what steps must be taken to reduce the error rate. The more he works with these problems, the more he can reduce the "bugs" until he has a relatively problem-free operation. If problems recur, an analytical, linear, logical thinking approach—vertical thinking—is usually appropriate and workable. Mechanical problems can be solved in this manner, as shown in Figure 7-3(aa).

Between yourself and the system or between yourself and authority people, interests often diverge, creating divergent problems.

The larger, more consuming problems that Dave faces are divergent ones, problems that involve opposing forces, such as his own independence versus the conformity expected by the store founders, Tom Hudson and Jack Willitt, and his manager, Pete Gross. Other opposing forces include his own desire for participative teamwork with his crew versus authoritarian direction the executives expect, and his desire to bend rules for his responsible supervisors versus the executives' expectation that he prove himself by following rules. These are versions of the underlying opposites of *freedom versus order* and *growth versus decay* that Schumacher shows are encountered wherever there is life, consciousness, and self-awareness and that create the divergent energy thrusts.

Dave's divergent problems also create a dilemma for him. If he continues to create a friendly, productive climate of teamwork, he'll lose the blessings of the executives. If he becomes more authoritarian, which his supervisors apparently want, he'll probably lose the support of his subordinates. Either way, he loses. If he uses the mechanistic, linear method of solving problems applicable to his technical, convergent problems, he's certain to lose and become defensive. He needs a more organic, flexible method that helps balance these opposing tensions or transcend them, such as drawing the circle bigger, as shown in Figure 7-3(bb). Then he can stay nondefensive. We'll see how he develops such an approach in Chapter 11.

Before describing this method more fully, let's consider what we mean when we say a problem is solved.

When Is a Problem Solved?

One way to know you've solved a problem—the more usual one—is to decide that *when a problem is solved, the present undesirable condition has ceased to exist.* You've gotten rid of the problem; it's dead.

This way of defining when a problem is solved clearly applies only to inanimate objects and processes, not to people. With our technological genius, we know how (or can figure out how) to manipulate objects, machines, mechanical processes, and money so that any undesirable conditions that pose problems can be made to go away and cease to exist. The moment people enter the picture, this definition is not useful. People don't cease to exist—unless you use the "final solution" and kill them all off! By this definition, to solve a problem is to kill it.[10]

Another way is to decide that *when a problem is solved, an undesirable condition has become more desirable for everyone involved.* The problem is not solved but resolved (or dissolved) for the time being. It doesn't go away and die.

This can happen in two ways: a new dynamic balance can be developed between the opposing tensions, or these tensions can be traced back to differing results people wanted, then integrating these goals in creative options that serve all interests. Both are shown in Figure 7-3(bb) as different aspects of placing the conflict in a larger context, more like a spherical, electromagnetic energy field. The area of the circle in now bigger than the conflict area.

When finding a dynamic balance between tensions, the resolution between opposites can be accomplished through an ongoing negotiation:

> Our logical mind does not like (opposites): it generally operates on the either/or or yes/no principle, like a computer. . . . [T]he mind may suddenly change sides, often without even noticing it. It swings like a pendulum from one opposite to the other, and each time there is a feeling of "making up one's mind afresh."[11]

This fluctuating, balancing renegotiation between opposing forces may be the most that Dave Eliot can expect to achieve from his subordinate position at Country Stores. The more he works with balancing the tensions between himself and the executives, the more he may find that these divergent problems "provoke, stimulate, and sharpen the higher human faculties, without which man is nothing but a clever animal."[12]

> Divergent problems . . . cannot be solved in the sense of establishing a "correct formula"; they can, however, be transcended. A pair of opposites . . . cease

[10]Ibid., p. 127.
[11]Ibid., p. 127.
[12]Ibid., p. 128.

to be opposites at the higher level, the really *human* level, where . . . higher forces as love and compassion, understanding and empathy, become available, not simply as occasional impulses (which they are at the lower level) but as a regular and reliable resource. [For example], justice is a denial of mercy, and mercy is a denial of justice. Only a higher force can reconcile these opposites: wisdom.[13]

Dave may develop considerable wisdom in reconciling his views in some kind of ongoing dynamic balance, but it will also take wisdom on the part of the executives to complete the larger circle that transcends—and dissolves—the divergent problem they share. Such problems arise because of human, not mechanical, concerns. We are always grappling with human needs for stability *and* change, for tradition *and* innovation, for order *and* freedom. Dynamic balances respect and allow for these differences. These are life's problems.

Logic doesn't help us because it insists that if a thing is true, its opposite cannot also be true at the same time. It also insists that if a thing is good, more of it will be better.[14] Life is larger than logic; therefore, we need methods larger than logic. Learning to live with ongoing dynamic balances between opposing forces is one way. Moving to a higher order of human experience is another.

The present norms of most traditional organizations probably do not allow room for more than renegotiating ongoing, dynamic balances. When we develop Dave Eliot's short- and long-term plans for handling his divergent problems at Country Stores, we'll see how this happens.

What Happens When Linear Thinking Is Applied to Divergent Problems?

When we place emphasis on linear thinking, we are likely to see all problems as convergent and treat them as if they were. Consider these questions about problems you've had:

- Do you have problems that you thought you had solved once and for all only to discover they keep coming back?
- Have you gotten exasperated with people who don't do what they're supposed to do and who continually create more problems?
- Do you sometimes feel that no matter what you do, there's not much you can do to solve certain problems?

[13]Ibid., pp. 126, 127.
[14]Ibid., p. 123.

If you answered yes to one or more of these questions, is it because you have seen these problems as convergent when they were actually divergent? Test this question on examples of your own.

Consider these three common ways that many people approach problems:

- Some ask a question, such as "What do you do when (describing some problem that often arises)?" They go looking for an answer, for something that works, often without considering further consequences of the action they seek. Their answer is evaluated on how well it works to get rid of the problem. What often happens is that the action causes new problems to crop up that need solutions that create more problems, and so on ad infinitum.

- Another approach many people use is to look for the one best way to solve a problem. They search for the formula that can be applied to all problems that look alike. The "right" formula is based on our dualistic, either-or, yes-no thinking—right-wrong, good-bad—without asking what the formula is right *for*. This approach ignores the question: "If a thing is said to be good but no one can tell me what it is good *for*, how can I be expected to take any interest in it?"[15]

  Pat answers are the usual result of this approach, such as "There's the right way, the wrong way, and our way," or "We've always done it that way." The answer is evaluated on the use of precedents. The problem may not go away, but it was handled in the so-called right way! The usual result is that the same old problems come back to roost and the same old ways of handling them are used even more vigorously, and so on ad infinitum.

- Another common approach is to use the more thorough, intellectual problem-solving methods that are widely taught in schools and organizations: analyze and define the problem, find alternative solutions, select the best one, implement it, and evaluate results. When a problem's causes, not just its symptoms, are analyzed thoroughly this method is well suited for certain kinds of problems: those that have arisen because of some undesired change in the mechanical sequences of the tasks being done or in the quality of materials being used.[16]

---

[15]Ibid., p. 132

[16]This basic method is well formulated by Charles H. Kepner and Benjamin B. Tregoe in *The Rational Manager: A Systematic Approach to Problem Solving and Decision Making,* McGraw-Hill, New York, 1965.

It doesn't do as well when the human element enters in. People don't behave like machines and don't want to be treated like one. To cope with this human failing, linear thinkers often become even more logical, having learned, "Deal only with ideas that are distinct, precise, and certain beyond any reasonable doubt; therefore, rely on . . . measurement and exact observation . . . [I]f only we abandon all sentiment and other irrationalities, all problems can and will be solved."[17]

Your eyes see what they are trained to see.

These problems remain unsolved or continue to occur because they are divergent problems being handled as convergent. People trained to think linearly, logically, and mechanistically are likely to see problems the same way—as convergent. Such people think in lines, boxes, and compartments and tend to approach problems by separating them into their component parts. They fix the parts, often looking for the key to the problem, as if it's a pyramid with a secret building block that will unlock its secrets.

This way of seeing is also consistent with competitive thinking. Expecting the world to be a win–lose game, logical thinkers often handle opposite in an either-or way: either you win or you lose. There is no other way; that's life. Problems and people are evaluated in this context. An ongoing dynamic balance, if it's thought of at all, may not be thought valuable enough to consider.

You are likely to get some undesired results when you use a method that doesn't match the problem. Figure 7-4(a) shows what happens when you apply the mechanistic, linear method (Figure 7-3aa) to a divergent problem (Figure 7-3b). When one energy thrust is made rigid, the solution stops the pendulum swing between opposing tensions. These tensions build up, adding to the accumulating momentum of the other energy thrust, which will strike back harder on its next swing. This occurred in the problems described above that didn't stay solved.

Even those problems that seem solved may not stay solved. Think back to Don Mitchell's grandstand play at the Adler, Benson, and Cutler presentation to their client, Bart Holman, where Don outshone senior partner, Ben Adler. As long as Dan can pull off these coups, he'll probably have Ben's admiration, even if Ben gives it grudgingly. Let him miss one and Ben's dormant, accumulating energy thrust may come out swinging and hit Don right out onto the street.

[17]Schumacher, *A Guide for the Perplexed*, p. 120.

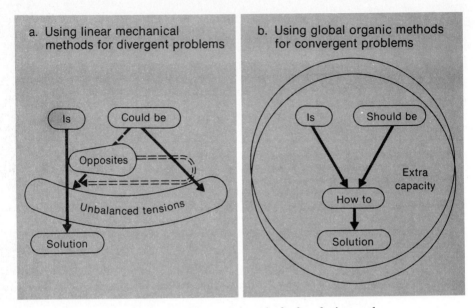

Figure 7-4. Problems and methods that don't match.

What Happens When Global Thinking Is Applied to Convergent Problems?

If you were to use only your intuitive, sensing skills, you might miss the obvious linear, convergent solution. Because of the intense intellectual emphasis in our education, there's not much danger of this occurring. However, many apparently convergent problems may include human aspects that are often ignored.

For example, in Dave Eliot's installation of the UPC scanners, there could be "bugs" because people weren't well trained or because employees are resisting the change and passively resisting his efforts. If he sees in a more global way when looking at his problems, he might find more than one problem, some convergent, some divergent. For example, a mechanical programming error may be made by a new programmer who claimed more experience than he or she actually has.

This is the advantage of using both sides of the brain when approaching a problem—you have spare resources available when needed. In Figure 7-4(b), that extra capacity is evident when you use the organic, global method (Figure 7-3bb) to work with a convergent problem (Figure 7-3a). Finding the appropriate balance in using both sides is vital; after you've explored the sensings, values, and options, your additional imagining and sensing may sidetrack you when it is time to make structured decisions by using logical analysis.

Use both sides of your brain to double your capabilities and cope-abilities.

As you add sensing and other creative capabilities to your mental reper-toire, you are more likely to be able to visualize human energy flows. You'll tend to think more often in flows, processes, and values. You'll tend to think less in either-or terms where you have to choose between energy thrusts. Ambiguity and confusion will be easier to tolerate because you'll be more able to accept these opposing tensions as part of your process of arriving at a new dynamic balance. You'll be more able to be involved and detached at the same time without having to compartmentalize yourself into fragmented, sequential pieces.

> While the logical mind abhors divergent problems and tries to run away from them, the higher faculties of man accept the challenges of life as they are offered . . . . knowing that when things are most contradictory, absurd, difficult, and frustrating, then, *just then,* life really makes sense. . . . The question is one of faith, of choosing our own "grade of significance." Our ordinary mind always tries to persuade us that we are nothing but acorns and that our greatest happi-ness will be to become bigger, fatter, shinier acorns; but that is of interest only to pigs. Our faith gives us knowledge of something much better: that we can become oak trees.[18]

The higher-order human values are needed for becoming an oak tree—for increasing your core of self from which you exercise self-choice. Whether or not you can always put these values into action, you're likely to become less defensive and more of your own person as you focus your visualization.

A Brief Historical Perspective on Change in Our Thinking

For a perspective on this process, let me include here a brief historical footnote.[19] The roots of our mode of thinking lie in the early Greek philosophy of the sixth century B.C. similar to Eastern thought at that time, in which science, philosophy, and religion were not separated. Gradually a separation of spirit and matter developed in Western thought, leading to the dualism that became the basis of scientific thought in the seventeenth

---

[18]Ibid., pp. 134–135.
[19]Adapted and reprinted by special arrangement with Shambhala Publications, Inc., 1123 Spruce Street, Boulder, Colorado 80302. From the *Tao of Physics* by Fritjof Capra, pp. 20–24. Copyright © 1975 by Fritjof Capra.

century, as formulated by Descartes and Newton. This separation of spirit and matter was paralleled by an image of a monarchial God who ruled the world from above, which led to a mind-body separation in our thinking. To split mind and body—spirit and matter—is to split you as a person.

This separation continues today, even though there has been a major shift in how we view the world since the turn of the twentieth century when the relativity and quantum theories demonstrated the interconnectedness of all energies. Segments of the scientific, psychological, and religious communities have more recently begun to shift toward a more holistic, organic view of the universe, more like Eastern philosophies, which continue to emphasize the basic unity of nature.

> [A]ll opposites . . . light and dark, winning and losing, good and evil are merely different aspects of the same phenomenon. . . . Since all opposites are interdependent, their conflict can never result in the total victory of one side. . . . This notion of dynamic balance is essential to the way in which the unity of opposites is experienced.[20]

> [As Capra sees it] we are now witnessing the beginning of a tremendous change, a cultural trend which I call an evolutionary trend of vast magnitude. You are witnessing the rising concern with ecology, a strong interest in mysticism, a strong interest in psychic phenomena, a rediscovery of holistic approaches to health and healing and last, but not least, a strong rising feminist awareness. Now I think that all of these phenomena are manifestations of the same cultural evolutionary trend, away from the overemphasis of the yang toward a balance between yang and yin, or between the masculine and feminine elements within all of us.''[21]

Many people seem to be seeking a more balanced way of being their own person—of being human—which will require a more dynamic balance in using both sides of the human brain. Let's see how that might be done for bringing about desired changes within yourself.

USING VISUALS FOR YOUR GROWTH – AND TO GAIN MORE RESULTS

The wisdom of "Watch out what you pray for, you might get it," applies here. Mental visualizing is as powerful as using your intellectual skills; the two together generate emotional and spiritual energy that nourish seeds of new beliefs that can guide your life experiences.

[20]Ibid., p. 146.
[21]Carol Foote, "Minding the New Physics," *Human Behavior*, October 1978, p. 31.

The Power of Mental Visualizing

You are now aware of what happens when you are on the defensive. And you know that when you can conjure up a picture of what you're like when you're off the defensive, you're on your way to becoming non-defensive. This process of visualizing how you are now and how you want to become is the same one that motivates people to clear their gardens of weeds—a vivid mental picture of flowers in riotous bloom.

Think of all energy being interconnected and interdependent. Modern physicists are now demonstrating that this is so, thereby confirming the beliefs of many philosophers and metaphysicians. Visualize that global network of universal energy. Then visualize *thought as energy* and consider this: If thought is energy, then *your* thought is also energy. If you could increase the potency of your thoughts by increasing the feeling and belief behind your thoughts, the greater the energy you could move through that interconnected network of universal energy. If you could do that and if it responds to the thought picture in your mind, that picture could—in its own time—materialize into physical form. Mental thought and physical form, according to both the physicists and metaphysicians, are simply different forms of energy. Let's see how this can work.

Give your visuals energy so you can affirm and form new experiences.

First, imagine yourself somewhere that allows you to relax, then feel yourself as being in and part of the global energy network—part of a universal energy that connects you with all life. Visualize that, feel it, and sense the release that comes as you accept that you are in an energy flow. Some people feel as if they are floating on a stream of consciousness, others as if they are charged with a circulating current of electricity.

Next, visualize yourself acting out what you want for yourself; be sure that nothing you want would harm people or take anything away from them. Make this a vivid, active picture in full detail. Put plenty of feeling into it; visualize how you want it to look after it's materialized into physical form. Stay relaxed with this visualizing until you sense that it's already taken form in thought and is probably in the process of taking form physically.

Then affirm that you have already received the results you visualized; accept them with a deep sense of appreciation and thanks. Stay with that feeling and belief until you have a sense that it's real for you.

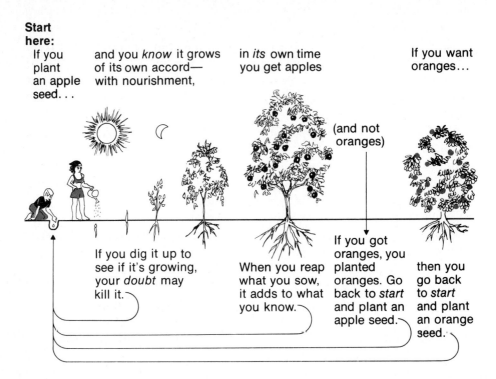

Start here:

If you plant an apple seed. . . and you *know* it grows of its own accord— with nourishment, in *its* own time you get apples If you want oranges...

(and not oranges)

If you dig it up to see if it's growing, your *doubt* may kill it.

When you reap what you sow, it adds to what you know.

If you got oranges, you planted oranges. Go back to *start* and plant an apple seed.

then you go back to *start* and plant an orange seed.

Figure 7-5. Visualizing the creative process.

Finally, release the completed picture into the larger energy network, letting it take form in its own time. If you have any doubts, go back to the first step to reaffirm your presence in the energy flow, and reaffirm your visual picture of the completed, desired situation. Expect to receive what you have put into the picture.[22]

If later you get other results than what you consciously put in your picture, you probably received something that reflects a stronger belief than those invested in your picture. The energy of the beliefs behind your thoughts can shape your experience. If you're having experiences you don't want, you can trace them back to the underlying beliefs that are creating these experiences and create new experiences by growing new beliefs.

In Figure 7-5 we see this process in a simple form. Plant seeds (beliefs) into the ground (your mind), where they grow through nurturing (your belief and faith, plus the larger energy of which you are a part), materializing into form (your experience). Notice how doubts can kill the process. Also notice

---

[22]Visualization techniques are taught by numerous metaphysical schools and individual teachers. This particular method was inspired by the philosophy of Ernest Holmes, author of *The Science of Mind* and founder of the United Church of Religious Science.

that if you don't get the result you expected, you go back to the beginning of the process and work with the initial visual that you planted in your mind, energized by your beliefs.

For example, if you want to increase your money supply, you first develop belief in the legitimacy of your having money. If you want more money (apples) but are getting little money (oranges), you probably have some beliefs about money that limit your supply. Instead of trying to get more money by making apples out of oranges, you start planting apple seeds instead of orange seeds. To do this, you work with changing your beliefs and mental visuals that produce your limited supply.

Let's see how this worked for Barbara Fraser, 51, who had tried a number of ways to increase her income from writing and speaking engagements without success. She spent some time reviewing her beliefs about money. Let's see what she found.

Visualizing Beliefs—and Powering Visuals with Beliefs and Action

Barbara Fraser had developed the habit of keeping occasional journal notes about what was happening to her and the things she told herself. Also after relaxing and asking inwardly for information, she recorded what came through her inner messages and visuals. She had been asking herself, "What do I believe about money?" with the expectation of receiving answers. Here are some of her journal notes as she was in the process of bringing these beliefs to the surface. Notice how many different senses she uses and how the images shift as they link together, like a moving montage. (Her arrows mean "leading to.")

I don't deserve to have money beyond my needs, and my needs should be simple. This just came to me. No wonder I don't have much! I learned that from my mother. Depression thinking of the 1930s. Also "Don't take gifts from strangers" which became *don't take gifts* (except on special occasions) → Take gifts only when appropriate or customary to receive gifts → It's not the gift, it's the thought → It's not necessary to spend the same amount in return. In fact, return-gifts are obligations and that's not *real* giving.

Somehow that ties with what I say so often—I have one of the most expensive educations around. I've paid dear for my experiences → I must pay for my mistakes. "Life isn't a bed of roses—you have to take the thorns too (that's my father). You make your own bed and you have to lie in it." Ugh. Beds have thorns in them? [Notice that this could be a bridge belief to other belief networks about sexuality or about sleeping and dreaming.]

Somehow this ties into → Luxuries and comforts are not for us— almost indecent. Think of the starving Armenians—save string—turn off the lights—save toothpaste tubes, grease, gasoline (Is this trip necessary?)—think of the boys overseas → Men should have money because they give their lives for their country → You should give up what you value →GIVE: Be a Gold Star Mother. Put your flag in the window.[23] GIVE without expecting anything in return.

It is more blessed to give than to receive.

It's a sin to have. Justify your need.

Can you make do? You should be thankful for what you have.

You shouldn't want more. To want money is to love it.

The love of money is the root of all evil.

It's a sin to want evil and I'll be punished—severely. Gawd, what a trip I've been laying on myself all these years. No wonder I don't have more money!

You can see how Barbara's early learnings from childhood admonitions, Sunday School lessons, depression years' frugality, wartime scarcities, and patriotic slogans had all served to knit a dense forest of corollary beliefs leading to her core beliefs that money for simple needs was all she deserved and that more was a punishable sin. Each of these beliefs may have been essential to her at some past phase of her life, but they had accumulated, intermeshed, and become convoluted. They remained tangled and unexamined as to their usefulness today. To be able to see herself as eligible to receive and own money beyond her basic needs, Barbara will have to thin out these beliefs of scarcity and moralistic negatives and replace them with more positive, abundant ones.

Consider this: Beliefs shape your experience and not the other way around.

Another underlying belief also has to be considered here. Let's say Barbara believes that her experiences create her beliefs. Since she knows she

---

[23]During World War II gasoline was rationed, and people turned in toothpaste tubes and grease for the war effort. Mothers could put flags in their windows to show they had sent their sons to war. Framed in blue and white, a red star was for a live son; gold was for a dead one.

can't change her experiences, she feels helpless to change her beliefs. With this picture, she's locked into her past and has thrown away the key.

However, let's say she can visualize her beliefs creating her experiences. Now she can look to past experiences and search out the underlying beliefs that created them. She can also ask herself, "What have I received that I wanted but didn't need?" She can direct her inner searchlight for these experiences and learnings and unearth other beliefs she learned.

Using the creative visualizing process, she can uproot the tangled trees of scarcity and sin and create a mental clearing. She'll need to till the soil of her mind to turn up broken root ends that could start growing again. Then she can go back to the beginning of the seed-planting process and grow new beliefs in her consciousness, perhaps picturing trees that give abundantly of their fragrance and fruit. Barbara's work is visualizing and believing in abundance as part of her experience; in time, results will automatically follow in forms most valuable in Barbara's life. It could be money, business contacts, an inheritance, or a new idea. Her thoughts, beliefs and actions will attract the right results for her. When you work with the creativity of universal energy in materializing beliefs, you always get responses. Some are humorous or unpredictable, such as events that seem too coincidental to actually be coincidental.

Make a new tape of new inner rules, dialogues and beliefs.

One way to change your beliefs is to reprogram inner dialogues. Here's how Barbara Fraser recreated her beliefs about money. She gathered four friends, two men and two women, and taped a session where she read them her journal notes, then asked what money meant to them, how they felt about it and what they had learned about it—all the rules, adages, sins and habits, as well as the fun of acquiring, spending, and investing money. After they left, she played the tape, writing in her journal all the additional material that seemed to also relate to her.

Then beside each item, she wrote down what she would like to add to her beliefs about money. Taking a new tape and visualizing herself with ample money, she spoke her desired new behavior and beliefs onto the tape, voicing them with conviction. She played it back and retaped sections of it until she was sure it felt right for her. Only then did she celebrate the destruction of her old tape.

Here are a few beliefs she put on her new tape:

- Money is energy that sustains life and affords pleasure.
- Plants always produce more than enough seeds to renew themselves. Nature is abundant in circulating its energy to sustain life; I am a part of nature; therefore I can have abundance to circulate. (Notice that she redefines money through her observations of nature, a good use of "The power to define is the power to choose.")
- I now let go of the scarcity of the 1930s and 1940s and all other that I've had. I replace it with a six-figure balance sheet composed of real estate, some stock, insurance and savings, and a larger five-figure annual income. (This was how much money she could visualize without doubting it. Later this could increase.)
- I see myself sitting down to deposit money and to write checks for my bills with an attitude of thanks that I have the money, that I've received value and can give value back.

Twice a day she listened to herself on her new tape, absorbing and affirming the new beliefs she had chosen. As she absorbed them, she needed to listen less often, using the tape mostly to counteract occasional inner messages from the old tape that repeated themselves out of habit. Her efforts went up and down for a while; she had many beliefs to change and frequently doubted this would work. But gradually she began getting invitations to speak, sometimes from sources she would never have thought to contact. This seemed like too much coincidence to be coincidence, which convinced her to keep on affirming her own beliefs.

This is just one example of how you can create ways to help yourself visualize and materialize more of what you want—as long as it's not at anyone's expense. As you work with both lateral and vertical thinking and determine whether you have a convergent or divergent problem, you'll find you can gain more of the results you want. As you use your lateral exploratory skills more, you'll also find you'll be thinking of more options—for personal as well as work situations. Gaining more results and having more options are particularly valuable in gaining more self-confidence. The more non-defensive you become, the less need you'll have for facades. You're becoming your own person—your authentic self.

LET'S GET STARTED

Choose one of the following items and experiment. (If you don't like any of them, invent one you prefer.)

- Think of a problem you've been having that doesn't seem to go away. Is it convergent or divergent? What method have you been using to work with it? What ideas can you develop that will help solve it—or balance the opposing tensions?

- Think of some aspect of your life that has not been satisfactory for you for a long time. Around that central idea, consider what you believe about it, such as the money example. Expect to find core and corollary beliefs, the smaller ones leading to the core. Make notes as ideas come to you on Notes to Myself. When you have the inclination and time, do some journal writing, allowing your mind and feelings to write themselves as you go, as if your eyes were closed. Try looking into space somewhere between your eyes and the paper as you write. Sense and see what happens.
- From your Incident Cards, think of a pattern that often repeats itself on these cards. Visualize that situation in your mind's eye. Now hear and sense yourself handling it with aplomb and confidence so everyone gains something each wants. When you've done this, congratulate yourself warmly. Does that feel good or embarrassing? Is the situation too small to deserve congratulations? Whenever you evaluate whether you *deserve* something, you may *de-serve* yourself! Listen to whether or not you limit yourself on self-affirmations.

IN THE NEXT CHAPTER

Next, we move into applying the ideas, skills, and concepts that we've been exploring until now. In Chapter 8 we develop quick responses for repetitious, irritating situations that may seem too small to make a fuss about but feel big enough to make us defensive. You'll learn how to gain results and generate options with extras in reserve.

From Chapter 9 on, we will use increasingly complex situations to show the Choosing Process in action, and we will describe some non-defensive endings for the situations we've introduced, such as Helen Henderson's and John Silberman's divergent problem in Chapter 10, and Dave Eliot's situation at Country Stores in Chapter 11.

Chapter 8 opens with the less complex, but tense, situation at XNG's industrial relations meeting. The scene is being replayed, this time using some non-defensive communication.

READINGS

Buzan, Tony: *Use Both Sides of Your Brain*, E. P. Dutton, New York, 1976. Designed for students to develop an organic study method that uses both sides of the brain. A basic step-by-step book on how to use the right brain to supplement the left brain. Shows how organic diagrams give better retention of material than you can get from outlines.

Couratin, Patrick: *Shhh!*, Harlan Quist, Vontobel Druck AG, Switzerland, 1974. Presumably a children's book, the unusual creativity of the art work may be better understood by children than adults. It can't be understood linearly; it has to be experienced imaginatively. Experiment with visuals and sensings with this one.

De Bono, Edward: *Lateral Thinking: Creativity Step by Step,* Harper & Row, New York, 1970. A basic text on vertical and lateral thinking, when to use which, how to develop skills in the lateral mode. Somewhat paradoxical in presenting the lateral, global thinking in a linear, vertical way. Useful.

Franck, Frederick: *The Zen of Seeing: Seeing/Drawing as Meditation,* Vintage Books, Random House, New York, 1973. Drawing while seeing what you're looking at, not your paper. Experiencing drawing as you draw it—a right-brain experience.

FILM

Joshua in a Box, Stephen Bosustow Productions, P. O. Box 2127, Santa Monica, Calif. 90406. Chicago International Film Festival, 5 minutes. A non-narrated experience that defies description.

For additional background reading, see bibliography entries 36, 39, 40, 43, 44, 45, 46, 48, 49, 50, 51, 52, 53, 57, 64, 90.

GETTING OFF THE DEFENSIVE

How to Think of Quick Responses in Time

DOOLEY'S WORLD By Bradfield

10-7

© King Features Syndicate, Inc. 1975.

Here's a quick recap of XNG's industrial relations meeting with a few changes and a different ending.

Remember that halfway through the meeting, Marie Taylor had expressed anger about the pattern she saw in selecting people to be laid off—they were mostly older women. Jack Angelo had cautioned her to be patient and she held her fire. Finally it was too much for her. "There now, see? Just like I said. You and your industrial relations. You're prejudiced against older women." As soon as the words were out of her mouth, she knew she had gone too far. She acted defensively and put Jack on the defensive. He exploded, "Oh f--- all those g--d--- broads."

Here's another version of the ending. This time Marie is centering herself. She quietly considers Jack for a moment while she buys some time, then comments with a thoughtful twinkle in her eye:

"I wonder if we have that option."

Everyone—even Jack—laughs as his remark hangs in midair, as if lit up in neon. The words slowly dim as the humor subsides. The issue of "using such language in front of a woman" doesn't come up. Jack blew it, and everyone knows it. He has to take responsibility for that. Yet he can still save face because Marie sidestepped his remark by not responding directly to it. Now, as the meeting moves on, Marie's chances of making her point are increased, provided she stops attacking others' attitudes and sticks to the data. If she stays centered, she'll have more options for handling double meanings.

THINKING OF QUICK RESPONSES

Most of us find ourselves in situations that occur time and time again, in which we don't know how to respond—we go blank, feel speechless, or perhaps think the situation is too trivial to bother with. Yet many times we may sense we haven't handled it adequately—there's an unresolved residual defensiveness left when the incident is over. We know it will probably happen again with no better results. So we swat at the gnats, miss them, and hope they will go away.

Many of these recurring situations seem trivial—minor putdowns, power plays, attempts to get credit for your idea (of which you have many more). A particular situation itself may be trivial; its *repetitiousness* is not. The situations continue to occur; you continue to feel more defensive.

If you find yourself in such repeated situations, they deserve your attention, no matter how trivial they seem. When you have a larger repertoire of available quick responses, you are more likely to dispose of these gnats. Then they won't be draining the energy you use in vague defensiveness. You can redirect it to more interesting activities. We'll start with building a repertoire; then we'll see how you can think of responses in time to do the job.

Giving quick responses does not necessarily mean delivering perfect squelches or fast put-downs that kill self-styled adversaries. Quick responses can be non-defensive ways to stay out of win-lose situations while you move toward as much mutual gain as you can.

Ten quick responses for handling double meanings are shown in Figure 8-1. Let's take each one of these responses and break them down to see how to apply them non-defensively in actual situations.

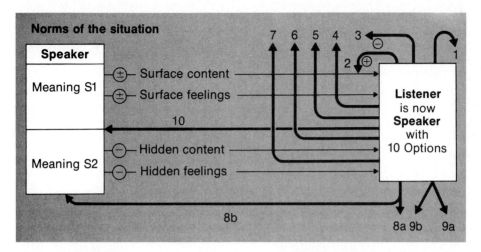

Norms of the situation

Speaker	
Meaning S1	±— Surface content
	±— Surface feelings
	10
Meaning S2	—— Hidden content
	—— Hidden feelings

7 6 5 4 3

2

1

Listener
is now
Speaker
with
10 Options

8b

8a 9b   9a

Legend: 1. Buy time
      2. Respond only to positive surface content
      3. If surface meaning is negative, reverse or divert it and shift its assumptions
      4. Name the process or game and stop talking
      5. Give and ask for feedback
      6. Surface the hidden content and stop talking

      7. Report (don't express) the feelings and stop talking
      8. Handle the hidden feelings or emotional load
        a. drop them
        b. send them back without adding to them
      9. Non-responsiveness
        a. change the subject
        b. diffuse with humor
   10. Use a close-off statement or action

Figure 8-1. *How the listener can get off the defensive.*

1. Buy Time

Let's say you're in a departmental meeting called by your supervisor, Warren Freeman, to discuss ways to rearrange the facilities for better work flow. A hidden agenda among the seven people present is who gets the higher or lower status spots as measured by the size of offices and desks. Since you've been acting as supervisor in Warren's absence and your work is closely linked with his, you think your status is close to his.

Looking at the floor plan under discussion, you point to the large office next to his; logically you think it should be yours. But Warren says, "No, I think you belong over here; I need you there as a quality control person." (He points to a smaller, distant office. Never has that subject come up before between you.) You feel a rush of confusion, some frustration, and you find yourself going blank, not knowing what to say. You decide to buy some time by counting to ten, but this time you've decided to do more than count. You're also going to figure out how to use the time so you can keep your hand in.

Buying Time to Gain Space to Think. You decide to keep it simple by saying non-defensively what you're doing. Here are some possible non-defensive quick responses with each one compared to a response that would be defensive, and why.

Non-Defensive	*Defensive*
"I'm taking a minute to think about that."	"Can I take a minute to think about that?" (Asks permission when not needed.)
"Hold it. There may be another way."	"Don't you think there may be another way?" (Gives away decision power.)
"I know we're under pressure, so let's stop to check that we've thought of everything."	"I know we're under pressure, but we want to be sure we haven't missed anything." (Invites a negative response. This could appear to block the decision or suggest personal unsureness.)

Another quick response from the psychiatrist's notebook is called "Hmmm . . ." If you want to add a little potency, nod thoughtfully and add "interesting," or "significant." All you're doing is making a neutral noise that keeps dibs on your place in the conversation.

With any one of these options you are buying time with the group to get room to think, to distance yourself from the surprise of Warren's double meaning: "You act for me when I'm gone; you check quality of work when I'm here." (You have status with me and you don't.) If you don't think of a response in time, you've still saved your place and saved your face.

Buying Time to Find a Way to Say No. If Warren Freeman is pushing for your consent to take the distant office, the option to say no simply may not occur to you. "I couldn't say no," you might tell yourself, "I might get fired." Or perhaps saying no feels like starting a fight, especially if there actually is an unknown hidden fight going on about who sits in the office next to Warren's. Rather than take any risks, you might feel you have no option but to go along with whatever is expected. If Warren is an arbitrary, authoritarian boss, this may be the best option until you ask yourself, "What results do I really want?" and know your answer.

Sometimes people know perfectly well they won't be fired for saying no, but they go along anyway, perhaps out of habit or to please others.

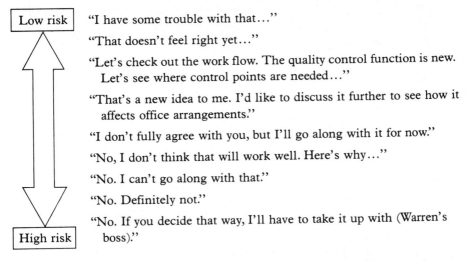

Low risk   "I have some trouble with that…"

"That doesn't feel right yet…"

"Let's check out the work flow. The quality control function is new. Let's see where control points are needed…"

"That's a new idea to me. I'd like to discuss it further to see how it affects office arrangements."

"I don't fully agree with you, but I'll go along with it for now."

"No, I don't think that will work well. Here's why…"

"No. I can't go along with that."

"No. Definitely not."

"No. If you decide that way, I'll have to take it up with (Warren's
High risk   boss)."

Figure 8-2   *Options ranging from low to high risk.*

There are a number of ways to work up to saying no to let Warren know that he cannot always have your unqualified consent under all circumstances. Figure 8-2 shows some options and risk levels.

Some of these options are high enough risk that you may indeed have your job on the line. However, only you can know how provocative no can be in your own situations. Only you know how strongly you feel about the issues involved and what your relationship is with Warren Freeman's counterpart in your life.

If no in any form is hard for you to say to your supervisor, practice using some of the higher risk options in situations in which your job is not on the line. For example, how easy is it for you to say no if someone comes by to go on coffee break and you don't have time right then? Or practice at home. Can you comfortably say no when one of your children wants you to buy something you don't want him or her to have?

On the other hand, you may be one of those people who say no so easily others seem to feel that further discussion is shut out—and they shut up. If you often do this or if you notice this response, practice using some of the lower-risk options. You leave the door open with "That doesn't feel right to me." You slam it shut with "No. Definitely not."

Buying Time to Get Your Feelings Under Control.   Here's a situation in which an unexpected remark aroused defensiveness.

Larry Grey, menswear buyer for a department store headquartered in San Francisco, is at the Los Angeles store where he runs into two head-quarter executives. One of them, Luther Keene, remarks, "Oh, *there* you are. Haven't seen you around lately." In the tone of voice, Larry hears a hidden accusation, "You haven't been working."

His anger rises sharply at the injustice and he lashes out. "If you think I've been goofing off, it's not true. How do you think we got that one million dollar increase in sales these last ten months?"

As they turn to leave, Luther remarks to the other executive, "God, he's touchy. Hope he doesn't act that way all the time. Better check him out."

Larry reacted defensively to the hidden meaning he *thought* he heard. As a result, he got no response, probably lost some credibility, and missed an opportunity to make his work more visible.

Was there really a hidden meaning? Was Larry justified in feeling as he did? These are pointless questions. Without feedback Larry can't find out Luther's real meaning. The defensiveness is Larry's feeling, whether it's a reaction to the executive's remark or his own defensiveness stored up from past experiences. It's there and requires no justification. Perhaps if you had been in Larry's shoes, you would have reacted differently. That also needs no justification.

However, Larry has to take responsibility for his own feelings and how they affect his communication. He didn't keep his anger low enough to maintain control of what he said, so he may have gotten results he wouldn't want. He *reacted*. But he had other options. Consider these:

- "Guess we've missed each other."
- "I've been moving around."
- "It's been a while."
- "Yes, that's right."

While Larry was buying time externally with Luther Keene, he might have been having other conversations internally between himself and his anger.

- "Hey, anger. Down, now. I can't afford the luxury of you right now."
- "After they leave, we'll get together and find out what was so volatile."
- "Give the benefit of the doubt. It's not personal. He sounds worse than he probably means to. Maybe that's his way of making small talk.
- "Easy now. Here's my chance to make points on my sales record."

If Larry's anger rose so sharply that he could think of nothing else, he might have exited with, "Excuse me, I'll be right back . . ." He could head for the restroom or stockroom where he can take time to collect himself. He may write out an Incident Card to work on later. These are some ways he can stay in charge of himself as long as his exit is reasonably composed. (Body language can reveal a lot. Skulking or scampering would probably say he'd lost his composure.)

2. *Respond Only to Positive Surface Content*

To use this option, you choose what you want to respond to and ignore any possible negative or double meanings. You act as if they didn't exist, even if you feel sure they're present. You can file these negatives away for future reference on your Notes to Myself if you want to. At the moment you focus only on the surface content, the one part of the meaning you're sure is positive.

Even if Luther *was* implying that Larry hadn't been working, Larry could talk to his anger, telling it to work *for* him while he turns the situation around. If he can cool his anger quickly, he could use one of these several options:

Options	*Odds and Probable Results*
"Right. Have to keep moving."	An end to the exchange as he physically keeps moving.
"I should hope not. That's how we made the one million dollar sales increase the last ten months. Have you been watching it climb?"	Responsive, giving information that makes his work visible and draws the others toward a favorable response.
"I haven't seen you either. Let's have lunch today and get caught up." (and if the answer is no) "Sorry you can't make it. We'll do it later up north."	If they accept the lunch invitation, he has a good chance to make his work visible and get information about ongoing problems. If they refuse, he can arrange a follow-up in San Francisco.

3. *If Surface Meaning Is Negative, Reverse or Divert It and Shift Its Assumptions*

"What are you so defensive about?" is a question that assumes you're defensive. If you do not shift this assumption but simply respond to the question, you may find yourself denying that you feel defensive. Before you know it, you'll *be* defensive. Assumptions act like hidden definitions, and the power to define is the power to control.

To stay out of this trap, you can shift the assumption by asking, "What leads you to think I'm defensive?" Another way to shift the assumption is to make an entirely different assumption by asking something like "Do you think we've covered everything we need to in this report?" (Notice that you don't ask, "What's so bad about this report?") The non-defensive comment assumes that both of you want to get the work done.

Here's another example in which fatherly advice from a supervisor carries some assumptions about a subordinate.

> Amy Pendleton was putting away her work at the end of the day when her supervisor, Ted Kraft, came over to chat a bit. He knew she was interested in getting ahead and that the next logical promotion was his job. After an opening comment or two, he advises her: "You know, you'll hurt your chances of getting ahead if you continue to be bitter about your past experiences."

Amy got defensive and asked where that judgment came from. When Ted said it was just his, she fended with, "There's no bitterness in me. If you see it that way, *you're* inferring it."

If Amy's voice rises or sounds adamant, her attitude could be perceived as denial of an accurate comment or a need to defend herself by striking back. Let's assume for the moment that Ted is making a power play, and his comment has these double meanings:

Surface Content (Negative):	You'll hurt your chances of getting ahead if you continue to be bitter about your past experiences.
Surface Feeling (Seems Positive):	I'm trying to help you get ahead.
Hidden Content (Negative):	You have a chip on your shoulder so I can't recommend you for a promotion yet.
Hidden Feeling (Negative):	You're not going to get my job if I can help it.

Amy can choose to pick up on the apparently positive feeling and ignore any assumption that she's bitter, that she has a chip on her shoulder, or that she's aiming for Ted's job. She can treat his comment as an assumption that he wants to help her get ahead by getting the job done more simply. She might say this:

Statement	Probable result
"I'm glad you brought that up, Ted. I've been working on how to smooth up the work flow in here. You know, I'm a realist. I've seen a lot of things happen that would probably make anyone, even you, feel bitter. I figure the best way to use that experience is to make the work easier for everybody."	Ted may not have time. She has diverted the focus of the surface content and hidden meaning back to the job. She hasn't been trapped into denying his charge of bitterness. She has owned it, extended it, and converted it to her own purposes, which could also help others, including Ted.
"Let me show you how I think we can simplify the paperwork." She reaches for a sizable stack of papers and asks, "Do you have time right now?"	If Ted feels he lost this round, he has a way to save face—he can leave. She has built a bridge for more job-related discussion so her work can become more visible. He can look good because of her ideas.

Let's see how Ted's comment would look if he had no double meaning. The surface content and feeling would be the same as before. The hidden meaning, if any, would be consistent with the surface meaning:

Hidden Content (Positive):   When you stop sounding bitter to me, I can consider recommending you for promotion.

Hidden Feeling (Positive):   If I can get her ready in time, I can show that I'm ready for my own promotion at my next review.

If this *had* been Ted's intended meaning, Amy's response would have fed right into Ted's undisclosed plans to advance himself—and her. Either way Amy gains, and odds are better that Ted also gains.

4. Name the Process or the Game and Stop Talking

This option is particularly potent because all your attention is on the process, game, or manipulation. When you listen to the actions instead of the words, you collect data and describe what you observe. For example, what is going on here when Hank asks for help?

Setting: The weekly poker game, which is at Joe Vernon's house tonight. As they start the ante, Hank Musker begins complaining about his boss. Recently, Hank had been named lead supervisor by Mike Flanagan, his foreman, who had promised him a raise in 30 days if he proved himself. According to Hank, it's now been over 60 days and no raise. Hank is sure his work is okay because Mike keeps telling him "Keep up the good work." Mike praised him again last week but still no money. "I've tried everything," Hank claims and asks his poker pals, "How can I make Mike give me the money he promised?"

Lots of advice and suggestions pour forth. They've all had similar problems. With each new idea, Hank says he's tried everything. "I've tried that and it didn't work," he assures them. Next he confides, "Let me tell you something," and launches a long tale of all the ways Mike has put him off.

Finally Joe notices what Hank's doing; he's playing helpless. Leaning back from the table, Joe quietly comments to Hank, "We've been making lots of suggestions and you keep saying 'Yes but..' and 'Ain't it awful!' It sounds to me like you're trying to prove how unfair Mike is to you." Poker comes to a stop as all eyes turn to Joe. "I don't know if Mike is being fair or not. I believe you've earned your raise. I'd like to know how *you* can sell that fact to Mike."

Joe has named Hank's "Yes, but" game. He's thrown the ball back to Hank and challenged him to catch it and run. Hank now has to stop raising objections to the advice given and start thinking of options of how to get what he's earned. He may feel he's tried everything, but if he gives up he won't get the raise. Joe is asking Hank to turn his thinking around toward what *might* work. Then they can explore possible options together.

Sometimes the most help is no help. Right now if Joe and the others say nothing, they leave the responsibility in Hank's hands. If just one of them waters down Joe's challenge, Hank is off the hook. Likewise, if someone rubs Hank's nose in his own game ("You sure got caught that time, didn't you Hank?"), he may justify himself and stay focused on what has not worked. If the others say nothing, Hank has to move ahead or drop it. Only when Hank is ready to help himself can Joe and the others be of help to him.

5. Give and Ask for Feedback

When you give and ask for feedback, you're checking with the speaker to find out if what you heard is what the speaker meant. It's simple to do. Before you respond, put the meaning you heard into your own words. Then ask the speaker to verify your understanding. Only when it's verified do you respond. Here's how it worked between a manager, Steve Harris, and a super-visor in his department, Jane Poulsen:

Dialogue	*Dynamics*
Steve: "You're pushing pretty hard on this cost-reduction plan you've got, Jane."	Implied: "You should back off."
Jane: "I should quit now while I'm ahead; is that what you're telling me, Steve?"	Jane asks for feedback by restating in her own words the content—sur-face and hidden—she heard.
Steve: "Kind of. The timing isn't right for any more changes now."	Steve confirms and gives more information.
Jane: "Oh, I hadn't thought about that. But isn't everybody interested in cutting costs?"	Jane pauses, but comes right back to her main concern.
Steve: "Sure, sure. But let's wait until they settle the new contract before we propose another project. But maybe we can lay some ground-work now."	Steve gives more information and offers initial support for Jane's idea, which she will need for getting action later.

Assuming that Steve's reading of management's mood is accurate and that he has no motive to stall Jane, both of them and the company can gain the results they all want.

Steve and Jane were able to communicate clearly with no hidden mean-ings. However, one person may often not want to communicate. He or she may be too busy, tired, worried about something else, or bored with it. Some may not know how to state clearly what they want to say. Others think their meaning is perfectly clear and the listener isn't listening. Still others think their meaning is so obvious that they may say to themselves, "I know what I mean, so why don't you? Any damn fool ought to be able to get it."

Ron Hathaway, public relations director of Consolidated Bank, has a habit of giving sparse feedback to his customer relations manager, Nancy Amerman. Let's see how she asks for more feedback.

Nancy's current task is to interpret a new bank policy that eliminates certain services offered by other local banks. She will use this information to train customer contact people—new accounts personnel, tellers, and loan servicing staff—to handle questions from bank customers. Nancy takes her second draft to Ron for comment.

Dialogue	*Dynamics*
Ron: "No, no, no. It's too defensive."	Ron makes a judgment that gives no information about what would be preferable.
Nancy: "What's wrong with it?"	Nancy asks for feedback in a way that invites more negative judgment.
Ron: "It's too negative, too long."	Nancy gets another non-useful judgment that doesn't point toward what would be better.
Nancy: "I'm not clear on how it comes across that way. I can shorten it, but I don't think that gets at what you're talking about. Can you try putting it another way?"	Nancy is now asking for feedback that asks Ron to give her observable data.
Ron: "It's not specific words, Nancy. It's the tone of the whole thing. Just try saying what we do compared to other banks, and why we do it that way. Keep it simple."	Ron doesn't give specific data, but as he talks Nancy sees why her material comes across as defensive. She's *feeling* defensive! Nancy knows why Consolidated has cut back its services but isn't clear how the customer contact people are going to sell it to them. So she asks.
Nancy: "Please go over once more how we tell our customers how they benefit from this change."	She takes the risk that Ron might think she should know this without being told.
Ron: "They don't, Nancy. We're selling safety while we cut costs, figuring the other banks will follow our lead. Money's tight, you know. So talk about safe, conservative practices that protect the customer's money."	But he levels with her, trusting her with the real reasons and what the bank wants to say. She has the information she needs. If she's uncomfortable with any of it, that would now be a separate issue.

6. Surface the Hidden Content and Stop Talking

To surface the hidden content, first you have to listen, then clearly identify what you think the hidden content is, and then make a separate decision about whether or not to say anything. A quick review of the results you want and the options you have can keep you from getting foot-in-mouth disease! Denise Townsend faces just this situation.

In a small manufacturing company, the annual budget meeting of the sales division heads and support staff is in progress. Sam Williams, division head, is sitting back to observe the discussion. His new sales manager, Burk Young, wants Bonnie Winters, a top-notch secretary who worked half time for Burk's predecessor, to work for him full time. He says he needs her experience to help maintain continuity while he learns the ropes from the inside.

Bonnie had worked the other half of her time for Denise Townsend, head of the order processing department (OPD), who says she, too, needs Bonnie full time. Denise claims that for the past two months, the salesmen have been making promises for delivery dates that Tony Castano, the production head, can't meet. OPD has had to handle the increased back-order complaints in addition to the usual customer follow-through with production, shipping, and accounting.

"That's just the kind of problem I need help with," Burk interjects. Persuasively he adds, "Surely you'd be willing to try it for just six months, wouldn't you Denise?"

("Ahh," thinks Sam Williams. "Bright boy. Knows how to go after what he wants. I knew I picked a winner in him. He'll whip the sales crew into shape before long. Denise will just have to manage for a while; she's done it before. But I'll have to ask Tony what's going on in production. Can't have him messing up my bonus this quarter.")

Sam decides it's time to speak up. Let's see what happens.

Dialogue	*Dynamics*
Sam: "Denise, you have to realize that sales is what business is all about. That's where the support belongs. OPD has to do that, too."	Sam explains the obvious to Denise, putting her down. His hidden meaning is, "Go along with Burk, little girl. If you don't, you're not supporting our department."
Denise: "That's what we're doing, Mr. Williams. The men are out most of the time, and we need Bonnie. She's especially good at calming down customers and writing the difficult follow-up letters. No one else knows how to do that, and I don't have the time."	Denise gets the message, but she decides to try showing Sam that OPD *is* supporting sales but needs more staff to do it well, since sales is creating the problem. (Notice she uses the deferential title, "Mr.")

Dialogue	*Dynamics*
Sam: "All Burk's asking is a six-month trial. If it doesn't work out by then, we can always reassign Bonnie back to you."	Sam's hidden message is that he is assigning Bonnie to Burk full time and that Denise should now be reasonable.
Burk: "Sure, and by then back-orders will be way down. We'll have to get with Tony. Right, Sam?"	Burk agrees and turns to Sam on a first name basis, discussing sales at Sam's level of operation, excluding Denise and others.

At this point, Denise is edged out. Not only is she not going to get Bonnie's help full time; it appears she isn't going to have her at all. She's hopping mad, not only at the cut back, but at Burk for cutting her out altogether. Since he's on the bonus plan and she isn't, it looks like she'll get no help from him.

Knowing Sam for the politician he is, Denise is sure he'll make Burk shine. Sales will push ahead no matter how many problems are created. It's no secret that Sam is set on making a new sales record this quarter after canning the last manager. Denise is still cleaning up that mess, which is all the more reason she needs Bonnie. But she figures Bonnie will do whatever Sam says.

Denise knows she now has to do three things: protect herself with Sam by keeping cool, support Burk (or at least appear to), and get more secretarial help. These are the results she wants for herself, her relationships, and her job.

What are her options? Here are a few ways to keep negotiations open by surfacing the hidden content:

Denise's Options	*Odds and Probable Results*
"It appears that Bonnie's time is taken so I'll have to put in for a new secretary. Without her experience, there's no question about needing full-time help. Much as I'd like to have Bonnie, she'll be lots of help to Burk and perhaps can train the new person."	She talks to Sam since he made the decision. She supports Burk but restates her own staffing requirements. Her odds for getting a new secretary may be about 50–50 since she's giving up Bonnie, an act of deference to a higher-level person. However, she assumes they agree that she does need full-time help.

Notice how quickly Denise moves from surfacing the hidden message (Bonnie's time is taken) to another option. She *stopped talking* about losing Bonnie. Had she gone on about how unfair or impossible it was, she would have lost control, credibility, and probably the chance of getting another secretary.

Let's take it one more step. Suppose Burk wants to appear budget conscious without putting down Denise, so he intervenes with:

Burk: "Why not try it for six months, Denise, or even four. It would make a real difference in profits this quarter."

Burk has done his homework well about Sam's goals. If he can get Denise to stretch, he will. But she's fast on her feet, too.

Denise: "One way that would work is for Bonnie to take the customer calls and handle the correspondence. You'll probably be out in the field a lot, and she'd be handling the accounts you'll be working on with Tony."

She's keeping cool, supporting Burk by referring to his work with Tony which Burk used to exclude her, and she's planning to get the job done somehow. She takes some risk in appearing less cooperative by shifting the customer function to Bonnie, but she thinks that's covered by tying it in with handling the problem accounts.

Not only is Denise keeping focused on results she wants, she's also considering appearances. She has to. In this competitive climate both Sam and Burk want immediate profit results so they get their bonuses and prove themselves up the line. Denise's concern for ongoing quality customer service has lower priority; and she has lower position power. She's in the dilemma of helping Sam and Burk get bonuses for which she's not eligible, while cleaning up problems with customers who were poorly treated by salesmen. She has responsibility for handling complaints and delays but has no authority to change the causes. OPD can reduce costs, but these are less visible and harder to measure as profits. The longer-term responsibility for losing a big customer rests heavily on these staff jobs and can create considerable defensiveness for people in Denise's position.

By joining forces, Sam and Burk are using sales goals as their means of looking out for themselves. They're going to win even if someone else has to lose. If Denise does not defend herself and her department, she's likely to overcommit herself and lose a customer in the long run. However, if she gets defensive, she's likely to lose staff in the short run. To defend herself non-defensively, she has to keep focused on gaining some of the results she wants while also helping Burk and Sam gain theirs—but not at her expense.

7. Report (Don't Express) the Feelings and Stop Talking

So far, Denise has done nothing about expressing her feelings in this situation. She has chosen to set them aside. Let's see how she might have reported her feelings without expressing them. Then we can see what makes the difference between the two.

Let's go back to where she was edged out after having been put down. She's momentarily without secretarial help with an increased workload. Here are some non-defensive ways that Denise can report—not express—her feelings.

- "I feel like the rug has just been pulled out from under my department."
- "It seems OPD is being made responsible for promises the salesmen make."
- "I'm beginning to sense that we're not on the same team."

Notice that Denise can depersonalize each reply by referring to OPD or the team. She reports feelings as factual data, then stops talking.

When Denise was edged out she was hopping mad. If she had *expressed* her feelings at that moment, she might have cast some accusations and raised defenses. For example:

- "You're decimating my department when it's the salesmen's fault that I have the problems I do. Don't you care about the customers?"

Accusations angrily hurled are likely to bring forth replies of "Let's be reasonable." If she were to continue, which is often the temptation, they might remind her of other problems she has and she may have to back off from blaming Sam or Burk. At that point, she would probably lose face as well as lose the fight. She would have lost her focus on results she wanted.

Whenever you report a feeling, you *must* stop talking when you've said it. There are few "musts" in non-defensive communication, but this is one. In situations like Denise's, many people's feelings become so aroused that their talking becomes almost compulsive. Even if they don't accuse others or otherwise express their frustration, they often explain, prove, and justify themselves. When your feelings are running high, this option is not usually the best one. You're likely to threaten or talk too much, lose sight of results you really want, and raise other people's hackles.

Let's go back to Denise's non-defensive options and assume she stopped talking at the end of the statement she chose. Others are then likely to respond, not as much to the feeling as to the content. Perhaps they will even come up with some options. A non-threatening comment, followed by silence, leads most people to say something to fill the silence. The worst they can reasonably come up with would probably be, "You shouldn't feel that way, Denise. That's not what we meant." Denise could then simply repeat that she does feel that way (not defending herself but reporting her feelings as facts) and stop talking again. She might also add a "buying time" comment, such as "I'd like to see if we can think of more options."

Sometimes it's better to follow than to lead.

Once others start taking responsibility for offering some options, Denise can offer her own. If she starts off with an option, such as "The salesmen should do their own follow-through," Sam and Burk are likely to see her as self-serving and non-supportive of the sales division or Burk. When *they* start proposing options, they're back into negotiations and Denise is out of the loser position.

8. Handle the Hidden Feelings or Emotional Load

Sam Williams sent Denise Townsend an emotional load when he said: "Denise, you have to realize that sales is what business is all about. That's where the support belongs. OPD has to do that, too."

Depending on Sam's tone of voice, some hidden meanings in that statement could be: "You're not very bright; you haven't learned anything on the job"; "You didn't know anything about business when you came and still don't"; "You have to be supportive and you aren't"; "You don't know how to be supportive so we will tell you in ABC terms"; "You're pretty stupid but we'll put up with you"; "I feel sorry for you", perhaps tinged with mild contempt.

Denise can't know whether Sam meant one, several, or any of these feelings, or how intense they were. In such patronizing comments, the Sams of the world are often only vaguely aware of the feelings that may lie hidden from their conscious attention. Such feelings might intrude on their main goals. In this case, Sam's goals are increasing sales to get the bonus and proving himself. As a result, he communicates emotional loads that are probably not consciously intended. However, a person in Denise's position—subordinate, staff job, potentially threatened, conscientious—is likely to be aware of the hidden feelings. Even if she distorts them somewhat because she feels threatened, she's likely to get the gist.

In response to Sam's patronizing teaching, Denise handled the emotional load by dropping it. It registered but she chose to not allow it to enter into what she was doing. Instead, she chose to focus on staffing OPD so the department could provide the needed support.

Dropping the emotional load is like being in your personal space bubble and controlling the screens so you don't let those feelings into your space. Visualize yourself at the controls deciding to let them drop outside. As you focus on this process, you're less likely to get defensive. You're in control.

Some people consciously load their comments by baiting or putting someone down. They intend that the listener get the load in a way that if confronted, they can deny or make light of the load, but make it stick. Stereotypes are useful for this purpose.

Consider, for example, those men who try to put down women by saying, "Women are their own worst enemies, you know." This can cover up hidden thoughts such as "You'll never get it together like we men do," or "You're not worth much and you can't change *that*. It's in your genes," or "Who wants to be beaten by a woman? I couldn't stand that." It can be an acceptable way of expressing superiority, conveying contempt, or hiding fear. Conscious baiting is an attempt to define and control others; it's a power play.

However, the power to define (and redefine) is also the power to choose. To drop bait sent your way, you can choose to separate yourself with a separator phrase, such as "as you see it," or "I don't buy that." Although the separator phrase is generally something you say to yourself, it can be your total response. Other options are:

- A non-commital glance back as you keep working or as you exit.
- "That's one view."
- "I hear you."
- "I'm glad we don't have to agree."
- "That was a loaded comment" (reporting the process).
- "Is that right?" (non-sarcastically).
- "Oh! I didn't know" (innocently).
- "At it again, I see" (making an observation).

Tone of voice can change the meaning, especially in the last three phrases. If you're feeling angry, these could become nasty barbs that could arouse more defensiveness in the speaker and keep the baiting game going.

When dropping others' bait, the result you probably want is a quick end to the conversation. Brief neutral responses work well when accompanied by body movements that say the same thing—walking away, looking down, getting back to your work. Your response will say, literally and figuratively, "I don't buy. I haven't time for it. End."

Another way to handle an emotional load is to send it back. It's like saying "Thanks, but no thanks. I don't want it. You can have it." It bounces off your separator screen and heads back to the speaker. This way you take no responsibility for what came your way because you don't take it into yourself. You let the speaker take responsibility for the load. If he or she refuses delivery, it stays out in limbo or drops of its own weight.

Let's see how this works in a man–woman baiting game:

Dialogue	*Dynamics*
Man: "Women are their own worst enemies, you know."	"Women" refers to all women, so woman now stands judged (down).
Woman: "There you go, putting down women again. You really hate women, don't you?"	The man is now accused (down) and typically will try to regain his position (up).
Man: "Of course not. The real tragedy is that women hate each other."	The man has simply restated his stereotype in different words— another power play (up).

Another possible response to "Women are their own worst enemies" is:

Woman: "Like men? You, for example?"	Another accusation (down) invites a down response.
Man: "Oh, you know better than that. Men stick together like women never will.	He sends a down by using another stereotype. The man is still up.

Suppose the woman doesn't accuse or add to the load in the original bait:

Woman: "Oh. I hadn't noticed any pattern unique to women."	The woman implies that men may also be their own worst enemies and sends back the load without adding to it (a draw).
Man: "You're not very observant, are you?"	The man tries to shift it back by judging the woman, trying to put her down.

Dialogue	*Dynamics*
Woman: "Oh, I'm quite observant" (leaving her comment hanging).	She can drop it ambiguously (draw). It's neither win nor lose; it goes nowhere.

Another option:

| *Woman:* "I've noticed *people* stab others in the back, some men and some women. No stereotypes needed. Now, let's get back to work. | The woman can take a stronger position by stating her view without using stereotypes. She shifts the assumptions. Getting back to work stops the game. No one has to lose face (although some people think they lose if they don't win). |

And one last option:

| *Woman:* "That's an old stereotype that has gone out of style. Look around you (walking away). | If this is said in an information-giving tone, it won't be a put-down but will end the conversation. |

9. Non-Responsiveness

Choosing not to respond to someone's meanings is similar to buying time. You stay centered where you choose to be and remain unaffected by the message by choosing to act on your own track. You may choose to make no response at all, but you can come back with an unrelated remark that gives you control over yourself.

Perhaps you've noticed conversations that are like two ships passing in the night: "I like cream cheese," followed by "My brother plays the violin." It's like "What are you so defensive about?" being passed by with "Did you see Johnny Carson last night?" Collect a few of these to have on hand when you want to play passerby.

Non-responsiveness is most useful when someone is trying to control you or your choices when you don't want them to. What can the door-to-door salesman say when you interrupt the spiel with "No thank you," and close the door? It works two ways, however. Sometimes the person with less power can use the same response. Has your child ever pulled down the window-shade and mentally tuned you out? It can be deadly.

When you keep control over yourself or your situation but don't try to take away control from a self-styled opponent, you're redefining the rules of the game. You're not playing adversary. You're not playing. You're serious about keeping your self-choice and self-control.

Although serious in the results you want, you can communicate them with humor. We'll see how that can be done in the next situation, in which you'll see one way to close off and close out an adversary who insists on win–lose rules.

10. Use a Close-Off Statement or Action

A close-off statement ends the exchange with a no-comeback comment, such as the perfect squelch or tension-relieving humor. When an adversary challenges you, there's a fine line between delivering the perfect squelch and throwing a curve designed to kill the adversary.

Humor can be used two ways: to diffuse the tension or to decimate the enemy. Timing and tone must be exquisitely tuned to stay centered in non-defensive self-control. Once more we enter the scene of action.

> Ann Morgan had been invited to speak to a manufacturer's trade association on the general subject of women in management. This program topic was being presented for the first time, even though equal opportunity laws had been in effect for over ten years.
>
> Ann's announced title was "Do You Take More Risks with Men than Women?" It drew an unusually large crowd, since the men who habitually attended used the occasion to invite their wives and women employees. Only two months earlier the regional trade magazine had featured a cover story on women in the industry's management. The editor of that trade magazine, Pat Doyle, was present and actively socializing during the cocktail hour.
>
> A buzzing tension pervaded the air—nervous bursts of laughter, serious discussions between intense pairs. Shifting clusters of people finally dispersed to dinner, followed by the warmly debated subject of the evening. Long familiar with such cross-currents, Ann was finely tuned. Her provocative talk, delivered in a whimsically humorous fashion, led into an invitation for questions from the floor.
>
> The first question came from an irate man, Duke O'Brien, known among industry people as an inveterate speechmaker. He shook his fist at Pat Doyle as he launched his attacks, using the feature story in her trade magazine as a springboard. "What do you women call fair anyway? You just want to take over everything without any experience. Women managers! Pooh, what do you know about it? You don't have any idea how long it takes to be a good manager in this business. And that

woman—what's-her-name over there—prints a whole feature article on women in management. Talk about discrimination! When do you ever see a feature on men in management?"

Ann's split-second humor cut in: "That's the other eleven months of the year!" Laughter and the applause of comic relief washed over the tension as Duke sat down shaking his head, quelled for the moment. Ann immediately invited other questions and the mood settled down as the meeting drew to a close.

Did Ann deliver a perfect squelch or throw a killing curve? As a speaker, she stimulated lots of feelings for opening up the discussion. She had to keep control of the meeting and bring the subject to a close if she was to maintain her credibility as a speaker. At the same time, she had to treat all participants with due respect, whether or not respect was returned. She had little to gain and much to lose if she decimated an adversary—or appeared to.

Duke O'Brien had come out fighting. He had taken the floor and had taken aim at Pat Doyle's article. Women managers were under attack, perhaps women in general, Pat, and perhaps Ann specifically, if not personally. Duke had every intention of winning his argument, concluding his tirade with what he must have thought was a clincher. By his rules, when he won, women in general and some women specifically would lose. By those same rules, if he didn't win, he'd lose. No room for mutual gain.

Define the results you want; define the rules of the game; harm no one; let no one harm you; and keep your options coming. Odds of non-defensive gains are then high.

Ann Morgan did some split-second choosing among her options. Duke was trying to define the scene, but Ann had to keep control of the meeting, take the heat off Pat Doyle, and call Duke's game without attacking him personally. If she could reduce the growing tension, all the better.

She handled his clincher, "When do you ever see a feature on men in management?" as if it were a serious question—the unexpected twist that seems to amuse us immensely. Keeping focused on the surface content only, Ann gave him the data he requested, and she won that round. The humor was relatively harmless to him. It broke the tension and helped move the questions on to other concerns.

Here are some of the things she didn't do:

- She didn't attack him personally, such as calling him a male chauvinist.
- She didn't tell him how he ought to behave, such as telling him to cool it.
- She didn't rub his nose in his loss, such as telling him he should know better than to take her on. What's more, she didn't laugh at him.
- She didn't try to renegotiate his win–lose rules, which might have made her appear to give in. To do that in that particular arena would have been her loss. Time was too short to work toward a gain–gain resolution.
- As a result, she didn't sink him; she only took the wind out of his sails.

Ann's timing was quick, her choice concise. Her humor diffused the tension while she retained control. Duke felt he had lost, and he had, fair and square by his own rules. That's the chance anyone takes when he or she insists on win–lose rules. By Ann's rules, it was a draw, and her rules prevailed.

There are a few ground rules for quick responses. If your fighting spirit gets aroused and you decide to smash 'em to the wall—and you do—others will get their faces bloodied. Not only do they lose the fight, they lose face. At times, your face won't look very good either. Their urge to deliver equal damage to you in the next round swells. To stay out of that lose–lose situation, your strongest position is to take a few moments to center yourself so you can deflect the attack, hold your ground, or take control in a gain–gain way so no one loses face.

On the other hand, if you usually back off into the wallpaper when you're defensive, *you* may lose face. That won't do either. Everyone's dignity must be preserved, including your own.

Most of these quick responses are optional things to say or do when you receive double meanings or direct attacks. None fit all situations. Think of the results you want and a few of the options you have and quickly select one that appeals to you. Say that option to yourself first; then decide whether or not you want to use it. When in doubt, don't. It's easier for others to hang you with your words than with your silence.

While you're learning quick responses, play safe. Because of the "keep cool" norm, you almost always take fewer risks when you seem calm on the outside, even if you're boiling inside. When you've learned how to boil over and calm down quickly, that can become one of your options. Even though it's often high risk, it has its place.

Remember that if you still have to take it on the chin once in a while, you can tell yourself you're on your way and will be "on center" soon. It's both a matter of having more available responses and thinking of them in time.

TIMING—HOW TO THINK OF IT IN TIME

Have you noticed how some people always seem to be quick on the uptake with a great reply? In comparison others seem like duds most of the time. What makes the difference? I think it has to do with feeling centered, turned on, confident—comfortable that if you don't make it this time, you will another. Few incidents are so vital that there won't be others as important on which to test your mettle.

Some people tell themselves they can't think fast enough or don't know how. Sure enough that becomes a self-fulfilling prophecy, and they really don't think fast on their feet. They know they can't—and they don't.

You're on your way to being centered when you face what you've written on your Incident Cards and when you don't require perfection of yourself.

If you are one of these people and would like to change that pattern, you can start by telling yourself, "I'm on my way." Even if you're just starting, you *are* on your way. Make your own list of quick responses for incidents that keep showing up on your Incident Cards. Make these responses a part of your automatic repertoire. If you don't demand instant perfection, you may discover that you can think of what you want to say faster than you think. (If one of your inner rules is "I have to be perfect," here's a chance to flex it, question it, and perhaps allow yourself time to learn.)

Let's assume you have noted on your Incident Card that what you want to be ready to do next time is, "To think of what I want to say in time to have the effect I want and which I will specify clearly." You might add, "To trust my creative self to flash the right pictures and words on my inner eye so I can see what to do." Once you start thinking and visualizing along these lines, you're on your way. In Figure 8-3 the "zap" is like your repetitious incident; notice how you can gradually think of what you want to say sooner than on the previous occasion. As you keep telling yourself, "I'm on my way," you are, even if it takes a while to get there. Stick with it, and soon you

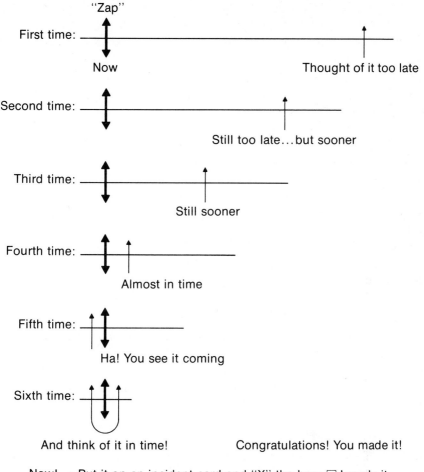

Now! → Put it on an incident card and "X" the box: ☐ I made it.

Remember: You're a success when you make it once!
(Forget the times you don't make it. They don't count.)

Figure 8-3. *Thinking of your response in time.*

can see it coming (fifth time or sooner), but *also* you'll think of what to say in time (sixth time or sooner). Once you start, the results you want and some options will begin to come more quickly. By centering in your strengths, you can make the self-fulfilling prophesy work *for* you.

Somewhere near the fifth time or before, you may become aware that people who zap make a preparatory signal—often a non-verbal sign—before they deliver their cargo. Think of someone who zaps you. Think sensingly now. Can you recall any characteristic signals he or she emits: sniffing in or out, recrossing legs, hitching up pants or smoothing skirt, leaning forward or back, an uncharacteristic silence?

Look for verbal signals too, such as "Um-mmm" or "We-e-ell"; listen for phrases such as, "Now, wait a minute" or "I don't know about that." You might be able to pick up subtle signals through changes in energy flow expressed by subtle body movements, such as a slight muscle tensing or an almost imperceptible drawing in of breath. Sometimes it's intuition, and you can't identify the source. These signals can often be sensed, even when they don't make sense in the usual way. With practice, you'll learn to trust them.

These signals are prologues to put-downs that can clue you to what's coming. When you're watching for them, you're paying attention to the other person's processes, which leaves less of your attention for feeling defensive. With this early warning system, you can be ready before the zap comes. Your odds will be better for thinking of what to say in time. Each time you do, notice it and write it on an Incident Card to help you keep building on your strengths.

PULLING IT ALL TOGETHER

After all the examples of quick responses and how to think of them in time, let's summarize. The following conversion table doesn't cover everything we've talked about, but gives a quick review of some ways to move from defensive to non-defensive responses. In table 8-1, you'll probably recognize some of the ways Marie, Jack, Nancy, Burk, Denise, and others used that you can use for your own incidents.

Buying time shows up frequently since it's often the first step toward becoming non-defensive. Remembering to stop talking long enough to think about what results you want and what your options are is often enough to turn things around.

Getting rid of or flexing some of the old rules can give you more room in which to operate. One old rule that many people learn is: 99 successes + 1 failure = 100 failures. (It may come from performance standards for male potency: 99 ups + 1 down = impotence.) Wherever it comes from, it's the rule that says, "I have to be perfect every day in every way (or appear to be)." If you keep score on yourself—an unkind rigor at best—try this rule: *You're a success when you make it once!* Forget the times you don't make it. They don't count today.

If keeping score gets in the way of learning, you can forget about scores. You score when you learn more.

Table 8-1. *Converting Defensive Responses to Non-Defensive Responses*

From Subordinate Defensiveness	To Self-Choosing Non-Defensiveness
Explain, prove, justify your actions, ideas, or feelings more than is required.	Report feelings or name the process; then stop talking.
Ask why things are done the way they are when you really want to change them. *"Why don't they...?"*	Ask *"How can we...?"* questions that point to results to be achieved and that include your personal goals.
Ask permission when it's not needed. *"Is it okay with you if...?"*	Report or recommend what you want to do and invite confirmation.
Give away decisions, ideas, power when it would be appropriate to own them. *"Don't you think that...?"*	Keep your own ideas, offering them with, I think... How does that sound to you?
Apologize, feel inadequate, say "I'm sorry" when you're not.	Buy time; ask yourself, "Is this what I want to do?" If not, take time to find other, better options.
Submit or withdraw when it is not in your best interest. *"Whatever you say."*	Buy time, listen to yourself and your feelings, choose appropriate action and timing to best suit your purposes and those of your system.
Lose your cool, cry, act angry, where it's inappropriate.	Buy time to detach yourself; leave the situation if necessary. Decide when and how to release emotional backlog to reduce odds of exploding.
Go blank, click off, be at a loss for words just when you want a quick response. "I should've said..."	Buy time; refocus on results you want; define issues, options, and risks; select options that will get results you want before you speak; consider the option of saying nothing.
Use coping humor or hostile jocularity when honest feedback might serve your purpose better.	Buy time to check if your choice is a safe one; select among available options; consider detachment.
Use self-deprecating adjectives and reactive verbs. "I'm just a..." "I'm just doing what I was told."	Use self-affirming adjectives. "I am..." (name a strength); "I do / question / decide..." (so you aren't acted upon by others).
Use the generalized *you* and *they* when *I* and personal names would state the situation more clearly. "They really hassle you here."	Use *I* and personal names of others to clearly define events and feelings. Use generalized *you* only when it fits. "I feel hassled and want room to make more of my own choices, here or elsewhere."
Smile to cover up feelings or put yourself down because you don't know what else to do and smiling says you're nice.	Smile when you feel a smile within, allowing that *you* to show. Honor yourself as well as others. Being nice when you don't feel it is insincere. You are real.

Perhaps it's time to invent a new yardstick: One success is all it takes to succeed. Ninety-nine failures is further evidence of the brilliance of the one success. The power to define is the power to choose, so choose what sets you up for success. This doesn't deny so-called failures or what you can learn from them. It just puts a different perspective on them.

TO GET STARTED

Think of some remark that puts you off balance, a gnat you'd like to handle better. It may come from someone at work, at home, someone you call a friend. Perhaps someone criticizes you by constantly telling you what you always do or never do. Maybe someone tells you, "You are too (emotional, rigid, fat, quiet, efficient)."

Listen for one that arouses your annoyance or irritation—when you usually tell yourself, "I shouldn't feel this way. It's not important." It *is* important if you're reacting to it. Whatever you are feeling is okay to feel, even if you don't like it. It's these niggly things that drain your energy because they get buried under the "shoulds." Take care of them, and you release your energy for more important things.

Be aware of the emotional energy you feel when you hear the gnat buzzing. As you turn that energy around to get off the defensive, ask yourself what results you want and what options you have. Then see how many *non-defensive* responses you can come up with. These responses are options you can choose from the next time the gnat appears. Now you are ready for it and can free yourself to move on to larger concerns.

IN THE NEXT CHAPTER

We move on to how you can *stay* off the defensive in more complex or longer-term situations. The Choosing Process is a way to regularly gain more of the results you want. First we will review how the seven steps flow together. Then we will see how to gather information about *attitudes* and feelings—your own and others. We'll also collect data about the events or activities that are occurring—the *content* of the situation—to prepare for defining the results you want. You'll be using both sensing and analytical skills to do these steps. Subsequent chapters cover the rest of the Choosing Process and what it looks like in action.

For additional background reading, see bibliography entries 7, 10, 13, 15, 16, 21, 29, 74.

9

GETTING OFF THE DEFENSIVE AND STAYING CENTERED

Choosing to Act, Not React

The Wednesday night NDC group was about to begin when Rachel Nelson arrived, shedding a pall on the gathering group. Usually she arrived with an energetic bustle, so immediately someone asked her what was wrong.

"My best friend was murdered this week," she explained tensely. "They're doing the autopsy now and the funeral is Saturday."

Everyone responded to this report in her own way, none comfortably. Most of them had not experienced the death of someone close to them, much less murder. What do you say at a time like this?

People murmured sympathetic comments; several asked questions about how it had happened. None said out loud that they felt helpless and uncertain about what to say to Rae.

We had already established high-trust, low-fear norms in this group. As leader I decided to risk suggesting that we use this stressful situation to see how the Choosing Process might help Rae. Everyone felt the inappropriateness of this suggestion, since societal norms about death, especially violent death, seem to require sympathetic comments and questions, but certainly *not* what then seemed like a cold, intellectual, heartless approach. However, Rae was willing, so we went ahead, writing down her comments on a chartpad. Here are some of her feelings and attitudes, mixed with more informational content:

- I've accepted the fact of murder. You have to.
- The funeral is what I dread. I'm petrified. (What was the threat?)
- The threat is I'll break down, and that means I'll be weak.

- Everyone expects me to be the strong one.
- I don't expect to be the strong one, but I'm afraid if I break down, I'll be letting myself down. (Notice the contradiction.)

As she continued to explore others' expectations about death, she blurted out "I hate funerals." She was angry at customs that require:

- Looking at the body.
- Listening to an eulogy by a man who doesn't even know Chris.
- Listening to talk about heaven and hell that I don't believe in and Chris didn't believe in.
- Listening to the man telling me who and what Chris was like. (Her fears and anger seemed to settle here.)
- I know they are going to violate Chris.

She was letting her feelings simply flow out. The group was with her process, not asking any questions that could divert the focus of her feelings. They listened to *her*, not themselves, and didn't evaluate any of her feelings. So more came:

- I feel like I'm letting him down.
- I feel guilty.
- He doesn't like these damn funerals.
- They don't *know* what he really wants or who he really is.

The group members continued to hear her pain, loyalty, and outrage. Sensing more anger and pain in Rae, I asked her if she wanted to work with some of her feelings. She did. She visualized first one person, then another, and told them all the bottled-up feelings and tears she had held within herself about each one. As she let her genie out of the bottle, she discovered these additional feelings:

- Much suppressed anger at the murder and its violation of Chris.
- Much more pain at the loss of her friend.
- A deep sense of being personally violated as Chris' friend.

Finally she felt some relief and release after freeing her multicolored genies and came to a surprised conclusion: "I didn't know I had such strong feelings about *all* those things!"

The people in the group had sensed them, shared and experienced her trip through pain, and were now relieved with her. No one was alone in this emergence from the valley of shadows. Quickly she felt new energy for working on the results she wanted at the funeral. Here's her list of possible results and some options for getting the results she finally chose.

Results Wanted (tentative statements as she considered some possibilities)

1. To accept the funeral ceremony as an exercise, not as symbolic of my relationship to Chris.
2. To fantasize Chris' wishes for the funeral and mentally picture it to completion. (This may be more an option than a result wanted.)
3. To feel resolution by adding a sense of eternity to the friendship.
4. To feel powerful in influencing the funeral service toward the values I shared with Chris.
5. To feel powerful in my own way of participating in the service.
6. Accept other people's need for the catharsis a funeral provides and to go along with that need, even though I don't need it.

Options (the group brainstormed options, then Rae added the risks)   *Risk*

1. Get to the ceremony-performer and tell him about Chris' *real* wishes for the service.   O.K.
2. Go and stop the damn funeral by taking control of it.   High
3. Not go to the funeral at all.   No
4. To ask or demand to speak about Chris in the service.   High
5. Go to the funeral with the idea that it's for other people (Chris would understand that). Keep my own feelings personal and private during the service.   O.K.
6. Be sure that a clergyman is not the ceremony-performer.   Medium

At this point Rae felt she had already made her choice—number 5. After her earlier recognition and release of feelings, she now felt comfortable with this choice of action, able to accept others' needs as well as her own. This settled the results she wanted—numbers 5 and 6—which gave a mutual gain to her and the others.

The NDC group was surprised that the Choosing Process could be used for an emotional event like violent death. One person sat back through it all, not believing it could be done. They had used it for work problems only where feelings were not as obvious.

They had just seen how, by simply listening to Rae's feelings, they could help her. They also saw that if she couldn't express her feelings at the beginning, she had another natural opportunity when she listed options. If her additional feelings changed the content and attitudes, Rae could go back and revise the results she wanted, and she did this. It wasn't the funeral that she dreaded as much as her fear of helplessness to prevent her anticipated violation of Chris.

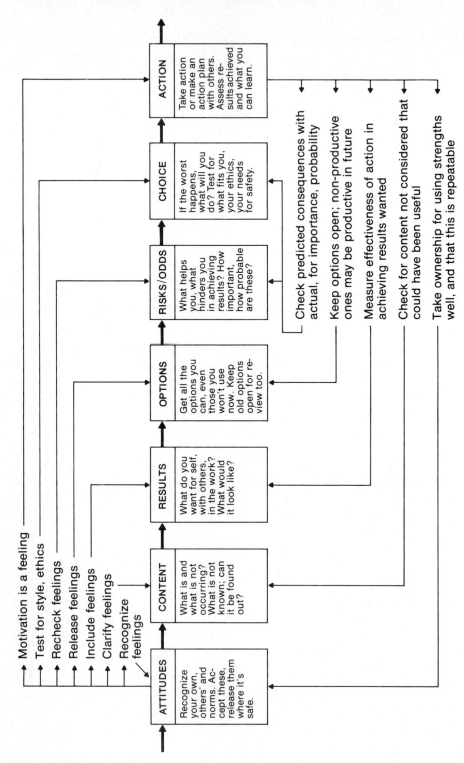

Figure 9-1. *The Choosing Process as a full-loop system.*

Once Rae found an option that gave her a sense of control over herself and a feeling of respect for Chris and for others who would come to his funeral, she made a decision that stopped the flow of options from the group.

Not all the steps of the Choosing Process were used in making her choice. However, Rae said that while she was choosing her action, she was testing her choice for fit to her personal style, her ethics, and for taking into consideration others' needs. She used the process in a fluid, flexible way to achieve mutual gain.

THE CHOOSING PROCESS IS FOR CHOOSING ACTION, NOT REACTION

The Choosing Process (Figure 9-1) is a way to gain results when opposing tensions exist between yourself and others or within yourself. When you use it, you can integrate all your ways of being human—the head, the heart, and the spirit—so that you can operate out of a cool, centered core of convictions, especially when you're under fire or personal stress.

Add feelings, subtract evaluations, and you give yourself the power to choose. You grow as a person as you honor yourself, stop criticizing and learn.

The central paradox of the Choosing Process is that to keep your cool, you allow feelings to be part of your process. This flies in the face of our conventional wisdom, which says that to keep your cool, you keep your feelings under wraps and stick to the facts. However, this very denial of feelings keeps people *reacting*, busily defending themselves against their own and others' hidden feelings. When you allow yourself to sense your feelings and consider them legitimate and valuable, they cease to be so threatening. Then you have a potent energy source for renegotiating your relationships and roles.

Another way the Choosing Process breaks with conventional thinking is the instruction to eliminate evaluation and substitute assessment. It may seem unnecessary to make this distinction between two words that seem to have similar meanings. However, their connotations are quite different. Evaluation implies judging, usually negatively; assessment suggests a nonjudgmental look at data from which to learn something valuable. The emotional response to each attitude is different.

Evaluation is a process that judges a person or action as good or bad, right or wrong, resulting in an either-or opinion. Many people panic when they are being evaluated. Their thinking gets muddled; clear, separate lines of thought lump together into a gray mass; inner questions jump around asking "What's wrong with me?" and "Can I measure up to someone else's expectations?" To these people, evaluation can feel like a life–death situation.

When an action is evaluated as good, it goes on the shelf to be used another time. If it doesn't work, it's dumped with the conclusion, "That's something we won't do again." Over the years, you can eliminate a lot of options—and people—by evaluating them.

Not only can you choose your actions, but you can know what you're choosing *for*. This gives you a sense of purpose and self-confidence.

Let's say you have taken an action and have gained most, but not all, of the results you wanted. If you evaluate—if you have an inner rule that says you have to be perfect—you might say you've failed.

In contrast, when you assess the effectiveness of each step in the Choosing Process, you learn to sharpen your skills of analysis, sensing, prediction, thinking of options in order to achieve more mutual gain in your results. Non-evaluative (non-judgmental) assessment gives you more information, helps keep options open, pinpoints skills that can be developed further, and even considers whether the problem warranted the time and effort spent on it. Your thinking remains sharp and clear when you're less dependent on others and when you use more critical judgment in your own interest.

Let's see how these two departures from conventional thinking can help you create a dynamic process for choosing your actions instead of merely reacting to others' actions.

In Figure 9-1 the steps of the Choosing Process are shown as the core in a full-loop system. The top loops flowing from left to right show the integration of feelings as facts at each step; the bottom loops flowing from right to left show the assessment of how well the action got the results wanted, plus several other learning outcomes.

Let's take a brief look at each step of the Choosing Process, how these steps interrelate, how feelings are used at each step, the underlying premises and values, and how it looks in action.

Examples are used from the case in Chapter 3 in which Helen Henderson is still trying to get the variance report from her assistant, John Silberman, while she is under fire from her boss, Bill Bendorff. When the scene ended, John had won a four-day delay with the apparent consent of Bill. Now we'll see what comes next when the Choosing Process is used.

Later in this chapter we'll see how Helen, having learned from using the Choosing Process, might have played the original scene less defensively. (In real life, you'd apply the learning to the next situation. For convenience, we'll use the same situation twice.)

Step 1. Sensing ATTITUDES

In this data collecting step, you sense what attitudes seem to be operating in the situation: your own, those of others involved in or who influence the situation, and relevant organizational norms. Attitudes include all the subjective information: feelings, assumptions, stereotypes, biases, beliefs, values, desires, expectations, motivations, priorities, even dreams! Attitudes also include norms for acceptable behavior and punishments for breaking norms, political motivations, power bases, who influences whom, who depends on whom for what, and who controls needed resources.

While collecting this information, you may incidentally gather some data about the content—the events that are occurring—or about influences affecting those events. No absolute separation has to be maintained because you'll be treating both as factual data.

Let's rejoin Helen, John, and Bill and see what's going on since the scene ended in Chapter 3. Recall that Helen had not received the variance report by Friday noon, so she called John and discovered that he had gotten Bill's consent to get it in by the following Tuesday. First, we'll listen to Helen's inner dialogue right after she receives this news; then we'll hear John's and Bill's inner dialogues as this situation develops.

Helen's Inner Dialogue	*How She Answers Herself*
1. What in the hell is Bill doing, undermining me this way?	Now hold on. You don't know what John told Bill.
2. I've been frustrated enough. This has got to come to a screeching halt. This is the third time John's stalled and gotten away with it.	No, it's my *efforts*, not me, that are frustrated. I need to distance myself and get another perspective on this.

Helen's Inner Dialogue	*How She Answers Herself*
3. So much rides on my succeeding in this job. I really want to make it in management.	For personal pride? For the future of women here? Money? Prestige? Being exceptional?
4. I've lost control of the first important project I've delegated so far. Bill doesn't seem sure I can manage. Does this mean I can't?	My confidence as a manger isn't very high yet. But I'm O.K. as a person. What *do* I think a good manager is?
5. I *say* I don't want to fire John, but am I really too scared to do it? How do I tell him he's about to be fired without sounding threatening?	I really don't want to lose John. I've worked with him for a long time, I like him, and I know he's good. That's real.
6. I've been going round and round with this thinking, and I just get more defensive. Time to buckle down and figure out what to do.	Hold it! Before you figure out what to *do*, figure out *what* you want to accomplish. What results do you want?
7. I could kill John for putting me in this spot.	You're off the subject again. Are you wallowing in self-pity?
8. He's too damn smug, knowing he's got me over a barrel.	I hate to be on the losing end, especially now. I'd like to feel as smug as he acts. AHA! Yes, that's exactly how I feel.
9. I want to regain control, first over myself, then over the situation and the report. I don't want to do it myself. It'd take too long and that's no way to manage.	I know I can't control John, so I have to find a way to influence him to want to come through.
10. I think I'm really angry at him for making me feel helpless, playing at his win–lose games with me losing.	Hey wait—who's helpless? I'm not going to give away my power to him any more.
11. I want to get more information from Bill. I may have lost this round, but I want to see that it doesn't happen again.	I also want a way to save face and regain my confidence. What if I level with him?

Helen's Inner Dialogue	*How She Answers Herself*
12. The result I want is to regain control, handle the present mess with dignity and establish more rapport with John.	I'll figure out my options after I find out what Bill was doing and where I stand.

Helen may have more feelings, but this shows how she works through some of her feelings, reviews some of the current content, decides on additional information she needs, and makes an early statement of results she wants.

Helen was also getting into the second and third steps of the Choosing Process—content and results she wants—while working with her attitudes. The process moves with the person. Helen's earlier feelings and thoughts flow into later ones so she no longer feels the same way as she did at the beginning. This is what happens when you *work through* your feelings—they move you toward some resolution.

Before we hear John's and Bill's inner dialogues, we need to know what transpired between them that led John to tell Helen that he would turn in the report on Tuesday, not Friday.

As it happened, John had recently run into Bill at the Midtown Jewish Community Center. They struck up a conversation that got around to the job. Bill casually asked John how it was working out with Helen, and John replied:

"Oh just fine, I guess. It takes a little getting used to, not answering to you anymore. There was less fencing around then and things were simpler. But I guess it takes her a while to get used to the job." His tone is somewhere between patronizing and patient tolerance.

"Something bothering you?" Bill inquires, sensing the ambiguity.

"Oh she's just pushing pretty hard on that variance report. When do you really need it anyway, Bill?" He's asking for the real, official word.

"Well I suppose we could manage if I had it by Tuesday, but she has to work these things out with you." Bill wanted to put Helen on her own.

"Oh. Okay. That's no problem. It'll get taken care of." He changes the subject to the evening's activities at the center, feeling he's back on the old footing with Bill again. His wife, Ruth, will like that.

John assumed that Bill had given his permission to extend the deadline until Tuesday, so here is his version after talking with Bill:

John's Inner Dialogue	*How He Answers Himself*
1. I fixed her. Never hurts to have a friend in the boss. Good thing I ran into him tonight.	It's kind of an empty victory though. Too easy.
2. I told her the best man would win.	And I have!
3. It'll be easier to face Ruth now.	Or will it?
4. I'd sure like to get a promotion soon to help pay the extra education expenses. They sure piled up fast.	That would probably set better with Ruth. I'll have to talk with Bill about that now that we're back on track again.

John is beginning to think of himself answering to Bill again, just as he did before Helen was promoted. So he's off the hook for Friday noon, giving him the weekend if he needs it. He didn't seem to hear Bill's intent that he work with Helen on their schedule.

Now it's late afternoon on Friday. Helen has cooled down after thinking through the attitudes and content. She calls Bill, and the scene shifts to Bill's office where he's picking up the phone. Helen asked to see him so he tells her to come in. But as he hangs up, an unexpected seriousness in her voice lingers. Suddenly he recalls his conversation with John at the center and wonders.

Helen arrives and comes straight to the point without her usual banter. (Experiment with the differences in tone of voice, pitch, and the pace of speaking that could make the following dialogue defensive or non-defensive.)

Non-Defensive Dialogue	*Non-Defensive Dynamics*
Helen (H1):* Bill, John tells me you gave him until Tuesday to finish the variance report. I had given him a Friday noon deadline. I think I need some clarification about how we're going to handle situations like this.	Notice that she doesn't accuse Bill of anything. She simply states her need non-defensively, inviting discussion about their roles.
Bill (B1): What did he say?	Bill is now listening carefully.
Helen (H2): He said he checked with you and you said you could wait a few more days—Tuesday, to be exact. I was surprised because this doesn't seem like your style.	She reports the information and invites more. She also reports her feelings, but again without accusing, judging, or evaluating Bill.

*These numbers will be used for later discussion of Helen's and Bill's conversation.

Non-Defensive Dialogue	*Non-Defensive Dynamics*
Bill (B2): It isn't, Helen. There must be some misunderstanding. We talked about it some, but I thought I made it clear that I wanted the two of you to work out your deadlines. I want you to handle this yourself without interference from me.	Bill has no need to become defensive. He hasn't been attacked and doesn't have defensiveness inherited from other unrelated situations. He keeps to the issues of timing, roles, and responsibility.
Helen (H3): That's what I thought, Bill. Right now I'm feeling he went over my head and that you went along with him. I'd like to get this sorted out.	She lets Bill know her feelings by reporting, not expressing, them; then moves on toward options, having confirmed that the result they both want is to keep John answering to Helen, not Bill.
Bill (B3): That's certainly not what I meant to do, Helen. I think I'd better talk with John about it. Let me get back to you.	Bill indicates his support of Helen's role, his need for more information from John, and an unspoken request for Helen to hold off.
Helen (H4): All right. I'll be interested in what happens.	She temporarily leaves the matter in Bill's hands.

At this point, Bill has his own inner dialogue about how Helen's promotion is being accepted in the day-to-day working relationships:

Bill's Inner Dialogue	*How He Answers Himself*
1. I told John he had to work things out with Helen. Sounds like he took my comment about Tuesday as if I was telling him to change the deadline.	I know he doesn't like having to work for Helen. Is he trying to use our common background and interests to avoid answering to her?
2. I want Helen to stand on her own feet but if John's trying to get around her, I'll have to stop that right now. I won't be a party to that.	If John's trading on that, I take great exception to it. That has nothing to do with the job. I'll see him Monday.

At this point, it appears that Helen's willingness to trust Bill to see that the new reporting channels are respected is well placed. John may or may not have been using a social connection to his advantage. But he did listen selectively, hearing only what he wanted to hear. He made the assumption that he could bypass Helen and win back the closer contact with Bill that he wants and control Helen at the same time. Before long, we'll see how well his assumptions work out. Right now let's continue with how the next steps of the Choosing Process were used.

Step 2. Analyzing CONTENT

This step is the more familiar data-gathering process in which you look for objective events that are, and are not, occurring. Think analytically, but you'll also need your imaginative skills. Helen and John have already asked the questions they needed to gather their content. Here's a more complete list of specific questions to consider in your own situations:

- What events are occurring? What events should be occurring?
- What events are not occurring that should be?
- What events might be occurring but remain hidden? These are the ones that are often political and can strongly affect your power position.
- Of potentially hidden events, which can you find out more about, and which must remain tentative risks?
- What's missing? (or who's missing?) Are there any conspicuous absences?

Helen and Bill have been using some of the questions in gathering data; John less so.

Another cluster of questions compares what is now occurring to what occurred at a previous time when there was a change:

- When did the change occur? Which people and what issues are involved?
- How serious is it? How far-reaching is it? How much does it matter?
- What is the probable cause of the change? What or who does the change help or hinder? Who cares enough to act? What tensions are increasing?

We already have this data in our present case.

A third cluster of questions considers additional resources that may be needed before taking action:

- Who else needs to be involved and why?
- Who else could become involved who also has such needed

resources as time, money, influence, access to information, power to lead others?

- How can these people be attracted to becoming involved?
- Who depends on whom, and who influences whom? Do some of the key people depend on many others to be able to do their job and are thus inclined to be more political?
- Who is interested in expediting the situation, and who can delay it?
- Where are other resources within or outside your immediate system?
- How important is this situation in the overall scheme of things?
- How much effort are you (and others) willing to invest in it?

This third cluster of questions is needed for more complex situations, such as Dave Eliot's at Country Stores. These questions go too far afield for this present case.

As we've seen, there's no clean separation between attitudes and content, just as there's no way to completely separate events from the people who create those events.

Collecting data doesn't usually raise defenses. Collecting too much may leave you with paralysis of analysis.

Helen, John, and Bill didn't ask all the above questions, nor was it necessary for their immediate purposes. It's easy to overdo gathering data. In interpersonal situations, just as in sales or inventory problems, you can use the Pareto principle.[1] This principle rests on the assumption that a "vital few" of the facts will usually account for most of the events that are going on. So if 20 percent of your effort turns up 80 percent of the data you need, you could spend another 80 percent of your effort to gather the other 20 percent—the "trivial many" details that would simply embellish what you already know.

When you're first working with the Choosing Process, you may think you've gotten 115 percent of the data you need, only to find out later it's more like 15 percent because you didn't know what questions to ask. Or more experience will show you through hindsight that you gathered more data than you needed. It takes some trial and error to develop a sense of when to stop. Often the time to stop hunting depends on how many and what kinds of

---

[1] For a graphic presentation of the Pareto principle, see R. Alec Mackenzie, *The Time Trap: How to Get More Done in Less Time*, AMACOM, a division of American Management Associations, New York, 1972, p. 52.

risks there are in your situation. When you sense that you have enough information, move on quickly to state the results you want. As you do that, you're likely to think of other specific, vital information you need. Odds are good it won't be trivial.

Step 3. Formulating RESULTS WANTED

In the two data-gathering steps—sensing attitudes and analyzing content—you may begin to formulate the results you want. Helen developed several possibilities during her data-gathering steps.

1. I don't want to lose John. He's good. (Helen's Inner Dialogue [HID]5, page 260.)
2. I'd like to feel as smug as he acts. (HID 8)
3. I want a way to influence John to want to come through. (HID 9)
4. I don't want to give away my power to John anymore. (HID 10)
5. I don't want to lose any more rounds with John. (HID 11)
6. I want a way to save face and regain my confidence. (HID 11)
7. I want to regain control, handle the present mess with dignity, and establish more rapport with John. (HID 12)
8. I want some clarification about my role from Bill. (Non-Defensive Dialogue [NDD] H1, page 262.)
9. The result wanted is to keep John answering to me, not Bill. (NDD, H3)
10. I want Bill's backing to keep John answering to me. (Although not explicitly stated, this was implied at NDD, H4.)

Some of these are interim statements as Helen develops her data and her goals. Some are immediate results she wants; others are longer-term. She can consolidate some of them, but she needs a separate statement for each aspect of the situation.

The complete results statement includes some gain for yourself, your relationships with others, and the job to be done.

After sorting and consolidating the results that Helen wants, the results she wants might be these.

Results Wanted	For Self, Relationship, or Task
1. I want to regain control, my confidence, and my personal power and dignity.	This fits my long-term personal goal for myself.
2. I want to establish more rapport with John and increase the mutual gain as we work together.	This establishes a direction for my longer-term relationship with John.
3. I want clarification of my role with Bill; also I want his backing about John answering to me.	This is what I want from my relationship with Bill, and clarifies the authority/power/control question.
4. I want my own work and the work that I delegate to be done well and on schedule.	I want the work to move ahead productively.

Notice that these all state *what* Helen wants but not *how* she'll get them. That comes in the options, risks, and choices steps.

Consider the results Bill has in mind. He wants to know whether John is using their private relationship for job purposes and, if so, to correct John's misperceptions. He also wants to ensure that John will acknowledge Helen's promotion and act accordingly. Restating these results in terms of what he *does* want, Bill apparently wants to back up Helen's promotion where needed, and he's prepared to take action to do that.

One person's wanted results may be another person's unwanted results. Then you have a divergent situation that requires balancing opposing interests. This could upset a third person's applecart.

As far as he knows, John already has the results he wants. He believes he's back on the old track with Bill and that Bill may help him line up another promotion somewhere else in the company. As he sees it, he's won this round with Helen and is in the driver's seat. He's made some assumptions but hasn't kept other options open in case his assumptions are incorrect. So he's due for a surprise from Bill. The next step of the Choosing Process will show the consequences of each person's decisions.

Step 4. Generating OPTIONS

Generating options might be called the freeing step of the Choosing Process. It frees you from evaluative either-or thinking that may not be appropriate for divergent problems such as the one John is now in. It's a formula without much flexibility, without grays. For example, when you assume you've found the solution and won, you may discover later you haven't (which is about to happen to John). By then you won't have many options readily available. Solution-mindedness tends to give a false sense of security.

When you have established the habit of thinking of options, you gain the missing flexibility that makes day-to-day living smoother. You have a negotiating frame of mind; if one option doesn't work out, you know there are always more. Option-mindedness tends to give you a more genuine sense of security.

Now we're going to look in again on John and Bill. It's Monday morning when our next scene opens. After coffee break, John accepts Bill's invitation for a few words back at his office. Shortly, Bill gets to the point. As we listen to them, we also listen in on John's inner dialogue.

Outer Dialogue: Bill and John	*Inner Dialogue: John Only*
Bill: I understand that you're planning on giving Helen the variance report Tuesday.	He's just checking out our understanding.
John: Yes. Everything's on schedule just like we agreed.	It sure feels good to be working together again.
Bill: Good. Except I hear it's not the schedule you and Helen agreed to. Is that right?	I guess I'm suppose to go through the formalities.
John: Well, she seemed overly anxious about getting it Friday. I'm glad we got it straightened out.	I'll let him know Helen is uptight, but we men can work these things out between us.
Bill: I don't think we have, John. I clearly recall telling you to work out the deadlines with her. That doesn't seem to be what you did. What happened?	Uh-oh... Did he say that? He sounds serious about this. Well, he's a good guy. I'll just explain...
John: I just told her you said it could wait until tomorrow and that she'd have it then. No problem.	He can be sure I'll get the report to *him* as promised.
Bill: The problem is this, John. You assumed I made a decision that bypassed Helen. *You* telling *her* makes	This begins to feel like trouble. He can't really be serious about this. If I observe the formalities...

Outer Dialogue: Bill and John	*Inner Dialogue: John Only*
it appear I'm your supervisor, not she. That's not how it is anymore. She's your supervisor, not me. It has to stay that way.	
John: I can go along with that as long as we know where we stand. I think you're being more than fair with her, Bill. I just want you to know that.	... everything will be OK. Never hurts to give a compliment.
Bill: I don't think you understand me yet, John. You and I don't stand where we used to. You now answer to Helen, not me. That has changed, even though nothing is different outside of work.	Hey, is he really serious? I can't believe it, but I think he is. Now that's betrayal if I ever saw it.
John: Well, that's certainly not what you led me to believe. Her promotion really is a demotion for me, isn't it?	How can I get Bill's help for a promotion now?
Bill: I was hoping you'd look at it differently, John. But that's something you have to decide for yourself.	I'm supposed to jump for joy when I have Ruth to face?
John: Yes, I sure do. (As he leaves, he looks as if the rug has just been pulled out from under him.)	I'd better get out of here and figure out what to do.

John's assumptions left him with no options except to get out and figure out what to do. Worse, he's feeling betrayed, apprehensive about facing his wife, dismayed that his access to a promotion seems to have gone down the drain. Not only does he feel demoted, he's feeling demolished.

"Now what?" He is angry and defensive, and sees only a bleak horizon.

When you're down, you can go further down before you turn around. Or you can choose to turn around right there by beginning the Choosing Process again.

At a time like this, you will probably need some breathing space and time to re-center yourself. Moments of the awful truth, such as John is now facing, can feel overwhelming for a while. Part of John's awful truth is that he did himself in. He saw only what he wanted to and made assumptions that proved incorrect.

John may *feel* betrayed by Bill, but in this case, Bill seems innocent of that. Even if Bill's intent had been malicious, John would still have his own feelings of dismay, disillusion, and demolition to manage. Blaming Bill, legitimately or not, would only serve to justify John's feelings of betrayal, to keep them boiling and clouding any possibility of working through them to a resolution. When John is ready to seek a resolution, the option of blaming Bill will hinder him more than it will help him. It's an available option but not one he'd choose if other options give him better odds of resolving his conflicts.

John has many other options, although he may not be able to think of them right now; he's feeling too defensive. As he's trying to sort out his own feelings and attitudes and those of Bill, Helen and Ruth, he's maneuvering himself right back to the beginning of the Choosing Process. And, in fact, this is exactly the most helpful place for him to be, painful though it is.

Growth can be painful. But there is much pain without growth. So if you have pain, you may as well grow *through* it. In the long run, it may be more painful *not* to grow!

John may agonize a while; he may shut down his feelings; he may go home and enlist Ruth's sympathy about how badly he's being treated. For many people, facing feelings at a time like this is almost more painful than they can bear, and they see no way out. John is going through this phase right now in his inner dialogue:

> Bill's a real traitor. He promotes Helen and then cuts me off at the pass. I resent the hell out of her, and Ruth makes me feel like a failure as a husband. I'm scared that I'm being put on the shelf. Am I really at the end and don't know it—after putting all that effort into getting my degree? Too old? Here I am pushing 40, and a younger woman beats me out. Am I dead in this company? Will it be any different anywhere else? I'm scared, and I feel defeated. To answer to Helen is the ultimate insult on everything I've ever done. And Ruth rubs it in where it hurts. Goddam Bill—he's knocked the pins out from under my whole life.

John's thinking has become circular and catastrophic. He sounds as if he's wallowing in self-pity, exaggerating, being unrealistic, irrational, unstable, and immature. Judgmental labels can add the final torturous twist to John's already painful process. To be able to accept his feelings for what they are, John must protect himself from such negative judgments right now—whether they come from Ruth, a psychiatrist, or himself. These *are* John's feelings at this moment, he *is* suffering his own agonies, and they feel terribly real. Whether or not you think he's being realistic, this *is* his reality.

No one has the right to deny another person's right to suffer. Nor has the sufferer the right to force another person to listen to his suffering. People who have shared good times may choose to share the bad.

It may be necessary for John to go through this agony before he hits bottom—the point at which he is ready to turn his pain into a growth experience. If he shuts off his feelings, they are likely to remain bottled up inside, ready to surface whenever he has to take orders from Helen. Or he may grow ulcers instead.

John may be ashamed of having these feelings; perhaps an inner rule says he should be man enough to take it. If he's like many men, he may be as distressed over Helen's sex as he is about her promotion. A common inner tape taunting many men is, "What kind of a man are you if you can't control your women?" Not only does he feel like a loser, he may feel castrated *because* of these inner rules.

Relief is available when John can release these feelings, own them as real, accept them as valid, recognize inner rules that lead him down painful paths, and start sorting out his own realities. Sometimes people can do this alone; often they need a friend who can listen and respond to the pain and anger with empathy, *without judging or evaluating*. For example, John might work through some of his feelings this way:

> Let's face it. I hurt, I feel insulted, I feel put down as a man. These *are* my feelings. It's okay to have them, even though I don't like them. My feelings are damned uncomfortable facts. It's also a fact that I still have to answer to Helen. Bill isn't going to back off about that. I feel castrated working for her, but Bill's backing her and I'd have to say he's a man. Maybe if I think of her as a person with a job to do, it won't be as bad as thinking of her as a woman who made me lose. Maybe if I think of myself

as a person with a job to do and with ambition to get ahead, it'll be easier to work *with* her. I still don't want to think of myself as working *for* her.

I don't think I have to dominate women to feel manly—or do I? Is that what's bothering me about Ruth rubbing it in? How do I handle that? (AHA! I *didn't* say, 'How do I handle her!')

With a start of this kind, John has taken the biggest step; he's turning himself around.

With new data about attitudes and content, you can revise the results you want, have new options and risks—a whole new ball game.

John is now accepting his feelings and visualizing possibilities as he experiments with flexing some of his inner rules that have distorted some of his relationships with Helen and Ruth. He may add another item about Ruth to the results he wants. He doesn't have to know *how* he'll get the results before he states *what* he wants. Here's his revised list of results he wants:

- Ruth's support (and absence of nagging) about the Helen situation.
- Bill's backing for a promotion as soon as possible.
- Relief from money pressures at home that a promotion would bring.
- To save face and feel effective on the job and as a man.

Sharpening his focus, here's how John will know when he's achieved the results he wants:

- I want to stay centered on following Bill's lead, and I want to level with Ruth and ask for her support. I will know I have achieved this when Bill makes a few favorable comments about how well I'm working with Helen, and when Ruth no longer talks about Helen getting the promotion and at least listens to what I'm trying to do without criticizing me.

Notice that John states first what *he* can do, then describes how he'll know he is being effective by what others will be saying or doing. If others don't do these things, he'll have to go back to what he can control—his own behavior.

John probably needs to brainstorm options for each separate result he wants. But for now, let's say John charges ahead and comes up with these options:

Results Wanted[2]

- Quit and leave them all hanging in the lurch.   No
- Let Helen sweat a while, but slowly I may come around.   ?
- Tell her she's smart once in a while. All women like flattery.   Yes
- Turn in the report to Bill. (That would feel good)   No
- Turn in the report to Helen with a deep bow of submission.   ?
- Turn in the report to Helen Tuesday as if it is on schedule.   Yes
- Treat Helen like a man.   ?
- Play it real cool at work, but develop Bill's friendship at the Center. Use both, but don't mix them. Follow Bill's lead.   Yes
- Eventually let Bill know I want his help about a promotion.   Yes—when?
- Get Bill's support by getting Helen's support.   Yes—how?
- Find out what Helen wants and give it to her.   ?—Yes
- Check out possibilities with other companies.   OK
- See if a transfer is possible through Personnel.   ?
- Ask Ruth to lay off. Explain what I'm trying to do.   Yes
- Develop more contacts outside of work, perhaps at the Center.   ?
- Do more things I enjoy.   ?—No
- Ruth has been talking about racquetball. Maybe we'll try that.   ?—No

This first burst of options is a rough cut and a good beginning. You can tell John didn't evaluate as he wrote them down; they're scrambled and diverse. At the end, he may have even wondered if he was getting off the track. Also notice that at the beginning he listed a few options that would allow him some revenge. He may decide later not to use them. But in this initial outpouring he's gotten out all the feelings he's aware of, and that is a critical first step.

Now let's see what happens at the next step where he begins to evaluate these options—the risk-rating step.

Step 5. Assessing RISKS and ODDS

The first step in assessing risks and odds is to assess how much each option gets the wanted results: John now asks himself: "Will this option get the results I want? If so, how much?" His notations are shown on his results-wanted list. On most of them, he's clear about Yes, No, Don't

---

[2]After brainstorming this list of options, John evaluates how well the option gets results he wants. See details below in the "Risks and Odds" section.

Know (?). On a few, he asks himself a question or indicates a direction, such as ?—Yes, which means, "I don't know if this would get results with Helen, but yes, it might."

John is having some difficulty evaluating these options for two reasons: He needs separate options for each separate result he wants, and options that seem to go astray may suggest other results he wants. For example, doing more things he enjoys, such as racquetball with Ruth, may lead to this desired result: Take better care of myself, especially when under stress. If it also leads to more support from Ruth, so much the better.

Working on several results simultaneously may lead to developing longer-term strategies at work and in your personal life. All this can evolve out of facing and handling a single incident.

The more you have at stake in a situation, the more it's worth to you to use the Choosing Process. For your long-term gain, set it up so others can also gain.

When there's a change such as Helen's promotion, the focus tends to be on the person whose role has changed. It *appears* she has the most at stake, although John may have as much and not know it, or he may deny it. Bill *seems* to have the least risk among the three of them, but we may not know the risks he feels in his non-traditional support of a new woman manager. Nor do we know how all this delay is affecting his credibility.

In the Helen-John-Bill triangle, a prediction about its outcome now is that John will turn in the report to Helen on Tuesday, she will accept it in a low-key way, Bill will feel comfortable about getting past the first hurdle of Helen's promotion, and everyone will be on good behavior for a while. Longer-term outcomes will depend a great deal on how Helen handles herself as she establishes new patterns in her relationships.

As Helen moves past early problems, let's see what she has learned from them. She's in the process of figuring out how to use what she's learned in later situations with John.

1. She allowed John to define the win–lose rules where he could win by not producing the report.[3] She has to take back the power to define the situation.

---

[3]See the analysis in Chapter 5 to refresh your memory on how John could win by *not* producing.

2. She didn't have enough information from Bill to be sure of her ground, and probably can get much more. Experience is the usual way to find out to what extent Bill would back her. To ask before you need it usually signals unsureness.

3. When she got defensive, she couldn't really listen to John; she was too busy protecting or justifying herself.

The no-nonsense manager might well get impatient with John and advise Helen to "Fire his ass out the door," justifying it with, "If he can't deliver, get him out and find somebody who can." This tough, hard-hitting approach may sound good, but you could lose good people that way, yourself included! It takes a stronger power base than Helen's to pull off a summary dismissal like that and not have it backfire.

Step 6. Testing CHOICES

So it's back to the drawing board for Helen. Using what she's learned and deciding to take responsibility for herself only (and *not* for John), she's focusing on the person-to-person relationships that determine whether the work gets done or is delayed again.

First she decides to review the Choosing Process; then she reviews some techniques for giving and receiving feedback while leveling with another person. She expects these reminders will help her regain the power to define the rules of future situations with John.

From her desk drawer, Helen pulls out Figure 9-2, a summary of the underlying premises and values of the Choosing Process. While reviewing the main headings beginning with "Know yourself," she begins to relax and accepts her frustrated feelings about John's delays. She also begins to accept John as a person to be respected, even though she doesn't always agree with his behavior. She gives herself credit for doing her homework but pauses at "Center in on gain." The results Helen wants are still the same, but she reminds herself that John must gain, too; and both of them must see that Bill receives his report.

On Figure 9-2, her eye moves on to "Have a rich supply of options," and she checks that as a self-assignment to brainstorm options. This leads to speculating that John might be a brainstorming partner; they're in this together.

"That feels scary," she notices within herself. "Yet, if he becomes involved in working it out, we could get on the same side of the fence. Then I wouldn't be sparring as John's adversary on Bill's testing ground." She flashes mental pictures in her head featuring the Bendorff Boxing Match

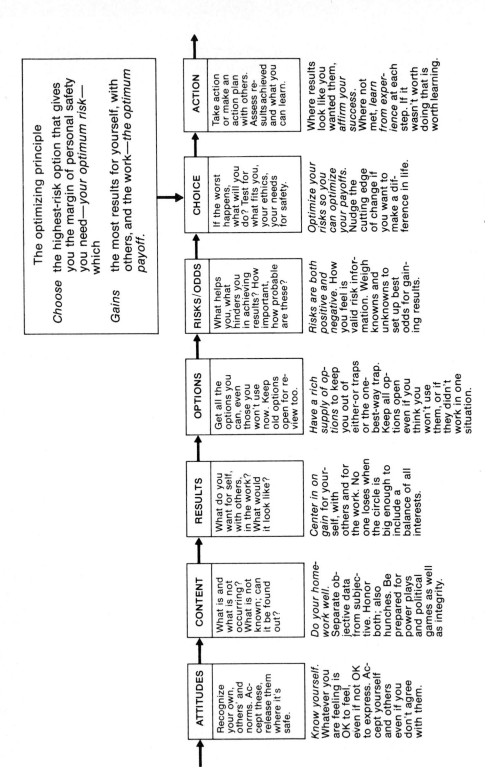

The optimizing principle

Choose the highest-risk option that gives you the margin of personal safety you need—*your optimum risk*—which

Gains the most results for yourself, with others, and the work—*the optimum payoff.*

ATTITUDES	CONTENT	RESULTS	OPTIONS	RISKS/ODDS	CHOICE	ACTION
Recognize your own, others' and norms. Accept these, release them where it's safe.	What is and what is not occurring? What is not known; can it be found out?	What do you want for self, with others, in the work? What would it look like?	Get all the options you can, even those you won't use now. Keep old options open for review too.	What helps you, what hinders you in achieving results? How important, how probable are these?	If the worst happens, what will you do? Test for what fits you, your ethics, your needs for safety.	Take action or make an action plan with others. Assess results achieved and what you can learn.
Know yourself. Whatever you are feeling is OK to feel, even if not OK to express. Accept yourself and others even if you don't agree with them.	*Do your homework well.* Separate objective data from subjective. Honor both; also hunches. Be prepared for power plays and political games as well as integrity.	*Center in on gain for yourself, with others and for the work.* No one loses when the circle is big enough to include a balance of all interests.	*Have a rich supply of options to keep you out of either-or traps or the one-best-way trap.* Keep all options open even if you think you won't use them, or if they didn't work in one situation.	*Risks are both positive and negative. How you feel is valid risk information.* Weigh knowns and unknowns to set up best odds for gaining results.	*Optimize your risks so you can optimize your payoffs.* Nudge the cutting edge of change if you want to make a difference in life.	Where results look like you wanted them, *affirm your success.* Where not met, *learn from experience* at each step. If it wasn't worth doing that is worth learning.

Figure 9-2. The Choosing Process: Underlying premises and values at each step.

276

with John coming out of the other corner swinging, then another picture featuring herself and John as the winning team on a television contest show.

The positive risks outweigh the negative, it seems to her. This may be a way to optimize her risks while also optimizing the payoffs. This smells like success, so she pats herself on the back and tells herself, "Not bad. You'll make it yet." Such self-affirming inner messages provide a powerful focus of energy on the task at hand. By affirming her success in a general way before it happens, she sets in motion a positive self-fulfilling prophecy. Instead of creating a vicious circle, she's drawing the circle bigger.

Feeling more centered now, Helen takes out the reminder card (Figure 9-3) that lists ways to give (and not give) feedback when you level with another person. She keeps this card with her Incident Cards. Notice that it's easy to identify your own or others' behaviors when you debate to win or when you dialog for mutual gain.

Step 7. Taking ACTION

Helen now feels ready to start at the beginning of the scene with John in Chapter 3 and play it through again. We have to imagine that Helen knew what she now knows, but that John is still trying to win by not producing the report. Remember that this is their third meeting on that subject, that it's still Tuesday, and the controversial Friday noon deadline hasn't been made. We're setting back the clock, with Helen as the only person with some experience in using the Choosing Process. This time, she's going to apply it and see if she can gain more of the results she wants in the same situation.

During this exchange, fill in the body language and inner dialogues that you think Helen and John might be having within themselves. Notice whether Helen sticks to the results she wants or gets sidetracked. Sense the positive and negative risks she takes as she regains the power to define the rules of their relationship.

Helen: Have a seat, John. I'd like to hear about how the variance report is progressing. Our time is running out.

John: You've given me so many projects that there just isn't time to do the legwork on this one.

Helen: Sounds like you're saying you're short of time just when there isn't much time left.

John: There's no way it can be done without extra help to do the probability programming.

DEBATE	DIALOG
LISTEN, THEN LIST YOUR REBUTTALS	LISTEN, THEN LIST THEIR POINTS
DEFEND YOUR POSITION	HEAR THEIR POSITION
GIVE ANSWERS	EXPLORE OPTIONS
INTERPRET, JUDGE others' behavior as right or wrong	OBSERVE, DESCRIBE others' behavior without evaluating
ASSUME YOU KNOW WHAT THEY MEAN	STATE WHAT YOU HEAR; CHECK IT
THINK EITHER-OR; find one best way	THINK MORE-OR-LESS without evaluating
GIVE ADVICE on what's best	SHARE IDEAS and INFORMATION
EVALUATE EACH OTHERS' VIEWS	ACCEPT AND DISCLOSE VIEWS
OVERCOME OBJECTIONS	RESPECT DIFFERENCES
ASK "WHY DON'T YOU?" QUESTIONS	ASK "HOW CAN WE?" QUESTIONS
STRIVE TO WIN	STRIVE FOR MUTUAL GAIN
MAKE POINTS NOW TO BUILD YOUR TRACK RECORD	BUILD RELATION-SHIPS TO CREATE ONGOING BENEFITS

Figure 9-3. *Debate-Dialog reminder card.*

Helen: You know, John, this sounds very much like the last two times we've talked. I'm feeling like there are roadblocks everywhere we turn on this assignment.

John: You just don't realize how much time it takes to do it.

Helen: John, I've been thinking a lot about what's been happening since I got promoted. We used to work together on these projects and knock them out on impossible schedules sometimes. Ever since the promotion, it's been different. I was thinking that if I were in your shoes, I wouldn't like it. I might even not want to do the work for someone who seemed to block my own progress. Tell me, John, what do you see as your next move in this company?

John: I don't see any. What's that got to do with the report?

Helen: If you don't see any advantage to yourself in doing these projects like we used to, I can't imagine that you'd put much steam behind getting them done. What for?

John: I do my work. When there's a job to do, I do it.

Helen: That sounds like grinding it out without any of the old enthusiasm.

John: What's there to be enthusiastic about? You got the promotion.

Helen: Yes John, I won that round. You lost. Worse, you lost to a woman. If you want to play by win–lose rules, you could probably make life very difficult for me. If you don't produce, I could make it difficult for you. I can play that game if I have to, and I'm in a position to win. Trouble is, nobody really wins in the long run. I'd much rather play by other rules—where we both can gain at least some of what we want and also see that Bill gains what he wants—the report.

John: Sounds good but things just don't work that way. You don't know that yet, but you'll find out.

Helen: We can make it work if we want to, John, although I guess you're saying you don't believe it can be done.

John: That's about it.

Helen: Well, here's one way it could happen. I can give you assignments where our findings affect policy. You could make the presentations to the executive group, which gives you a chance to show what you can do. Or I could give you assignments that never take you outside the department. It seems to me some exposure upstairs would be useful to you if you still want to go somewhere in this company.

John: Why would you do that? You'd want that exposure for yourself.

Helen: I'll get the exposure I want. I'd be at those briefings, but you'd do the presenting as the real expert. I get points because I know how to work with brains; you get points for having the brains. Bill gets points for having a good department. The execs get good work that saves them money.

John: Well, I don't know...

Helen: Think about it, John. It may have some possibilities. Now, back to the immediate situation...

John: How much time do we really have?

Helen: The outside limit is ten days, or a week from Friday. That's pushing it to the limit though. Bill says he'd really like to have it by this Friday, or Monday or Tuesday at the latest for him to feel safe.

John: Do you know what his pressures are?

Helen: No. Would that make a difference?

John: If I knew the pressures, I might be able to shortcut something, or loosen the tolerances.

Helen: Then go ahead and get his priorities. Good idea. Let me know what you find out and what day we can deliver, will you?

John: Yeah.

As John leaves, Helen calls Bill before John can see him. Fortunately she gets through to him:

"Bill, I think John's moving again." Hearing Bill's interest, she tells him John is coming to see him about how to shortcut the technical work. "It's a calculated risk, Bill. John finally took hold of figuring the angles to meet your pressures. Clearly his contact with you is important to him, which is fine with me as long as he's not going over my head. You and I have talked about that. I'm also working with him on his longer-range goals," and she summarizes the executive briefing idea.

"Sounds good, Helen. I can go along with that. What day can I expect the report?"

"After John sees you and does some quick calculations, I'll call you back. I'm betting on Monday."

What is your *prediction? On what do you base it? What kind of control is being used here, by whom? To what extent is control being shared? Can John save face while he becomes involved again? If we assume that John is still thinking in win–lose terms, can he still win by not producing the report? On what do you base your opinion?*

Helen, John, and Bill are now renegotiating their conflicting but intermeshing interests and roles. Each person's interests are complex, constantly changing, and subject to pressures from many directions. Each time the Choosing Process and its values are put into action, more trust can develop. The more the trust, the less need for defenses and façades. If you're the first to risk lowering some defenses, you can't do it when you're looking at potential losses. You *can* do it when you're centered and focused on your potential gains. The Choosing Process and its values provide a way to maintain that focus.

IN THE NEXT CHAPTER

Next we see how to state the results you want so you increase your odds of gaining them. We also see how *not* to state them. Then we review some beliefs that can lead you into defensive traps and see some ways to get clear of them.

Finally we pick up on Dave Eliot's situation at Country Stores as he develops his wanted results. In Chapter 11, we continue with some of Dave's options and possible strategies. As he uses the Choosing Process, we'll see how he can negotiate from centered flexibility.

For additional background reading, see bibliography entries 21, 31, 58, 59, 63, 83.

10

GAINING RESULTS YOU WANT AND OPENING OPTIONS

For Yourself, Your Relationships, and Your Activities

Ace Franklin, an engineer at City Gas, has just been put on the defensive by his coengineer, Dan Gruber. He's jotted it down on the Incident Card shown in Figure 10-1. Notice the initial results he wrote in "What I want to be ready to do next time."

Not only is Ace going to show Dan why his own design is better (even though Ace knows Dan's is better), but he wants to feel vindicated. Ace sounds committed to lying in wait for Dan until he gets the chance to win his point. He's not likely to voluntarily change his engineering design, even if it would cost City Gas and its customers substantial money or dangerous exposure. Ace is going to show Dan.

Before we analyze the results Ace Franklin wants, we'll outline the criteria he used when stating results non-defensively. Then we'll apply those criteria to his statement, see whether they are met or not met, and the probable results if Ace acts on his initial statement. Then we discuss the inner rules and underlying beliefs that apparently led Ace into his potentially costly defensiveness. Finally, we suggest another results statement that gives a clear understanding of what to do if you're not getting the results you want. We'll repeat the analysis steps using two additional incidents that create defensiveness.

Then we'll revisit Dave Eliot at Country Stores where we left him feeling defensive and powerless. Since he's reading along with us, he may have some ideas by then for formulating the more complex results he wants.

INCIDENT CARD Date_____ Number_____	

Situation
DAN ASKS ME WHY I'M
NOT DOING MY DESIGN
THE WAY HE SAYS TO
DO IT. HE APPEARS
TO BE RIGHT ——

What I did was

DEFEND MY REASONS
FOR DESIGNING THE
WAY I DID ——

My feelings were
WHY DIDN'T I THINK OF
IT? I FEEL STUPID

What I want to be ready to do next time is

I'LL SHOW HIM WHERE
HE'S WRONG AND WHY
MY DESIGN IS BETTER

So I can feel

VINDICATED !

☐ I made it   My next step is: Scheduled for
                Do nothing _____
☒ I avoided it   Work on it_____ _____
                Think about it later __ _____
☐ I blew it   Other_WAIT FOR_
                      MY CHANCE

Additional comments

Copyright © 1974 by Theodora Wells

Figure 10-1. *Ace Franklin's Incident Card.*

HOW TO STATE NON-DEFENSIVELY THE RESULTS YOU WANT

Figure 10-2 shows a reminder card that shows the four criteria against which you measure your results-wanted statement; the fifth criteria describes how you'll recognize the results when you see them.

Ace Franklin: "I'll Show Him"

First, let's look closely at Ace's initial statement of the results he wants and see how it meets the criteria.

Next time, I want to be ready to:	*Discussion of Whether Criteria 1 through 4 Are or Are Not Met*
I'll show him where he's wrong and why my design is better *So I can feel:* VINDICATED!	1. Met. Ace states what he *does* want, although in right–wrong, win–lose terms.
	2. Not met. Ace assumes that he can show Dan he's wrong and change his view or opinion.
	3. Not met. Ace refers primarily to himself, negatively to Dan, with no results for task.
	4. Not met. Only gain is for himself, none for Dan, none for task (or negative).

If Ace follows this course of action, he'll probably find a way to prove he's right, even though he knows he isn't. He'll save face. However, Dan will probably see through it and may or may not call him on it. Their working relationship is likely to become less compatible, and Dan may be less willing to offer suggestions to Ace. This could lead to a deterioration in design quality.

Next, let's go back to the beginning of Ace's Incident Card and look for assumptions, unknowns, and possible inner rules he may have.

CRITERIA FOR STATING
RESULTS WANTED

1. State what you DO WANT to happen when results have been achieved.

2. Focus on what YOU can control or influence.

   Assume you cannot change or control another person.

3. Include the results you want for:
   - yourself
   - your relationships with others
   - job or task achievement

4. Arrange that YOU AND ALL OTHERS GAIN SOME of what each wants; and that you give similar importance to task results wanted as you give to human results wanted.

   ★ ★ ★ ★ ★ ★ ★ ★ ★ ★ ★ ★ ★

5. What will people be doing and saying that indicate you have gained the human results you want?

   What indicators will show you have achieved the job results you want?

   ★ ★ ★ ★ ★ ★ ★ ★ ★ ★ ★ ★ ★

   REMEMBER!

   Two small, clear statements are better than one big fuzzy!

Figure 10-2. Reminder card for stating results.

Ace Franklin's Situation:	What Makes It Defensive (or Non-Defensive), Unknowns, Assumptions and Possible Inner Rules
Dan asks me why I'm not doing my design the way *he* says to do it. He appears to be right.	We don't know the manner Dan used, his tone of voice, whether or not there was provocation or a put-down. We also don't know their preceding relationships or other personal factors. These can influence their communication but don't have to control it.
What I did was: Defend my reasons for designing the way I did.	Ace gets on the defensive and closes off Dan's option, which Ace suspects is better than his own. Ace's inner rules seem to be "I have to be right, be perfect, prove myself, win." Dan seems to have become a threat to Ace's ego or self-concept, since Dan's idea is discarded even when Ace agrees that it may be right.
My feelings were: Why didn't I think of that? I feel stupid.	Ace may have another inner rule, "I have to think of it *first*," and if he doesn't, he condemns himself as "stupid." If he feels in competition with Dan, Ace is now losing. For him to face losing may mean to lose face.

The intensity of feeling in Ace's desire to be vindicated suggests some strong underlying beliefs, such as these:

- Might makes right.
- To be wrong is to be vanquished.
- The vanquished must be vindicated.

If these are among Ace's underlying beliefs, he must come out on top, like the virile warrior. An additional thrust could be a strong pride in craftsmanship. In this utility, one could almost feel that pride being poured into the engineers' work, as if pride were the core of their professional identity. None seemed likely to *consciously choose* risking the quality of their designs for this sort of internecine warfare. Yet here, in his own words, Ace is *doing* it.

Ace's pervasive tone sounds vindictive: "I've been hit where it hurts and come hell or high water (including, 'To hell with my design'), I'll *show* him. I'll vindicate myself and get my revenge." The feeling might look like this drawing.

Revenge is sweet.

William Steig, *The Lonely Ones*, Duell, Sloan & Pearce, New York, 1942, p. 44.

Ace may not feel this strongly about a single incident, yet there seems to be an intensity about his urge to be vindicated. While respecting that feeling within himself, he can also visualize himself functioning with different feelings, even if he doesn't yet know how he can choose to feel different feelings. For example, let's say that Ace has a deep pride in craftsmanship and appreciates professional excellence wherever it occurs. Then he can appreciate Dan's ideas even while he resents them for not being his own. Ace may know intellectually that Dan didn't intend anything personal, yet be emotionally unable to accept that.

Ace's first non-defensive statement of results may concern only himself working with his own attitudes. For example, consider this restatement that meets most of the first four criteria:

Possible Restatement of Results Wanted	*Discussion of Whether Criteria 1 Through 4 Are or Are Not Met*
To consider Dan's comments as impersonal suggestions about my design, not as personal threats.	1. Met. It states what Ace does want.
	2. Met. It deals only with what Ace can control.
	3. Met part way. Does not yet deal with Dan or other coworkers, nor the task.
	4. Met part way (same as 3).
So I can feel: Confident in using my own expertise and become open to give and take.	

Ace has such strong win–lose feelings that this first iteration is probably best focused on his own strengths and values. As he accepts himself more and his fears of being a loser gradually melt away, he'll be more ready to develop results he wants in his relationships and work. If he wants to work more closely with Dan, he'll be more able to do it on the basis of professional craftsmanship instead of using a win–lose scorecard. If he prefers to keep some distance from Dan, he might add only a little more to the above restatement, such as: "With an attitude of open exchange, take Dan's and my suggestions to other engineers and involve them in generating ideas that affect our work." This distances Ace from Dan, exposes Ace to the same risks as Dan, involves others, and circulates information about interrelated designs.

When underlying feelings hinder you, look for other feelings that can help you. As you offset "hinders" with "helps," you gain more balance and more options.

Notice that Ace has gone through a process of following his feelings to his inner rules; these led him to understand some of his own underlying beliefs. Ace then brought these underlying beliefs to the surface, to his conscious awareness, and accepted them. At this point, Ace would be asking his core-of-self (where his central values reside—his self-choice area) a key question. That key question is, "If I set aside my defenses, what do I really want to happen?" Notice that this is a "what" question, not a "how" one. As he listens for his answers, he is likely to state results that will produce gain for himself with other people, and in doing the work.

Now let's consider a different situation in which the person tends to short-change herself.

Sue Isaki: "I Signed a Review That I Felt Was Unfair"

Sue Isaki is a government clerical worker at a naval installation. On her Incident Card she didn't state whether her supervisor, Lee Logan, is a man or a woman. Her situation is described below, followed by comments.

Sue Isaki's Situation	*What Makes It Defensive (or Non-Defensive): Unknowns, Assumptions, and Possible Inner Rules*
I was given a performance review that I felt was unfair.	We don't know how her review was given, what advance preparation there was, what criteria Lee used, and whether criteria were made explicit. We also have no specific perceptions of Sue's performance as seen by either Lee or Sue.
What I did was: To sign the report and to say nothing, hoping the next one would be better.	Sue gave Lee no feedback about her feelings of the review, so Lee doesn't know that there is a difference of opinion. Lee can reasonably assume that Sue agrees with the review. Also Sue has done nothing that could give her hope for a better review next time because Lee did not work with Sue to agree on objectives for Sue to achieve by the next review— another unknown.

Sue Isaki's Situation	What Makes It Defensive (or Non-Defensive): Unknowns, Assumptions, and Possible Inner Rules
My feelings were: I should not have signed the review and should have spoken up and given my true feelings.	Notice that Sue is still not stating her feelings but is reprimanding herself for what she *should* have done. Her inner rules may be, "I have to be a nice girl, be liked, not question authority, not make waves." All her feelings are directed against herself, with none toward Lee or toward the "unfairness" of the review. Sue tells herself what an inadequate girl she is, thereby reducing her self-confidence and giving Lee more power over her.

Next time, I want to be ready to	Discussion of Whether Criteria 1 Through 4 Are or Are Not Met
Be tactful in giving my reasons why I feel I'm an outstanding employee in many areas. *So I can feel:* At ease with myself and satisfied.	1. Not met. Being tactful is a method—a "how"—for gaining a result. But Sue does not specifically state what she would consider a fair review. 2. Met in part. Sue can control her own behavior, but she's not dealing with the content—the issue of fairness. 3. Not met. Feeling good about being tactful won't change her review; no results wanted are stated about negotiating with Lee, signing the review, or the new outcome she wants. 4. Not met (same as 3).

If Sue takes her present course of action, she'll be tactful and at ease with herself, but may continue getting the same kind of reviews. Lee may listen to Sue's polite reasons why she's an outstanding employee, but if Sue requests no feedback from Lee, she may not find out what she has to do to change her review. Sue could go on feeling victimized until she decides to leave—or is fired.

Some of the underlying beliefs that Sue seems to have are these:

- Be good and you'll be properly rewarded.
- When you tell yourself what you should have done, you have finished punishing yourself. (Notice her should's didn't become results wanted.)
- The way to gain agreement is to be tactful.

It sounds like Sue has entered into an unnegotiated contract: "If I do what I'm supposed to do, you'll give me what I deserve." Visually, it might look like this:

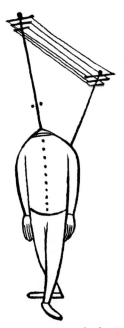

I do what is expected of me.

William Steig, *The Lonely Ones*, Duell, Sloan & Pearce, New York, 1942, p. 12.

This "good girl/guy" pattern creates a singularly cruel trap. Many people genuinely believe that they are doing everything they can to earn their just reward, which will follow as night follows day. Their *specific*, personal belief is rooted in a *general*, societal belief in the work ethic, which promises rewards for good behavior. Occasionally this happens, but it's naive to count on it. To avoid this trap, specific, personal expectations must be negotiated with another specific person. It's the squeaky wheel that gets the grease!

If Sue wants to get a performance review that reflects more accurately what she believes is a fair report of her work, she'll have to initiate some communication with Lee. Sue may not know how to initiate this contact, but until she decides that such contact is essential, she won't be looking for ways to do it. Too often people set aside *what* they want because they don't yet know *how to get it.* Stating the results wanted *first* opens up the flow of options for how to get them.

Let's see how a less defensive restatement of Sue's wanted results might be stated.

Possible Restatements of Results Wanted	*Discussion of Whether Criteria 1 Through 4 Are or Are Not Met*
Reopen discussion with Lee about performance review with intent to get it changed to what I consider to be fair. *So I can feel:* More self-confident.	1. Met. It states a desired outcome. 2. Met. It focuses on personal intent and what Sue can control—herself and how she handles the discussion. 3. Met. Self, others, and task are included. 4. Met generally. We still don't know what "fair" means to Sue's or Lee's perceptions.

Sue might have a second, backup position such as: "To get my views considered in the next performance review." In this statement, she doesn't mention Lee, so the personnel department might be an added resource for her. It increases her range of operations.

Now Sue can apply the fifth criterion—a statement of what people will be saying and doing so that both the human and the task results are achieved. For example, Sue might be satisfied with this, "To have open discussions with Lee within two weeks, present a summary of my strong points in a confident voice, listen to Lee's feedback, decide then if I've been sufficiently heard by Lee. No, I want something in writing. At minimum, I want a note about my viewpoint in my personnel file."

Sue may not be quite ready to state the maximum results she wants, but at least she's stating *some* tangible result she needs. Notice that she doesn't state who would write the note for her file. If necessary, she might do it herself. She's making a start toward speaking up for herself instead of continually leaving her fate in the hands of other people, especially people with authority.

Women may learn to give away their power this way from traditional expectations of what is proper for their sex. Values in Sue's Asian background may have reinforced these expectations, depending on how her parents lived their values. Men may also learn to give away their power from military experience, where they are expected to respect the uniform even if they don't respect the man wearing it. Rules requiring deference and obedience to rank require the good soldier to subjugate his person power to someone else's position power. This may be necessary in front-line battle conditions, but it may be a habit difficult to unlearn in civilian life. No matter *why* people give away their power, today's need is to reclaim it for their effectiveness as people.

Now consider the last incident we will include in this chapter. Getting needed information is the problem.

Ken Kendall: "Vic Won't Give the Information I Need"

Ken Kendall manages a technical department. He needs project information from another department head, Vic Knudsen. When he has difficulty getting it, he involves Vic's supervisor, Jess Roberts, who is a division head. Here's how Ken noted it on an Incident Card.

Ken Kendall's Situation	What Makes It Defensive (or Non-Defensive): Unknowns, Assumptions, and Possible Inner Rules
I need information from Vic. He's reluctant to divulge any information this early in the project. (I need it to start preparation.)	Vic is apparently withholding information because of timing, although that doesn't seem relevant to Ken. We don't know if this is Vic's real reason. We also don't know past work relationships between Ken and Vic, or if there are any residual feelings from past projects that might be barriers that need to be reduced.
What I did was: Complain to Vic's boss, Jess, who agrees that I need the information. Vic still doesn't cooperate, claiming that he's seen no	Ken apparently assumes that when he can't get action from Vic, it is logical to go through channels to Jess. (He seems to disregard the

Ken Kendall's Situation	What Makes It Defensive (or Non-Defensive): Unknowns, Assumptions, and Possible Inner Rules
output from me from a previous project (which was cancelled).	political implications of going over Vic's head.) Since Jess seems to agree with Ken, he may assume that Jess will make Vic deliver. So far, no results. We don't know if Jess did anything about it, if Vic has other reasons for doing nothing, if Vic didn't like Ken going over his head, if Vic is judgmental inappropriately regarding the previous project, or if Vic is playing a win–lose game. If he is, he's winning.
My feelings were: Defensive. I'm not given the real reason for his not communicating. Vic shifts the blame to me, referring to a past cancelled program.	Ken feels like a loser and blames Vic. Ken seems more focused on defending his position than on getting the information. Question: Is Ken taking the blame he says Vic is shifting to him? If Vic wants power over Ken, he's doing fine. Control of information is a potent source of power. Ken seems to feel it's unfair to bring up past events.

Next time, I want to be ready to	Discussion of Whether Criteria 1 Through 4 Are or Are Not Met
Point out that Vic is failing to communicate. Whether or not I produce from his information (in the past) is not the point. *So I can feel:* Not on the defensive.	1. Not met. Ken wants the information. Pointing out Vic's lack of communication won't get it. 2. Not met. Ken can't control, and apparently can't influence, Vic or his boss, Jess. 3. Not met. It doesn't deal with Ken's need for information (self and task) and doesn't state what result Ken wants with Vic. 4. Not met. No gain anywhere is likely as Ken's results are now stated.

It's not clear to whom Ken intends to point out Vic's failure to communicate. He's already gone to Jess without results so far. Repeating his complaint to Vic isn't likely to produce much more, except to give Ken some sort of emotional ventilation and perhaps further solidify Vic's resistance. Ken's inner rules may be, "I have to be in control, be right, go through channels, justify myself." He doesn't seem to have an active inner rule that says, "I have to produce," even though that's the reason he gives for asking for the information. The probable result of Ken's present course of action is no change.

Ken's stance suggests that he has these underlying beliefs:

- When I have justified myself (or my request), others should do what I ask (especially when their boss agrees with me.)
- When you find out why someone else does what they do, you have the answer to the problem. (Even if Ken could find out Vic's reasons for withholding the information, he still won't have the information. He'll only know why he *isn't* getting it.)
- When you've fixed the blame, you've fixed the problem. (Ken doesn't like Vic putting the blame on him, but Ken seems to want to put the blame on Vic. Ken seems convinced that once that point is made, the problem is solved. But he still won't have his information.)

Ken's tone seems to be coming out of the universal bemoaning question, "Why doesn't everybody else play by the rules of fair play like I do?" Visually it feels like this:

I am blameless.

William Steig, *The Lonely Ones*, Duell, Sloan & Pearce, New York, 1942, p. 32.

Ken is so busy justifying himself that he seems to be listening to no one but himself. Possibly Vic is doing the same thing. When two people listen only to themselves, not much communication takes place. Something about mutual listening needs to be included in Ken's restatement of results wanted.

A few small, clear statements of wanted results may be easiest for Ken to work with. These can avoid the vagueness of fuzzy, hard-to-quantify language that is often used to describe a larger, longer process. The restatement that follows is a big, fuzzy statement; the next restatement has several small, clearer statements.

Possible Restatement of Results Wanted	*Discussion of Whether Criteria 1 Through 4 Are or Are Not Met*
Initiate some mutual listening with Vic in our communication. When we are both hearing each other, let Vic see for himself that my having the information now will expedite the coordination among his, mine, and other departments. Get the information.	This statement covers several steps of a process between Ken and Vic without intervening points to check progress of their relationship. Let's see how it meets criteria 1 through 4: 1. Met. It states he wants better communication that will result in getting the information. 2. Met. It states what Ken can control and how he wants to influence Vic. 3. Met. It includes results for Ken, with Vic, and about the job to be done. 4. Met. Gain is included for all parties and task.

Although this restatement meets the first four criteria, it's too fuzzy to meet the fifth one where it's necessary to describe what people will be saying and doing when the results have been achieved. Odds are also good that Ken is not ready to make such a statement right now. He still has too much of the injured martyr in him.

More realistically, Ken might go through the following reasoning process, if he is willing to face himself. Here he makes a series of smaller, clearer steps, each of which will be easier to recognize when they occur. He also gives himself time to consider more options.

Process of Restating Ken's Results Wanted	*Ken's Inner Dialogue as He Develops a Series of Steps in His Wanted Results*
I want that information now so my department can get prepared.	This is the end result I want to do a good job and keep my department on schedule. Question: Am I jumping the gun on timing? How much time can I take and still get my department prepared?
I must have the information in one week for best preparation; at worst, if I get it in three weeks, I can manage without overtime.	I want to do this project perfectly to make up for problems on the last project. I won't admit that to Vic, but I can still do it if he fights me a while longer. I can't run up overtime, so I have to find a way to get the information in three weeks. I have to find a way to talk with Vic.
I want Vic to listen to me, hear my priorities, and give me the information I need.	I'm perfectly justified in getting the information now. Even Jess agrees with me. But that isn't getting it for me. Vic is unfair to bring up that last project. But he's in the driver's seat and shouldn't be; we're both department heads. I want him to listen to me. I suppose that means I have to listen to him to get things started. Maybe I have to appeal to his self-interest.
Find out what Vic's concerns are and see if I can offer him some assistance.	I don't really want to help him out, but maybe if I at least offer, he might come around for me. I'll try listening carefully to his problems and feedback what I'm hearing so he knows I understand. I'll have to hold my tongue and wait to see what results this brings. If I can help him, I will, even if it kills me. I think he may give in return.

Process of Restating Ken's Results Wanted	Ken's Inner Dialogue as He Develops a Series of Steps in His Wanted Results
I think Vic is basically a fair person. He often helps people out.	I think Vic wants this new project to go well, same as I do. Once we start talking, I can offer proper coordination that will support his efforts. Then I think even he can see that I'll need his information so my department can give that support. But I'll have to shut up and let him offer it. That feels like giving up control. How can I do this and stay off the defensive?
Stay centered on what Vic and I are both interested in doing and that we are both basically fair people.	I don't have to keep concentrating on what I don't like about Vic. He has some good points, too. If I put my attention on these, he may come through because that would make him feel good as well as getting the job done. I'll get that, too.

Ken is now less concerned about saving face, justifying himself, fixing the blame, and appearing holy pure. His odds are now much better that he'll have the information within the time limits he's specified.

The effective results statement is bite-size—small enough to chew. Ingest the whole meal at once and you risk indigestion, sometimes constipation.

Ken can also monitor progress as he goes along, looking for specific actions and words that he and Vic are using that indicate improved communication in their relationship. Now Ken is taking responsibility for his part of the relationship. He and Vic are negotiating requirements for getting the job done with fewer barriers between them. As Ken listens more to Vic and as he begins to get results, self-confidence in his competence in handling people relationships will increase. Thus encouraged, he's likely to continue gaining results he wants.

COMPLEX SITUATIONS REQUIRE MORE FORMULATION OF THE RESULTS YOU WANT

The situations we've just analyzed are relatively simple. Ace, Sue, and Ken each had a person-to-person confrontation in which they became defensive. Defensiveness showed up in their initial statement of results they wanted and pointed the way to underlying beliefs and inner rules that were impeding their efforts to gain more results. Attitudes were affecting content as well as the way they defined the results they wanted. Once these attitudes, feelings, inner rules, and beliefs were faced, they began to see their situations in a different light; they considered more aspects of what was occurring, and they chose different priorities. The results they really wanted could then be more clearly stated. With more focused statements, the greater their odds of gaining results they want.

In more complex situations, the process is the same except that you have more factors to consider and weigh. For example:

- When several people are involved, their places in the hierarchy are a consideration. They participate in a network of people who influence each other and control various resources.
- The political climate and power differentials between yourself and the people you seek to influence, or to whom you are accountable, are potent factors.
- The degree of dependency you have on others, dependencies they have on you, and the scarcity of your services in the market are considerations.
- The norms, taboos, and rituals that have grown with an organization can affect your authority, credibility, power, influence, and control. Your current status and the general assessment of your future potential by higher-level authorities as well as by your peers and subordinates are among these factors.
- Timing is often crucial. Sensing when to move ahead aggressively and when to fade into the woodwork may be a critical skill. Access to the informal grapevine, knowledge of recent events and reading nonverbal body and facial signals are important. As you become non-defensive, you'll probably find yourself tuning in to more subtle signals and may learn to trust your intuition as you listen more sensitively.

- Effects on profits, cost effectiveness, pressures, and deadlines are additional factors to consider.
- Innovation that results in improving the company's market position, such as being first with a new customer benefit, may operate in your favor.

These are among the factors that Dave Eliot has to consider as he handles his current situation at Country Stores. Recall that in Chapter 4 we left him in a defensive, low-power, down position. Old-timer Ed Jones from Payroll had tripped him up for not putting a disciplinary memo in the personnel file of his night crew supervisor, Juan Martinez, for Juan's tardiness. Having warned him against fraternizing, Dave's boss, Pete Gross, refused to discuss the matter. Dave felt the pull of the reins and was apprehensive that something worse was in store.

We explored the conflicting values underlying the issue Dave raised when he didn't follow the rules. Dave's participative style didn't fit well with the old-timers' authoritative styles. They held the power. Although Dave's group was highly productive and his own work was technically excellent, this didn't offset his youth, inexperience, and low seniority at Country Stores. As a novice in the company, not observing the rules rendered him ineligible to enter the men's hut as an initiate. In fact, his initiation ritual began so badly that full membership in the executive club is further away than when Dave was hired.

When you have divergent interests to balance and you're low on the totem pole, add others' wanted results to your own. Odds are good you won't lose if you set up good odds for everyone to gain.

As we become more acquainted with Dave, we discover that he is not one to compromise himself much. He's one of the New Breed who is committed to becoming his own person while also being committed to technical and professional excellence. He wants to choose for himself; however, he's flexible enough to make compromises and negotiate out of his trade-off area. He's already learned that when he violates himself or his values, he suffers more pain, anger, and guilt than he wants in his life.

Pete Gross and the founders of Country Stores, Tom Hudson and Jack Willitt are all twice as old as Dave and, in their minds, many times more experienced. Being traditional, they expect their juniors to defer to their experience and wisdom. They believe in using their power to control the operations and the operators. That's how business is run. They see no inconsistency between this viewpoint and the recruitment flyers they write that advertise "unlimited advancement opportunities." They do what's necessary to make more profits every year.

In a general way, the conflict between Dave's values and those of the executives is predictable. (Look again at Figure 2-3, *The nature of conflict between traditional employers and new breed employees*, p. 29. Differences that create a vacuum are more easily ignored than others—doing a competent job, questioning authority, having fun and a playful attitude, exercising more independence, thinking for oneself—which create conflict. Dave's values are among those that create conflict. He has to assume that the executives aren't likely to change very soon. Dave needs to figure out how he can live by his values and also gain more results as DP manager.

Let's see how Dave can approach gaining more of the results he wants—non-defensively. As we rejoin him, he's still feeling defensive and down, now recognizing the dynamics we've just reviewed. In fact, Dave has been reading along with you in this book and is now ready to experiment with non-defensive ways to keep his cool while under fire from Ed, Pete, Tom, and Jack. He begins by talking to himself. Here's what he says and how he answers himself back.

Dave's Inner Dialogue	*How He Answers Himself*
Here I thought I was doing fine because my crews are producing so well, and I've done some great design work. I thought that's what they hired me for. I don't like playing these corporate games.	You may not like it, but that's the reality. Are you going to stay defensive or breathe deeply and start on a new track?
(He turns his attention to his body messages and notices his shallow breathing. Slowly he exhales, visualizing all his tensions leaving; then allows his lungs to fill at their natural pace, imagining himself breathing in peace and relaxation; repeats it several times, thinking "I'm centering.")	There it goes (talking to his breathing). Goodbye. Feels good. Go relax my neck, my brain, throughout my whole body. Ah yes, now I'm coming into focus.
With all four of those men putting on the screws, I don't look too good right now. Wonder if I should stay.	You know that's an easy out. Keep it as an option, but if you stay, what results do you want?

Dave's Inner Dialogue	How He Answers Himself
I suppose I have to put that damn memo in Juan's file. But now we know that's only the tip of the iceberg. It's cold here.	Okay, it's cold. Set that aside for a moment and think of results you really want.
I don't like the cold climate. I've got a good operation and don't like getting this treatment over a lousy memo. Don't they care that Juan's a good man? And me, too?	Yes, you're a good manager. But there's more to managing here, and you'd better face it since you're staying.
If I could have what I really want, they'd leave me alone and let me run my shop the way I am and quit fussing about silly rules.	Good start, except you have to deal with probabilities, and this isn't one of them.
Okay, I'll list what results I really want, but it seems like an exercise in futility. There's no hope of getting it right now.	Keep that up and you'll get your self-fulfilling prophecy. Just start . . .

So Dave decides to stop fighting himself and go ahead. Gradually he finds himself becoming involved with some angles he hadn't thought about before. Here is his first cut at possible results he would like to achieve.

- Continue managing in my present style. We like working our way. We consistently produce well. I may not get up points for that, but if my people don't produce, I'll get down points.
- Do something about the memo to get them off my back. Maybe put one in that is so innocuous it can't hurt Juan.
- Talk with Juan (and maybe the others) to see how we can protect the great teamwork we have. (I think this is an option. It's an activity, not a result.)
- Build a stronger power base for myself and my group so others give more respect for our function.
- It's not just respect I want; I need political leverage.
- Develop ways to make allies out of Tom, Jack, and Pete. I don't care for Ed and don't think his influence is as high as the others. (What am I doing? Setting priorities? Risk-rating?)
- Change my present image from the naughty boy to the fair-haired boy. (They'll probably see me as a boy for some time so I may as well accept it.)

- Make myself more visible in ways that make Jack glad that he re-cruited me. He wants to back a winner. (A possible ally?)
- Become more active in the Association of Data Processing Execu-tives and Managers Association (ADPEM), present some papers, get published, earn some awards.

At this point, Dave feels he's beginning to wander, so he reviews the list to see how he might sharpen its focus. Then he realizes that he's thinking of how Jack might gain, so he continues on the mutual gain theme.

- What does Tom want for Country Stores from me? The ads say: First with the Best in the West. Guess he wants to be first with product code scanners, and I'm the one to do it. Tom knows that Jack thinks I'm the best DP manager in eleven western states. What if another chain installs scanners first? I do have some potential here.
- What does Pete want for himself or Country Stores from me? He makes points with Tom and Jack when I make points. How does he make points with Tom? Innovation, I think. Maybe in saving money, too. As controller, saving money makes points, even though making money usually counts for more.
- What does Ed want? I don't really want to give him anything, but I don't want him as an enemy either. Nit-picking is his schtick. How can I use that?

Dave is now thinking about gain–gain trade-offs, what matters to some powerful people in his life, and some organizational goals, which, if met, could enhance his own goals. Strategies are beginning to form in his head when he stops short, realizing that he still needs a clear statement of results he wants or a series of short, clear statements.

He experiments with clustering immediate results he wants, then in-termediate ones that involve more research or data gathering, and finally his longer-range objectives. He consolidates and reshapes his wanted results to look like this:

Immediate Results Wanted
1. Follow all the rules as much as possible—or appear as if I am. Give token deference and gain more credibility and political leverage.
2. Develop ways within each crew to also appear to follow rules for the next three months; then discuss it again at a weekly meeting.
3. With Juan's involvement, devise a harmless memo for his file.

Intermediate Results Wanted (more information is needed and available)
4. Find out more about what each executive wants from me for himself and for Country Stores. Include their assistants or secretaries.

5. Develop ways to meet those wants while also increasing my power base.
6. Study who depends on whom for what, and how I can use that to increase my power base. What can I give and take in negotiations?
7. Publish an article in the right place to add to my reputation and visibility and to Country Stores' image of being forward thinking. Define this better after researching it and estimating my writing time and their publication schedule.

Longer-Term Results Wanted
8. Legitimacy for managing in my participative style. Legitimacy may mean convincing the executives that I can be trusted to obey the rules so they can responsibly close their eyes when I break them. I expect this will give me space to operate more freely within the system's rigidity.
9. Keep centered and turned on so I continue to grow as a person while growing as a political, technical, ethical professional—here or elsewhere.

(Notice that these results do not include income or position goals, although they could. We have limited Dave's wanted results to his situation in Chapter 4. This is not intended to be a complete career plan.)

Now Dave reviews his results statement to see if they state only what he wants. He realizes that if he has options, content, or other steps of the Choosing Process mixed in with his results statement, he may not yet be clear about what he wants. Consequently, he may reduce his odds of gaining them. As he sorts out his statements, he decides whether each one states *what* he wants. If so, that's a RESULTS WANTED. If it states *how* to get a result, he knows that is an OPTION. If he needs more information, that is data to gather about ATTITUDES or CONTENT. Here is how his analysis comes out.

Results Statements (in segments)	WHAT or How	Choosing Process Step
1. Follow rules (or appear to)	How	OPTION
Give deference	How	OPTION
Gain more credibility	WHAT	RESULT WANTED
Gain more political leverage	WHAT	RESULT WANTED
2. Ways for crews to follow rules	How	OPTION
Discuss in three months with crews	How	OPTION or ACTION
3. Write harmless memo about Juan	How	OPTION
Involve Juan in writing memo	WHAT	RESULT WANTED

Results Statements (in segments)	WHAT or How	Choosing Process Step
4. Gather data about what each officer wants from me and for Country Stores. Use their assistants to gather data or to verify it.	Data	ATTITUDES or CONTENT
5. Ways to . . .	How	OPTIONS
Meet executives' wants	WHAT	RESULT WANTED
Increase my power base	WHAT	RESULT WANTED
6. Study who depends on whom	Data	ATTITUDES or CONTENT
How can I use dependencies?	How	OPTIONS
Increase my power base	WHAT	RESULT WANTED
What can I give or take?	Data	ATTITUDES or CONTENT
Negotiations	How or WHAT	Negotiations might be an OPTION, or Negotiating may start a RESULT-WANTED statement
7. Publish an article in the right place	How	OPTION*
Add to my reputation	WHAT	RESULT WANTED
Add to my visibility	WHAT	RESULT WANTED
Add to Country Stores' image of being forward thinking	WHAT	RESULT WANTED
Define and research writing time, publication schedule	Data	CONTENT
8. Legitimacy for my participative management style	WHAT	RESULT WANTED
Legitimacy means I can be trusted by the executives so they can ignore it when I break a rule	WHAT	An indicator of having gained a RESULT WANTED
Space to operate within this rigid system	WHAT	RESULT WANTED
9. Stay centered and turned on	WHAT	RESULT WANTED
Grow as a person	WHAT	RESULT WANTED
Grow as a political, technical, ethical professional	WHAT	RESULT WANTED
Here or elsewhere	Where	OPTION (*Where* is a form of *how*. Dave can work elsewhere—an OPTION)

*Publishing an article could also be a RESULT WANTED. However, for Dave's conflict situation, it's more of an OPTION that he later assesses for how this activity would help or hinder him in gaining results he wants.

When Dave summarizes his analysis by the Choosing Process steps, he sees a new pattern emerging. First he collects all the OPTIONS and sets them aside for later consideration.[1] Then he lists the data-gathering items under

[1] We will use Dave's OPTIONS in the next chapter as he develops his strategy.

the first two steps, Sensing ATTITUDES and Analyzing CONTENT. Dave sees that he can decide later whether or not to get that information. First he clusters the RESULTS he wants. Later he will give them priorities. Here's how Dave's information looks now.

Choosing Process Steps	*Dave's Information*
Step 1. Sensing ATTITUDES	Gather data about what each executive wants from me and for Country Stores. Use their assistants to gather data or to verify it.
Step 2. Analyzing CONTENT	Study who depends on whom for what What can I give or take? Define and research writing time and ADPEM's publication schedule
Step 3. Formulating RESULTS WANTED	⑤ ─── Gain more credibility ① Gain more political leverage ③ ── Involve Juan in writing memo ④ ── Meet executives' wants ── Increase my power base ── Negotiate ── Add to my reputation ── Add to my visibility ── Add to Country Store's image of being forward thinking ── Gain legitimacy for my participative style ── Make space to operate in this rigid system ② Keep centered and turned on ── Grow as a person and as a political, technical, ethical professional

Dave now clusters and restates the results he wants and notes the basis for clustering.

1. Increase my power base to gain more political leverage so I have more space within which to operate (regarding the system).
2. Keep centered and turned on as part of growing as a person and as a political, technical, ethical professional (regarding myself).
3. Gain legitimacy for my participative management style, including willingness to negotiate and involve other people (regarding relationships in all directions).
4. Meet executives' wants, one of which is the image of forward thinking (regarding relationships upward).
5. Add to my reputation and visibility; it may gain me more credibility. The three are so intertwined, I can't separate them (regarding attitudes wanted from the executives; others, too).

Dave isn't sure whether he's clustered his results too much; he also wonders where to begin. First he decides to rank his results; then he'll take them one at a time to see if they meet the criteria for a good results wanted statement. Then he can specify how he'll know the results when they have been achieved.

Dave uses a paired comparison method of prioritizing that he has found to be easy and effective. Here's how it works.[2] First he builds a grid on which to make the comparisons among his five statements. (Simply extend it if you have more items.) It looks like this:

A	B	C	D
1 2	—	—	—
1 3	2 3	—	—
1 4	2 4	3 4	—
1 5	2 5	3 5	4 5

Beginning with column A, Dave then compares the first result he wants with the second, asking himself, "If I had to choose between only these two results, which would be most important to me, given my situation at Country Stores?" He circles his choice and continues down column A, then completes the table. Here are his choices and the number of times he chose each result.

					Priority
A	B	C	D	Result 1 = 3 times	2
1②	—	—	—	Result 2 = 4 times	1
①3	②3	—	—	Result 3 = 1 time	4
①4	②4	③4	—	Result 4 = 0 times	5
①5	②5	3⑤	4⑤	Result 5 = 2 times	3

Dave now reorders his list of results by how many times he chose each one when he was forced to choose between pairs. Here are his priorities:

1. Keep centered and turned on as part of growing as a person.
2. Increase my power base to gain more political leverage.
3. Add to my reputation and visibility to gain more credibility.
4. Gain legitimacy for my participative management style.
5. Meet executives' wants.

Dave's final step is to look over his list and see whether the priorities feel right to him. He decides that he's already working on the first results he wants through developing his non-defensive communication processes, and

[2]For a detailed demonstration of this prioritizing method, see Richard N. Bolles: *The Three Boxes of Life and How to Get Out of Them*, Ten Speed Press, Berkeley, Calif., 1978, pp. 420–423.

he feels some urgency to work on increasing his power base so he can some-how gain more political leverage. He knows he'll link this to his first priority by keeping focused on mutual gain and the ethical considerations that are part of being his own person. He also sees that he can gain some of the other results he wants while he's working on this one. In fact, meeting some of the executives' wants may be an option for gaining political leverage.

As he begins to see some options, Dave becomes excited at the prospect of gaining more control over his situation. He has to slow himself down to check that his top priority results meet the criteria. He decides to shorten his statement to: *Increase my power base to gain more political leverage.* He figures that if he gains this, he may gain more than operational space; there may be other gains he can't predict yet. He doesn't want to limit himself by expecting too little. Even though Dave's present situation doesn't look prom-ising, he decides to do all he can to stimulate the self-fulfilling prophecy to work in his favor.

Now he double-checks his results statement with the criteria.

1. Yes, it states what he does want—as an end to achieve and not as an activity or an option for getting there.
2. Yes, it is stated in terms of what he can control or influence and it doesn't assume that he can change or control another person.
3. No, it does not include relationships or tasks. Dave feels that rela-tionships are included in his other results statements; he also has some tasks in mind as options. He decides to leave his present state-ment as it is for now, even though it doesn't fully meet this criterion.
4. No, it does not include gain for relationships or tasks, but only gain for himself. However, Dave knows he's centered in mutual gain and feels he won't play win–lose games. He applies similar thinking to this criterion as in 3.

Dave now goes on to the fifth criterion:

5. What will people be doing and saying that indicates you've gained the results you want? Here's what Dave says would satisfy him that he has increased his power base:
   - Ed reports no broken rules from my department for one month.
   - My crews feel decently treated by all old-timers for one month.
   - Most comments about my fraternizing with my employees will have ceased for one month. Even better would be some kidding remarks from one or more of the executives, especially from Pete.
   - Evidence of acceptance, such as the beginning of an initiation ritual—a lunch invitation, an after-hours' meeting to which I'm normally not invited, or even a warmer-than-usual exchange

over coffee during executive time in the lounge. I'd like to have
stronger recognition, but this will satisfy me for now.
- At the end of one month, I'll review these indicators and decide
if these have occurred and whether I really am satisfied.

This is a good start. In Chapter 12, we'll see how useful these descriptions can be. It helps to know a result when you see one!

IN THE NEXT CHAPTER

We'll continue with Dave Eliot's use of the Choosing Process and see how he generates his options and assesses both his positive and negative risks to come up with his odds of gaining results. We'll also see how he optimizes his risks and payoffs, then how he tests his tentative choices for worst consequences and for fit to his personal style and ethics. By then he'll have an integrated strategy for going into action.

READINGS

Bolles, Richard N.: *The Three Boxes of Life and How to Get Out of Them,* Ten Speed Press, Berkeley, Calif., 1978. This introduction to life/work planning goes hand in hand with Bolles' earlier, popular book, *What Color Is Your Parachute?* This new book shows you how to bring a better balance among your learning/working/playing lives during your lifetime. Rich in ideas, it is also based on mutual gain.

Mager, Robert F.: *Goal Anaylsis,* Fearon, Belmont, Calif., 1972. Mager holds little reverance for fuzzies—statements such as "having the proper attitude" or "take pride in your work." He asks, "How would you know one when you see one?" With humorous clarity, he shows how to state a goal or result you want, and how to describe what people will be saying or doing when they've reached that goal. Descriptions replace evaluative statements, similar to the *do's* and *don'ts* of listening.

For additional background reading, see bibliography entries 13, 15, 33, 85.

11

GENERATING OPTIONS, ASSESSING YOUR RISKS AND ODDS, AND TESTING YOUR CHOICES

So You're Ready for Action

To develop a power base, Dave knows he needs a two-phase strategy plan. During the first phase, he has to handle the immediate problem of Juan Martinez' disciplinary memo and the related issue of socializing after work among Mary Galloway's day crew and some of the night crew. During the second phase, he will work toward integrating a network of actions that will increase his long-term position power. He expects to be able to meet his strategic goals by using person power and by staying centered. He also expects to use mutual gain values in the way he develops his strategies with upper management. Not only will development of a mutual gain strategic plan increase his odds of gaining political leverage, he knows he gets the best cooperation from store managers and his own crews when he functions this way.

To stay centered and avoid becoming sidetracked, he uses a summary of the Choosing Process steps that he keeps with his Incident Cards. He refers to these steps and their underlying values to remind himself where he is in the process and what to do next. Figure 11-1 shows the summarized steps.

Now Dave has his point of reference. He also states again the result he wants to focus on: *Increase my power base to gain more political leverage*. Dave's thinking processes are written in detail, although the process actually occurs in a very short period of time.

TAKE CARE OF THE CONFRONTING ISSUE FIRST

The first phase of his strategy is to handle the confronting issue of the disciplinary memo. He figures that if he doesn't do this, he hasn't gotten off

THE CHOOSING PROCESS STEPS

Sensing ATTITUDES
- *What are your feelings, inner rules, biases, beliefs, priorities?*
- *What are others' attitudes?*

Analyzing CONTENT
- *What are facts, opinions, unknowns, about the events, recent changes?*
- *What else might be occurring?*
- *What additional data do you need?*

Formulating RESULTS WANTED
- *What results do you want for you, with others, about the work?*
- *What indicators will satisfy you that results have been achieved?*

Generating OPTIONS
- *Brainstorm all your options.*
- *Include those you'll probably not use. DO NOT EVALUATE THEM YET.*

Assessing RISKS and ODDS
- *Rate each option by what HELPS and what HINDERS you, and how well it gets the results you want. Take*
- *OPTIMUM RISKS FOR OPTIMUM RESULTS.*

Testing CHOICES
- *Test for worst consequences and what you'd do if that happens.*
- *Test for fit to your style.*
- *Test for fit to your ethics.*

Taking ACTION
- *Act on your choice, or make action plan with others. Assess how well results are achieved.*
- *Assess what you can learn from your use of each step. Claim credit for what you did well.*

Figure 11-1.   The Choosing Process steps.

first base toward gaining political leverage. Here's how he thinks about it, assuming the executives are competitive in their thinking.

> Pete, Jack, and Tom have listened to Ed and interpret my not following that rule as fraternizing—a cardinal sin to them. If I'm going to gain

credibility in their eyes, which I have to have to gain political leverage, I need to see myself as they now see me. They're going to minimize their risks with me and maximize their payoffs. They want to get as much out of me as they can with no further investment—or through fear. Operating from that premise, here's how my odds look if I do or if I don't write the memo.

Dave's Payoff Matrix[1]		*Decision to Put Memo in Juan's File*	
		Yes	No
Credibility in the eyes of "minimax" executives	Gain	0	−30
	Loss	0	−10

If yes, put the memo in Juan's file, I won't gain any credibility either way. I'm just doing what they think I should have done in the first place. However if no, my odds of gaining credibility are −30 or more—it'll never happen. Odds of losing credibility aren't as great—only −10—because I'm already on the down side. I dig my own hole a little deeper. Put in a memo consistent with my values.

Referring back to the Choosing Process reminder card, Dave notes that he's actually working with three of the results he wants—gaining credibility, keeping centered in his management values, and getting a footing for political leverage. He now needs options for the harmless memo.

Dave goes back to the options he collected in the last chapter (pp. 305–306) and X's the ones that seem to be possibilities.

Step 4.	X	Follow rules (or appear to)
Generating OPTIONS	X	Defer (to executives)
		Devise ways for crews to follow rules
		Discuss with crews in three months
	X	Write harmless memo about Juan
		Devise ways to (meet executives' wants)
		How can I use dependencies?
	X	Negotiations
		Publish an article in the right place
		Work elsewhere

Using these options to start with, Dave generates all the options he can think of, including those he knows he probably will not use. Tempting as it

[1]For further explanation and applications for using the payoff matrix, see R. Richard Ritti and G. Ray Funkhouser, *The Ropes to Skip and the Ropes to Know: Studies in Organizational Behavior*, GRID, Inc., Columbus, Ohio, 1977, pp. 66–100.

is, he refrains from evaluating these options as he brainstorms them. Here's his list:

Table 11-1. *Options and Risks About the Memo.*

Options About the Memo	Risk
1. Negotiate with Juan on how to write a memo that's harmless to him.	+
2. Write a tough memo; follow it up with one that takes Juan off the hook.	+
3. Tell Juan to get in on time so we don't rock their boat.	−
4. Meet with crews to figure out ways to cover for each other so their attendance looks okay on the time clocks.	−
5. Get a good excuse from Juan, "good" meaning one that will satisfy the old-timers that I've taken "corrective action."	+
6. Send copies to Pete, Jack, Tom, and Ed, as well as to Personnel.	−
7. Act as if I'm properly chastised.	−
8. Admit I made a mistake.	?
9. Defer to the rules as a fact of life here.	+
10. Defer to the executives because they made the rules.	−

Dave now goes to the risk-rating step and does a simple first cut by marking them with (+) for least risk and good odds, (?) for questionable, and (−) for those he doesn't like. His notations are shown above in Table 11-1.

Before discarding the negative or questionable risks, he does some consolidating and combining, and makes notes about why he rated each one as he did. (This step can often be omitted; however, it can be useful in identifying clearly how you perceive a situation and what your feelings are about it.) Dave found he could rank the items on his list as he worked with it without using the prioritizing technique. Table 11-2 shows his consolidated list of options, arranged from least risk to most risk with his reasons. The numbers in parentheses refer to the original options on his list in Table 11-1.

Table 11-2. *Options from Least to Most Risk.*

Options From Least Risk to Most Risk	Reasoning
1. Negotiate with Juan on best way to write the memo so he's satisfied he won't be hurt while we satisfy the rules. Show him my options and find out his thoughts. Also see how he can work with his crew on this (1, 2, 5).	Juan is affected, so he has to be involved. Want his support and cooperation personally, as well as with his crew.
2. Defer to rules as a fact of life here with Juan as well as with the executives. Show him and Mary the need to balance productivity with deference (9).	Discuss these norms with Juan and why it's important to all of us; trust he and Mary will see the sense in it for themselves. Get their reactions and ideas.

Dave has now consolidated his pluses. Next he'll see if he can do something with his question in Table 11-1 other than discard it as an option for this particular situation.

3. Admit I made a mistake to any one of the executives (8). Admit to myself I made a mistake and learn from it. (*Decision: Learn from it only.*)	To the execs, no. They would see this as weakness and give me minus odds again. I don't think I made a mistake by my values. I underestimated the importance of rules compared to productivity.

Now he considers the minuses in Table 11-1 and does a quick calculation using a scale of 10. He weighs how much he thinks the option will help and hinder him to gain the results he wants and scores it accordingly.

4. Tell Juan to get in on time (3). As it stands, *it scores −3.* Ask Juan to get in on time to take off the pressure and see what ideas he has for the crew to stay responsible for their production without getting turned off by rules that don't help them. *Score is now +3.*	We've never operated that way and I don't want to start now. It's not my style, but . . . This is more my style. With his background, I bet he has some ideas. It must be an old game to him.
5. Defer to the executives because they made the rules, acting as if I am properly chastised (7, 10). *Score = −3.*	I might make some points (+5) by brownnosing, but this one really violates me (−8). It's not worth it.
6. Send copies to the execs as well as to Personnel (6). *Score = −8.* It's safer to get the word out informally after taking action. *Score = 0.*	Feels good at first. But it doesn't deserve that much visibility. Better to simply put the memo in Juan's file and let Pete know it's done.
7. Meet with crews on how to cover each other so everyone's time clocks are punched on time (4). *Score = −10.*	It's practical but not for me. It would break a much more serious rule and would appear dishonest if discovered— a basis for being fired. No. Much as I hate time clocks, that's an issue for another time.

Dave is now at the action step of the Choosing Process. He has already considered his style, his ethics, and the worst consequences for most of the options and has tested them as choices. He can keep available his rejected options 5 through 7 for another time or place where other people are involved and when the risks are likely to be different. However, for here and now, he chooses to act on options 1, 2, and 4, which he has converted to a plus. He's now choosing his actions instead of reacting to other people's actions.

After practicing the application of the Choosing Process to this relatively simple first phase, Dave sees how it works and expects to move more quickly in the second, more complex phase.

REVIEW DIFFERING VALUES AND DEVELOP INTERMEDIATE RESULTS STATEMENTS

As Dave starts to develop a series of actions that will result in an integrated strategy, he realizes that his results statement: *Increase my power base to gain more political leverage,* is too global. It states only the general direction for action. He has specified in part what he meant in the last chapter when he outlined how he'd know he had increased his power base (pp. 309–310). However, absence of Ed's reports of broken rules and absence of comments by executives are negative indicators. They may say the same things but not in his presence. How his employees feel the old-timers have treated them is not relevant to his power base nor to his credibility with executives. Evidence of acceptance by one of the executives is the only positive indicator he has so far. Then he remembers that an effective results statement is bite-size—small enough to chew. He sees he has set out the whole meal.

As he finishes the review of his process so far, he looks back at the data-gathering ideas he had in the last chapter (p. 307): find out what each executive wants from him and for Country Stores, study who depends on whom for what, research the article idea. These scattered ideas leave him feeling fragmented, not sure where to start. He decides to pull back and review how power is used with authority to exercise control. He wants to control himself and his operation; others want to control him. How does one go about building a power base? How do you exert influence? What factors are involved in renegotiating your position?

To put your wanted results in smaller packages, you may need to back up in the Choosing Process to get more details about attitudes or content.

As Dave considers these questions, he realizes he doesn't know very much about power nor how to acquire it. For most of his time at Country Stores, he'd been so involved in the technical processes of installing the UPC scanners and keeping his crews at peak production levels that he hadn't thought about power. Through his computer sciences training and experience, he has acquired the habit of doing his homework well before designing any program. He approaches these questions in the same manner, except this time the software is people and how they influence each other. With this shift in focus, he now recalls some information he has picked up along the way, but which he now hears and sees with an entirely different perspective.

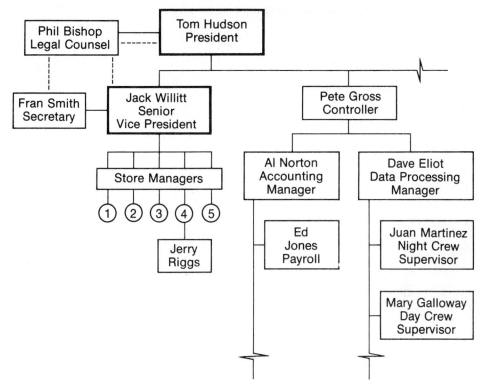

—— Solid lines = formal responsibility and reporting relationships in Country Stores.
------ Broken lines = formal relationships outside Country Stores.

Figure 11-2. *The formal organization chart: Dave Eliot's contacts at Country Stores, Inc., founded by Tom Hudson and Jack Willitt.*

While coordinating the installations between corporate offices and the stores, he has picked up information from suppliers, store managers, and their assistants and secretaries. Gradually he sees some patterns forming. He's used to diagramming flowcharts, so he experiments with rediagramming the chart of formal organization relationships shown in Figure 11-2.

Using the people shown on the linear chart, Dave draws the influence diagrams in Figure 11-3. The size of the circles and the amount of overlap represent Dave's accumulating impressions of the intermeshing network of private, personal, positional, and political relationships among the people he's had the most contact with to date.[2]

For example, Dave has inadvertently discovered that the legal counsel, Phil Bishop, is a power behind the scenes. Not only does he counsel Country

---

[2]I am indebted to an unknown person for this technique for diagramming influence. Among trainers useful material is often borrowed. Proper credit is sometimes lost in the process.

The People At the Top

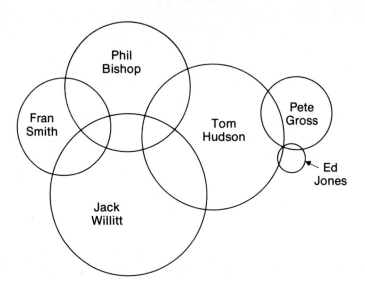

Store Managers Added

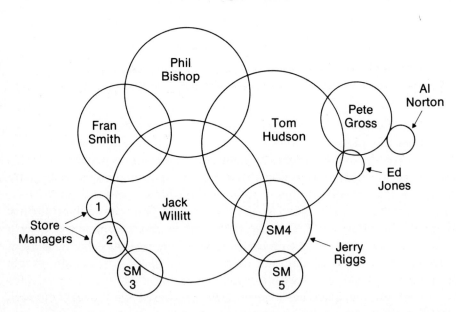

Figure 11-3. *Dave Eliot's influence diagram showing circles of informal influence.*

Stores, Inc., he also counsels Tom and Jack privately in a joint real estate venture, which Phil manages for them. Dave has also learned that Fran Smith, Jack Willitt's secretary, assists Phil in administering this joint venture. Apparently she doesn't have direct influence with Tom Hudson, but Dave assumes she probably has considerable indirect access to him through Jack and Phil.

Dave's primary information source is Jerry Riggs, 37, manager of Store 4, the largest of the chain. When Dave was designing the store's installation, they had talked about many things besides store operations and gradually had developed some trust and respect between them. Dave now realizes he could learn from watching how Jerry uses power. Jerry, it turns out, is the most influential of the store managers. He has a style that inspires trust; people love to tell him their troubles because he listens and seems to care about them. He does care, but Jerry has found that this trust also builds strong customer ties. He says this was one of the reasons he was elected to the district school board.

It's also Jerry who told Dave that Ed Jones' sister married a cousin of Tom Hudson's, which gives Ed some limited influence with Tom. In addition, Ed was the one who, many years ago, found Pete Gross for the controller spot. Tom took an immediate liking to Pete and soon invited him to join the Valley Country Club, the only private membership club for miles around. Tom and Pete are very much alike; both are outgoing, community-conscious and conservative. According to Jerry, their wives also get along well.

In old-line, stable systems, old history may influence current affairs. Find a pipeline into the past to more accurately read the present.

When Jack Willitt hired Jerry 13 years ago, he spent a lot of time seeing that Jerry got the needed backing to build Store 4 into the highly successful operation it is today. Thanks to Jack's connections, Jerry has been able to negotiate some contracts with suppliers that have given him cost advantages, some of which he's been able to pass on to other stores. Tom also likes Jerry and was instrumental in introducing him to several powerful community and regional people, some of whom have subsequently sponsored him in his election campaign. Among the store managers, Jerry is clearly the model for the others. Store Manager 5 is the only one Jerry sees as having growth potential. Dave thinks Jerry is probably a threat to the other store managers; he's become the standard for comparison and he's a hard act to follow.

As he studies the power structure of Country Stores and as he's gotten to know Jerry, Dave finds that he admires Jerry's mind, which seems to be always clicking with new ideas that make unexpected connections. He's willing to spend time filling Dave in on past history, and it appears to Dave that Jerry also knows when to be discreet. Jerry's ideas for promoting the scanner changeover formed the basis for Tom's advertising campaign, which builds on Country Stores' basic theme of The First with the Best in the West.

As Dave sketches in his impressions on his influence diagrams, he discovers that he knows very little about Al Norton, the accounting manager. The next time he's at Store 4, he makes an opportunity to ask Jerry where Al fits in.

"That's where Pete was smart," he tells Dave. "In Al, he found a man who likes nothing better than his accounting, so the work always gets done right and on time. Al is no competition for Pete, and he's too square to pay any attention to Ed's shenanigans. He wouldn't know what to do about it anyway."

Dave hasn't told Jerry about the memo, but his ears perk up at the word "shenanigans." He asks Jerry what he means by that.

"He's an old crony that they keep around as part of the furniture. Don't pay any attention to him. He's the mop-up committee."

With that, Dave tells him about the memo incident and is surprised at Jerry's reaction. "That's different," he says. "I thought you knew. Mary in your shop is some shirttail relative of Ed's that he brought in a few years ago. Ed always picks Mary's brains about what's going on. He uses anything he can pick up that he thinks will keep him in solid with Pete or Tom. He knows he's on the shelf so this is how he makes himself feel important. Since you're still new though, Tom might listen to him. Best to keep your act extra clean for a while—maybe quite a while."

This new bit of information unsettles Dave and he wonders, "Is Mary the trusted supervisor I thought she was? Is she an inside informer? How does she interpret my way of managing? Is she using her perceptions against me?"

When in doubt, give the benefit of the doubt. Then state your assumptions and what-ifs, and visualize alternative scenarios.

Then Dave realizes he is taking everything Jerry says at face value. His old habit of doing his homework well nudges at him; "Trust your own judgment. You've liked her work so far, and you have no reason to question her." His self-doubt also nudges him, "But you haven't been thinking in political terms before now. Look at it again." Then his subjective good sense tells him, "You're running a little scared right now, Dave. Cool it. Put this Mary thing on the back burner and see if you can find out more, preferably from her." His pragmatic, objective mind tells him, "Jerry was giving you his view. Check your own. Check with others. It's possible that Mary thinks she's being helpful and is unaware of any other implications. The more important questions are: 'If you assume she's not an ally, how might she become one?' and 'If you assume she is an ally, how much risk do you take?'"

By doing these influence diagrams and filling in the blank spots, Dave becomes aware of how much data about people he has been ignoring. He also notices that he already had most of the information he needs but wasn't aware that what he knew was, in fact, useful information. He'd been focusing his attention on technical, not political behavior. As he studies the relationships he's drawn and also considers the norm that productivity is expected but not rewarded, Dave sees he'll have to use other ways to increase his power base. But how?

Dave recalls that Jerry was about his own age when he first came to Country Stores and that he's done very well in his 13 years. Here's a live example of how one person acquires and uses power and influence at Country Stores. In addition, Dave, thorough as usual in doing his homework, does a little research and comes across an article on power and dependence in management, in which he finds four ways in which successful managers establish power *over* others in their relationships.[3] Dave doesn't want power over others as much as he wants power *with* others, but he also wants to increase his political leverage. Not sure if this is an inherent conflict in terms, he decides to see if the way Jerry uses power is like the way the article describes the use of power and whether the recommended actions would fit his own values.

Testing Traditional Ways of Establishing Power Against Your Own Values

1. Create a sense of obligation by doing favors that cost you little but that others who are dependent on you appreciate very much.   The article calls this "true friendship," but this isn't Dave's idea of friendship. To him it's more like negotiation—or manipulation. But he considers his relationship with Jerry. Dave is somewhat dependent on him for information; Jerry's enthusiastic interest and support in the scanner installation makes

---

[3]John P. Kotter, "Power, Dependence, and Effective Management," *Harvard Business Review*, July–August 1977, pp. 125–136.

Dave's work much easier; his talk about past history helps Dave and doesn't cost Jerry anything except time; and he offers a few suggestions about how to play the game at Country Stores.

Dave wonders what Jerry will want from him in return and starts to feel manipulated. However, he also would be glad to do what he could for Jerry in return for the time Jerry has given. Dave realizes he would *choose* to help Jerry. To Dave that's different from an obligation. He likes Jerry, but even if his acts of friendship are given only to create an obligation, Dave knows he can respond from appreciation and still keep power over himself. So far, so good—but not a basis for building a personal friendship.

Dave recalls that when Jerry started out, Jack Willitt gave him a lot of backing. Did Jack set up an obligation or was it mutual gain? Both wanted a successful operation and got it. The same process seemed to work when Tom introduced Jerry to the right people to help his election to the school board. The effect was a negotiated trade-off: "I scratch your back, you scratch mine."

Dave makes a note to himself to analyze later: "Who depends on me for what?" as well as "On whom do I depend for what?"

2. *Build a reputation as an expert on certain matters through visible achievement, recognizing that experts are typically deferred to.* Dave sees this is where his ADPEM article fits in. He's aware that he's the only manager at Country Stores who has computer sciences expertise, but so far he's not used it for building a reputation, nor have his achievements been as visible as they could be. Again he considers Jerry's methods.

Jerry has no specialized knowledge to qualify him as an expert; however, the other store managers think he's an expert on purchasing. He passed on some cost advantages he gained from suppliers—a highly visible act. Jerry has no expertise as an educator but he's on the school board—a highly visible position. He has built a reputation as an involved citizen concerned with building the community. If he can run a successful business, the reasoning went, he can run a successful school district. The reasoning may or may not be faulty, but it added to Jerry's power base when visible support and involvement of other powerful persons was provided through the less visible support of Jack and Tom. Inside Country Stores as well as outside in the region, Jerry has a reputation as a winner.

Dave notes the question, "How can I make my computer expertise more visible through achievements I can point to?" He likes the idea of this kind of power—as long as it's authentic.

3. *Foster in others an identification with yourself, your ideals and values, or what you stand for.* Dave is cautious about this one; it sounds like building a cult around yourself. On the other hand, if values are genuinely shared and people are working together to make them active, that fits Dave's values. His concern is the potential of abusing power through the use of charisma and dazzle.

As Dave sees it, Jerry has acquired power by his track record at Store 4. Not only do other store managers think of him as the model to follow, the executives seem to point to him as the shining example. Perhaps Jack Willitt takes pride in having spotted a winner and in helping Jerry become one. Jerry may do the same thing for Store Manager 5, whom he sees as having growth potential. As he mulls this over, however, it occurs to Dave that he has no idea what Jerry's values are or what he stands for. He wonders if he's unconsciously idealized Jerry because of his easy, outgoing personality and obvious success.

Dave adds to his notes: "Not comfortable with this one if it's based only on personality, even though it's an option that works. I also want shared values so people give their personal commitment."

4. Feed other people's beliefs that they are dependent on you, either for help or for not being hurt. The more dependent they think they are, the more they will cooperate with you. Dave knows this works but it sounds like coercive control. However, it's an option and he decides not to evaluate it before he finds out how it works. So he reads on.

First you identify and secure resources others need and don't have and that aren't readily available elsewhere. These resources might be authority to make certain decisions; control of money, equipment, or office space; access to important people; specialized information or control of information channels; even your own subordinates.

Then you let the other pepole know you have these resources and that you stand ready to help them or hurt them, depending on how well they cooperate with you. (Dave's reaction is "gentlemanly blackmail.") In many cases, it won't matter whether you actually control these resources or if others gain the impression that you do. Impressions of power are often as powerful as actual power, he learns. They didn't talk about this in college.

For the moment, Dave sets aside such questions and considers scarce resources over which he has control.

- Only I can make certain technical decisions on the scanner project.
- Only I understand *all* the interfaces between the scanner project and the other data processing programs here.
- I have excellent technical resources through ADPEM and a few computer suppliers. I have some but not total control over these information channels.

- My expertise is specialized but is also somewhat available in the market.
- My subordinates are loyal, committed, and productive. (I still have to find out more about Mary.)

Dave also considers whether he would personally cooperate with someone who purposely hoarded needed resources to make him dependent and force his "cooperation." Although he might go along for a while, he doesn't ever want to become so dependent on a job that he would have to submit to such coercion for long.

As far as his own control of scarce resources is concerned, he knows it is limited to the time he survives at Country Stores. Because of this, he accurately estimates he would take a high risk if he becomes coercive in using this leverage. They'd fire him if they found out. He might survive longer if he exercises covert control, such as requiring his sign-off on key documents as part of the ongoing scanner system. He could make this appear as an internal safeguard when it would really be maintenance of his personal leverage. He knows other DP managers do this, but Dave rejects this option. It's not his style and doesn't fit his ethics.

Dave notes down another question: "How can I build on my scarce resource power so I gain, so others higher up gain, and so Country Stores gains?" He's thinking of options such as Jack Willitt's initial selection of him. Jack may want to prove that his choice was right. If Dave can use his resources to prove Jack right and also contribute something to Tom's advertising campaign, he might achieve mutual gain in several directions. Dave is now beginning to build a strategy that brings together several pieces of information he's been gathering. But that's jumping the gun a little. To complete the picture he now answers his own questions so he can state the immediate and intermediate results he wants in a workable form.

From his research about gaining political leverage, Dave now has three questions to answer:

1. Who depends on me for what, and on whom do I depend for what?
2. How can I make my computer expertise more visible through achievements I can point to?
3. How can I build on my scarce resource power and still use mutual gain?

Who Depends on Whom for What? Analyzing the Dependency Balance

Dave now summarizes his data-gathering steps of the Choosing Process. He realizes that his responsibility for the total data-processing system at corporate and remote locations is a highly interdependent one. This makes him quite dependent on a great many people. Even with built-in controls, the sytem works best when other people work the system correctly and promptly.

When he's integrating a new technology into the existing system, he relies heavily on the store managers to handle the changeover properly during installation and while it's being "de-bugged." Dave recalls that when the scanner installation was in the design stage, he was dependent on clearances from legal, internal auditing, security, and the outside auditors. Although it was true that they usually took his advice, he couldn't go ahead without their approvals. Before that, he had relied on the computer company for expert advice on key critical points. From the beginning, he has been dependent on Pete on the financial side, on Jack for smooth internal operations, and on Tom for the advertising and customer relations side. After the installation is completed and fully operational, Dave will still be dependent on these same people, but with different emphasis. Others may be added to the list, such as trainers in technical skills to operate his system.

Looking at interdependence again, he considers what these people depend upon him for. An efficient, easy-to-operate system with consistent feedback and follow-through and minimum disturbance to operations is the goal. This is directly related to profits in the highly competitive, low-margin business that Country Stores is in. Reaching this goal may earn him regular pay increases, but not necessarily power increases. Much as Dave would like the quality of his work to be the basis on which he gains both economic benefits and power, he sees that he's going to have to become more politically active if he's going to gain the leverage he wants. His present staff position doesn't give him nearly as much formal power as people like Jerry get from line operation positions. Dave's job requires his technical expertise, which gives him more informal person power than most line managers have when they come into Country Stores. To him this seems a strong asset that he can use for leverage.

Dave has made a point to keep current his ADPEM associations. Occasionally he has called on other DP managers for advice, ADPEM is an easy channel for getting published, and there's an active grapevine about positions that become available and what goes on in those companies. This adds to his personal power leverage because he considers himself always available to move to a better position. Some DP managers identify more with their profession than with their company, which reduces their dependence on any single employer. Dave also feels this way because currently he has few associations at Country Stores that give him the friendship and exchange his colleagues do. Sometimes he feels almost lonely at work. Even so, he likes feeling he doesn't have to conform to everyone's expectations. This feeling gives him a sense of independence he would not have without ADPEM. It may also give him leverage for maintaining his different style of managing his department. On the other hand, if line managers can command larger salary increases for their employees than Dave can, that could reduce his leverage. Ability to compete successfully for financial resources is power in virtually all systems.

Also, the higher you go, the more difficult it is to measure what you do. Appearances may substitute for substance. So never underestimate the power of personality. The higher you go, the more potent it becomes.

Now Dave considers some of the personalities he's been studying and the way people use their affiliations to enhance business relationships. Jerry hasn't mentioned his social connections with Jack, Tom, or Phil, but Dave makes a good guess that Jerry is a member of the Valley Country Club. Tom, Jack, and Phil Bishop probably have social personal ties in their joint real estate ventures, which may include the wives. Tom and Pete and their wives probably make another social grouping with some substantial power. As Dave sees social networks take form, he realizes that he's been seriously neglecting this vital area from which considerable political leverage often comes.

He wonders in passing how serious it may be to these people that he hasn't married yet. One day he brings this up casually with Jerry.

"Well, I don't think it makes much difference to Jack, but I'm sure it matters to Tom." And Jerry goes on to tell Dave about Tom's cousin having met Ed Jones' sister when they both worked at Country Stores several years ago. As far as anyone knows, they *had* to get married—something Tom refuses to talk about.

The light dawns on Dave. "*That's* why I got those comments from Pete about not fraternizing after work with my crews. And that explains Ed's manner; he acted almost vengeful. Mary must have told Ed about our socializing after work."

"Of course she did," Jerry assumes. "And Ed's convinced he'd be accounting manager now if it weren't for his sister screwing up. And now you're getting mixed up with Mary after working hours—at least that's what Ed will think and so will Tom, probably. Are you?"

"You know better than that, Jerry! I'm surprised you even ask." But Dave finds himself explaining, "We're all just friends who enjoy unwinding a little after finishing a heavy run. You know that."

And Jerry replies, "Hmmm. Friends, huh?" with a slight smirk. "Okay, so maybe now I know better, but who else does?" He stands up and ends the conversation with, "Well, it's your business, Dave. But it sure doesn't look good." With a sinking feeling, Dave senses that the final pieces are falling into place. Much as he dislikes these innuendoes, he realizes he will have to take them into account in his strategy.

After giving himself time to let his emotions settle down, he restates the results he wants in briefer, more workable statements.

1. Take care of immediate barriers to acquiring power: Juan's memo, Mary's part in the situation, socializing.
2. Develop more of a relationship with Pete. I need his support to gain acceptance and leverage.
3. Use mutual dependence for mutual gain. Find ways to do this.
4. Use special expertise as a scarce resource to help, not hurt, others.
5. Make myself more visible through publications and community activities.
6. Keep eyes open for other mutual gains that would give me leverage.

Developing a Flexible Strategy in a Complex Situation

Dave now has a fairly complete picture of the many factors that affect his present power position and his political future at Country Stores. He has not yet developed his own long-term career plans, but he knows he can move without loss of professional credibility any time after the scanner installation is debugged. That will take only a few months more. He continues his strategic planning by doing an analysis of his interdependence among the people and groups at Country Stores and clusters them:

High	Fairly High	Medium to Low
Pete Gross	Pete's secretary	Ed Jones
Tom Hudson	Phil Bishop	Training Staff
Jack Willitt	Jerry Riggs	DP suppliers
ADPEM	Other store managers	Security staff
Juan, Mary, crews	Internal auditors	
External auditors		

Dave now develops a list of actions that is his working strategic plan. First he lists immediate actions.

1. Write the memo with Juan's knowledge, involvement, and, hopefully, his consent.

2. If the opportunity arises, sense whether Juan has gotten indicators from Mary that suggest she's misrepresenting her relationship with me.

3. Let Mary and Juan know the importance of following rules as a way to buy consent for (or waiver of) our unusual teamwork style. Seek their cooperation, preferably their ideas and commitment.

4. Open communication with Mary to get a better idea of her motives, how much she talks to whom about what, the nature and strength of her relationships with Ed. Perhaps share with her some of my concerns if she seems aware and reliable.

5. Provide for socializing, but make it less visible to other people. Perhaps don't stay and drink as long as before, but keep involved with the crews. Check Mary's nonverbal body language for indicators.

6. Be aware of innuendoes, but don't let them influence my basic way of managing unless something else comes up that suggests I have to reconsider my risks.

Then he lists those intermediate actions that have more unknowns and will likely take longer to achieve.

1. Put myself in Pete's, Jack's, and Tom's shoes; consider how DP information could make their lives easier; give them more control over operations; give early warnings of potential trouble spots; or quickly identify successful promotions. Test to see if computer time and processing costs could be reduced at the same time.

2. Increase dialogue with Pete. How can I give him something he needs to make life easier for him or to make him look better to Tom or Jack? Is he being criticized because of me? Can his secretary be helpful to me?

3. Write an ADPEM article about the sophistication of Country Stores' system and tie it in with the advertising theme of being First with the Best in the West. The article will increase my visibility and the desire of Country Stores' executives—especially Tom—to have an innovative image. Remember they want company data kept private.

4. Use the article as one means of opening up more communication with Pete. Make changes he suggests and seek his support in getting Tom's okay. As a result of this article, I'd like a positive change in attitude toward me from both Pete and Tom.

5. Assuming that Pete, Tom, and Jack have good working relationships with the external auditors, find a way to involve auditors in better controls and gain their support for my ideas. I hope they

might toot my horn for me, especially to Pete. He's one key to Tom and Jack.

6. Find a logical avenue to gain Jack's support. Tie into his having recruited me and his apparent willingness to give support to newcomers. Build on his apparent desire to prove his ability to spot a winner.

7. Look for a way to be invited to join the country club. This is where business–social activity seems to occur and membership is probably a status symbol. Play this one by ear; it could be part of the initiation ritual.

8. Make an ally out of Ed. He seems to be the local recruiter. Through Mary, ask if he knows anyone to fill the research jobs I need done. He needs to feel valued. I don't like him much, but can respect that need.

9. Look around for a community activity in which I could get deeply interested that would give service, give me visibility, and provide a bridge to social connections.

At this point, Dave decides he has plenty of ways to start achieving the results he wants. He also recognizes that he will have to trust his intuition and sense of timing. He also sees that as events develop, he can move around his priorities and follow-through actions, while always keeping in mind the key questions, "What results do I want?" and "What are my options right now?"

Dave recognizes that he has to be cool in this system, partly because he's presently under fire and partly because keeping cool is without a doubt a dominant norm. The more ways he sees to gain what he wants through non-defensive means, the more comfortable he becomes with this norm. If he doesn't make headway in a reasonable length of time, he knows he can come up with more options. If he finds he's seriously blocked because of attitudes that won't change, he's confident he can go elsewhere and make better progress.

★　★　★　★　★　★　★　★　★

In fact, Dave's flexible approach worked. At Jerry's suggestion, he went to the public relations director, Stan Stover, about his ADPEM article and eventually they became friends. With Stan's active support, most of Dave's results were achieved over the next two years, except that he was not able to manage his department with as much freedom as he wanted. The major breakthrough came when Dave headed up the United Fund campaign. During that time he became acquainted with bankers, many of whom were among the power people in the region. Many were Tom's friends and were also people who supported Jerry Riggs' school board election. Tom offered Dave's DP expertise to the president of the largest bank to solve some unusual problems they were having. Dave later joined the Valley Country Club and at last contact, Dave was considering establishing an independent DP consulting firm with Stan as his managing partner.

IN THE LAST CHAPTER

We have now seen many people use the Choosing Process to solve work problems non-defensively. Sometimes authority people did not change styles; others became more collaborative when subordinate people persisted in non-defensive behavior and communication.

In the last chapter we consider more fully some effects of becoming more of your own person—of increasing your person power—when you relate to someone who has more position power. We also see how this change might affect how you each use power: for dominance and submission, or to integrate results you each want so that the combination is greater than the sum of both. At the same time, we look at the difference in energy flow between the two of you. We use a simple example to show these actions and interactions: the universal coffee memo.

For additional background reading, see bibliography entries 13, 15, 66, 85.

12

USING YOUR POWER NON-DEFENSIVELY

In Authority–Subordinate Relations and Future Potentials

Consider this universal coffee memo, which has appeared in some form at least once in virtually all offices in this country.

MEMORANDUM

DATE: January 14
TO: Mezzanine Floor Staff and Officers
FROM: I. M. Madden
RE: Coffee Stains

Effective immediately all coffee, tea, soft drinks, etc., must be consumed in the staff room provided for that purpose! Our carpeting is now permanently stained because people have been careless. Our new premises are beginning to look like a pig pen. Without question, desks cluttered with half-empty styrene cups do not enhance our professional image. Your strict adherence to this rule will be appreciated.

Reactions to this universal put-down range from feeling angry or indignant to feeling that it's pretty ridiculous. Say you received the memo and are now classified as a staff person who behaves like a pig. You want to take an action to let Mr. Madden know that this or similar memos aren't appreciated. You guess accurately that most people will ignore it or gripe about it in the staff room but do nothing. You don't want to blow it out of proportion, nor do you want to ignore it.

Here's where the power of no power comes in. If unanimous action (a source of power in itself) is not feasible, consider the power of anonymous action. For example, in one company this response was posted the next day on the bulletin boards and in the restrooms and was distributed to all mezzanine desks:

MEMORANDUM

DATE: April 1
TO: I. M. Madden
FROM: We
RE: Your memo Re: Coffee Stains

We salute and commend your position about the coffee, tea, soft drinks, etc. Rest assured we will cooperate in every way possible. It is maddening that our Mezzanine Floor Staff and Officers, at least some of them, act like pigs, which certainly does give off an unprofessional aura. Since we are all penned up together, we are glad that you have seen to it that at least the carpeting and desks are rescued from this abominable disregard. Here are some ways we will cooperate with your new rule:

1. When customers ask for coffee, we will tell them they cannot have any because we no longer allow piglike behavior in carpeted areas and they are not allowed in the staff room.
2. When the Board of Directors or the President asks for coffee to be served, secretaries will refuse and discontinue providing maid service.
3. We will be sure that the external auditors do not bring coffee with them while working here. This will also have the benefit of reducing the time they spend, thus reducing audit costs.

Thank you for taking such effective action on this high priority matter, which has such profound effect on our bottom line.

Results were immediate. Everyone speculated about who did it. Management wrapped the blanket of silence around the whole issue by having the memos quickly removed and acting as if nothing had happened. When asked about it, they murmured something about observing the rule by being careful about spills, but to go back to work and forget about it. Clearly the subject was closed.

Was this a mutual gain action? The answer depends on your time perspective. In the short run, the line was drawn against I. M. Madden's action, which let all managers know there are limits. The date and content suggest the absurdity aroused by Madden's memo, which apparently was embarrasing to other managers and perhaps to him. More than likely he wrote it when he was irritated about something else. The source kept quiet and couldn't be positively identified, although many curious rumors circulated. Even if "We" had been discovered, any further action would have made a mountain out of a mole hill. The point was made and the staff could get back to business.

In the longer run, managers at that company may think twice before starting up a steamroller to squash a gnat. Whether the reason for revising their tactics would be to avoid embarrassment or to consider the underlying issues is not certain. The fact that such memos are circulated often and universally suggests that the self-esteem issues are not considered. To many managers, the "We" memo would feel like an attack on their ability to control subordinates. That many managers are afraid of losing control is well documented and is easily observable, especially in traditional, paternalistic systems.

If a manager thinks in win–lose terms, the "We" memo may represent a technical knock-out in this round of the fight for control. The gentle, though public, ridicule provided comic relief for employees but may have been hard for Mr. Madden to take, even though he appeared to invite it. (Perhaps this is why such memos often come anonymously from the personnel department.) Whether or not Mr. Madden makes more of this issue or responds inappropriately to other issues in the future will depend on his need to defend his self-esteem, his commitment to competitive values, and other personal priorities and pressures.

Problems that involve opposing interests—divergent problems—don't stay solved when traditional, logical methods are used. Ignored interests and accumulating anger eventually require a new dynamic balance.

Taken by themselves, minor incidents such as the coffee memo are not worth the time we are now spending on it; however, it may be worth the effort because such incidents rarely occur by themselves. Usually they represent a pattern, a way of thinking about managing behavior. Consequently they tend to occur repeatedly in many forms, often done by managers who are not aware that these minutiae become grains of sand in the wheels of productivity. You, the subordinate, may be blamed for being too sensitive, or you may be perceived as petty. Even though some managers can sometimes be insensitive and petty themselves, they can shift responsibility for such behavior to sub-ordinates. Given that reality of how position power is often used, you need your person power to deflect responsibility that has been improperly shifted to you. Then your emotional reactions are less likely to become a pool of quicksand in which you, not the thoughtless manager, will get stuck. Drawing the line against arbitrary action is one available option to use before you come to a grinding halt.

DRAWING THE CIRCLE BIGGER COMPARED TO DRAWING THE LINE

Drawing the circle bigger is another option, but one that requires people in higher positions to participate. Also the values in a more participative system make possible more use of the organic, global method for working with divergent problems (as shown in Figure 7-3bb, page 208).

The coffee problem is a divergent one. Under pressure, the opposing interests move farther apart. The traditional, linear problem-solving method doesn't solve it (as we saw in Figure 7-4a, page 214). Instead, the method we need is oganic, having complex but necessary interrelationships of its parts, similar to living organisms such as ourselves.

Now let's move to another company where we see in some detail a more open climate that has a built-in organic structure for resolving conflicts. We'll continue with the coffee incident as a convenient, simple vehicle for describing the more complex people processes.

PromOtions Personalized (POP) is a fast-growing, high-pressure marketing company specializing in promotional items sold only to large accounts. POP's climate is much more participative than the one at Madden's company. Here everyone believes that all conflicts, no matter how small, have the potential to generate something new. No one has much time for resolving conflicts, but everyone consistently gives his or her best creative effort to find answers. The name of the game is: *What profitable new POP promotional item can come out of this conflict?*

The coffee conflict has now come up. It is approached seriously instead of being brushed off as an annoying gnat. According to the rules of the game, anyone can call a POPMEET, which is a quick stand-up meeting of five or six people conducted at tall, small, round tables on wheels. These are available everywhere, including restrooms. Each table has a NEW POP sign with a rack of cards attached. The group that meets will create a new promotional item out of the causes of the conflict, if they can do it in 15 minutes. The

POPMEET-caller and the adversary consult together to determine who else might be affected by the conflict. Potential customers for the yet-to-be-created NEW POP are always included. One representative for each of the affected groups will participate in the roundtable discussion. External groups are represented by employee volunteers, internal groups by someone from the affected department. The people in conflict make the final selections.

To keep it simple, let's assume that the same events about coffee are now occurring at POP—stained carpets, messy desks, officer and auditor habits, etc. Let's also say that you, a POP employee, hear manager Irene Maxon complain about the new showroom looking like a pig pen and advocating that coffee should be limited to the staff lounge. To you, that's conflict!

You call a POPMEET. You and Irene consult according to custom, and you decide you need someone to represent customers who frequent the showrooms; they drink a lot of coffee and also spill it. You also need someone from the maintenance department and a rep for the officer–auditor group. Six is the maximum number of people who can stand at a round table, each of whom has an equal voice. As you and Irene gravitate toward a NEW POP table, you are joined by volunteers from whom you select two as customer reps. You put out the word for reps from the internal groups. The new POPTEAM quickly encircles the table; you briefly summarize the conflict. The brainstorming begins.

After 15 minutes, your POPTEAM has generated 18 ideas from which you identify one potentially profitable NEW POP. The six of you pick a time to meet after hours, and all of you sign a NEW POP record card. As POPMEET-caller, you write up the POPTEAM's idea and turn in the card to the NEW POP DEPOT, keeping a copy.

In meetings after working hours your POPTEAM designs a coffee cup with these features: it has a unique base that catches side drips so no rings are left on surfaces; it is next to impossible to tip over; it makes no noise when set down; it holds in the coffee's heat and also hides cold, unsightly dregs. A company's logo can be displayed so it's seen with every sip, yet flows with the cup's contour. With purchase of a medium-priced machine, each cup could be individually personalized by the purchaser.

Your POPTEAM then analyzes the market, estimates production methods and costs, outlines a marketing plan and projects the profit potential, which must come within a predetermined range. Resource information is available from the business development people. When you've taken your idea as far as you can, your POPTEAM meets with the business development committee where their role is to play devil's advocate. The results will be GO, NO GO, or KEEP GOING. When all criteria have been met, POP will put your NEW POP on the market, with your POPTEAM acting as advisory consultants. After product development and initial promotional costs are covered, each POPTEAM member will receive an equal, small percentage of the gross sales for as long as POP sells it. When POP discontinues it, all rights revert to your POPTEAM with no strings attached except you can't sell to POP customers for five years.

Executives of POP point proudly to several former employees who saved and invested their NEW POP royalties and are now in their own businesses marketing their products to smaller accounts. Other employees save their products to develop as retirement ventures. Occasionally POP has purchased the entire output of former employees' companies, and have even helped finance a few; POP has struck a neat balance between collaborative effort and competitive payoff in both the short and long runs. Employees also see the possibilities for themselves, which, paradoxically, results in lower turnover. As they say, "Where else can you get a deal like this?"

What Makes the Difference at POP? Integrating the Needs of People with the Needs of the Task and the System

Executives at POP have found a different dynamic balance among the potentially opposing interests of employees and the work of the organization. In many innovative ways, they have turned these interests toward a shared vision and have consequently created a stimulating place for people to work, grow, and make money, with a potential for future economic security that results from their own efforts. This releases energy that is channelled to increase POP's competitive market position. Their experience has shown that the company makes money because its people do; that the company grows because its people do; that the company increases its share of markets because its people increase their potential share of other markets.

Employees who can't or don't want to participate in these ways don't have to. They have the option to work in more traditional ways, but no one at POP has the time nor inclination to stand over them telling them what to do. People who need that security go elsewhere, or become stronger persons while performing in their subordinate positions. Those who stay don't want a dominant–dependent way of working; they prefer the autonomy and interdependence here. Then when they integrate their diverse interests, all gain.

Does this sound ideal? It is. As far as I know, POP doesn't exist. I've never heard of a company resolving conflicts by using POP's organic process of product development. Some companies support their people's growth but for different reasons. No company I know of encourages people to become entrepreneurs who might leave and later become competitors.

Dreaming up new ways to structure work is not necessarily idealistic nonsense. It's possible that living our old ways of structured work is realistic non-sense! Visualizing an alternative is the first step toward realizing it.

Few of these ideas are new. Some evolve out of thinking in the 1920s and earlier.[1] In more recent years a number of organizations, including subsidiaries of large corporations, have been experimenting with open systems—participatively designed structures, tasks, and relationships. Success has been mixed, and in most cases, the experiences have not moved beyond the first several years of experimental phases. Why not? Here are a few hints.

- Sam Culbert and John McDonough are consultant-writers who talk about a collaborative experiment with about a hundred engineers in a large corporation. It went awry because people needed to present themselves as *objective* and rational, and no process was provided for dealing with the necessary realignment of *subjective* interests. Discussion of task efficiency was done, but there was no safe way to open up the personal, self-serving politics that usually determine people's priorities.

- These same consultants found that asking engineers to expand their responsibilities to include coordination and integration of their work with other engineers brought little action. The engineers knew they were evaluated on their own individual technical output. The existing reward system didn't give payoffs for collaborative behavior.[2]

- David Crandall heads NETWORK, a non-profit educational service, and is committed to creating a collaborative system. Among the difficulties he has encountered are power distribution issues; specifically, if participants believe they can win only at the expense of others, no collaboration is possible. Apparently for collaboration to occur, people must believe that it is possible for everyone to achieve his or her most important goals. He also noted the need for competence in the collaborative process and in task content, both of which

[1]In particular, see Mary Parker Follett, *Creative Experience*, reprinted by Peter Smith, New York, 1951, by permission of Longmans, Green, London, 1924.

[2]Reproduced by special permission from The *Journal of Applied Behavioral Science*, "Collaboration Vs. Personal Alignment: An Experiment that Went Awry," by Samuel A. Culbert and John J. McDonough, vol. 13, no. 3, 1977, pp. 351–359, NTL Institute for Applied Behavioral Science.

have to be supported by organizational norms that encourage collaborative problem solving.[3]

■ John Donnelly heads Donnelly Mirrors, Inc., (DMI), one of the most visible successful, for-profit, participative organizations. He thinks people who are skeptical of open systems are afraid of losing authority; to the extent a manager has to rely on the authority of his or her position, that person is a questionable manager. Many managers who have a high need for authority don't do well at DMI because they focus on personal, not group, achievement.

In Donnelly's opinion, industrial organizations tend to stifle achievement because they reward individual achievers who hog the psychic increment of work: the enjoyment of success. If each employee is going to feel effective as a person and work at achieving something that makes a difference in her or his life, enjoyment of success has to be widely available. Donnelly is willing to put his faith in the good sense of people, their ability to take care of themselves and to work well together, if given the chance. DMI appears to structure its climate, resources, work, and human systems in a way that allows people to exercise considerable power and control over themselves, with others, and in performing their work: a nondefensive system.

In a decade of rising labor and material costs (1965–1975) DMI not only held the price line on most items, it actually *reduced* its prices on some. At the same time, its sales volume increased six-fold, from $3 to $18 million, while the staff increased only two and one-half times, from less than 200 to over 500 people. Profit information is not public; however, these indicators seem to spell authentic time-tested success.[4]

Clues for Recognizing a System's Climate from Limited Information

When you are moving from one organization to another and want to identify a climate that encourages you to become more of your own person, you'll need some clues. Let's see what clues we can glean from the slice of the POP system revealed by the coffee incident.

---

[3]Reproduced by special permission from The *Journal of Applied Behavioral Science*, "An Executive Director's Struggle to Actualize His Commitment to Collaboration," by David P. Crandall, vol. 13, no. 3, 1977 pp. 340–350, NTL Institute for Applied Behavioral Science.

[4]From an interview with John F. Donnelly, "Participative Management at Work," *Harvard Business Review*, January–February 1977, pp. 117–127.

- *Considerable organizational energy is focused on results wanted:* NEW POPs. The portion of the reward system that we saw supports this focus, both in the short and long run. If other rewards are consistent with this pattern, POP will not fall into the trap of expecting one thing while rewarding another, as happened with the engineers above.
- *Hierarchy seems relatively flat.* Anyone can call a POPMEET; anyone can volunteer within the structured limits of the game. The maintenance rep has equal voice with an officer–auditor rep. Business development people are available, but decisions are based on predetermined guidelines. Guides were probably determined with the participation of interest groups and constituencies, similar to the POPMEET process.
- *Psychological and social distance between employees and managers is probably short.* In the philosophy statement explaining the NEW part of NEW POP, the letters stand for Negotiating Equals Win. Whether you read it as Negotiating = Win, or as equal persons who negotiate together both win, people seem to be expected to work together as peers.
- *The ability to suspend judgment and refrain from evaluating seems evident.* Ideas brainstormed at a POPMEET aren't evaluated, but are boiled down for usefulness for a NEW POP. If a conflict doesn't lend itself to a new product, the POPMEET can brainstorm options for handling the conflict more directly after defining results wanted.
- *Work and play are not mutually exclusive.* To many it seems like a crazy place to work—spontaneity, playfulness and thinking for yourself are valued, rewarded, and supported by the norms. Any boredom from routine, repetitious activities is likely to evaporate in the excitement of creating a NEW POP.
- *NEW POPS are developed on a shared time and effort basis; some on company time; mostly on their own time* sharing some business development resources. The company markets the NEW POP in its existing channels after the POPTEAM has developed the basic marketing plans and approaches, returning the rights for later development in other markets. This approach seems to use creative and pragmatic thinking and action in a useful sequence as one way to develop profitable products.
- *Neither competition nor fear of competition seem to be excessive.* Safeguards have been provided; the excitement of competition used with collaborative excitement is working; no evidence of destructive competition shows so far, but may need monitoring. For many people, it's a habit.

- *Trust seems high among the various groups.* The company's commitment to its stated philosophy seems high; apparently for a long time managers have done what they said they would do.
- *Group effort is rewarded.* In the short run individuals receive equal rewards; in the long run, rights revert back to the group with undivided interests. This is evidence that the underlying philosophy holds that group effort is more innovative than individual effort for creating NEW POPs.
- *POP seems to optimize efforts, risks and payoffs through its reward system.* As a marketing organization, sales is a top priority. Sales efforts are probably also rewarded on the basis of wanted results, with no rewards for results not wanted. POP sales guides may require account executives to specify the results the purchaser wants to gain with its customers and then to match the promotional item's functions to those specifications.

  Rewards for fitting the product to customer needs would tend to focus the sales efforts on best-fit items that the customer will buy in large quantities, not necessarily on one's own NEW POP. Another account executive may do very well on your NEW POP, and you'd also be making money on it. If you're selling, you could also do well on someone else's NEW POP.

  Another option POP might use to increase sales would be to encourage the account executives to call POPMEETS on customer specifications to develop NEW POPS especially for them; POPMEETS might also be extended as a way to develop new channels of distribution, using similar incentives to mutual gain.
- *Perhaps most improtant of all, there's a vision*—the fulfillment of the American Dream—of one day being your own boss in your own business. At POP this is a realizable dream for financial security during retirement. The boredom trap is avoided by the retiree's keeping involved with the others in the POPTEAM as they develop and market new products. If some people want the money only, other options are likely to be available.

Notice that the Choosing Process is built into the slice of the POP system we've seen. When conflicts are accepted, attitudes are easier to sense. Content is analyzed for a potential NEW POP. Results are clearly formulated: a profitable NEW POP. Options are generated at the POPMEET with an initial assessment of risks and odds. The POPTEAM tests choices and takes action as they develop the product, the production and marketing plans, and profit potential with the business development group. The full loop is completed when members of POPTEAM receive their royalties based on sales volume, and later the rights to their product. Non-defensive processes seem to be integrated into the POP system, and the mutual-gain philosophy supports these processes.

Notice, too, that the POP system seems to have norms that allow for both the objective and subjective processes to occur simultaneously, which is vital for a climate of non-defensiveness and for being more of your own person (as we saw in Figure 1-1, page 5).

Communication is less likely to be in the form of power plays and other defensive-creating styles; their style tends to keep defenses down. Feedback is less likely to be distorted or non-existent because differences are more respected and accepted. Both levels of meaning—content and feeling—are likely to be communicated and listened to (as we saw in Figure 5-2, page 132).

Values held by higher-level POP people seem to be more like New Breed values than those of traditional employers (as we saw in Figure 2-2, page 28). They seem to be exercising more power *with*, and less power *over*, others. Putting heads together when working as allies can be as exciting as banging heads together as adversaries, and sometimes is more gratifying.

NOW THAT YOU'RE CENTERED, CONSIDER YOUR IMPACT ON OTHERS

As you become more of your own person while becoming non-defensive, as you increase your core of self, as you create a larger trade-off area and are less willing to give away your person power to others, you may need to consider the impact of these changes on people with more position power than you now have. They are the ones who decide whether or not you gain more position power. You have better odds of increasing both person and position power when you can recognize the kind of authority person who is most likely to be supportive of the changes you are making.

Many people in authority positions are going to have to cope with such changes, if a recent survey is any indication. Experts at Opinion Research Corporation in Princeton, New Jersey, have gathered data over 25 years and have verified what many people have observed: There has been a major shift in the attitudes and values of employees in the private sector.[5] Today's greatest dissatisfactions are about self-esteem issues, and these researchers

---

[5]M. R. Cooper, B. S. Morgan, P. M. Foley, and L. B. Kaplan, "Changing Employee Values: Deepening Discontent?" *Harvard Business Review*, January–February 1979, pp. 117–125.

predict no reversal in the future. Key findings among clerical and hourly people are these:

- A majority do not see opportunities for advancement as good.
- A majority felt that they were not treated with respect as individuals.
- The majority found their companies unwilling to listen to their problems and complaints.
- Not only did companies not listen, but the majority felt that even fewer companies did something about these concerns.
- The majority were especially critical about fairness in dealing with employees. Playing favorites was a key concern.

Employees felt respect for their supervisors and also rated pay and benefits high. But these factors didn't outweigh the self-esteem issues. These same self-esteem issues were also among the chief concerns of managers, although they consistently rated their companies higher than clericals and hourly workers, probably due to what the authors call the "hierarchy gap."

If we assume that employees' dissatisfaction about self-esteem issues indicates an increase in person power (with less increase among managers), these trends can show changes in authority–subordinate relations, as in Figure 12-1a. Notice that the four quadrants show high and low person power (PERp) and position power (POSp). In the subordinate column, the shaded area indicates substantial increase in a sense of self-esteem. This seems similar to wanting to be, or becoming, more of your own person. The authority column shows less growth in self-esteem factors, although there are indicators of some, such as growing respect for supervision. (The shaded areas that indicate increases in expressed self-esteem and expectations are not based on exact survey data; only on my interpretation of the trend.)

It's also my guess that the pressures to make no change and to maintain the status quo, indicated by the downward arrows, are different on each group. As a subordinate, you seem to be generally freer to grow as a person up to a point; as long as you can't seriously influence the company's resources, you aren't perceived as a threat. Authorities, on the other hand, are often more closely watched. More pressure is brought on them to adhere to tried-and-true ways, even when they no longer apply. Due to such pressure, it's my further guess that authority people won't keep all the growth they've attempted; some have been squashed in their growth goals.

Looking at Figure 12-1b, we see the subordinate and authority columns separated and numbered, with the four conditions of your relationships to authorities briefly described. For example, when you are in Condition 1, you have low person power and low position power. When you relate to an authority person in Condition 3 who has low person power, you're likely to find indicators of low self-esteem: defensiveness, façades, minimal feedback,

a. Changes

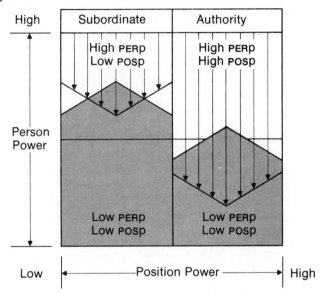

b. Effects of changes

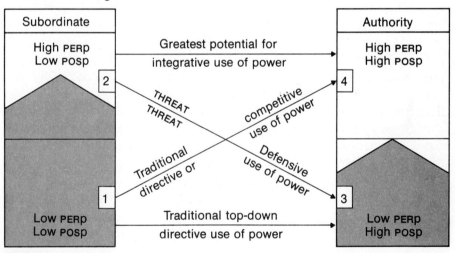

Figure 12-1. *Changing your use of power in authority–subordinate relationships.*

closely protected behavior. Traditional top-down use of power would be comfortable for this person; it would give him or her some security that may not be available among other authority associates.

When you are in Condition 1 relating to an authority person in Condition 4, who is high in both person and position power, you may get the traditional treatment if you are self-effacing. However, if you are growing, you may be treated competitively, as if you're a contender for a winning position. This authority person might be similar to the creative gamesman that Michael Maccoby described.[6] You'd have to know more about his or her values to make a more accurate prediction.

Moving up now to your being in Condition 2 relating to an authority person in Condition 3, you're a threat. Even though you have less position power, with your increasing person power, you might be perceived as a threat to 3's position power, and you are likely to "come on too strong" for this person's comfort. You may get more than defensive responses; a threatened person can become quite repressive or work behind the scenes without your knowledge. Again, you'd have to know more about the person's values and habits to make a better prediction. Since there are probably more managers and supervisors of this kind than any other, all your non-defensive skills will become very useful in this transition.

When you are in Condition 2, an ideal person to work for is an authority who is in Condition 4, high in both person and position power. You would probably both find each other stimulating, if you also share interests and values. This person can be a candidate for developing a highly productive mentor relationship. Among these people lie the greatest potential for integrative use of power, similar to the way power was used at POP and DMI. Position power was used to enhance person power, not substitute for it. Therefore, people could combine and integrate their diverse interests into creating something new that was valued by both the people and the system.

Higher power people—those high in both position and person power—have less need for the security of hierarchy. Some may even enjoy exploring ways to shake things up occasionally. Many will do it with a sense of perspective—and humor.

IMPLICATIONS OF BECOMING YOUR OWN PERSON— NON-DEFENSIVELY

As this analysis shows, you will need to reassess your positive and negative risks as you change yourself and when you change your job. You could move to another company and eliminate some negative risks, but

---

[6]Maccoby, *The Gamesman*, pp. 121–171.

you're likely to pick up other ones. In your present system you probably already have good inside information or can get it. Think of whom you would choose to work for if you could. Does she or he have the basic power dimensions that could help you move? What about values, style, personality, teaching ability? What can you offer that would be of value to her or him?

We're now back to the Choosing Process, gathering data about attitudes and content. Whatever change you are contemplating, the initial questions still work: What results do I want? What are my options? What else do I need to find out? Who can help me? The more important the situation, the deeper you'll go into the Choosing Process, the more you'll make sure that you and others always have space to save face, and the more you'll focus on mutual gain.

The more your actions enhance others, the more you increase your odds of being enhanced yourself. This circulation in the bank of life's energy returns to you many times over in unexpected ways. Although easier said than done, when you stay centered in the values most vital to you, the rest falls into place.

> Once you know
> That nobody
> Can take from you
> What is really yours
> You stop trying
> To protect it.[7]

For additional background reading, see bibliography entries 13, 15, 25, 32, 35, 39, 40, 45, 54, 57, 59, 61, 65, 68, 69, 70, 79.

[7]Bebermeyer, . . . *And Master of None*, p. 31.

ANNOTATED BIBLIOGRAPHY

Books and articles are followed by suggested periodicals. Entries are arranged by six general topics:

A. Interpersonal Communication: Verbal and Nonverbal
B. Human Development and Personal Growth
C. Creativity and New Ways of Experiencing When Approaching Problems
D. Organizations, Managers, and Change
E. Women, Men, and Organizations
F. Societal Values and Change

At the end of each annotation, the chapters to which the entry is most applicable are noted in parentheses.

A. INTERPERSONAL COMMUNICATION: VERBAL AND NON-VERBAL

1. Bennis, Warren G., David E. Berlew, Edgar H. Schein, and Fred I. Steele: *Interpersonal Dynamics: Essays and Readings on Human Interaction,* 3d ed., Dorsey Press, Homewood, Ill., 1973. An excellent book of readings that amply demonstrates emotional expressions, self-confirmation, personal change, and improving interpersonal relationships. The contributors are outstanding. (1, 2)
2. Birdwhistell, Ray L.: *Kinesics and Context: Essays on Body Motion Communication,* University of Pennsylvania Press, Philadelphia, 1970. A classic study in body language, this book is for serious students of kinesics. A complex notation system describes the way the body is used to communicate certain kinds of information. (3)
3. Capaldi, Nicholas: *The Art of Deception,* Donald W. Brown, New York, 1971. An excellent summary of how to raise defenses by deceptive win–lose communication methods. Important for identifying subtleties and knowing what you can expect in competitive communication. (3)

4. Fabun, Don: *Communications: The Transfer of Meaning,* Glencoe, Encino, Calif., 1968. Originally developed for Kaiser Aluminum and Chemical Corporation (who holds the copyright), this colorful pamphlet makes visible many common communication problems with options for clearer transfer of meanings. Now a classic, it is an excellent summary of a complex process. (5)

5. Goffman, Erving: *The Presentation of Self in Everyday Life,* Doubleday Anchor, Garden City, N.Y., 1959. A classic in how people present themselves, as if on the stage of life; how we play out our roles and live our values; how we use façades, play games and protect ourselves. Insightful, interestingly presented, it's a "must" for seeing through the ways in which people present and preserve their personal dignity. (3, 5, 6)

6. Goffman, Erving: *Interaction Rituals: Essays on Face-to-Face Behavior,* Doubleday Anchor, Garden City, N.Y., 1967. Further development of themes begun in *The Presentation of Self in Everyday Life.* Of particular interest is the chapter on deference and demeanor. (3, 6)

7. Gordon, Thomas: *Leadership Effectiveness Training, L.E.T.: The No-Lose Way to Release the Productive Potential of People,* Wyden Books, New York, 1977. Dr. Gordon draws on many of the same principles that are used in non-defensive communication. However, L.E.T. addresses people in leader roles; NDC addresses people in subordinate roles. L.E.T.'s underlying values are directed toward no-lose results; NDC moves toward gain–gain results. Most readers will find rich additional material in this book. (1, 2, 5, 6, 8)

8. Haley, Jay: *The Power Tactics of Jesus Christ and Other Essays,* Viking Penguin, New York, 1969. A collection of essays that clearly demonstrates how one-upmanship works in psychotherapy, in Christ's development of his personal following, and in other provocative ways. His simple clarity and gentle humor can bring awareness that might have taken longer to gain. (3)

9. Henley, Nancy M.: *Body Politics: Power, Sex, and Nonverbal Communication,* Prentice-Hall, Englewood Cliffs, N.J., 1977. Focuses on how nonverbal communication is used to maintain power in the social hierarchy, especially between men and women. Excellently researched and documented by the psychologist-author. (1, 3, 6)

10. Jacobsen, Wally D.: *Power and Interpersonal Relations,* Wadsworth, Belmont, Calif., 1972. An excellent review of the research on power, its bases, methods, attributes, group attributes, effect of the situation, leadership styles, and in various types of systems. Summarizes power principles and provides an extensive bibliography. Good reference text. (3, 4, 8)

11. Jellinek, J. Stephan: *The Inner Editor: The Offense and Defense of Communication and How it Applies to Advertising, Politics, Education and Marketing,* Stein & Day, Briarcliff Manor, N.Y., 1977. Although this book focuses on advertising, politics, education and marketing, it describes how people's inner editor deals with the offense and defense of communication. The inner editor includes many of the rules and underlying values discussed in non-defensive communication. (3, 4)

12. Johnson, David W.: *Reaching Out: Interpersonal Effectiveness and Self-Actualization,* Prentice-Hall, Englewood Cliffs, N.J., 1972. A textbook of readings and exercises to build your interpersonal skills and effectiveness. Although designed for classroom use, it could also be a valuable personal workbook. (5, 6)

13. Karrass, Chester L.: *The Negotiating Game,* World, Cleveland, 1970. An easily readable report of findings from doctoral research on the effects of self-esteem, aspiration levels, power, and negotiating skills. External power was found to be less potent than one might expect when the other factors were high. Internal power sources of self-esteem, aspiration, and skills can be developed to work with external power factors. Good background reading for communicating non-defensively. (8, 10, 11, 12)

14. Mehrabian, Albert: *Silent Messages,* Wadsworth, Belmont, Calif., 1971. This collection of research findings is easy to read. Chapter 3, "The Double-Edged Message," is of particular value here. (5)

15. Nierenberg, Gerard I.: *Fundamentals of Negotiating,* Hawthorne Books, New York, 1973, 1971, 1968. Combines and expands on two earlier books, *The Art of Negotiating* and *Creative Business Negotiating.* Much of this excellent book is about developing attitudes for creating options in negotiations where all parties gain something they want. Useful applications are offered for negotiations in purchasing/selling, real estate, labor relations, lawsuits, and other specialized fields. (8, 10, 11, 12)

16. Rogers, Carl, and Richard Farson: *Active Listening,* University of Chicago Press, Chicago, 1957. Among the first materials on how to listen actively to others with the idea of hearing their feelings as well as their words. Risks of really hearing the other person's meanings are discussed. (5, 6, 8)

17. Rogers, Carl, and F. J. Roethlisberger: "Barriers and Gateways to Communication," *Harvard Business Review,* July–August 1952, pp. 28–34. Now a classic, this early article focused on the tendency to evaluate as a key barrier to mutual understanding. Active listening is illustrated in action. (3, 4, 5, 6)

18. Scheflen, Albert E.: *Body Language and Social Order: Communication as Behavioral Control,* Prentice-Hall, Englewood Cliffs, N.J., 1972.

Heavily illustrated with pictures showing facial and body expressions that connote social control of people and space, this book includes subtleties not found in the pop literature on body language. Useful for a good understanding of such behavior without getting heavily technical as in Birdwhistell. (3, 6)

19. Smith, Gerald Walker: *Hidden Meanings: Decoding the Common Words and Expressions We Hide Behind,* Celestial Arts, Millbrae, Calif., 1977. Many word clues indicating hidden meanings are given, with translations of what is really meant. Useful for identifying double messages, but doesn't tell what to do after you recognize them. (3, 5)

20. Thorne, Barrie, and Nancy Henley (eds.): *Language and Sex: Difference and Dominance,* Newbury House, Rowley, Mass., 1975. Many contributors offer an overview of sexual implications in the use of language that emphasizes differences between men and women and that establishes dominance of men over women. (6)

B. HUMAN DEVELOPMENT AND PERSONAL GROWTH

21. Bebermeyer, Ruth: *...And Master of None,* Ruth Bebermeyer, 218 Monclay St., St. Louis, Missouri, 1976. (Order directly, not sold in stores.) Short poems, mostly four-liners, that succinctly go to the core of humanistic, non-defensive ways of being yourself. A short short course in non-defensive communication. (1, 2, 3, 6, 8, 9)

22. Cole, Jim: *The Façade: A View of Our Behavior,* cartoons illustrated by Tom Woodruff, distributed by Ed and Janet Reynolds, Mill Valley, Calif., 94940, 1970. A collection of drawings and captions that show the processes of acquiring façades, fears of dropping them, and how taking the risk of dropping your own façades leads to others doing the same. A clear, simple portrayal of the complex process of how to come out of hiding non-defensively. (3, 5, 6)

23. Erikson, Erik H.: *Toys and Reasons: Stages in the Ritualization of Experience,* W. W. Norton, New York, 1977. This well-known psychoanalyst reviews how parents and society provide rituals at each stage of development in the life cycle. This ritualization gives an individual a group and personal identity; a sense of belonging while deflecting feelings of unworthiness onto outsiders; some definitions of what's right and legally good or guilt producing; and sanctioned ways for doing daily activities. (3)

24. Farson, Richard: *Birthrights,* Penguin Books, New York, 1974. A humanistic attitude toward raising children with deep regard for their rights as people and the kinds of needed supports for growth to develop

as healthy, self-defining adults. Builds on belief in the essential goodness of the child. (3)

25. Gibb, Jack R.: *Trust: A New View of Personal and Organizational Development.* The Guild of Tutors Press, Los Angeles, 1978. The first compilation of Dr. Gibb's long development and use of the TORI process—Trusting, Opening, Realizing, Interdepending—to help individuals and organizations release their energies for greater productivity and creativity. Valuable for becoming your own person—that is, being who you are more fully. (1, 2, 12)

26. Hampden-Turner, Charles: *Radical Man: The Process of Psycho-Social Development,* Doubleday Anchor, Garden City, N.Y., 1971. Hampden-Turner brilliantly synthesizes a massive body of research, primarily from psychological and management literature, to formulate his model of a healthy and creative psycho-social development, and what happens when people feel anomie—at loose ends, anxious, and defensive. He also reviews how formal systems encourage this anomie and how it can be changed. Especially useful to people wanting to add depth to their conceptualization of non-defensive processes. (2, 3)

27. Levinson, Daniel J., et al.: *The Seasons of a Man's Life,* Knopf, New York, 1978. The major stages of adult development in men's lives are studied in depth. Problems of transition between stages are featured. It seems to record how major social expectations affect men's life cycles without discussing sex-role implications. (3, 4)

28. Maslow, Abraham H.: *Toward a Psychology of Being,* Van Nostrand Reinhold, New York, 1962. Maslow's direction of working from an assumption of health and moving toward desired personal growth goals is the same assumption underlying non-defensive communication. (1, 2, 3)

29. Novaco, Raymond W.: *Anger Control: The Development and Evaluation of an Experimental Treatment,* Lexington Books, Heath, Lexington, Mass., 1975. A technical research report outlining ways to self-manage one's anger. It will add to your intellectual knowledge, but it is not a self-help book. (6, 8)

30. Piaget, Jean: *The Moral Judgment of the Child,* The Free Press, New York, 1965. A study of how moral judgment evolves in children, covering such values as respect for rules among children; moral rules laid down by adults and what children learn from these; and ideas of justice, equality, and authority. (3)

31. Rogers, Carl: *On Becoming a Person,* Houghton-Mifflin, Boston, 1961. Probably the best resource for describing how to become your own person. Of particular interest are the chapters on what it means to become a person and the description of the fully functioning person. (1, 2, 9)

32. Rogers, Carl: *On Personal Power: Inner Strength and Its Revolutionary Impact,* Delacorte Press, New York, 1977. Rogers clearly demonstrates the conflicts that can arise in organizations when people become more of their own persons and how these can be worked through even from a relatively powerless position. He also discusses the revolutionary impact of developing human excellence, since this questions and threatens several basic American values. He incorporates ideas developed in his earlier writings, which are useful for background in non-defensiveness. (1, 2, 12)

33. Rosenberg, Marshall B.: *From Now On: Without Blame and Punishment,* Community Psychological Consultants, Inc., 1740 Gulf Drive, St. Louis, Missouri 63130, 1977. (Order directly, not sold in stores.) A deeply perceptive book, gently written, to help be in touch with one's feelings as a means of becoming more capable of intimacy and personal effectiveness. (1, 2, 5, 6, 10)

34. Sheehy, Gail: *Passages: Predictable Crises of Adult Life,* E. P. Dutton, New York, 1974. The predictable crises of adult life for both women and men are entertainingly and informatively presented. Some ways of coping with change are offered. You can reduce defensiveness by being prepared ahead of time. (3)

Periodicals

35. *The Self-Determination Quarterly Journal,* 2435 Forest Ave., San Jose, Calif., 95128. Publication of a new personal/political network of California people who are concerned with influencing politics to allow for more self-determination. (12)

C. CREATIVITY AND NEW WAYS OF EXPERIENCING WHEN APPROACHING PROBLEMS

36. Adams, James L.: *Conceptual Blockbusting: A Guide to Better Ideas,* W. H. Freeman, San Francisco, Calif., 1974. Great for unblocking just about every kind of barrier to creativity. (7)

37. Bolles, Richard N.: *The Three Boxes of Life and How to Get Out of Them,* Ten Speed Press, Berkeley, Calif., 1978. This introduction to life/work planning goes hand in hand with Bolles' earlier, popular book, *What Color Is Your Parachute?* This new book shows you how to bring a better balance among your learning/working/playing lives during your lifetime. Rich in ideas, it is also based on mutual gain. (10)

38. Buzan, Tony: *Use Both Sides of Your Brain*, E. P. Dutton, New York, 1976. Designed for students to develop an organic study method that uses both sides of the brain. A basic step-by-step book on how to use the right brain to supplement the left brain. Shows how organic diagrams give better retention of material than you can get from outlines. (7)

39. Craig, James H., and Marge Craig: *Synergic Power: Beyond Domination and Permissiveness*, ProActive Press, P.O. Box 296, Berkeley, Calif., 94701, 1974. A study of how power operates when the predominant value is domination and how it can operate to provide synergy. A workable model for moving from exercising power over others to using power to co-create and integrate diverse interests. (7, 12)

40. Csikszentmihalyi, Mihaly: *Beyond Boredom and Anxiety: The Experience of Play in Work and Games*, Jossey-Bass, San Francisco, Calif., 1975. The core chapter, "A Theoretical Model for Enjoyment," is one of the few descriptions written on the flow process in creative effort. (7, 12)

41. De Bono, Edward: *Lateral Thinking: Creativity Step by Step*, Harper & Row, New York, 1970. A basic text on vertical and lateral thinking, when to use which, how to develop skills in the lateral mode. Somewhat paradoxical in presenting the lateral, global thinking in a linear, vertical way. Useful. (7)

42. Franck, Frederick: *The Zen of Seeing: Seeing/Drawing as Meditation*, Random House, New York, 1973. Drawing while seeing what you're looking at, not your paper. Experiencing drawing as you draw it—a right-brain experience. (7)

43. Holmes, Ernest: *The Science of Mind*, Dodd, Mead, New York, 1938. Based on findings from science, religion, and philosophy, this metaphysics shows ways to experience abundance of supply, good health and positive energy in your daily life by affirming your oneness with universal energy and laws. (7)

44. Houston, Jean: "The Mind of Margaret Mead: How She Democratizes Greatness," *Quest*, July–August, 1977. A fine word-picture of how images link across time and space, using all of one's senses, making the extraordinary seem ordinary. Suggests ways we can learn to use the powers we've been given instead of structuring them to cultural expectations. (7)

45. Karagulla, Shafica: *Breakthrough to Creativity: Your Higher Sense Perception*, DeVorss, Santa Monica, Calif., 1967. After eight years of research, this neuropsychiatrist discovered that people with higher sense perception abilities are far more numerous than previously supposed. The observations of "sensitives" who could see energy states were found to correlate accurately with medical findings. In addition, percep-

tions about energy-sappers and the energy exchange between actor and audience raise provocative questions about further development and use of higher sense perception. (7, 12)

46. Koberg, Don, and Jim Bagnall: *The Universal Traveler: A Soft-Systems Guide to: Creativity, Problem-Solving, and the Process of Reaching Goals,* William Kaufman, Los Altos, Calif., 1974. An integrated summary of creative ways for getting personal and organizational results. Draws from many different disciplines and combines functions of both hemispheres of the brain. Entertainingly written and artistically presented, it'll give you some ideas when you feel short of options. (4, 7)

47. Mager, Robert F.: *Goal Analysis,* Lear Siegler/Fearon, Belmont, Calif., 1972. Mager holds little reverence for fuzzies—statements such as "having the proper attitude" or "take pride in your work." He asks, "How would you know one when you see one?" With humorous clarity, he shows how to state a goal or result you want, and how to describe what people will be saying or doing when they've reached that goal. Descriptions replace evaluative statements, similar to the *do's* and *don'ts* of listening. (10)

48. Pirsig, Robert L.: *Zen and the Art of Motorcycle Maintenance: An Inquiry into Values,* Bantom Books, New York, 1974. In this man's odyssey of self-discovery and search for truth, you explore with him different ways of analyzing and solving problems based on different themes in Western thought and philosophy. (7)

49. Roberts, Jane: *The Nature of Personal Reality,* Prentice-Hall, Englewood Cliffs, N.J., 1975. Whether or not you can accept the idea of a psychic entity speaking through a person while in a trancelike state, there is wisdom that comes via Jane Roberts on how beliefs shape experience and how to get in contact with beliefs to extend your perspectives and probabilities. Well worth considering; if you're a skeptic, a good mind-stretching experiment. (7)

50. Schumacher, E. F.: *A Guide for the Perplexed,* Harper & Row, New York, 1977. The author of *Small Is Beautiful* develops a philosophy for creating an inner unity by progressing through four levels of being. Inner unity is defined as a center of strength and freedom—an inner space out of which to act, instead of merely being acted upon. His ideas expand on the non-defensive concept of a core of self, and he offers a much broader philosophical base and vision of what's possible. He also discusses divergent problems more thoroughly. (7)

51. Stevens, Barry: *Don't Push the River (It Flows by Itself),* Real People Press, Box 542, Lafayette, Calif., 94549, 1970. Expect a new experience in reading. Ms. Stevens bends the language to make it flow for her personal expression. Although it makes many references to gestalt

therapy, most of it is her being in her own process, which lets you be in yours. She *is* her experience instead of talking *about* it. (7)

52. Tucker, Anne (ed.): *The Woman's Eye*, Knopf, New York, 1973. Behind the camera's eye is a woman's eye. Another experience of seeing through another pair of glasses. (7)

53. Watzlawick, Paul: *The Language of Change: Elements of Therapeutic Communication*, Basic Books, New York, 1978. Discusses the varying language patterns used from the left and right hemispheres of the brain; demonstrates how change occurs more readily when communication is from the right hemisphere language patterns, which suggests listening to messages from both sides of our brains can help us make desired changes. Psychologically focused. (7)

Periodicals

54. *Quest: In Pursuit of Human Excellence*, P.O. Box 3720, Greenwich, Conn., 06830. This new magazine pursues its purpose well without getting the Pollyanna touch. Beautifully written and illustrated, it offers new challenges to be your best. (12)

D. ORGANIZATIONS, MANAGERS, AND CHANGE

55. Argyris, Chris, and Donald A. Schön: *Theory in Practice: Increasing Professional Effectiveness*, Jossey-Bass, San Francisco, Calif., 1975. Reveals how executives' espoused theories are often different from their theories in use, resulting in double messages that get results they didn't expect or want. Also shows a specific program for identifying the differences and how to move to more effective communications and results. Provides models for moving from defensive to non-defensive values. (4, 5)

56. Culbert, Samuel A.: *The Organization Trap and How to Get Out of It*, Basic Books, New York, 1974. This book shows how you can participate in *not* getting ahead when you listen to organization rules for getting ahead. Proposes ways for people in subordinate positions to get together to bring about change through shared interests. Integrates consciousness-raising with group process to gain results collaboratively. Easier said than done, but this book presents some concrete effective ways. (4)

57. Follett, Mary Parker: *Creative Experience*, reprinted by Peter Smith, New York, 1951, by permission of Longmans, Green and Co., London,

1924. As an industrial and government consultant with legal expertise, Ms. Follett has an unusually rich background from which to draw her proposals for new uses of power and the integration of differing interests so all parties gain. Although written in 1924, her ideas and observations are as fresh today as they must have been ahead of her time then. (4, 7, 12)

58. Kepner, Charles H., and Benjamin B. Tregoe: *The Rational Manager: A Systematic Approach to Problem Solving and Decision Making,* McGraw-Hill, New York, 1965. How to specify and analyze a problem to discover its most likely causes; defining what outcomes must be gotten and what is wanted so that rational decisions are made. Probably the best book on the linear method for solving convergent problems. It does not deal with organic methods of resolving divergent problems. (4, 9)

59. Likert, Rensis, and Jane Gibson Likert: *New Ways of Managing Conflict,* McGraw-Hill, New York, 1976. A textbook that brings together excellent work in developing a system of integrative-interaction networks in the process of changing from competitive to more collaborative organizations. Extensive, solid work done by respected researchers and consultants in this field. (4, 9, 12)

60. Maccoby, Michael: *The Gamesman: The New Corporate Leaders,* Simon & Schuster, New York, 1976. The gamesman is the competitive American male at his best or worst, depending on your views and values. The core chapter is about the separation of head and heart, which is what we are bringing together in non-defensive communication. Readable, revealing, and cause for reflection. (4)

61. McClelland, David C.: *Power: The Inner Experience,* Irvington Publishers, New York, 1975. Based on years of research, this book reports on experiencing, accumulating, and expressing power. McClelland's findings report results ranging from interpersonal to international power factors. The most reported finding was that mature people with high leadership potential have high power motivation with high inhibition and a firm faith in people, calling on their strengths and originality of ideas. These leaders do not dominate nor treat people like pawns. (4, 12)

62. McLean, Reston G., and Katherine Jillson: *The Manager and Self-Respect: A Follow-Up Survey,* AMACOM, A Division of the American Management Associations, New York, 1977. This report summarizes the damaging effects of competition on managers, their relationships, and their effectiveness in their use of power. It tends to confirm other information reported in Chapter 4. (4)

63. Morrissey, George: *Management by Objectives and Results for Business and Industry,* 2d ed., Addison-Wesley, Reading, Mass., 1977. Morrissey

is one of the major writers in the field of management by objectives (MBO). However he goes beyond objectives and places more emphasis on results that are wanted and achieved. (4, 9)

64. Pilhes, Rene-Victor: *The Provocateur,* Harper & Row, New York, 1977. Translated from French, this engrossing novel shows what happens to corporate executives who aspire to build one corporation that encompasses the world. Three seemingly unrelated events occur: the death of an executive on his way to the office, the appearance of parchment scrolls tied with black and green ribbon on every employee's desk the same morning, and discovery of a crack in the building's foundation. The plot thickens, and the executives' values shape their actions and finally . . . Read it to discover if it's their final demise or destiny. (4, 7)

65. Pressman, Jeffrey L., and Aaron B. Wildavsky: *Implementation,* University of California Press, Berkeley, 1973. Its subtitle annotates it: *How Great Expectations in Washington Are Dashed in Oakland: Or, Why It's Amazing that Federal Programs Work at All, This Being a Saga of the Economic Development Administration as Told by Two Sympathetic Observers Who Seek to Build Morals on a Foundation of Ruined Hopes.* (4, 12)

66. Ritti, R. Richard, and G. Ray Funkhouser: *The Ropes to Skip and the Ropes to Know: Studies in Organizational Behavior,* GRID, Columbus, Ohio, 1977. A delightful unorthodox textbook, *Ropes* reads more like a novel. You'll recognize key organizational types engaging in typical behavior. For example, Ben Franklyn, production manager, is always "getting the product out the door." Stanley, the universal subordinate (which is why he has no last name) is guided by Dr. Faust, consultant and Stanley's former university professor. Bonnie is the universal woman—secretary. Ted Shelby is the staff man always promoting a new program . . . and others. A realistic guide through the organizational maze about what really goes on in fifty-five brief chapters, summarized in seven sections showing some principles. (4, 11)

67. Steele, Fritz: *The Open Organization: The Impact of Secrecy and Disclosure on People and Organizations,* Addison-Wesley, Reading, Mass., 1975. An easy-to-read description of the norms and risks of disclosing information in systems. Of particular interest is the discussion on control, power, and disclosure. (4, 5, 6)

Periodicals

68. *Journal of Applied Behavioral Science,* NTL Institute for Applied Behavioral Science, P.O. Box 9155, Arlington, V., 22209. For those who are working with organizational change, this journal offers research

results and is the best in this field. The occasional thematic issues are excellent, such as on self-help groups and power. Highly recommend the 30th Year Commemorative issue, "Collaboration in the Work-Setting." (12)

69. *Journal of Applied Psychology,* American Psychological Association, 1200 17th St., N.W., Washington, D.C., 20036. This journal carries many new findings about effects of the workplace on people. (12)

70. *Washington Monthly,* 1028 Connecticut Ave., N.W., Washington, D.C., 20036. Exposes the culture of bureaucracy, including Tidbits and Out-rages, and Memos of the Month that speak for themselves. They have had an excellent series on Work in America, including Suzannah Les-sard's "America's Time Traps: The Youth Cult, the Work Prison, the Emptiness of Age," David Hapgood's "An End to Demeaning Work," and Lucy Komisar's "Violence and the Masculine Mystique." (12)

E.   WOMEN, MEN, AND ORGANIZATIONS

71. Battalia, O. William, and John J. Tarrant: *The Corporate Eunuch,* Crowell, New York, 1973. Describes how executives and managers have been psychologically castrated into being channelers and keepers of corporate systems instead of contributors or creators. Offers some strategic approaches for taking more control over one's life. (4)

72. Ferguson, Charles W.: *The Male Attitude: What Makes American Men Think and Act as They Do?* Little, Brown, Boston, 1966. (Out of print; available from University Microfilms, Ann Arbor, Mich., 48106.) Prob-ably the most important book written on the subject; he gives an histor-ical review of the American development of male attitude. The section on "The Sea" shows the total control of sea captains over our early founders and their impact on values in early communities. "The Gun" deals with the effects of war on Western development and the present day views toward guns. "The Slave" shows the effects of slavery on male attitudes of power, dominance, and control. "The Scribe" shows male control over the writing of history, the educational process, lan-guage and the written word. "The Machine" holds out a faint hope that the interconnectedness in the activities of men is an alternative to the power/dominance/control. Ferguson is an historical novelist, and this book reads like one. (4, 5, 6)

73. Goldberg, Herb: *The Hazards of Being Male: Surviving the Myth of Masculine Privilege,* Nash Publishing, New York, 1976. An excellent psychological analysis of the effects of social expectations on men's

behavior, styles of thinking, their values, and defenses. The chapter entitled "Feelings: The Real Male Terror," describes common façades and defenses among men that contribute to the kinds of norms in work systems. (4, 5, 6)

74. Harragan, Betty Lehan: *Games Mother Never Taught You: Corporate Gamesmanship for Women*, Rawson Associates, New York, 1977. Addressed to women, it will also be useful to many men because it covers "the unwritten rules that men use to play the power game and everything else you'd like to know that your male colleagues will never tell you." Many men won't talk to women competitors at all and often don't talk with each other. Written in game language, it outlines "the Game, the Board, the Rules," "the Players, the Penalties, the Objectives," and "Symbols, Signals, Style, and Sex," all of which is an excellent interpretation of what goes on and the ways to cope with it. (4, 5, 6, 8)

75. Hennig, Margaret, and Anne Jardim: *The Managerial Women*, Doubleday Anchor, Garden City, N.Y., 1977. Well-considered directions for women managers; many good ideas to consider and solid information (although the reported research is somewhat dated). Does not address the effects of the male value system, but only how to work in it; therefore, in my opinion, it stops too soon. (4)

76. Kanter, Rosabeth Moss: *Men and Women of the Corporation*, Basic Books, New York, 1977. Most of this book is an original analysis about the effects of organizational structures on men and women. She shows how power, opportunity, and numbers (ratios of men-women, minority-white, etc.) influence people's effectiveness. She implies that organizations will have to change their structure before much change will occur for people, especially between women and men. She may be correct, but personally, I don't have that much time. I would like to hear her ideas on how to expedite such change. (4)

77. Loring, Rosalind, and Theodora Wells: *Breakthrough: Women into Management*, Van Nostrand Reinhold, New York, 1972. Addressed to managers, this book takes this position: Change has occurred—now what do we do about it? A practical approach to changing men–women work relationships, for understanding this aspect of organizational dynamics, and for how to identify and use available capabilities. (4)

78. Pleck, Joseph H., and Jack Sawyer: *Men and Masculinity*, Prentice-Hall, Engelwood Cliffs, N.J., 1974. A collection of excellent articles describing how masculinity requires men to seek achievement and suppress emotion, which restricts their ability to work, play, and love fully. It also shows how organizations exploit the masculine role to promote their own goals, such as measuring masculinity by the size of the paycheck. (4, 5, 6)

Periodicals

79. *Sex Roles—A Journal of Research,* Plenum Publishing, Box 569, Old
    Chelsea Station, New York, N.Y., 10011. Covers current research on
    the effect of role expectations on both women and men. Tends to focus
    more on academic than corporate environments. (12)

F. SOCIETAL VALUES AND CHANGES

80. Anderson, Walt: *A Place of Power: The American Episode in Human
    Evolution,* Goodyear, Santa Monica, Calif., 1976. A sweeping historical
    perspective of where American human evolution fits in the context of
    the world ecological framework and a current look at power arrange-
    ments. Well-seasoned with pictures—each one "worth a thousand
    words." Very readable, current, humanistic. (1, 2, 4)
81. Cohen, Peter: *The Gospel According to the Harvard Business School,*
    Doubleday, Garden City, N.Y., 1973. An irreverent diary of the author's
    education at HBS where he learned competitive values and its conse-
    quences, including death. It sets you to thinking when you realize how
    many large corporations are managed by HBS graduates who are in a
    position to affect the lives, aspirations, and values of employed millions.
    (4)
82. Fromm, Erich: *The Revolution of Hope: Toward a Humanized Technol-
    ogy,* Bantam Books, New York, 1968. The chapter on "What Does It
    Mean to Be Human?" is particularly relevant to the definitions and
    values for non-defensive communication. (1, 2)
83. Fromm, Erich: *To Have or to Be?* Harper & Row, New York, World
    Perspective Series, 1976. Best known for *The Art of Loving,* this psy-
    chiatrist and social analyst compares two underlying themes of life: the
    having theme, which values acquiring material possessions, competi-
    tiveness and aggression, which leads to greed, envy, and violence; and
    the *being* theme, which is based on loving, the pleasures of sharing, and
    on productive instead of wasteful activity. He outlines a socioeconomic
    program of change that offers a place for being human. (1, 2, 9)
84. Heilbroner, Robert L., et al.: *In the Name of Profits: Profiles in Corpo-
    rate Irresponsibility,* Doubleday, Garden City, N.Y., 1972. A collection
    of actual cases of corporate irresponsibility that have gone to court or
    congressional committees. Useful for recognizing corporate double
    talk. (4)
85. May, Rollo: *Power and Innocence: A Search for the Sources of Violence,*
    W. W. Norton, New York, 1972. Of particular interest is Dr. May's

distinction between genuine innocence and pseudoinnocence—making a virtue out of helplessness, weakness, and powerlessness as a means of exercising power. His clear defintions of power are useful, and he makes a strong case for the human need for a sense of significance; the ability to influence others; the humanity of the rebel as compared to the destructiveness of the revolutionary; and the need for compassion in our human interdependence. (10, 11)

86. Schön, Donald A.: *Beyond the Stable State,* W. W. Norton, New York, 1971. An examination of the inability of bureaucratic systems to adapt rapidly to the accelerating rate of change. When slow change provided more stability, actions based on knowable predictions were possible. Now these institutions must become learning systems, Schön proposes, where "we must act before we know in order to learn." Provocative reading by a challenging thinker. (4)

87. Silk, Leonard, and David Vogel: *Ethics and Profits: The Crisis of Confidence in American Business,* Simon & Schuster, New York, 1976. Based on off-the-record discussions held by the Conference Board, leading American businessmen discuss values, views, fears, and conflicts about payoffs, bribes, lying, and other questionable practices that have eroded public confidence in these leaders. (4)

88. Slater, Philip: *Earthwalk,* Doubleday Anchor, Garden City, N.Y., 1974. An insightful analysis of our basic thoughts, themes, and values in Western culture about progress, scientific rationalism, the goal of self-sufficiency, leading to a schizoid detachment. Helps you see yourself in another perspective and stimulates ideas for new options. (1, 2)

89. Terkel, Studs: *Working: People Talk About What They Do All Day and How They Feel About What They Do,* Random House, New York, 1974. As Terkel interviews people about what they do all day and how they feel about what they do, a rather dreary picture emerges. About two-thirds of the way through this book, I found myself anxiously looking for *someone* who found significance in his or her work. Eventually there are a few. Documents the inhumanity or inaneness of work—from top to bottom. (1, 4)

90. Thayer, Frederick C.: *An End to Hierarchy! An End to Competition! Organizing the Politics and Economics of Survival,* New Viewpoints, Franklin Watts, New York, 1973. Thayer proposes a new way of seeing things as they are today—the alienating effects of hierarchy and the absurdities of competition. He proposes a new social theory for change where some people cease to be masters over others, and the interdependence among people has avenues for creative expression, productivity, and growth through structured *non*hierarchical interaction. Covers interpersonal, organizational, and political processes. (4, 7)

CAST OF CHARACTERS

Names of people in the cases are indexed by first names since this is the way they appear in the book.

INDEX

Actual situations are indexed under Defensive communication: examples and Nondefensive communication: examples. Dialogues when talking to oneself and other dynamics are indexed together under Dialogues. Exercises for getting started, experiments for sensing feelings and other suggested experiences are indexed under Self-Experiencing. Authors' names are in italics.